THE TEXAN–SANTA FÉ PIONEERS

The
TEXAN-
SANTA FÉ
PIONEERS

by
Noel M. Loomis

NORMAN

UNIVERSITY OF OKLAHOMA PRESS

BY NOEL M. LOOMIS

Rim of the Caprock (New York, 1952)
The Buscadero (New York, 1953)
The Twilighters (New York, 1955)
Johnny Concho (New York, 1956)
The Texan–Santa Fé Pioneers (Norman, 1958)

Library of Congress Catalog Card Number: 58–6848

Copyright 1958 by the University of Oklahoma Press,
Publishing Division of the University.
Composed and printed at Norman, Oklahoma, U. S. A.,
by the University of Oklahoma Press.
First edition.

A Dedication and an Acknowledgment
TO DOROTHY, MY WIFE, WITH LOVE
She's the kind of girl in her fifties that
a man dreams about in his twenties.

INTRODUCTION

THIS BOOK grew out of an impulsion to find the answers to two questions:

1. Was the Texan–Santa Fé Expedition a wild-goose affair, as it was called, or was it a reasonably intelligent attempt by President Lamar to solve Texas' pressing financial problems?

2. Was the expedition designed as a military conquest of Mexican territory?

As will be seen, the way has been devious, but answers have been found to these and other intriguing questions.

Some three to four hundred hard-boned men and boys cut a tortuous path through the wilderness from Austin, Texas, to New Mexico in 1841. They were called the Santa Fé Pioneers, but they never reached Santa Fé at all. Through mismanagement, starvation, thirst, Kiowa hostility, Mexican cunning, and Texan treachery, the expedition came to a tragic end.

It has been compared to the Lewis and Clark Expedition. The two expeditions were similar in concept but quite different in execution. The Pioneers seemed plagued with an incredible succession of misfortunes—or was it that they lacked a Sacajawea?

Historians generally have called it the Texas Santa Fé Expedition. It set out into unknown wilderness and made the first westward crossing of the fearful Llano. Its trail across the scorched prairies and through the rocky canyons of West Texas is marked by such entries as this: "It was now discovered that two of our men were missing, unable . . . to keep up with the main body . . . . We could only hope that they might be able to follow our trail. . . . it was impossible . . . to go back in search of them."[1] These two men never were heard from again.

When they finally did reach the New Mexican settlements—gaunt from thirst, dirty, and starved—they immediately fell captive to Mexican militia and were sent on a two-thousand-mile journey on foot to the City of Mexico; to smallpox hospitals, lepers' prisons, and the dreaded *Acordada*.

While the prisoners, with clanking log chains at their ankles, cleaned human offal from the streets of Mexico, they had no way of knowing that the expedition, ignominious as its end then seemed, would in a few years bring on the Mexican War and result in the greatest single territorial addition to this nation—one-third of the continental United States—an area bigger than the Louisiana Purchase.

The rank and file had no thought that it might be considered a military expedition, as shown later by the testimony of many of them, and most of the volunteers went for their health, for the great adventure of traveling an unknown country, fighting wild Indians, and visiting fabled Santa Fé, ancient city of revelry and dark-eyed women.

The Pioneers' route was north from Austin to the Cross Timbers, and then west to Santa Fé—a thousand miles more or less. They lost thirty men on the vast Texas prairies and suffered inordinately from lack of food, from thirst, and from diarrhea, but they slowly and painfully continued. Just before reaching Santa Fé, however, they were made prisoners and started on the second leg—a long, long *jornada* to the south. They lost forty more men on this part of the trip and during

---

[1] George Wilkins Kendall, *Narrative of the Texan Santa Fé Expedition*, I, 259. Kendall, co-owner of the New Orleans *Picayune*, went on the expedition as an observer, and was captured and imprisoned. His two-volume *Narrative* sold over 40,000 copies, was published in ten or twelve editions in the United States and in Europe, and is still very readable. The only biography of Kendall is Fayette Copeland, *Kendall of the Picayune*. Kendall's two-volume work, which will be noted many times in this book, will be referred to as Kendall, *Narrative*.

their subsequent imprisonment, and many—too many—do not seem at this date to have been accounted for at all.

From San Miguel to the City of Mexico they went on foot, sometimes with lariats around their necks. The other ends of the *cabristas* were tied to the saddlehorns of Mexican soldiers. They marched through the desert in bitter cold, without shirts or even shoes. Most of their scanty clothing already had been traded for a hard ear of corn to eat or a few miles' ride on a mule when it seemed they could walk no farther. They staggered on with rifle muzzles in their faces, the lash at their backs. Sometimes they had a pint of corn meal a day for food—and they used some of that to bake cakes in which they hid money and watches.

But even though their situation was grim, there were pleasant moments. They were allowed to bathe in the hot springs at Ojo Caliente, below Chihuahua, to get off some of the vermin and filth. An Anglo-Saxon can imagine their astonishment when the Mexican women, laughing over such a good joke, removed their own clothes and came in to bathe with them. But theirs would seem to have been only a token consternation, for Kendall asserts stoutly that this was not immodest of the Mexican women by their own standards. Both sides appeared to favor fraternization—a word which was not to appear in this connection for another hundred years, although the principle must be somewhat more ancient. As far as the Texans were concerned, if it had not been for the charity of the Mexican women, more of the prisoners would have died of starvation.

Although their morale as Pioneers was execrable, as prisoners it was excellent. They held a kangaroo court and convicted a man of "the simples" for being a member of the Santa Fé Pioneers, his presence with them being considered prima facie proof. They fined him two dollars which was spent on native liquor and "revelry" (which made the budget for revelry a little over one cent apiece).

Most of those who escaped or were released made their

way back to Texas, and some of them died soon after while again facing the Mexicans; some were killed trying to escape; some were recaptured and returned to the same prisons.

If all of the Mexican officials had been as kind as Ochoa, who had charge of the prisoners from Paso to Chihuahua, the expedition might have been a minor incident, but unnecessary indignities and hardships, privations and cruel punishments, brutal killings and executions gave it a political significance that Mexico as a nation was powerless to combat. Not only did the Republic of Texas become inflamed, but serious repercussions were felt throughout the United States. Mass meetings were held in New Orleans and other cities demanding harsh retribution, for most of these "Texans" had friends and families back home in the United States.

There were many rumors of punitive expeditions by both Mexico and Texas, which soon were substantiated by General Woll's attack on San Antonio, Caldwell's battle on the Salado, the Dawson Massacre, the Somervell Expedition, the Mier Expedition, the breakout from prison in Mexico, the drawing of the black beans of death, and the execution of eighteen Texans. From indignation to incredulousness, there was presently a full-blown war between Mexico and the United States.

It should not be inferred that all Mexicans favored harsh treatment of the prisoners. Those who did, in fact, were in the minority, and most Mexican civilians were more than kind. There were protests of their official treatment even in the Mexican press, and Dámaso Salazar, the most hated of all the brutal commanders, was ordered court-martialed by the Mexican President. Many of the commanders of the prisoners allowed them a great deal of liberty on their own parole, and some went to extreme lengths to feed and clothe them and provide horses for the lame and wagons for the sick. Others were said to be "as bad as Salazar."

The Pioneers split into two main parties before they ascended the Caprock from Camp Resolution. This event marked the physical disintegration of the command. The first of these two parties to cross the Llano—and the first to be captured—is generally known as the Sutton-Cooke party. Originally it was composed of almost 100 men. The second party may be known as the McLeod party; it consisted of about 180 men who stayed in camp below the Caprock when the Sutton-Cooke party went ahead. Both parties surrendered without firing a shot.

Most of those in the Sutton-Cooke party were started down the trail to the City of Mexico on September 20, 1841; the McLeod party set out one month later—on October 17. The two parties went to Mexico, as the city was frequently called, by slightly different routes. The Sutton-Cooke men (those who survived) reached Mexico December 26. The McLeod men (those who survived) reached Mexico about February 1, 1842. A good many remained at various points along the way, seriously ill with smallpox.

Following, then, is the story of the Texan–Santa Fé Pioneers. The emphasis is on the human element, for in the final analysis it was men who made this monumental piece of history. They were men with wives and children and grand-children; men who were bachelors; men of sixty and boys of twelve. They were men who reached high to scratch their names, all unknowingly, on the great wall of history. Some died, and their bodies were thrown to the wolves; at least one was grateful to sink into obscurity; a few elected to stay in Mexico. Many died of *la viruela* (smallpox) or the dreaded *vómito* (yellow fever) and were denied burial in a Christian cemetery; one professed the Catholic faith at the last moment of life in order to give his bones a secure resting place; one died of yellow fever at sea on his way back to Texas.

Many of them returned home to fight again for the Lone Star Republic. At least twenty fought against Mexico in the series of actions that ended with the Mier Expedition, and about half of those were dead before the skirmishes were over. Many of the Pioneers went on to illustrious careers; many were in the Mexican War; some died fighting for the

[xiii]

Confederacy. Many have descendants in the state of Texas; one has a living son in Galveston.

They were Indian fighters and "amateurs," neurotics and "originals," men looking for adventure, men wanting to travel and see the country, men trying to cure an "inflammation of the lungs" on the great western prairies,[2] men who hoped to make a profit on the goods they would sell in Santa Fé, men who looked to the glory and honor of the Texas Republic, and men who hoped to see strange sights and have unusual adventures and afterward write newspaper reports and books that would bring them fame and money.

They all got more than they expected. For some of them the price was very high. But whatever these men had or whatever they lacked, they all possessed that driving impulsion to "see the elephant"—which, under other names, has not entirely left us yet.

[2] It may seem strange, in this day of hospitals and sanatoriums, that men went on such an expedition for their health, but this was common practice. George Frederick Ruxton, Frederick Law Olmstead, and Josiah Gregg are notable examples. None of these was with the Pioneers, but each became famous through his travels for health. See LeRoy R. Hafen (ed.), *Ruxton of the Rockies*, 309. Frederick Law Olmstead, *A Journey Through Texas*, "Note by the Editor . . . the hope of invigorating weakened lungs by the elastic power of a winter's saddle and tent-life"; Josiah Gregg, *Commerce of the Prairies* (ed. by Max L. Moorhead), *xix*.

CONTENTS

Introduction   .   ix

1. Background and Preparation   3
2. North from Austin   22
3. Through the Cross Timbers   37
4. Through the Breaks to Camp Resolution   54
5. Sutton and Cooke Across the Llano   67
6. Surrender of the Sutton-Cooke Party   81
7. McLeod Crosses the Llano   96
8. *La Jornada del Muerte*   114
9. Salazar, Armijo, Santa Anna, Carlos   134
10. Navarro; Kendall's Passport   141
11. Was William P. Lewis a Traitor?   148
12. Was a Military Conquest Intended?   161
13. Treatment of the Prisoners   173
14. Repercussions   182

Appendices

A. Preliminary Biographical Roster of
     the Texan–Santa Fé Pioneers   193
B. Transfers and Lists   255
C. Commanders on the March to Mexico City   258
D. Others Encountered in
     Study of the Expedition   261

E. Mexican Prisons   273
F. Ships   274
G. Kendall's Itinerary   275
H. Advance Parties   281

   Bibliography   283
   Index   299

ILLUSTRATIONS

George Wilkins Kendall   *opposite page*   46
General McLeod Orders the March   47
The Buffalo Chase   62
Thomas Falconer   63
George C. Grover   63
General Order at Camp Resolution   94
Where the Pioneers Descended the Caprock   110
General Manuel Armijo   111
H. R. Buchanan   158
Passing Through Guanajuato   159
Peter Gallegher   174
Page from the Gallegher Diary   175

MAPS

The Route Taken by
the Pioneers   *opposite page*   14
(Adapted from Kendall, *Narrative
of the Texan Santa Fé Expedition.*)
North from Brushy Creek   *page*   31
North Through the Cross Timbers
and West Along the Wichita River   43
West Along the Wichita River and
Northwest to Camp Resolution   59
Across the Llano in Two Parties   71
West to the Descent of the Llano   93
Route of the Main McLeod Party
to Paso del Norte   115
South from Paso del Norte to Cuencamé   125
South and East from Cuencamé to Mexico City 129
From Mexico City to Vera Cruz   133

THE TEXAN–SANTA FÉ PIONEERS

1. BACKGROUND AND PREPARATION

INCONSPICUOUSLY, on the upper right-hand corner of the editorial page of the *Austin City Gazette* for April 28, 1841, appeared the call for volunteers to the Texan army. The notice, signed by William G. Cooke, was overshadowed on that page by a lengthy harangue on the coming presidential election in Texas, but, as it turned out, the call for volunteers was more significant.

Cooke's notice was as follows:

> Having been authorized . . . to organize a military force for the purpose of opening a commercial intercourse with the people of Santa Fé; for which purpose troops are necessary to escort the merchandise through the Comanche wilderness. I therefore respectfully address myself to the young men of the country. . . . All who arm, mount and equip themselves, will receive the pay of mounted gunmen. . . . Ten large road-wagons will be furnished by the government to the merchants . . . this expedition will furnish an ample field for adventure . . . I am authorized to announce the names of Edward Burleson,[1] Antonio Navarro, G. Van Ness and myself to represent our Government with the people of Santa Fé.

The call was issued at the order of Mirabeau B. Lamar, president of the Texas Republic. The words were plain enough:

[1] Burleson gave place to Dr. Richard F. Brenham before the expedition started. Burleson had an illustrious career of his own and was to be elected vice president of the Republic five months after the call for volunteers.

[3]

to open trade with Santa Fé and to raise a military force sufficient to protect the merchants and their goods through Indian country. There was also the intention to extend Texan sovereignty to the Río Grande. This was no great secret, but it was not publicized.

At the time the notice appeared, it caused great excitement and enthusiasm throughout Texas—indeed, throughout the entire South. Many Texan newspapers long had been clamoring for this enterprise to be undertaken, and there was a rush of volunteers from all classes of men.[2] In Austin, in Houston, in San Antonio, in Gonzales, in Victoria, the pulse of Texas' adventurous men beat high. They talked about nothing but the expedition—the wild Indians ahead and possible scrimmages with them, the buffalo hunting, the bears and rattlesnakes, and the excitement of exploring country unknown to white men.

In Houston, all was hurry, preparation, and excitement. Men cleaned rifles and pistols, made bullet pouches, and repaired saddles and bridles.[3] In Austin, "preparations were going on in every quarter." Merchants were packing their goods and mending and strengthening the heavy wagons.[4] Officers were busy organizing companies, discussing the route and the probable reception at Santa Fé, and, perhaps, trying to find guides. Major George T. Howard went to New Orleans to buy supplies. But "hardly a word was said of any hostile collision with the inhabitants of New Mexico."[5] As a matter of fact, there was reason for believing the inhabitants of New Mexico would welcome them.

[2] The volunteers included many men who had their crops in and were leaving the summer work to their wives and children while they went out to make a few dollars; there were quite a number of merchants and "tourist volunteers" or professional soldiers. There were lawyers, druggists, surveyors, physicians, printers, mechanics, engineers, blacksmiths, carpenters, loafers, clerks, horsejockeys, and two or three comedy actors. (Gathered from scattered sources.)

[3] Kendall, *Narrative*, I, 21. This refers to a company of volunteers gathering at Houston.

[4] *Ibid.*, 63.

[5] *Ibid.*, 21.

In that spring of 1841 the young nation was approaching a financial crisis. Texas had been a republic for five years—since March 2, 1836, when delegates from over the state met at Washington-on-the-Brazos and, in a rough, unfinished building whose door and window openings were still without glass, drew up the Texas Declaration of Independence.

It was cold that day, and cotton cloth was stretched across the openings to keep out the March wind.[6] Nevertheless, the convention reminded the world of the rights of free men, set forth the denial of those rights by the Mexican government, and declared Texas free and independent.

The subsequent battle at the Alamo, the massacre at Goliad of Fannin's 340 surrendered men, the defeat and capture of Santa Anna himself at San Jacinto—all are known, by legend at least, to most persons in the Southwest.

But many factors complicated the existence of the new Republic. There was continued threat of conflict with Mexican troops; there was trouble with the Comanches and Kiowas on the northwest and the Lipan Apaches on the west; Texas' area was large but her population small, so the per capita cost of all governmental functions was high; she had a long coast line but no navy to protect her trading vessels; and she was confronted almost immediately with the panic of 1837.

A final factor was politics, for in the Republic of Texas men took political affairs very seriously.

Houston served the first full term of two years as president and, under the constitution, was ineligible for re-election.[7] Perhaps it was good for him that he could not run again, for he was already in trouble. It was said that he drank too much and that he quarreled with his friends while in office. He was able to treat with some of the Indians, and so spent little money on frontier defense, concentrating instead on maintaining the Republic's fiscal structure. But, even so, "star

[6] H. Yoakum, *History of Texas*, II, 72n.

[7] William Kennedy, *Texas: The Rise, Progress, and Prospects of the Republic of Texas*, Appendix VIII, p. 896 (the Constitution of the Republic of Texas).

money" fell to eighty cents on the dollar before his term was over.[8]

Lamar succeeded him in 1838 for a term of three years. Lamar envisioned roads and schools and public works—a fine dream but one hampered for lack of money. Houston opposed Lamar at every step. Lamar has been called a dreamer and Houston a bad loser. It depends on who is calling.

By 1841, Texas was broke; her expenses for the year were $1,176,288; income was $442,604, mostly in her own low-value paper. The public debt was over $7,000,000, and the interest on that debt alone was $400,000 a year—almost as much as the national income.[9]

Business in Texas was at a standstill; one of the few sources of income was the money paid to soldiers in the Texas Army. Lamar tried to get a loan from the United States, from England, or from France; he tried to establish a bank; he tried to sell land scrip—land being the one thing of which Texas had plenty.[10]

None of these efforts was successful. The loan failed because of the panic and the uncertainty about Texas' ability to defend herself against Mexico. Land scrip had little value because of the antagonism of both Mexicans and Indians.[11]

However, early in his term, Lamar had broached the subject of an expedition to Santa Fé[12] to establish a firmer claim

[8] Marquis James, *The Raven*, 302.

[9] Yoakum, *History of Texas*, II, 333–34.

[10] For a general discussion see Thomas Maitland Marshall, "Commercial Aspects of the Texan Santa Fé Expedition," *The Southwestern Historical Quarterly*, Vol. XX, No. 3 (January, 1917); A. K. Christian, "Mirabeau Bonaparte Lamar," *The Southwestern Historical Quarterly*, Vol. XXIV, No. 1 (July, 1920).

[11] James T. DeShields, *Border Wars of Texas*, 371–72, suggests that the loan, if successful, would have resulted in a great folly—the invasion of Mexico by an army from Texas—and that on this account it was better for Lamar and Texas that the loan was not granted.

[12] Evidence for the accent in "Santa Fé" is conflicting. It seems to have been used until late in the nineteenth century, and this writer believes that the advent of the Linotype, with its multiple fonts of matrices and the consequent difficulty of maintaining some 1,200 to 1,300 "fancy letters" in each font, had much to do with its omission. This was made official by the *Second*

to the Río Grande as the western boundary of Texas, and in 1840 he had issued a proclamation inviting the people of Santa Fé to join the Texans in "full participation in all our blessings."[13] But now he had a most impelling motivation: to salvage Texas' disintegrating financial structure. This could be accomplished, many believed, by the establishment of trade relations with Santa Fé and Chihuahua.

Those two areas, isolated from the City of Mexico by distance, Indians, mountains, and desert, depended on two sources for manufactured goods. One was Independence, Missouri, two-thirds of the goods from which were consumed in Santa Fé, while the rest went on south to Chihuahua. The other source was the Pacific Coast, where British traders, operating largely through the port of Guaymas, supplied goods for the Chihuahua area over the roughest seven-hundred-mile mountain trail then known. The total value of foreign goods brought into the two areas was between three and five million dollars a year. Much of it was contraband, but that was a detail. It was a *cosa de México*—one of those things—and the fact of its illegality had little effect on its movement.

Those two consuming areas also were rich in gold and silver, furs and hides, and other products easily turned into liquid assets.

In 1839, Lamar advocated a Santa Fé expedition in his message to the Texan Congress. He pointed out that the route from St. Louis to Chihuahua was three thousand miles, but from Austin to Chihuahua it would be only two thousand miles, via Santa Fé; also that a road from Austin would establish a short route from Havana, Cuba, to Santa Fé. Texas herself had little to sell, but could profit from a flow of traffic.

Havana at that time was an important wholesale center,

Report of the United States Board on Geographic Names, 16, where the board recommended, "The avoidance of the use of diacritic characters" in geographical names.

[13] Christian, "Mirabeau Bonaparte Lamar," *The Southwestern Historical Quarterly,* Vol. XXIV, No. 2 (October, 1920), 96.

receiving goods from England and from the northeastern manufacturing area of the United States, and the routing of several million dollars' worth of goods a year through Texas would mean a great deal in employment, in duties, and in the standing of the Republic among other nations. But politics intervened, and the Texan Congress did not authorize the expedition; therefore nothing official was done about it.

Before Lamar's scheme is labeled visionary, remember that in the spring of 1839 a party of Mexican traders from Chihuahua, headed by Henry Connelly, transported one-third of a million dollars in gold and silver bullion and specie to Jonesboro, Arkansas—across Texas but not through a settled district.[14] This would seem evidence enough that the Mexicans wanted goods and that they had hard metal to pay for them.

Texas newspapers repeatedly pointed out the importance of the Santa Fé trade and urged the President to open the route. Letters written by officials and public utterances by Lamar referred to it again and again. In April, 1840, Lamar issued his invitation to the citizens of Santa Fé, and the following November the Texan Congress convened again. This time Lamar was ready. However, the opposition was equally prepared, for Sam Houston was sitting in the Texan House of Representatives, elected from San Augustine. Houston's influence was always powerful in Texas; he and Lamar had clashed many times, and Houston did not like men who opposed him; he was not backward in giving his opinion on "the full extent of Lamar's stupidity."[15] Houston said, "The sole object of Lamar is to insure . . . his re-election."[16]

---

[14] *The Southwestern Historical Quarterly*, Vol. XX, No. 3 (January, 1917), 244. It is interesting to note that in 1789 Governor Fernando de la Concha proposed a route from New Orleans via either St. Louis or Natchitoches to Santa Fé—which he said would save 40% over the cost of goods from Mexico City.

[15] Donald Day and Harry Herbert Ullom (eds.), *The Autobiography of Sam Houston*, 163.

[16] *Ibid.*, 167. This is a strange statement in view of the fact that under the constitution Lamar was ineligible to succeed himself.

The two men clashed over another issue, the Franco-Texienne bill, and Houston lost. Lamar seemed to have control of Congress, and the future looked bright for an expedition to Santa Fé; but then came the first of the long series of misfortunes that plagued the expedition to its disastrous end: Lamar became ill and on December 12, 1840, had to go to New Orleans for medical treatment.

The Texan Congress was left in the hands of the vice president, David G. Burnet, and for a while the "Bible-thumping" Burnet seemed able to handle the body. The Texan Senate passed Lamar's bill to open communications with Santa Fé, but when this bill reached the Texan House, a substitute was offered to authorize an expedition to Santa Fé—Houston opposing both bills. Congress adjourned without having passed either bill.[17]

Perhaps Houston's opposition went a step too far, for, before adjourning, the Texan House voted twenty to ten to disband the regular army.

Lamar returned a few days later[18] to face Indian pressure on the northwest and the ever present possibility of active fighting with Mexico—but no soldiers. Defense of any kind would be difficult, and many young men were deprived of the small income on which they had depended. It is fair to say the situation was desperate.

At this point, Lamar, noting that both houses of the Texan Congress had approved the Santa Fé venture in principle, ignored the fact that nothing legal had been done about it and proceeded to organize an expedition, setting up machinery to finance it to the amount of $80,000 or more.[19]

J. B. Shaw, controller of the Texas treasury, refused to allow the bills until Lamar gave him specific instructions.

[17] *The Southwestern Historical Quarterly*, Vol. XXIV, No. 2 (October, 1920), 98–99.
[18] Lamar had returned by March 8, 1841. *The Papers of Mirabeau Bonaparte Lamar* (ed. by Charles Adams Gulick and Harriet Smither), III, 496.
[19] *The Southwestern Historical Quarterly*, Vol. XX, No. 3 (January, 1917), 257. Yoakum, *History of Texas*, II, 323, says more than $89,000 was spent. Another figure given is $78,421.51.

[9]

This Lamar did.[20] Then he instructed William G. Cooke to issue a call for volunteers, sent Major Howard, an old Indian fighter, to New Orleans to buy supplies, and chose Hugh McLeod, inspector general of the Texan Army, to lead the expedition.[21]

The call was made, and the men gathered in and around Austin, which was only two years old and had only five hundred inhabitants. There seem to have been four points of concentration near the town: Camp Cook,[22] Camp Bell,[23] Walnut Creek Camp,[24] and Camp Cazneau on Brushy Creek (usually called Brushy Creek Camp).[25] Brushy Creek, about fifteen miles north of Austin, was the take-off point.[26]

Supplies came in. Bargaining for horses began, and cattle were rounded up both as draft oxen and as beef cattle.

Seventy head of beef cattle were bought at the beginning.[27] They would be herded with the expedition, to be butchered as needed—the mainstay of subsistence.[28] But men held in one place for six or seven weeks, even though relatively inactive, have to eat, and so a considerable portion of the beef was consumed before the start.[29] This shrinkage in the beef herd did

[20] Yoakum, *History of Texas*, II, 322–23.
[21] McLeod signed the first military orders as "H. McLeod, Col. Comdg." Bancroft Papers, 696. (This is a reference to microfilm of transcriptions of documents in Mexican archives, supplied by the Bancroft Library, Berkeley, Calif.; page references are to numbers on the microfilm. See the bibliography.) On June 19 he first signed himself "Bvt. Brgt. Genl. H. McLeod." Bancroft Papers, 704.
[22] General Order No. 2, May 31, 1841. Bancroft Papers, 697.
[23] Special Order No. 3, June 4, 1841. Bancroft Papers, 798.
[24] Special Order No. 5, June 11, 1841. Bancroft Papers, 799.
[25] General Order No. 6, June 19, 1841, in Bancroft Papers, 704, is dated at Camp Cazneau, as is Special Order No. 7, Bancroft Papers, 800, which says they will "take up the line of march tomorrow morning."
[26] George W. Grover, "Minutes of Adventure" (a journal kept by one of the Pioneers; a very important source, referred to hereafter as Grover, "Minutes"); *Austin City Gazette*, June 23, 1841.
[27] Thomas Falconer, *Letters and Notes on the Texan Santa Fé Expedition 1841–1842* (ed. by F. W. Hodge), 37. Falconer, too, wrote copiously of the expedition, and his journals constitute a very important source. (Referred to hereafter as Falconer, *Letters and Notes*.)
[28] The menu contemplated is given in Kendall, *Narrative*, I, 85.
[29] *Ibid.*

not, however, bring about any rationing, for the beginning allowance was three pounds of beef a day per man.[30]

In addition to beef on the hoof, they had coffee, sugar, salt, and dried beef, but no breadstuffs or vegetables. Instead of bread, Kendall says, a quantity of tobacco was provided, and coffee enough to give each man two pints a day, with the necessary sugar.[31] The omission of some barrels of flour, says Falconer, was an "injudicious economy."[32] This lack of bread would plague them perhaps more than anything else. Kendall mentions it the first evening they camped: "No breadstuffs were provided, unless a small quantity of rice can be dignified with that title."[33] The time would come when the craving for bread would be almost overpowering—second only to thirst. The time would come when Kendall would feverishly buy all the bread he could pack into his saddlebags, even though plenty was on hand.[34]

The total number of men on the expedition was well over 300 (the usually accepted figure is 320),[35] and one of the most important items of supply undoubtedly was horses. It seems likely that Companies A and B were designated and equipped as cavalry, Companies C, D, and E as infantry. Lewis's company was artillery.[36] All volunteers were mounted, however,

[30] *Ibid.*, I, 85.

[31] *Ibid.*, I, 85.

[32] Falconer, *Letters and Notes*, 77.

[33] Kendall, *Narrative*, I, 73.

[34] Except for the complete absence of flour, this diet was not unusual on the frontier. Some twenty years later, Charles Goodnight, as a member of the Texas Rangers in the broken badlands of the Caprock—the same country through which the Pioneers were preparing to travel—said: "Meat was our main fare. We rarely had bread, but we always tried to have a little flour on hand to thicken soup. . . . We always had plenty of bacon. . . . Tobacco-chewers seemed to feel the hunger less than those who did not use it." J. Evetts Haley, *Charles Goodnight*, 45.

[35] See Appendix A.

[36] As far as the United States Army is concerned, the word "troop" was dropped from 1832 to 1883—but this is Texas cavalry. Bancroft Papers, 259, shows "Company C First Regiment of Infantry" of Texas was issued "1 horse, 1 saddle, 1 bridle, 1 pair of spurs, 1 surcingle, and 1 larriett." Obviously, in Texas there was little difference between infantry and cavalry.

and the purchase of three hundred horses was an important responsibility.[37]

It is interesting to note Kendall's evaluation of the different kinds of horse available in Texas: the heavy American horse, the wiry-looking Indian pony, doubtless broken down and short-winded, the light but game Mexican, and the barely broken mustang. Kendall bought a powerful American horse for four times the price of a proud, delicate Spanish pony, and never regretted the cost. He called the horse Jim the Butcher; Jim was later confiscated by the Mexicans.

There were other factors more worrisome than horses. To those seasoned mountain men or frontiersmen who had some knowledge of the unknown territory ahead, it was a source of increasing concern that the expedition had no guides. Guides, of course, would have to be Indian, for no others knew the country, and probably they would be Lipan Apaches. But regardless of tribal affiliation, guides were necessary.

Even worse than the lack of guides was the late date of departure. It was now almost the first of May, and the date itself was a warning. A controlling factor in expeditions in the West was availability of grass for the animals. It was impossible to carry feed for them on a long trip, and therefore every expedition's aim was to start as soon as grass was available and get as far as it could before it ran into summer drought on the plains.[38]

In July and August—especially on the Llano—they might

[37] On page 72 of the *Narrative*, Kendall says, "The different companies of volunteers, all well mounted and well armed and riding in double file." In General Order No. 5 McLeod says, "Such men . . . will . . . join the main body at San Saba, after having received their horses." Bancroft Papers, 703. Falconer, *Letters and Notes*, 35, says, "All the men were mounted."

[38] Randolph B. Marcy, *The Prairie Traveler*, 20, says the grass on all roads leaving Fort Smith was high enough for grazing by April 1. Nor would it seem unseasonably cold, for Falconer, *Letters and Notes*, 67–68, says of the country around Houston, "The trees were in leaf [sometime between March 12 and March 23], and, I was told, that the season was as far advanced as at Richmond in Virginia in the month of May. . . . The cotton seed was at this time being sown."

be hard hit for grass, certainly for game for human food, and probably for water for both men and animals. The Llano was a fearsome place in late summer because there were no running streams across it, and few lakes. The lakes that did exist might be so heavy with alkali that the water would be poisonous to man and beast. Horses and cattle, if allowed to drink freely, sometimes died; mules were said to be cautious, but men suffering from thirst often had to be restrained.

McLeod set June 5 as the starting date,[39] but the expedition did not get under way at that time, and there was muttering. Major Howard, Tom Hancock, and William Cooke, as well as Mathew Caldwell and Samuel Howland, the official guide for the expedition, were familiar with conditions northwest of Austin, even if their knowledge of the country itself did not extend very far. Perhaps that was when Major Howard, aide-de-camp,[40] began to disagree with McLeod.

Other plans for the take-off seem to have developed, but were not carried out. The first plan was to go up the San Saba River, roughly northwest of Austin,[41] where they would meet some Lipan Indian guides,[42] pick up reinforcements on the

[39] General Order No. 1, Bancroft Papers, 696.

[40] Appointed by McLeod in General Order No. 6, Bancroft Papers, 704.

[41] Falconer speaks of this route in his Notes, and says the shortest route is from the San Saba to the Pecos; Letters and Notes, 37. McLeod mentions meeting the "rest" of the command at San Saba; this probably referred to the long-abandoned fort and mission of San Saba, northwest of Austin, whose inhabitants had been massacred in 1758 by the Comanches and whose garrison was permanently removed in 1769. The San Saba flows into the Colorado River (upon which Austin is located) ninety miles above Austin. Frederick R. Bechdolt, Tales of the Old-Timers, 220, says, they had intended to take the old route by which the padres had crossed the Llano when they founded the San Saba mission. This is a geographical error, for the Spanish priests came from San Marcos, which is southeast of San Saba and not across the Llano. Carlos E. Castañeda, Our Catholic Heritage in Texas, III, 397–98.

[42] The most direct reference to the Lipans appears to be in Kendall, Narrative, I, 365; he implies that failure to meet the Lipans caused the change of itinerary from directly northwest to due north. However, it could not have been a matter of meeting the Lipans, for they did not proceed in that direction at all.

[13]

Brazos,[43] cross the Llano,[44] and reach Santa Fé in six to eight weeks.[45]

Another plan, mentioned by Falconer, was to follow the Colorado River northwest to the Pecos River—which was more direct than the route they did take.

While they were waiting, companies were formed, officers appointed, supplies apportioned, wagons allotted to the merchants, and invitations issued to men of standing to accompany the Pioneers as scientific observers, historiographers, or honored guests.

Cooke, Brenham, and José Antonio Navarro of San Antonio were to be civil commissioners of Santa Fé, and George Van Ness, twenty years old, was to be their secretary.

Cooke, as civil commissioner, was over the military. Staff officers of the military escort were Hugh McLeod, brevet brigadier general; Major George Thomas Howard, aide-de-camp; Theodore Sevey, adjutant; H. L. Grush, commissary of subsistence; Major Valentine Bennet, quartermaster; Benjamin B. Sturgess, paymaster; Francis A. Whitaker, surgeon; John Holliday, assistant commissary of subsistence; J. M. Alexander, assistant quartermaster; Samuel W. Howland, guide; and Joseph H. Rogers, wagonmaster.[46]

The companies were commanded as follows: Captain J. S.

[43] The *Austin City Gazette* of June 23, 1841, reports, "They expect to be joined on the Brazos by 121 volunteers from the East." This seems to imply Americans from beyond the Sabine River.

[44] In 1841 the Llano had not been crossed by white men for more than two hundred years. Coronado crossed it in 1541, De Salas in 1632. Martin and Costillo crossed the southwestern corner in 1650—but the Santa Fé Pioneers would make the first westward crossing. Many crossings had been made along the Canadian River, but that is off the Llano to the north.

[45] Kendall, *Narrative*, I, 84: "Not more than two months at the very farthest." "Nobody in Texas at that time thought it was more than 500 miles." *The Southwestern Historical Quarterly*, Vol. XXIV, No. 2 (October, 1920), 114. Oxen might be expected to make from ten to twelve miles a day. Therefore these two figures are in accord. The closest route by road today, according to a Rand McNally map of 1953, is 707 miles. The latitude and longitude of Austin were not known, as shown by a letter from Falconer to Lamar (Falconer, *Letters and Notes*, 123), and it is quite likely that Santa Fé's position was still undetermined. Hence the misassumption.

[46] Taken from Charles J. Folsom, *Mexico in 1842*, 249.

Sutton, Company A; Captain W. D. Houghton, Company B; Captain Radcliffe Hudson, Company C; Captain Mathew Caldwell, Company D; Captain J. H. Strain, Company E;[47] Captain William P. Lewis, artillery. Each company had from forty to fifty men, and the artillery company had a brass six-pounder pulled by mules.[48] There were seventy-seven "merchants, amateurs, drivers, servants, etc."[49] Of these latter, eight or ten, or possibly a dozen, were merchants; since there were twenty-three wagons, there must have been that many drivers or more;[50] there were a number of personal servants, poorly accounted for by name or number; and, presumably, the word "amateurs" covers the rest.

Hunt was a guide, but Howland was appointed official guide, for he was a well-known man in whom all had confidence; apparently Hunt assisted him.[51]

Some of the men furnished their own mounts and supplies, but supplies in bulk were largely furnished by the Republic.[52] H. Bailey Carroll gives a considerable list of supplies, which includes 2 pounds of calomel, 37¾ pounds of horseshoe nails, 4 pounds of epsom salts, 12 violin strings, 3 barrels of tar, 251 pairs of white cavalry pants, 1 clarinet, 2 tin lanterns, and 55 frying pans.[53]

The call for volunteers promised ten large road wagons for the merchants' goods; Falconer says there were fourteen merchants' wagons when they left,[54] and Kendall complains

[47] Companies and commanders' surnames taken from General Order No. 4, Bancroft Papers, 702; initials supplied.

[48] Taken from Kendall, Narrative, I, 71, and the Austin City Gazette, June 23, 1841.

[49] Austin City Gazette, June 23, 1841. This was later corrected to 37.

[50] In the Grand Reference Sheet, Grover lists thirteen "teamsters" by name. However, each writer's classification differs; Grover, for instance, lists nine merchants, one of whom is Major Howard, second in command. Howard was a merchant and he may also have had goods, but the term is inadequate here.

[51] Bancroft Papers, 931.

[52] See Cooke's call for volunteers, above.

[53] H. Bailey Carroll, The Texan Santa Fé Trail, 11–12.

[54] Falconer, Letters and Notes, 77.

that "the government of Texas did not furnish wagons and oxen enough to transport the goods of the merchants."[55]

It is generally agreed that each military company had one baggage wagon, and that the commissioners, the staff, and "guests" such as Kendall, Falconer, and Franklin Coombs (a boy of seventeen, son of Kentucky's governor), had all together two wagons. This makes twenty-two; adding one for the ambulance or Jersey carryall for the sick and injured brings the figure to twenty-three. Grover agrees with this figure; Kendall mentions twenty-four. The right number probably is twenty-three.

Falconer says each wagon was drawn by six or seven pairs of oxen, and the brass six-pounder by mules. This means nearly three hundred draft oxen alone.

The preparation stretched into seven long weeks, and this did not sit well with men who disliked inaction and indecisiveness. These were mainly men of action—impatient by their very nature—and on June 3 occurred a symptom of their restlessness when a private, John C. Snow, was killed by a sentinel. A court of inquiry was convened—a mild introduction to the long series of courts-martial that was to follow and which would not end until, almost under the rifles of Mexican soldiers, Captain Houghton, commanding Company B, should request his own court-martial October 1 near Tucumcari for making a dry camp at night only 150 yards from fine springs.

The sentinel was tried and acquitted. Colonel McLeod said of Snow: "A brave man, and one who had fought for his country, when she needed the aid of every son."[56] He added, "The safety of the camp depends upon the vigilance of the sentinels, and his hail, if unanswered, is the peril of those who advance upon him." Strong words—the words of a soldier. They would be remembered when the Kiowas, unopposed and apparently unnoticed by any sentry, stampeded the

[55] Kendall, *Narrative*, I, 365; in his summary of the causes of failure.
[56] General Order No. 3, Bancroft Papers, 701. This seems to imply that Snow had fought in the Texas Revolution.

stock at Camp Resolution and drove off eighty-three horses, leaving most of the starving command on foot. Perhaps they would be recalled when Lieutenant Hull and four of his men were cut off by the Indians, massacred, scalped, and mutilated. But now, in Austin, they were just words, and were lost in the general excitement.

There was also a squabble because the men of Captain Sutton's company demanded the right to elect their own officers. McLeod said this had not been the agreement; he ordered them discharged, forbade their re-enlistment in any other company, and ordered the company disbanded, but added: "If the Company return to a sense of duty immediately they will be received and the past forgotten." He was not a man to hold a grudge.

Presumably the company returned to its sense of duty, for Sutton's company was one of those to take up the march from Brushy Creek.

They lost another member of the Pioneers before departure, however. On June 12, Private A. Jackson Davis of Company C was killed by the accidental discharge of his own gun, and Colonel McLeod said: "His body will be interred with military honors so soon as a coffin can be obtained."[57]

Eventually the expedition was ready to move, but the exact date of its leaving is not agreed on.[58] Since nearly all of the concurrent journals were taken by the Mexicans, this is not astonishing, especially when coupled with the difficulty of keeping accurate count of days in the field. It is further complicated by the fact that all units of the expedition may not have started from the same place and therefore perhaps not at the same time.

H. Bailey Carroll sets the date at June 19, because, he says, that is the day of the month put down by Gallegher, and Gallegher's Diary, as a whole, is more accurate than any other.

[57] Special Order No. 6, Bancroft Papers, 799.
[58] June 10 had been another tentative starting date, for McLeod, under date of June 10, 1841, said, "Four companies leave this morning, two tonight." *Papers of Lamar*, III, 535–36.

Carroll's reconstruction of the Austin–San Miguel itinerary certainly will be the last word for a long time to come, but the starting date requires further consideration.

Gallegher's Diary says "June 19 (Sunday)." Carroll says that Gallegher wrote this diary in a notebook for the year 1840, which leads into an involved mixup, for June 19, 1841, was not Sunday, as Gallegher puts it down, but Saturday. Sunday was June 20.

Grover says the artillery company left June 21. Falconer, in his Letter, says June 21; in his Notes he says June 19; in his Account he says June 21. Kendall says June 21. A letter from Samuel A. Roberts, acting secretary of state of the Texas Republic, to Barnard E. Bee, dated June 21, 1841, says "on the morning of the 20th instant."[59] Special Order No. 7, dated June 19, signed by General McLeod, says: "Companies will . . . take up the line of march tomorrow morning."[60] The *Austin City Gazette,* in its issue of June 23, says: "The Santa Fé Pioneers left their camp on Brushy on the morning of Sunday last."

It is worth noting that the two official documents indicate June 20. But to a long-time editor the use of the word "Sunday" in the *Gazette* is almost conclusive, for a newspaperman lives by the day of the week—not by the day of the month. He has a press day coming up every Wednesday or Thursday, or oftener as the case may be, and everything happens "last Saturday" or "this Monday" if it happens after the last press day. (This was even more likely a hundred years ago, before accounting systems had ever been dreamed of in connection with a small newspaper.) The editor would not, even today, likely be mistaken in the day of the week; he can't afford to be. This also points to June 20.

Accepting Carroll's reconstruction of the itinerary, it is necessary only to note that the command stayed in camp sev-

[59] George P. Garrison (ed.), *Diplomatic Correspondence of the Republic of Texas,* II, 91. (Referred to hereafter as Garrison, *Texan Diplomatic Correspondence.*)
[60] Bancroft Papers, 800.

eral days—the accounts vary—at the site of an old fort on Little River. At that point the starting dates can be reconciled.

From Little River on to San Miguel, no reason appears for not following Carroll's dates as given in his narrative, *The Texan Santa Fé Trail.*

"The Santa Fé Pioneers left their camp on Brushy on the morning of Sunday last, and took up the line of march for Santa Fé. Heaven speed them! Success attend them!!" So said the *Austin City Gazette* on June 23, 1841.

Perhaps it was a premonition—that second exclamation point after "success attend them." For although the Pioneers themselves were far more interested in getting on with it, those who were only watching—the men and women of Austin, wives and children watching their husbands and fathers preparing for the trip, voiced grave doubts. They pointed out the delay of six weeks, the Kiowa- and Comanche-controlled wilderness, and the dreaded Llano with its blazing sun, its blistering wind, and no water. They shook their heads when the report was circulated that there were no Indian guides.

Some noted grimly that the attitude of the men was not suitable for such a serious undertaking. For most of the volunteers, the adventure seemed to be a great lark, and they thought of it only with excitement. (Not to be unexpected, for most of the Pioneers were under thirty years of age; a large number were under twenty.)

President Lamar, Secretary of the Treasury Chalmers, and some other officials of the Republic visited Brushy Camp the night before departure, and all "roughed it" with the volunteers—the President of the Republic cooking his own steak on a ramrod before an open fire and sleeping on the ground with the volunteers, a single blanket forming each man's bed.[61]

This demonstration of democracy was very impressive to those who saw it, but it served only temporarily to becloud still another adverse factor that would emerge immediately after the take-off.

[61] Kendall, *Narrative,* I, 69–70.

Every home in Austin was affected by the preparations. Houston men argued fiercely with Lamar men concerning the wisdom of the expedition and, when they could not prevail, fell back on the question of constitutionality. The former said Lamar was ignoring the laws of the Republic; the latter said he was justified by the law of necessity.

Children were wide-eyed with excitement and awe. The small community had been turned upside down with bustling men riding back and forth on horseback, soldiers in spanking cavalry uniforms, frontiersmen in brand new buckskins and moccasins. Every day there was something new; cattle, mules, horses, wagons loaded high with boxes and hogsheads.

For the women it was an anxious time: while pulling children out of the way of wagons and horses in the dusty streets and holding babies in their arms, they could not help but wonder if their husbands would return safely from the fabled, distant land of New Mexico. The wives were the ones who had the silent, anxious hours. Sometimes they pleaded, all the while knowing their arguments would not have any effect.

For this was Texas, and it was the great adventure. Kendall says, "Never since the discovery of America had such a journey been undertaken,"[62] and there were many who agreed with him—even those guards who herded the oxen and horses on the prairies around Austin—for at night around a hundred campfires they listened to tales of hunting exploits, Indian fights, and the black-eyed Spanish girls in Santa Fé, and they had no patience for talk of caution.

There was some criticism of the choice of McLeod as a commander of the expedition. McLeod was a graduate of West Point, but he was only twenty-seven years old. It is a little difficult to know exactly why his appointment was opposed. It could hardly have been for lack of experience, for he had entered Texas from Georgia in July, 1836, and had served in the army until December, 1837; he had fought with Thomas Rusk against the Kickapoos in 1838 and again against

[62] *Ibid.*, I, 70.

[20]

the Cherokees in 1839, under Lamar's expulsion order; he was the ranking colonel at the famous Council House Fight with the Cherokees in 1840.

James T. DeShields suggests a reason for his selection as leader, that might have had much to do with the disharmony between McLeod and the men under him; he says McLeod was a brother-in-law of President Lamar.[63] Whatever the reason for the dissatisfaction, McLeod's deficiencies as commander of such an expedition would appear soon enough.[64]

[63] *Border Wars of Texas*, 362. This was no more than speculation until the last moment of preparation of this manuscript. At that time a letter from Mrs. Lilla M. Hawes, director, Georgia Historical Society, cited H. D. LeMar, *History of the Lamar or LeMar Family in America*, to the effect that in 1842, General Hugh McLeod married Rebecca, sister of John T. Lamar, who was a first cousin of Mirabeau Lamar; McLeod was Rebecca's second husband. This would have been sometime after the *Rosa Alvina* sailed from Vera Cruz on August 12, for presumably McLeod was on that voyage. However, there is other evidence that McLeod was a strong family friend earlier than that. McLeod had sisters at Macon, Georgia, in or near which many of the Lamars had lived. *Papers of Lamar*, II, 169. And on June 19, 1838 (over four years before the marriage), John T. Lamar wrote to his cousin Mirabeau: "I feel like a Brother to him [McLeod]." *Papers of Lamar*, II, 170.

[64] There is evidence of dissatisfaction in the *Papers of Lamar*. In Vol. II, 209, I. W. Burton felt called on to defend him: "McLeod is a most able officer." In Vol. III, 514, James H. Durst, in a letter dated April 24, 1841: "There is also a great objection to Col. McLeod. . . . I think the objection is the want of Courage." However, there is no evidence that McLeod lacked courage on this expedition; perhaps the real reason was McLeod's lack of leadership ability—which would have been hard to put on paper.

2. NORTH FROM AUSTIN

SLEEP WAS FITFUL the night before the start, and by daylight the excitement among the men, assembled fifteen or twenty miles from Austin, was at a high pitch. Breakfast was eaten, fires extinguished, horses saddled, and teams harnessed. Then, with the men gathered, President Lamar made a "neat and appropriate address,"[1] reminding the men of the great service they were about to do the Republic by opening a trade route to New Mexico, and wishing them good luck.[2]

For a few moments the men were awed and silent, eyeing the huge wagons of merchandise with respect.

Cooke, the commissioner-to-be of Santa Fé at thirty-three, and McLeod, a general at twenty-seven, both were impressed with their heavy responsibilities and accepted their missions with considerable emotion.

McLeod gave the order to go forward, and the band broke into a stirring march. The first company, with horses impatient in the early morning, swung out in column of two's.[3] Captain Caldwell's Company D guidon fluttered at the point, and behind it, with the General's party, the Lone Star flag of Texas rippled in the breeze and the rising dust, and the

[1] Kendall, *Narrative*, I, 70.
[2] To the writer's knowledge, no eyewitness view of the start exists in documentary form; this is a reconstruction from facts known and some deduced (such as details of the speech by Lamar).
[3] Kendall, *Narrative*, I, 79.

iron tires of the heavy wagons pulled dirt from the surface and sifted it back to the ground as the oxen bowed their necks and the oaken oxbows squealed at the tremendous pressure.

Caldwell's company led off, for McLeod depended on him to do most of the scouting.[4] One other company followed Caldwell's; then the twenty-two wagons, pulled by oxen, and the Jersey carryall, pulled by mules, followed in single file; then came the beef cattle, herded; then three companies as rear guard, including the artillery company with its six-pounder—which turned out to be surplus baggage, to speak mildly. One company was detailed for fatigue duty—driving cattle and cutting away the banks of creeks and removing obstacles. The companies were to take turns at this duty.[5]

A later writer speaks of "rows of white tents, the lone star banner in the breeze, companies drawn up in double ranks, the undulations of the prairie. Yoke oxen and beef cattle. A band of two clarinets, four bugles, and half a dozen fifes and drums."[6] A sort of montage effect, for men marching over the prairie "in sets of four," as he suggested, are hard to reconcile with rows of white tents.

The *Austin City Gazette* said 362 men[7] left Brushy Creek

4 Caldwell was an experienced frontiersman and a signer of the Texan Declaration of Independence; he had been in the Council House fight with McLeod; he had been present when the Cherokee chiefs, John Bowls and The Egg, were killed; and at the famous Battle of Plum Creek he had led eighty-two men forward to attack a thousand Comanches. He was very popular with the men.

5 Kendall, *Narrative*, I, 71.

6 Bechdolt, *Tales of the Old-Timers*, 215. The case for the band seems a little overstated, although Kendall (I, 74), says they had "some two or three clarionets, a horn and bugle, besides fifes and drums." In a later letter, Amos F. Kendall (no relation to George W.) says he was the leader of a band which included three other musicians. Bancroft Papers, 649; Brief, 345. (Because many items included in the Bancroft Papers are identifiable only by the number scratched on the writer's microfilm, a further reference is sometimes given to the Brief, which is a compilation of typed copies of microfilm and other material. In any place where other page numbers exist, they will, of course, be given.)

7 The *Gazette* said a total of 321 men, but its own company and classification totals add up to 362. See Appendix A. The *Gazette* later reduced the total figure by forty, as related.

[23]

that morning. They made ten miles the first day and en-camped on the San Gabriel River, north and a little west of the Brushy Creek camp. This was a good day's march, even "over beautiful rolling prairie," for it was the first day, and many of the oxen never had been yoked before; a number of the wagons were turned over, Kendall says, and it was almost night when they reached their camping place.

Some of those who had arrived there ahead of the main body went fishing and tried shooting alligators in the San Gabriel River. The fun had started.

In a well-organized expedition, nobody would have gotten there ahead of the main body and had time to fish and shoot alligators. Here, perhaps, was McLeod's first real brush with undisciplined men—and his first failure. Too, they might have eaten alligator tails and saved beef, but nobody mentions it. Apparently they shot alligators just for sport.

That night they roasted or broiled beef on sticks or ram-rods, and the experienced frontiersmen began to spin yarns for the benefit of the wide-eyed pilgrims, who furnished an attentive audience, for they had come for just such doin's. A dying campfire, coffee simmering on the coals, wood smoke in the quiet air, brilliant stars above, a bobcat squalling in the distance—with stories of the Alamo and San Jacinto, of buffalo hunting among herds of millions, of Indians bent on raising hair during the Comanche moon in September—this was the stuff of dreams.

And so the old-timers whittled and chewed and told tall tales, while the newcomers hung on every word and tried to hide their squeamish stomachs as they became acquainted with chewin' tobacco.

George Wilkins Kendall spent his time looking and listen-ing and favoring his game leg.[8] He was 32 years old, a New England bachelor, a printer, traveler, and editor, described as witty, genial, and gentlemanly. A portrait of him shows a

[8] Five days before the Pioneers left Brushy Creek, Kendall broke a bone in his right ankle, but he went anyway. It is not an untypical incident.

rather handsome man, probably tall, with dark, thick, wavy hair, eyes large and deep set, a long, patrician nose, lips full and with an upward quirk at each corner, and a full, heavy strip of chin whiskers encircling his face from ear to ear; his hands look large and strong but well shaped; he is fashionably dressed, and there is a strong suggestion of good humor in his eyes. He was an intelligent and aggressive newspaperman, and that was a large part of the reason for his being on the expedition. He was interested in the Republic of Texas and aware of the importance of the trade route to Santa Fé. By being with the expedition, he would—as he had done so often —scoop his competitors on the news of the great western country, which was one of the most important subjects of that era. His subsequent writings are evidence that he did not pass up many stories.

The next morning they were awakened by reveille, of which Kendall was "heartily tired before the campaign was over." That day, in spite of the early start, they made only five miles, and McLeod admitted the need of another wagon. Perhaps he was under pressure, perhaps he saw it himself; it is likely the wagons were too heavily loaded and too highly piled for stability. At any rate, he sent Major Grush to Bryan's settlement to buy a wagon and four yoke of oxen, with the necessary chains.[9]

On June 22 they made six miles and camped on Opossum Creek. This day they passed the site of Major Howard's famous fight with the Comanche Indians. This had been a daring affair, and its retelling was heady stuff.[10] That day, too, they saw their first buffalo. During the night a tremendous storm of thunder, lightning, and wind came up, and the tent covering Kendall's party was carried away completely. The rest of the night, he said, they "took plain without kiver."

[9] Special Order No. 8, dated June 21, at "H.Q.S.F.P. Camp Archer." Bancroft Papers, 800.

[10] Kendall reports this fight in his *Narrative*, I, 74. For Howard's official report, dated October 26, 1839, see DeShields, *Border Wars of Texas*, 305–307. Howard's report is modest.

On June 23 they were still in rolling prairie country. On June 24 they made eleven miles to Little River, where there was an old fort. At this time (and presumably from the start), Kendall and Navarro were riding in the Jersey wagon. Navarro was lame for a reason not explained by Kendall.[11] On this day the expedition traveled into an immense herd of buffalo, and at that point the command took its second step toward disintegration.

The merchants and those in the commissioners' party were not under the military, but all others were.[12] Those not in the military were free to leave the line of march to shoot buffalo whenever they pleased, but all the rest were in the army and under officers. Nevertheless, the excitement of the fabled herds that covered the prairie like a black cloud was too much for the rank and file. "Notwithstanding orders had been given . . . not to break ranks, nothing could restrain the youngsters . . . every two minutes a Texan malcontent would leave the ranks at full gallop, and dash off after some huge animal . . . Perchance a bull—for the 'green-horns' generally select the largest."[13] It would seem a liberal assignment of extra fatigue duty would have brought this enthusiasm under control, but there is no record that it was dispensed.

Sometimes a bull, wounded only, would charge the hunter, but the bulls were not as vicious as Kendall imagined, for, whatever their valor, none of the greenhorns was hurt. A number of buffalo were killed, and several calves were "taken prisoners." That night they feasted on hump ribs, tongue, and marrow bones, along with buffalo veal.

About this time, however, in the midst of an unlimited supply of buffalo meat, it was decided they needed more beef cattle, and Major Grush was sent back for thirty head.[14]

[11] A reason is given in the Bancroft Papers, 1023, in a letter from Navarro asking for five minutes with Armijo: "My ulcered leg, inflamed with the cold. . . ." On p. 1065, in a letter to Santa Anna, he says he broke the leg in childhood and has had no use of it for over thirty-five years.
[12] General Order No. 2, Bancroft Papers, 697.
[13] Kendall, *Narrative*, I, 79–80.

Falconer sounds a warning note when he says that even on the buffalo range beef was distributed as if buffalo meat was offensive,[15] and Kendall reports that the men threw away the coarser parts of the beef, and clouds of buzzards alighted within the lines, fighting over them. The commander can hardly be excused for allowing such waste.

Major Howard and Archibald Fitzgerald, a San Antonio merchant who had been a professional soldier in many parts of the world, were sent to the Falls of the Brazos from Little River to get more teams.

Nor were affairs quiet in a disciplinary sense. One Private Kellett of Company D was charged on June 25 with sleeping on post. He was tried the next day, pleaded guilty, and was sentenced to a reprimand and loss of one month's pay. General McLeod noted that the court-martial had been very lenient and hoped the prisoner would not repeat the offense.[16]

Private Gates of Company E was charged with taking bread belonging to the hospital stores and refusing to give it up. He was fined a half-month's pay.[17]

Private Glass of Company E was charged with stealing sugar, but was acquitted.[18] Glass, too, was doomed. In September he would be killed and scalped by Kiowas while out picking mesquite beans for food.

Nor was all well with the officers. On June 25, McLeod told the expedition that because of ill health he was forced to return to civilization for treatment, and that Captain J. S. Sutton, the senior captain, would be in command until the return of Major Howard.[19] McLeod, attacked by a fever, was

[14] The reports of this mission are confused. There is no military order covering it. There were several missions back to the settlements, but little definite information about them.

[15] Falconer, *Letters and Notes*, 37.

[16] General Order No. 8, Bancroft Papers, 706–707.

[17] Special Order No. 10, Bancroft Papers, 801.

[18] Special Order No. 13, Bancroft Papers, 801.

[19] General Order No. 9, Bancroft Papers, 708. Sutton's seniority is mentioned in Special Order No. 2, June 3, 1841. See Bancroft Papers, 78; Brief, 157.

taken in a wagon to Bryant's Station, twenty miles east. Sutton was only twenty years old, and it is now apparent that Howard's appointment as aide-de-camp was considerably more than that in fact.

On the same day a young man named Lockridge, a Louisianan who had once been in independent circumstances, killed himself by shooting—probably with intent. He had been a lawyer, modest and retiring and good mannered, but he became despondent over loss of property and ended his life.

That night there was a false alarm of Indians when a Dutchman, a servant of Cooke, was fired on by a sentry in the dark, but fortunately was missed.

For several days the expedition was in this area, and bears and New Mexican hogs (*javelinas*) were plentiful in the bottoms, but still the men threw away the less choice portions of beef, and still the buzzards came over, and again the old campaigners began to mutter. The expedition had been on the road only a week.

No excuse appears for the officers' allowing this waste. The danger of the journey must have been apparent to all who were in a position to know the facts.[20] As for the volunteers—the enlisted men—the best explanation is given by Kendall, who says they did not question. In other words, they did as enlisted men have done all over the world.

On June 25, McLeod had left the expedition. On June 29 the Pioneers went ahead under Major Howard. The days' marches were conservative: eight, seventeen, fourteen, and four miles.

The "spy company" was formed about that time. A spy company was a scouting party. Some such arrangement was necessary in moving a large body of men through unknown country, for the importance of water, grass, fuel, security,

[20] There was no lack of warning. In 1841 alone several open conflicts had taken place. In May, Tarrant had destroyed several Indian villages on the Trinity; this had led to the great fight on Village Creek; these events were reported in the same issue of the *Gazette* that reported the departure of the Pioneers. Hays, Major Gage, and Captain Chandler all fought the Indians in June. All this activity should have given ample notice.

and wild game was multiplied when the number of men went into the hundreds; and with wagons the terrain also had to be considered.[21]

Kendall noted that hardly a day passed that they did not have wagons upset, accompanied by terrible swearing. "For originality, deliberate utterance, and deep wickedness, I have never heard [it] equaled."[22]

Private Campbell of Company A was tried for falling asleep on post between 1:00 and 2:00 A.M. He pleaded not guilty, but the court sentenced him to fourteen days of fatigue duty and to two days of leading his horse and packing his luggage on the line of march.[23]

On July 4 they crossed the South Bosque and went ten miles to the North Bosque. That night a man named Flint, having eaten too freely of unripe grapes or berries, developed a severe case of colic. Whitaker worked on him, but nothing helped; Flint died, and was buried the next day with military honors.

The additional beef cattle arrived, presumably under Major Grush, and at least two additional volunteers, Thomas H. Spooner and a man named Mercer, came from the Falls of the Brazos—Spooner for the purpose of attacking an Indian village on the route.[24]

That day they hit rugged going. They had to cut a road through a thick belt of woods on both sides of the Bosque and dig away the steep banks. When the wagons went down, they locked the wheels and held the wagons back with ropes. To get up the opposite side, they hitched together twenty yoke of oxen and used the ropes besides, pulled by fifty or sixty of the fatigue party, and Kendall says there was "jumping, whipping, cracking, yelling, pulling, cursing, and swearing."[25]

[21] In 1840, Burnet had approved a law providing three companies of fifteen men each to act as spies on the frontier. Walter Prescott Webb, *The Texas Rangers*, 32.

[22] Kendall, *Narrative*, I, 90.

[23] General Order No. 11, Bancroft Papers, 710.

[24] Bancroft Papers, 618; Brief, 375.

[25] *Narrative*, I, 95ff.

That night, while they were making camp, a number of men were detailed to get wood for fires. One of them cut down a small tree and tied it to his Mexican horse's tail with a rope to haul it to camp. (Again, we must remember that many of the "men" were under the age of a present-day high school graduate.) After the work of the day, the horse had no patience for shenanigans. When the Pioneer walloped it across the rump with his hat, the horse began pitching[26] to free itself from the strange weight. It broke into a gallop and headed straight for the middle of camp, with the tree bouncing wildly from side to side behind it. No trail driver would be astonished at what happened next. All the horses, mules, and oxen in the area looked up; their nervousness was not soothed by the sight of men running to get out of the way, each shouting to the next man to stop the runaway. The horse cut a swath through the camp itself. It galloped wildly down the middle, the dragging tree scattering pots, strips of meat cooking on sharpened sticks, and burning brands from the fires.

Suddenly and concertedly, consistent with traditional habit, every horse, mule, and ox gave a snort, curled its tail, and took off at top speed in whatever direction its head was pointed. A moment later most of them swung together, and the stampede was on, the animals taking off as a fairly cohesive unit, disregarding men, fires, and other objects in their path.

Kendall, apparently not caught in the general line of the stampede, was impressed. This was the first one he had ever seen, and he was fascinated by the sudden and inexplicable way in which the animals moved at exactly the same time. Fortunately, the stampede did not become a unit until most of the animals were out of the campground, so there was no serious damage to property, but it took several hours to round

---

[26] In many parts of the West a man is told that the word is "bucking"; that "pitching" refers to the movement of a ship. However, where the writer was raised, on the South Plains (not far from the site of Camp Resolution), the word was "pitching," and Ramon Adams, *Western Words*, 116, says pitching is "the Texans' name for bucking."

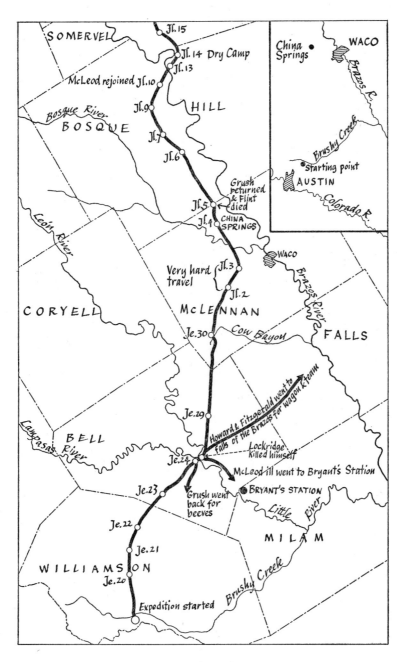

North from Brushy Creek, June 20–July 15, 1841. (County lines shown are modern counties.)

up the stampeded animals—an added trial to a hard day. After supper the stampede provided a fresh subject for the edification of the greenhorns, and it is evident that Kendall was tremendously impressed by the Texans' stories of other and greater stampedes. In fairness to Kendall, a full-scale stampede is terrifying, and it is doubtful that even the Texans much overstated the facts.[27]

Beyond the Bosque they hit a gullied region where Falconer says they had to travel twice the distance they gained, for not being able to keep a straight course. The Gallegher-Hoyle *Journal* says it was very hot.

On July 10, Falconer says they came in sight of Comanche Peak.[28] Carroll says this was actually Bee Mountain; this statement is supported by Colton's map of 1855.

The Brazos water was brackish, and they camped at a spring near the river. They stayed there three days to repair wagons, and Kendall got acquainted with rattlesnakes. He says, "The first intimation we had of the vicinity of his snakeship being his crawling over one of us in an attempt to effect a lodgment under some of the blankets." Doubt as to Kendall's direct observation of this incident is justified, for he adds, "I rolled myself, head and all, under my blanket, and lay perfectly quiet until daylight."[29] It is hard to believe that any resident of rattlesnake country would be so complacent. Perhaps Kendall, after the lapse of a year that seemed like ten, had forgotten the details and actually was relating something that had happened in some other tent. It is not believed that the men in any tent had the self-control to crawl under the blankets and remain there the rest of the night with a rattlesnake loose among them.

[27] Kendall's remarks on this incident and stampedes in general appear in the *Narrative,* I, 95–98.

[28] This is an adjusted date, to reconcile Falconer's Notes with the present schedule, which agrees with Carroll's. All dates from this point on also will be adjusted. Different chroniclers vary several days until an important event, when they agree almost unanimously. Such an event is the massacre at Camp Resolution.

[29] The rattlesnake material appears in the *Narrative,* I, 91–92.

They were almost due north of Austin, and in the valley of the Brazos was good grazing, along with grapes, plums, honey, trout, elk, deer, bear, wild turkey, and buffalo and mustang in season. What Kendall considers the season for mustangs is not clear. Perhaps he is referring to buffalo, which migrated regularly. If he is correct in mentioning elk, this is one of the very few bits of evidence that elk at one time inhabited the interior portion of Texas.[30]

Indians had been on the Brazos the year before, and volunteer corn had grown in their abandoned fields. Prudence would have suggested cutting down on the beef ration and filling in with other foods, but this apparently was not done. Major Howard was in command.

General McLeod returned on July 12, but he likewise took no action to conserve the beef herd. Whatever McLeod lacked, it is now apparent that he had plenty of courage, for, knowing the disciplinary problems of the expedition and knowing also that his officers were in disagreement with him, he nevertheless caught up with the command as soon as he was able and continued with it.

They started north again. Howland must have been acting as guide, though without any knowledge of the country. Cooke and Thomas Hunt had been briefly on the Red River. They crossed the Brazos, with McLeod again in command, and the expedition stopped for the midday meal—still, in many parts of Texas, called dinner. Scattered out along the river's edge, the men built many small fires to cook food and boil water for coffee. What happened, Kendall says, was accidental, and probably resulted from carrying fire from one spot to another.[31] There was a flash of fire, and Kendall, glanc-

[30] Kendall, *Narrative*, I, 102. Henry R. Schoolcraft, *The Indian Tribes of North America*, I, 433: "The elk was an inhabitant of the North Atlantic forests [in the sixteenth century] and was found . . . as far south as . . . the prairies of Texas." Vernon Bailey, *North American Fauna No. 25, Biological Survey of Texas*, 60, discusses the lack of evidence.

[31] In 1833 the phosphorus friction match was made on a commercial scale, but it seems more likely that men on a long trip in 1841 depended on flint and steel. The campfire, therefore, would be the source for most uses.

ing up from his own suspended strip of beef, was blinded by the blaze that flashed up like gunpowder. It was their first prairie fire.

It spread along the high, dry grass at the edge of the river with astonishing speed. A gust of wind would sweep it a hundred yards ahead and then blow steadily while the fire spread out and down the river. Before anyone who understood prairie fires could get there, the fire was beyond control and burning on a broad front—a wide band of leaping red flames, sometimes twenty feet high, turning into yellow flame and then swirling columns of black smoke; the rushing of the flames and the crackling of the burning grass were sounds that had all the newcomers hypnotized for a few moments.

Some of those at the south end of the camp, urged by experienced hands, tried to beat out the flames, but the wind was strong and the fire had too great a start. And so they had still another introduction to the hazards of the western prairies.

Fortunately the wind was from a northerly direction, and carried the fire west and south. If the wind had been behind them and had carried the fire along their path, it would have burned the grass ahead of them and severely complicated the problems of grazing.

With most of the men somewhat dazed by the lightning-like development of the fire and a little awed by its primitive violence, they gathered their equipment to go forward that afternoon. They stopped to camp at a mudhole, and all night long the bright line of fire swept across the prairie to the west, and the next morning it was climbing the narrow strip of low hills or breaks which led up from the Brazos valley to the prairie.[32]

They traveled over a dry prairie ridge all day under a hot sun, without water. The men suffered from thirst, but the horses and cattle were harder hit. They left the next morning

[32] Kendall, *Narrative*, I, 103; also mentioned in Gallegher's Diary and the Gallegher-Hoyle *Journal*.

without breakfast, for eating would increase thirst. They traveled all day, and late in the afternoon a spy reported that a large spring lay near their course. "The line of march was now instantly broken," says Kendall. Those who had good horses beat them into a gallop, while the ox-drivers used their blacksnake whips and "imprecations if possible more horrible than ever."

The spring flowed out of "an immense natural bathing tub," a basin sixty feet wide and ten feet deep, filled with cool, sweet water. Kendall soaked his swollen ankle. The men took baths, and they left the spring with regret the next morning.

Both Gallegher and Hoyle say, "From this spot on we knew nothing of the country as it never before had been traveled by a white man."

They made twelve miles, ten miles, six miles. On July 18 they found the "skull" of a white woman "but recently killed."[33]

Then eleven miles, then six miles, and on July 21 they moved into the southeastern tip of the western Cross Timbers. Up to this time their route had been almost due north and over prairie country. Now they encountered that peculiar tongue of land that seems entirely out of place in the area northwest of what is now Fort Worth. It is a long, narrow strip of blackjack country that extends down from Oklahoma. It is very rough and difficult to travel, cut up by ravines and grown up with brush and post oak that made wagon travel almost impossible. They would be in the Cross Timbers a week, and it would be a trying week. Kendall was to hear

[33] The implication is plain that they assumed she had been a prisoner of Indians, but the fact that they could identify the skull (or head) as that of a white woman suggests the woman had not long been a captive, for a white woman in Indian captivity soon grew to look like an Indian. It would have been very unusual for a Texas Indian to carry the head of a victim any distance; however, by migration, sale, and resale, a captive might have moved a long way very soon. Far the most curious feature is *why* she was killed, for captive women were property in every sense of the word, and exchangeable for goods. This one must have been particularly intractable and must have enraged her Indian owner at this spot.

[35]

for the first time the expression, "I have seen the elephant," and Major Howard was to resign as second in command— whether forced to do so by McLeod or whether as a protest, is not known.

3. THROUGH THE CROSS TIMBERS

"WE HAD BEEN cutting away trees," says Kendall, "crossing deep ravines and gulleys, turning and twisting 15 or 20 miles to gain 5." The streams in the Cross Timbers were supposed to have water in July, but they were nearly all dry. However, bears, deer, and some buffalo were found in the Cross Timbers, and a great deal of wild honey, which helped to take the place of bread. They discovered a deserted Indian village. The oxen were travel-worn and the horses needed shoeing, so on July 23, in the middle of the Cross Timbers, they camped on the Trinity River and set up a blacksmith's forge. The carpenters got to work repairing the wagons. There must have been water in the Trinity, or the journals would speak eloquently.

It is hard to understand, this long afterward, why they were carving their way through the Cross Timbers at all. They entered the Cross Timbers on its southeastern point and followed it north and west for some fifty miles, coming out on the western edge.[1] Furthermore, topographical maps show that if they had turned northwest from the July 20 camp, they would have had prairie country all the way to the Wichita

---

[1] According to John Pope, the upper Cross Timbers was ten miles wide, east to west. John Pope, brevet captain, United States Topographical Engineers, *Explorations and Surveys for a Railroad Route from the Mississippi River to the Pacific Ocean*, II, 4th part (included in the volume with separate pagination, but undesignated), 40.

River. The spy company could not have been operating very efficiently, and there must have been serious dissension among the officers.

Kendall says every attempt to find a way out of the belt proved futile. He says, too, that on one or two occasions they saw distant fires upon the hills at night—meaning Indians.[2] Since at no point were they ever more than ten miles from the prairie, it seems clear that feeling between McLeod and his officers must have been very high and resulted in extreme non-co-operation, for there were at least a dozen men in camp who could have gone on foot, discovered the prairie, and returned in a single day.

Perhaps it was this situation that brought about the show-down in the middle of the blackjack. Kendall says the officers held a consultation to devise means for more rapid progress. On reflection, that would seem to be a euphemism.

The "consultation" was held, however, and it was conceded (by whom, Kendall doesn't say) that the wagons had been too heavily loaded even for the prairie, and the first step toward lightening them was to throw away a large quantity of dried beef that had been brought from Austin. It was said to be spoiled anyway. It was also decided to do away with the tents, with the exception of one to serve as a hospital, and, so that there would be no argument about it, all the tentpoles were burned.

During this tumultuous meeting of the officers of the command, the fatigue party was digging away the steep banks of the river and cutting a road through the heavy timber and chaparral of the bottoms. The way would go through a stony and hilly country, Kendall notes.

Lightening the wagons was not the answer to all their troubles, and apparently there were those who thought it a mistake to throw away the dried beef and who did not believe it was spoiled at all. It should not have been if it had been

---

[2] Kendall may be mistaken. It seems strange that wild Indians would build fires on hills at night for all the world to see; this was not customary.

dried properly. At least McLeod found it necessary to issue an order appointing a committee to pass on the condition of what was to be discarded.[3]

Gallegher says flatly that "a council of officers requested Gen. McLeod to resign," and this is repeated by Hoyle. Kendall apparently was off looking for honey. Falconer, too, is discreetly silent; perhaps he was busy helping his fellow-countryman, Lieutenant Hull (formerly of the English navy) take astronomical readings.

It is notable that all journalists tread very lightly on this occurrence. It would seem to deserve more attention. The most eloquent comment is the long list of regulations for the future laid down by McLeod in General Order No. 12,[4] for these must have resulted from considerable criticism of some weeks' standing. Perhaps it was brought to a resolution over the abandonment of the dried beef, or even of the tent poles. Until new material is found, conjecture is the principal tool of understanding in this matter. It seems that the absence of criticism of McLeod by the journalists is significant, coupled with a similar absence of criticism of other officers. Whatever else the journalists said, they did not criticize McLeod directly—nor did they defend him. If they had felt McLeod to be in the right, it would seem normal for them to support him. But nobody even offers the excuse that he was doing his best.

It must have been a severe test for McLeod. He, a stripling of twenty-seven, molded in the traditional West Point pattern,[5] was opposed by a company of older men who were experienced in the ways of the wilderness. But McLeod, with the backing of his rank, maintained the upper hand; it was Major Howard who resigned as second in command. He stayed with the expedition, but was no longer aide-de-camp to McLeod.[6]

[3] Special Order No. 14, Bancroft Papers, 801.
[4] Bancroft Papers, 712–13.
[5] McLeod resigned a commission in the United States Army to join the Texan fight for independence.
[6] Major Howard also was a veteran Indian fighter, as indicated before. He

[39]

Presumably to satisfy the other officers and perhaps to satisfy himself, McLeod, there in the middle of the Cross Timbers, issued rules designed to speed up the march. "The following regulations," he said, "will be rigidly adhered to," and he forbade useless baggage, firing without orders, straggling from the ranks, and individuals' going after water at a distance. "The leading captain will be particular in observing the proper distance between the wagons and the companies in front of them, not allowing this distance to exceed one hundred yards." A few days later it would be fifteen miles.

On July 26 the expedition moved ten miles north and a little west through the blackjack and chaparral. The way was broken every two or three hundred yards by deep gullies; there was a heavy undergrowth of briars and thorn-bushes, "impenetrable even by mules," and the passage cut by the large fatigue party, which had gone in advance with shovels and axes, was necessarily narrow. The way was so rough that Navarro, although very lame, could not ride in the Jersey wagon and mounted a horse, and the merchant, Archibald Fitzgerald, drove the wagon that day. His style of handling the reins, Kendall says, was of the breakneck order—but so was the road.

It was an unusually hot day, and no air stirred within the Cross Timbers. At the first gully two wagons upset, and it took two hours to get them back on their wheels and the loads repacked. By that time it was hotter and the road was worse. By dark they were only halfway; the oxen were balking and the men were blasphemous; neither had had water all day in the hot and dusty blackjack. Several wagons had been

---

was in the battle at Plum Creek, among others, and went through the Council House fight with Colonel McLeod (Howard was then a captain); he limped from an Indian wound, probably received at the battle on Opossum Creek, about which Kendall tells. Having been sent to New Orleans to buy supplies for the Pioneers, he must have had, at that time, the confidence of both Lamar and McLeod. In 1852, according to Carroll, McLeod certified that Major Howard had resigned in the Cross Timbers, but did not further explain. Apparently some speculation had come up that Howard had been court-martialed.

upset, broken up, and left behind, and the expedition was scattered along the narrow trail for miles, everyone looking for water, "uncontrolled and uncontrollable."

At midnight they were still on the march. The Jersey wagon was in line behind all the road wagons, and consequently could move only when they moved. The six-pounder got stuck in a gully, and most of the fatigue men mounted their horses and went off to look for water. Kendall, hampered by his lame ankle, lay down inside the wagon and went to sleep.

They went on the next day, without water and without food. They finally emerged from the Cross Timbers about noon and found those who had been on horseback comfortably camped around a spring of fresh water a few miles across the prairie from the edge of the Cross Timbers. All afternoon and into the night more wagons and more oxen emerged from the timber and made their way to this new camp. With plenty of fresh water and with full stomachs, everybody began to feel optimistic again. The blacksmith set up his forge once more and went to work on the wagons.

They had spent seven arduous days in the Cross Timbers and had traveled fifty miles; they had had a full-time detail of twenty-four men engaged in cutting a path.

In spite of the fact, now quickly forgotten, that the expedition's discipline had come apart at the seams, they felt reassured, for to the northwest, as far as they could see, only smooth, gently undulating prairies were in evidence, and they believed their troubles were over.

They saw a line of distant timber and supposed that it marked the Red River, and, although they did not know it, they were only a short distance from a historic Wichita Indian village.[7] Howland advised against traveling close to the

[7] See Herbert E. Bolton, *Athanase de Mézières and the Louisiana-Texas Frontier 1768–1780*, II, 85 ff. Although Kendall says this was a noted camping ground for the Pawnees, he probably means the Pani Piqué or Tattooed Pawnee, as the Wichitas were often called. See Frederick Webb Hodge, *Handbook of American Indians North of Mexico*, II, 947. Historically, the Wichitas and the Pawnees of Nebraska are related and associated, but around 1800 in the Southwest a reference to Panis or Pawnees usually means the Wichitas.

Red, because the river water during the summer was almost unusable, and the banks would be cut with frequent deep gullies by the many tributary streams. The decision was to keep back from the river to "head the gullies" and travel on the prairie. It was an intelligent move, but almost immediately they hit the Wichita River, and, thinking it the Red, began following it in the general direction of southwest.

In the meantime, they crossed the trail of the Chihuahua traders, made the year before by Connelly's expedition—American and Mexican merchants in Chihuahua who themselves were trying to shorten the trade route. Those were the merchants—Henry Connelly, James Wiley Magoffin, and others—who, anticipating Lamar's effort, had loaded seven hundred mules in Chihuahua in the spring of 1839 and had taken them across Texas, then had loaded eighty wagons with goods in the spring of 1840 for the return trip. They had great trouble in the "dismal bogs and fens" of Red River, made worse by constant rains, and spent five months, Kendall says, cutting their way through the Cross Timbers.[8] This was the company with which an American circus went to Mexico and had considerable success.[9]

But now there was more trouble; beyond the trail of Connelly's expedition they found the prairie burned over, which made grazing for the animals a serious problem. That day Dr. Whitaker, the staff surgeon, was lost or missing, and that day also there was plenty of Indian sign.[10]

[8] This is not the trip of Josiah Gregg in 1839, mentioned in *Commerce of the Prairies* (ed. by Reuben Gold Thwaites), II, 100ff. Gregg followed the Arkansas and the Canadian Rivers.

[9] Although this group is invariably referred to as a circus, Kendall further characterizes it as "a company of American equestrians, with all their horses, canvass, and circus appointments generally." In 1841 the circus was largely equestrian. See *Hobbies* for January, 1936, p. 24, and for March, 1955, p. 34; *Illustrated News*, 1853, p. 372. Kendall's mention of five months is exaggerated, but not too much. Connelly's Expedition made the trip from Chihuahua to Jonesboro, or Pecan Point, in six weeks; the return started in April and ended in August, with some delay at Presidio del Norte.

[10] "Sign" meant any kind of evidence outdoors. "Indian sign" meant abandoned villages or campsites, discarded clothing, ashes of campfires, the bones of animals consumed, footprints, or any other indication that Indians had been

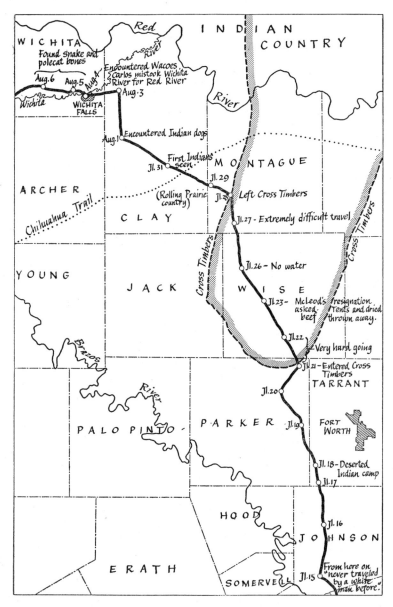

North through the Cross Timbers and west along the Wichita
River, July 15–August 6, 1841. (County lines shown
are modern counties.)

Now, too, there was more dissension. Some, realizing the tremendous waste of effort in the Cross Timbers, argued that they should not have crossed the Brazos at all, but should have stayed on the ridge between the Brazos and the Colorado, thus traveling a shorter course and avoiding the Cross Timbers altogether. Others said the prairies along the Brazos-Colorado ridge were watered only by salt lakes. Kendall was able to say, a year later, that perhaps it worked out for the best as it was.

Obviously the veteran Cooke was thoroughly lost. He had laid out a section of the Texas Military Road (a chain of frontier forts) from the Brazos to the Red River in 1840 and had established Fort Johnson above one of Holland Coffee's trading stations as a supply base;[11] he had also established Fort Preston some twenty miles west of Fort Johnson. The Military Road could not have missed the Cross Timbers very far—but "not very far" was a long way in the wilderness.

The band played and fires were burned at high points of the prairie that night in the hope that the lost Dr. Whitaker would hear or see and be led to them, but he did not appear. The six-pounder was fired the next morning (the most useful function it ever performed), but when Whitaker still did not arrive, the expedition went on, and there is no record that anyone was sent to look for him.

On July 31 they saw their first wild Indian, A buffalo cow ran past the Jersey wagon, pursued by an Indian armed with a long lance. His clothes and chaps were of buckskin, and a yellow band was around his head. He was followed by two others.

Navarro, in the Jersey wagon, shouted, "¡Los indios!" and snatched at a rifle.

Fitzgerald shouted "Comanches!" and whipped the mules into a gallop.

---

present. Eliminatory evidence of man or beast was very important on the frontier.

[11] Near the present town of Denison, Texas.

The Indians passed so close to the wagon that the dirt from their horses' hoofs rattled against the curtains of the wagon, but Kendall says the first two Indians paid no attention to the wagon. The third Indian wheeled about and went back. The first two continued after the buffalo. The Pioneers' encampment, however, was not very far ahead, and the buffalo ran into the lines, where it was shot by Lieutenant Scott. The Indians, obviously disappointed, turned and disappeared over the prairie.

That night the Pioneers made another dry camp. On the next day they picked up Indian dogs, "some twenty or thirty half-starved curs." These dogs were to be more valuable than anyone then imagined.

The frontiersmen pointed out immediately that the Indians must have been desperate for food, not to be alarmed by the wagon, and the discovery of a deserted Indian camp soon after verified the conclusion that game was scarce on the prairie that summer, for the camp refuse showed the bones of fish, snakes, terrapins, and polecats—the last resort, for few Plains Indians would touch any of these animals—except possibly terrapins—until they were starving.

By this time the men themselves resembled Indians. Their faces were mahogany brown, their hair was uncut ("long and matted," says Kendall), and their shirts torn and greasy. As a matter of fact, Major Howard chased a man known as Larrabee and almost shot him before he found out he was not an Indian. Larrabee would die later on the road to Mexico.[12]

The country west from the Cross Timbers is predominantly prairie, rising in a series of long terraces or steppes; they were usually described as "undulating prairies," and so the prospect

[12] Larrabee is called a volunteer by Kendall, but his name does not appear on any of the lists unless it is one of the illegible names on the Grand Reference Sheet. Grover lists a "Larabe" who died "on the Concho in October," but this probably is a geographical error, for Grover was several hundred miles away at the time.

For an anecdote about Larrabee, see *The Southwestern Historical Quarterly*, Vol. IX, No. 3 (January, 1906), 149; he was a servant or hired man of Major Bennet.

for travel—if a man overlooked the closely picked bones in the Wichita camp—was promising.

On August 2 they saw an eclipse of the moon, which is evidence that they were up early, for the eclipse began at 3:19 A.M. and lasted until the moon set at 4:55.[13]

On August 3 there were more courts-martial. José Jimerez (probably Jímenez) of Company B was charged with sleeping on post but found not guilty; he had lain down on his post but not slept. P. Bickford of Company C was charged with mutinous conduct for refusing to stand his turn at guard duty; his pay was stopped for one month and he was given two months' fatigue duty. Spencer Moffitt of Company E was also charged with mutinous conduct and gross disobedience, and got the same sentence, with recommendation for leniency because he had not served before as a soldier. H. P. Little of Company A was found guilty of using contumelious language toward the officer of the day and was fined two months' pay and sentenced to permanent guard duty for the duration. McLeod concurred with the court in all sentences and remitted Moffitt's sentence, but warned: "He must remember that the court will never recommend him the second time."[14]

That evening Franklin Coombs, son of the governor of Kentucky, and Curtis Caldwell, twelve-year-old son of "Old Paint," were missing for a short while, but came in after the fires were kindled. At 9:00 P.M. they had a tremendous rain which continued all night. Kendall slept soundly wet through to the skin, and they started the next day's march in wet clothes and a drizzling rain.

Now occurred another in that long chain of incredible circumstances that could lead to nothing but tragedy. It was a mistake, unintentional and unforeseeable, but it was nevertheless a link in the series of events.

A Mexican named Carlos told the men around him that he had trapped up and down the Red River when he had lived

13 *The Farmer's Almanack, for the Year of Our Lord 1841*, 3.
14 General Order No. 14, Bancroft Papers, 715-19.

George Wilkins Kendall

From an oil portrait by Thomas Hicks, about 1837

Special Order
No. 7

Head Quarters Santa Fe Pioneers,
Camp Cazneau, June 19th 1841.

The commandants of Companies
will hold themselves in readiness to take up
the line of March tomorrow Morning immediately
after Guard Mounting

By order of
1st Brig. Gen. H. McLeod

Theodore Livey
Adjutant

_____

Special Order
No. 8

Head Quarters Santa Fe Pioneers
Camp Archer June 20th 1841.

Major Grush with a
sufficient guard, will forthwith proceed
to Bryants settlement and purchase one
wagon and four yokes of oxen, with the
necessary chains &c, and join the Command
with the same as soon as possible

Theodore Livey
Adjutant

By order of B. Brig. Gen. H. McLeod

_____

General McLeod Orders the March

in Taos, and knew it well—that this country resembled it very much.

Carlos had worked as a mail carrier for several years between Austin and San Antonio and was known to be honest and trustworthy. He was promptly transferred to the spy company.

Kendall says Carlos' work and reputation were known, but gives no authority, for, after all, Carlos was a Mexican, and it was not customary in those days to give a Mexican more than summary treatment. Probably Carlos was known to men like Cooke and Fitzgerald, both of whom lived in San Antonio.[15]

That day the spy company met some Waco Indians. The Indians were well armed and mounted on large, powerful American horses which Kendall says "had evidently been stolen." Many had American rifles, and they were better dressed than "Camanches or Caygüas."[16]

The imperative need now was geographical: Where were they? In which direction was Santa Fé? How far was it?

Carlos addressed the Indians in Spanish and tried to verify his own impressions.[17] They were not informative. They said —probably with self-satisfaction—that they had been watching the party for several days. Captain Caldwell tried but could not get information from them, and finally the Indians rode off. Caldwell sent Tom Hancock and another man to follow them, and these two were led to a large Indian village.

---

[15] Juan Carlos is listed as a member of Company B by Folsom, *Mexico in 1842*, 250. A full discussion of Carlos' probable motivation in this matter will be given in a later chapter.

[16] The Wacos were one of the Wichita tribes. Kendall says (*Narrative*, II, 403) that later he talked with "Mr. Gregg" (undoubtedly Josiah Gregg) and Gregg thought they were not Wacos but Cherokees. If, however, they were inhabitants of the village the Pioneers were about to discover, they probably were Wacos. The Cherokees had been expelled in 1839 and the leaders killed, and, with the Texans on the move, no group of Cherokees would have allowed themselves to be seen, much less contacted.

[17] The Spanish language to a certain extent was the common language of the Southwest—the Indians having been exposed to it for hundreds of years.

Fifty Texans[18] rode toward it with a flag of truce, but the Indian inhabitants—women and children and old men—began to flee, driving their horses before them. Van Ness and Carlos went forward with the white flag. A second phase of the village's desertion took place, in which the fleeing Indians were warriors, and it was fairly apparent that these Indians were of the same tribe as those to whom they had recently talked. By the time Van Ness reached the village, there were no Indians left. Fires were still burning, pumpkins boiling, and animal skins full of corn were left there.

McLeod had given strict orders that the Pioneers were not to molest anything, and they camped near the village that night, anticipating trouble that did not come. The river water was too brackish for drinking, however, and they could not locate whatever springs the Wacos must have used.

Kendall says the houses were conical and built of poles, buffalo hides, and rushes. The poles were straight up for ten feet and then bent over at the top until the houses looked like beehives.[19]

Carlos now was confident that they were on the Red River, some distance above a well-known trading house, Coffee's Upper Station.[20]

Grover reports that about this time they were beginning to use mesquite beans for coffee. Kendall says they took some pumpkins from the Indian village; Falconer says they were watermelons, and he adds that sentries were set to keep the men from molesting the village. On the whole, it would seem the Wacos had little to complain about.

[18] There is a confusion here which Kendall does not clarify.

[19] These are typical Wichita dwellings. For a drawing, see George Catlin, *Letters and Notes on the . . . North-American Indians,* II, plate 173, opposite p. 70.

[20] Holland Coffee, working out of Fort Smith, established a number of trading stations, but presumably this refers to the one highest on the Red River—in the extreme southwestern corner of Tillman County, Oklahoma—which he established in 1833. This Upper Station, as it was called, was about seventy-five miles above the mouth of the Wichita, and careful measurement shows that the Pioneers on this date, instead of being above Coffee's Station, were fifty miles below it.

That night they had boiled beef, pumpkin, and fried cat-fish, which they caught in the stream. They had eaten no vegetables for two months, and the pumpkin was well received.

The men detected Indians watching them from the distant hills that day, but they made no move to attack them or stampede the stock.

On the evening of August 5, Dr. Whitaker rejoined them. He had fallen asleep and the expedition had gone off without him, and then he had gotten lost. Apparently the intervening six days in the open had not hurt him. It would be interesting to know how he survived alone in a country filled with Indians and how he evaded them. But these details are lacking. Kendall does not elaborate.

Kendall joined the spy company August 6. They were still following the Wichita, believing it to be the Red.[21] The water was low, and they were traveling south of west, but no one worried for a few days.

Gallegher says it was good land, with plenty of timber but bad water and broken country. The beef cattle were becoming very gaunt from lack of grass and water. The sugar was gone and the coffee almost gone. They still had three pounds of beef a day, but were feeling the lack of bread.

The found a stream which Carlos said was the Río Eutaw, where he had trapped, and there seemed to be a wagon road on the opposite side. Carlos was positive that he knew this country as well as his mother's backyard, and said the *Angosturas* or Narrows of the Red River[22] were only seventy miles beyond, and once they reached the Narrows, they would have

[21] There were a number of Red rivers in the Southwest. The word *colorado* in Spanish means "ruddy," and this applies to the Red or Canadian, especially at flood time when the water is loaded with red silt. The Colorado River which empties into the Gulf of California originally was called the Napestle; the present Red was known as the Red River of Natchitoches. Austin, the capital of Texas, is on still another Colorado River. The present Canadian, where it rises in New Mexico, was also called the Colorado (Kendall, *Narrative*, I, 249), and quite possibly Carlos was fooled by the appearance of the water as much as anything else.

[22] Narrow canyon in the mountains of eastern New Mexico, through which the Canadian flows.

[49]

only seventy more miles to the Mexican ranches around San Miguel.[23]

Carlos spoke with authority and gave the men confidence. They began to feel that their endless toil and hardship were approaching the end and that the familiar sights of civilization were near.

They prepared their night camp with lighter hearts, although it began to drizzle and the rain soaked them through to the skin. Even this discomfort was endured in fortitude, however, because of the feeling that they were near the end of the trail.

The night noises began as the campfires died down. Hoot owls hooted from the cottonwood trees—almost overhead, it seemed—and wolves howled unusually close to the fire.

The frontiersmen, putting their rifles inside their blankets to keep the powder dry, muttered, "Indians!" and the green-horns began to get nervous. Perhaps Santa Fé was farther than Carlos thought. It seemed pretty far at that moment.

No one reconnoitered to find out for sure whether or not the sounds came from Indians. No man wanted to be wandering around in the dark with Indians on the loose, and apparently the talk did not reach McLeod, for he appointed no scouting detail.

Eventually the camp grew quiet and the men slept. Then, without warning, pandemonium broke loose. The bellowing of oxen sounded through the camp, and the thunderous pounding of hoofs, carrying through the earth, brought the men awake. Instinctively they scrambled for their lives, while the entire herd of oxen stampeded straight through the camp, over the ashes of the campfires, over sleeping men and their equipment. In a moment the whole camp was demolished; the embers of the fires were scattered, the men were plastered with mud, the equipment was trampled by hundreds of hoofs.

[23] Actually they were about 560 miles from Santa Fé (instead of 200)—and the Llano Estacado was still before them.

[50]

The oxen bellowed, scattering into the darkness. In the short space of a moment the camp had been disrupted, and there would be no sleep the rest of the night, for the frontiersmen had been right: the night noises—hoot owls and wolves—had been Indians, up to their old, familiar trick of stampeding the cattle. It may be that some of the youngsters who had so lightheartedly joined the expedition to attack Indians along the route, at this point began to wonder if the shoe was possibly on the other foot.

They rounded up the cattle and continued west. Buffalo were no longer seen, and even Indian sign became scarce. The country grew more broken, and they were forced to cross and recross the river under great difficulties.

At about this point Falconer says casually that "little credit was given to calculations opposed to" the opinion that they were nearing Santa Fé.[24]

On August 10 they reached the area known now as the Moonshine Breaks in central Baylor County.[25] Here they found fresh mesquite grass and mesquite bushes "about the size of a peach tree"; Kendall says the Comanches used the mesquite beans to make meal, while the Mexicans used them to make beer and sugar.

On this day there were three more courts-martial.[26] Tompkins of the artillery company was found guilty of sleeping on post and fined one month's pay. Private White of Company B had refused to assist Major Bennet in removing an obstacle from the road, had spurred his horse and ridden off; he was sentenced to fatigue duty all the way to Santa Fé, but the court recommended the sentence be remitted. H. B. Sutton

---

[24] *Letters and Notes,* 37.

[25] Carroll, *The Texan Santa Fé Trail,* 99.

[26] It is a strange fact that the several chroniclers almost—if not completely—ignore the courts-martial, of which there were sixteen en route—one for each seventeen men listed in the military. It is an eloquent silence. If the number of courts-martial seems unusually large, it is interesting to know that a check by the National Archives revealed that in the United States Army in 1840 there were 10,570 officers and men, and in that year there were 675 courts-martial—one for each 15.7 persons. That was for a full year, however.

of Company C was sentenced, for sleeping on post, to wear a ball and chain for a month and other penalties, but the ball-and-chain portion of the sentence was remitted for impracticability.

McLeod still did not see eye to eye with his officers, for he rebuked them as follows: "The commanding officer . . . is astonished that the Court should have deemed the offense of sleeping on post, the highest offense, except mutiny, of which a soldier can be guilty, worthy of so slight a punishment. . . . The mitigating circumstances gave just grounds for a recommendation by the Court; and they surely could not but believe that their recommendation and the testimonials appended, would have equal weight with the commanding officer."[27] Apparently McLeod did not object to remission of the sentence, for he granted it—but he thought the sentence should have been more severe.[28]

August 11 was a fatal day. On this day Kendall's life was saved because of his pack mule. The spy company was broken up (or had been already), with implications that the action resulted from discord between McLeod and Caldwell. McLeod sent Samuel Howland, their official guide, with Alexander Baker and William Rosenberry, ahead to San Miguel to buy coffee, sugar, and bread to be sent back to the expedition, and to advise the populace that the Texans were on the way and find out what sort of reception they might expect in the Santa Fé country.[29] Kendall says, "I wanted to go along

[27] General Order No. 16, Bancroft Papers, 721–23.

[28] McLeod's persistence in criticizing the "light" sentences and the court's persistence in handing out its own punishment, are also eloquent. Remember that the personnel of the court changed constantly. Presumably McLeod thought at that time they should throw the fear of the Lord into the volunteers by a sentence of death or possibly whipping, for he was young and probably considered that severity of punishment was the answer to his problem of discipline. The courts' repeated ignoring of his feeling indicates that the other officers felt that much of the fault for the expedition's disciplinary troubles lay with the commander. When men are allowed to break ranks, seemingly at will, the theft of a loaf of bread by a hungry man does not seem a very heinous crime.

[29] This was hardly the action of a would-be conqueror.

but my pack mule would have been an incumbrance." He was later to see Howland and Baker executed a few feet from his prison window.

4. THROUGH THE BREAKS

TO CAMP RESOLUTION

HOWLAND had lived several years in Santa Fé and knew many persons in that area, besides having a fluent command of the Spanish language.[1] The three men were to travel by night and lie concealed during the day, to avoid trouble with the Comanches. They were to find the Narrows and then San Miguel, and were to send back guides. They left, traveling light and fast.

On August 12 the main expedition continued slowly west. They saw cedar trees for the first time, but drinkable water was scarce, and they made a dry camp that night. They were now eating mesquite pods freely, and had found that a piece of rawhide in the mouth helped thirst, while a bullet was still better. They were forced to travel far to the south, away from the river, to head the ravines. On August 13 they once again made a dry camp. They started the usual fires for cooking, and, although they had had one graphic warning of the inflammability of the prairie grass, again somebody was careless. The grass was several feet high and very dry. Kendall, scraping in the sand along a stream bed to find water, heard

---

[1] *Funk & Wagnalls New Standard Dictionary* (1930) is cautious about "breaks" and "brakes"; it defines a brake as a thicket. These, however, are breaks in the ground.

an explosion and looked up to see clouds of black smoke ascending. The grass was burning fiercely around two wagons, and the flames raced over the prairie, propelled by a sweeping wind.

One wagon was saved—probably by men taking the tongue and others literally putting their shoulders to the wheels and manhandling it out of the fire area. The second wagon, however, with its dry wood and canvas, caught fire from the wind-driven wisps of burning grass and became a torch before they could get it moving. Men beat at the fire with blankets, hats, even bare hands. Those merchants whose goods were in that wagon worked in frenzy, shouting futile orders that turned to cries of dismay.

Falconer's eyebrows were burned off while he tried to save the wagonload of goods. When Kendall galloped up, Falconer's face was blistered and sooty, and some of his clothes were burned from his back.

The only fortunate thing was that once again the wind was in their faces, and it swept the fire across the prairie behind them. Gallegher says they could see the flames of the burning grass for several nights. And some merchant or merchants (nobody says who) must have looked with sick regret upon the ashes of seven thousand dollars' worth of trade goods.[2]

Then they learned how near they had come to real disaster. The wagon that had been pulled out of the fire barely in time was the ammunition wagon.

Carpetbags, clothing, and other items were lost, but Ken-

---

[2] Both Gallegher and Hoyle estimated the value at $7,000, which gives us an idea of the load. Trade goods generally had a rough valuation of $2,000 a ton, and experienced traders hauled as much as two tons in a wagon. But the journalists have been pointing out the great size of the loads, and now we can estimate that each wagon contained about three and one-half tons. This is not beyond reason. Charles Zabel and J. L. Beardsley, in an article, "Before the Railroad Came," *Outdoor Life*, August, 1933, speak of three wagons coupled together and drawn by twenty oxen; the first wagon held 7,000 pounds, the second 5,000. Charles Goodnight once freighted 13,000 pounds of salt in a single wagon.

dall never explains what caused the explosion that started the fire.

They saw mountaintops far to the west, and Carlos said they were the Cuervos, landmarks for the Narrows.

On that day parties of men hunted water in all directions without success; horses and oxen suffered more than mules, and Kendall says they became nervous and exhibited a broken, unsteady action. The expedition descended a steep bluff to a river—which was found to be very brackish.

But the worst blow was yet to come. That morning Captain Caldwell had ridden to the south. At evening he returned with the incredible news that the river to the south of them was not filled with reddish-colored water. They knew by hearsay that there was a river between the Red and the Brazos (the Wichita) that carried water like that in the Red, and the river to the south should have been the Wichita, but it wasn't red and its water was loaded with mineral salts, which positively identified it as the Salt Fork of the Brazos.

Had they been on Red River and above Coffee's Station, where Carlos thought they were, they would now be within sixty miles of San Miguel. As it was, they did not know where they were or how far it was to anywhere.

On August 14, thoroughly lost, they traveled the divide between the Brazos and the Wichita. Here the road was easy and the grass was good, but there was no water, and criticism began to center on Carlos—for he was, after all, a Mexican, and Mexicans in general had a poor reputation among the Pioneers, as with all Texans, even though José Antonio Navarro was one of the Santa Fé commissioners and highly respected. Following the massacre of Goliad, it was not, ordinarily speaking, patriotic to trust a Mexican in Texas.

In reciprocation, the Mexican *paisano* was inclined to picture any Texan as a fire-breathing monster on horseback, a *bárbaro* (savage). It did not make for mutual confidence.[3]

[3] Kendall, *Narrative*, I, 132 (speaking of Carlos): "A character for probity which few of his countrymen of the same class receive or deserve." See also

So it may be assumed that the "criticism" aimed at Carlos was more than that; undoubtedly it was harsh and brutal abuse coupled with dire threats of mayhem and emasculation.

The only water they found that night was impregnated with gypsum. Great discretion was indicated in its use. Although the animals seemed to like it, in men it caused nausea, stomach-ache, and diarrhea, and did not seem to quench the thirst.[4]

Kendall says everyone in camp who spoke Spanish was questioning Carlos. He says no threats were made, but this is hardly credible. These were undisciplined men on short rations, without fresh water, and completely lost on the vast western prairies.

The next morning Carlos and an Italian named Brignoli were missing. With them went all hope of being within sixty miles of the New Mexican settlements, for Carlos would not have deserted if they had been that close.

Fresh water was three days' travel behind the Pioneers. They waited until nine o'clock, but Carlos did not appear, and the Pioneers pushed on west—now without even the hope offered by a Mexican guide. Now they realized that the presence of someone who *thought* he knew where they were was

George Frederick Ruxton, *Adventures in Mexico,* for more pointed remarks. See also Waddy Thompson, *Recollections of Mexico.* On the other side, see García Conde's proclamation to the people of Chihuahua, July 28, 1841: "Do you know who are the Texans? They are some adventurers who deprecate us as savage and corrupt idiots." Bancroft Papers, 844ff. Or hear the words of Santiago Vidaurri, reporting to Antonio Cortasar on May 5, 1841: "The major part of the population of Texas is composed of infamous criminals, vomited by Europe, North America, and various points of the earth, who . . . have transformed it [Texas] into a den of malefactors afflicted with the most depraved vices." Bancroft Papers, 358ff. The distrust was not one-sided. Needless to say, these harsh feelings were not unanimous even then, and by now a great deal of the old animosity has disappeared.

[4] There were several indigenous specifics for diarrhea, but none of the journalists make any note of their use. Goodnight said snakeroot tea was good, and, as a last resort, tea made from the inner bark of a cottonwood tree. He said the latter made a "hell of a drink," but it always worked. Haley, *Charles Goodnight,* 85. On December 5, 1956, a guide at the mission of San Diego de Alcalá said the early priests planted and cultivated prickly pear cactus on the grounds of the mission so they could use the apples as a specific for diarrhea and dysentery.

better than the inexpressible helplessness of being lost in that vast wilderness.

Captain Caldwell led a party of thirty men to the north to explore the Wichita Mountains—then unknown, Kendall says, on any map.[5] They knew it was hopeless to go back, but Caldwell found nothing but the print of a white man's shoe —made by one of Howland's men or by Carlos or Brignoli. Caldwell satisfied himself that they were not close to the Narrows and went back. He shot a fat buck, and his men ate it, and they rejoined the main command about 10:00 P.M. at a dry camp.

More spies were sent out the next morning, and some of them, instead of spying, catered to their thirst and rode ten miles on the back trail to a spring they had passed the day before. They tarried long enough to wash their clothes and joined the expedition again at night, finding it encamped by what became known as the One-Minute Spring.[6] The water was impregnated with copperas and magnesia, which acted as a powerful cathartic on the men—but they drank it in large quantities anyway.

On August 17, Caldwell was sent to the north with fifty men and instructed to find Red River and locate a good wagon road and send back guides.

At a council held after Caldwell left, it was decided to reduce the beef ration to one and one-half pounds per day per man. By this time the beef, being tough and stringy, had lost a substantial part of its value as nourishment. Deer and antelope were around them, but they could not kill enough to take care of their needs. One buffalo was shot in four days.

On August 17, Dr. Brashear, the assistant surgeon, died of a liver complaint.[7] He was buried with military honors.

[5] Not the present Wichita Mountains in Oklahoma; probably the broken country east of the Llano.

[6] Falconer, *Letters and Notes,* 83; according to Falconer the water was clear and bright as it came out of the ground, but turned bitter and nauseous soon after exposure.

[7] So says Kendall. Grover says he died of consumption.

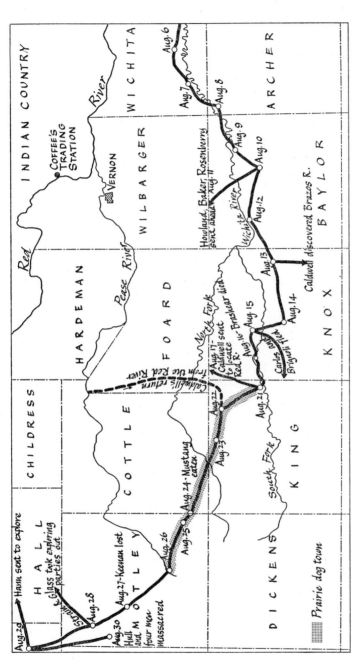

West along the Wichita River and northwest to Camp Resolution, August 6–August 30, 1841.
(County lines shown are modern counties.)

All were now sick and extremely weak from the purgative water, and they were overjoyed when a guide returned on August 20 to say that a passage had been found to the northwest.

They went through an immense prairie dog town, and one man armed with a double-barreled shotgun, one with a Colt's repeating rifle of small bore, and Kendall, with his short, heavy rifle (twenty-four balls to the pound),[8] went to shoot some of the animals, for they were told the flesh was excellent.

They soon discovered, however—as innumerable small boys have discovered since, trying to shoot prairie dogs on the South Plains with a .22 rifle—that prairie dogs are hard to kill. A hit animal would turn a somersault and get into his hole,[9] and even hit with buckshot at ten paces, he would manage to get away. Kendall tells a story that sounds fanciful, of one prairie dog, cleanly killed, that was dragged into its hole by a companion.

Presumably they did get a few whose heads were knocked off with Kendall's Dixon, for he says each of the three men had a dog[10] to eat, and they found the meat exceedingly sweet, tender, and juicy—like squirrel but much fatter.

That night they had supper of poor beef, and it rained torrents for hours. The next morning they finished the prairie dogs—so they must have had more than three—wrung out their blankets, and dried out their clothes. That day the spy company returned, believing they had located the Red River, and the expedition turned northwest and for four days traversed a great flat pasture with good grass, during all of which time they were in the prairie dog town. Traveling was easy, but rations were short and the water was bad.

[8] Kendall says in the beginning that his rifle was made by Dixon of Louisville. It must have been a little over .60-caliber. See Edward L. Sabin, *Kit Carson Days*, 86–87.

[9] We used to say—and believe—that prairie dogs could duck bullets. More likely it was a reflex action on being hit, plus an instinctive seeking of refuge in the burrow.

[10] Most persons know the prairie dog is not a dog but a member of the squirrel family. See Vernon Bailey, *Biological Survey of Texas*, 90.

On August 22 they had their first contact with hostile Indians. They were now approaching the Caprock and getting into Kiowa country, and one night six horses were stolen.[11] Dr. Brenham lost a fine white horse tied within six yards of sleeping men; the Indians evaded the guard, came into camp, cut the lariats holding the animals and led them out again past the guard—all without being detected. One of the artillery mules was found shot through with an arrow, but this must have been outside of the camp.

The next day they found ponds of rain water that "saved the expedition," according to Kendall. That night he had a sumptuous meal of broiled antelope, fine mushrooms, and young buffalo. He was considerably astonished, however, to discover later that the buffalo meat in reality was mustang meat.

On August 25 they traveled hard all day, but the country was so rough they made only two miles. They camped near a salt spring. Lieutenant Hull made astronomical observations and thought they were not over one hundred miles from the New Mexican settlements.

At this camp there were three more courts-martial. Private Moore and Private Watkins were found guilty of fighting and fined two months' pay and sentenced to fatigue duty. A musician, Alphonse Pisarzewski, was acquitted of selling a sword that belonged to the Republic.

Kendall records the continued disintegration of the company's discipline: "One party would go in this direction in quest of grapes or plums, another in that, hunting for game or water, and nearly all discipline was lost. . . . midnight coming before all the different parties arrived in camp."[12] They

[11] Navarro said the Indians were "Caygüas," with that spelling, but pronounced "Kiwaa" and generally written "Kioway." Kendall, *Narrative*, I, 198n. Thus casually do we learn that the Indians who would harass the expedition were not the deadly, ubiquitous Comanches at all, but the equally deadly—if not as far-traveling—Kiowas.

[12] Kendall, *Narrative*, I, 200–201.

were lucky that no Kiowas were in the neighborhood when they made these night excursions.

On August 27 they came out of the breaks onto a beautiful tableland covered with mesquite trees, and here, for the first time, they saw the Caprock, which some of them thought might be the Cuervos of which Carlos had spoken.

That day a soldier, Francis Keenan, was missed from the expedition. A party was sent to look for him, but he was not found. More Kiowas had come across their trail and now, unseen, were watching every move.

The next morning more horses and mules were missing. The night had been clear and there had been no alarm, but the animals were gone. The Pioneers crossed another salt stream in broken country and, at evening, reached the "Quintufue,"[13] where the waters, says Kendall, "were bubbling along over a bed of golden sand."

Just above their camp was a deserted Indian campground which the Kiowas apparently had left in haste, taking time only to drive their horses with them. The expedition found some dried meat of buffalo, deer, and mustang, which tasted wonderful.

Captain Strain was ordered out with twenty-five men to contact the Indians, preferably to find out the position of the expedition, but at least to ascertain whether the Indians intended to be friendly or hostile—surely the most unnecessary question of the nineteenth century.

The next day they went on, but encountered ravines impassable even for mules. The expedition halted. Captain Strain had not returned, so Lieutenant Hann was sent out with ten

[13] Hodge thinks this was the Quitaque in southern Briscoe County. Carroll identifies it as Los Lingos Creek, a tributary of the North Pease. Most early Texas writers say that Los Lingos Creek was a famous rendezvous for the Plains Indians, and was so called from the many languages spoken there when the Indians met to sell or trade horses and human slaves. Captain Henry W. Strong takes issue, however, in language too vehement to be convincing: "Why do people manufacture such lies just in order to make it appear that they know something?" But he offers no alternative. See *My Frontier Days and Indian Fights on the Plains of Texas*, 49.

The Buffalo Chase

From George Wilkins Kendall, *Narrative of the Texan Santa Fé Expedition*

Thomas Falconer

From Thomas Falconer, *Letters and Notes on the Texan Santa Fé Expedition*

George C. Grover

Courtesy Walter E. Grover

good men to find a road that would head the ravines. They camped that night without water; their principal food was hackberries—and only those who have eaten wild hackberries can believe there is so much seed and so little meat in them.

The next morning the report went around that fresh water was available at a spot two miles away, and all the animals were driven there at once, but there was no water; the weather was insufferably hot, and by eight o'clock they straggled back to camp.

A council of officers was held, and it was decided to return to the Quintufue; the various parties away from camp could easily find the trail of the expedition. Captain Strain had been out thirty-six hours, and forebodings for his safety were expressed on every hand.

The horses and mules were gathered up and saddled, the oxen yoked, the wagons lashed tight—and rifle fire was heard in a part of the prairie hidden from view by a slight rise. Fifty men mounted and galloped to the scene—but they were too late. Lieutenant Hull and four other men—Robert or James Dunn, Samuel Flenner, Francis Woodson, and William Mabee —who had gone out to scout for game, had been surrounded, attacked, killed, stripped, scalped, and mutilated by a party of one hundred Kiowas.

The men chased the Indians, but their horses were inadequate. They surveyed the scene of the massacre. Hull had thirty lance and arrow wounds; the bodies were carved from head to foot; some of the men's brains were scattered over the ground; Mabee's heart was cut out of his body. Mabee's hands still grasped the broken stock of a Colt rifle,[14] which he prob-

---

[14] Kendall, *Narrative*, I, 190, mentions the Colt's repeating rifles of small bore used to shoot prairie dogs. Grover says Hull and his men defended themselves with "patent 16-shot rifles," and Kendall says Mabee's broken rifle was a Colt.

This writer has not been able to substantiate this apparent reference to a 16-shot Colt's rifle. Neither Charles Edward Chapel, *The Gun Collector's Handbook of Values,* nor James E. Serven, *Colt Firearms 1836–1954,* lists anything resembling a 16-shot Colt rifle, even in experimental models. There were only two production model Colt rifles and one production model carbine

ably had broken over a Kiowa's head, although Grover thought Mabee's head had been smashed by the rifle.[15] It is possible a Kiowa rifle figured in his death.

While fifty men with shovels went to bury the five massacred Pioneers, McLeod started the rest of the expedition back toward the Quintufue. Captain Strain reappeared then, knowing nothing of the massacre, and said he had found no road except to the east. Some of his men had already gone to the Quintufue, they too having found nothing but salt water.[16] Strain had tried to talk to various parties of Indians without success.

Three more men—Donovan, J. Kenyon, and Klein—got too far from camp and probably were killed by the Kiowas, for they were never heard from again.

The expedition was in extremely serious condition. All dried meat, coffee, sugar, and salt were gone, and the allowance of fresh meat, says Falconer, was reduced to one and one-half pounds per man. Whether it had previously been increased after the first cut we do not know.

Kendall says "nearly all discipline" was lost; parties of three

---

available to the Pioneers. Both rifles were 5-shot to 8-shot (occasionally 10-shot), and the carbine was 6-shot. These rifles came in calibers as small as .31. The only explanation seems to be that the Pioneers' rifles had extra 8-shot cylinders which could be loaded separately and substituted to save time reloading. Metallic cartridges were not in use. This might have been called a 16-shot rifle by Grover, but from Serven's reproduced clippings on the difficulty of quick replacement, it seems more optimism than firepower was present. James Hobbs, *Wild Life in the Far West*, 347, mentions 16-shot Henry rifles, but that was 1868. Green, *Mier Expedition*, 70ff., speaks of firing nine shots from his repeating rifle as a signal; he must have been shooting government powder.

[15] It was a quick fight, but not an easy conquest for the Kiowas. They lost at least ten warriors, including a chief. James Mooney, "Calendar History of the Kiowa Indians," *17th Ann. Rept.*, B.A.E., Part 1, 277: "Winter 1841–42. Ä' dalhabä -k'ia Ehótal-de Sai—The winter that Ä' dalhabä -k'ia was killed." He was a noted war chief, says Mooney. The massacre occurred on a small stream which the Kiowas called *Tóñ-zó'-gódal P'a*, or Swift Water River, but in commemoration of the many horses they took from the Pioneers, the Kiowas renamed the stream *Päbo P'a*, American Horse River.

[16] The word "salt" used in this connection, of course, means any kind of alkaline water or water so loaded with minerals that it is not potable.

and five were wandering everywhere at will, hunting food and water.

With tragedy threatening on every hand, they ate Lieutenant Hull's horse, which had been killed by the Kiowas, and another horse that had been killed by the Indians at the same time. By now they were not throwing away the rough parts; they ate everything—blood, hide, and entrails.

At a council of officers that night, they considered their situation: lost, provisions almost exhausted, the men enfeebled by long marches, surrounded by powerful and well-mounted Indians. There were only two possible courses: to destroy the wagons and retreat toward Austin, or to divide the command and send one party forward with the best horses, to try to reach the settlements and send back help.

Both Falconer and Grover say that at that time they had only "four or five days' rations" on hand, and Grover says immediately afterward that the expedition had but four days' provisions.[17]

After long deliberation the council agreed to divide the command. It was the traditional and historic decision that in the West often presaged tragedy. It was not always a fatal decision, but inevitably it meant dividing strength, and it meant one party would be formed of the strongest, the other of the weakest.

[17] A little arithmetic will help to clarify the picture. The cattle they started with were not the Herefords we have today, but range cattle with more bone than meat. They probably did not weigh more than 600 to 800 pounds each at the start, and this was reduced by thirst and lack of grass until it is possible that the average weight was not over 500 pounds. Beef-bred cattle today dress out about 50 per cent. If those trail-worn longhorns dressed out 60 per cent, then one ox would produce 300 pounds of beef. Add another hundred pounds or so for skin, intestines, and other edible parts and one beef might supply rations for a day for the command of some 300 men. But this was poor beef—and their entire subsistence.

It is inescapable that at the start nobody figured how much beef the expedition would require. The starting ration was three pounds a day; if they were to reach Santa Fé in fifty days (just over seven weeks), the expedition would need 45,000 pounds of beef. At this rate, each of the seventy starting animals would have had to produce 643 pounds of meat. Kendall, *Narrative*, I, 85, does some fast figuring when he says thirty head were required for three weeks. This coincides with our estimate.

Cooke was to proceed northwest with one hundred men, mounted on the best horses available, each man with five days' provisions in his saddlebags. Captain Sutton, an excellent officer, was to be in charge of the military with him. There were to be from ninety-seven to ninety-nine men all told in this party, including Kendall and Grover. Captain Lewis and Lieutenant Lubbock were to go with the Sutton-Cooke party, as well as Dr. Brenham, Major Howard, George Van Ness, Archibald Fitzgerald, and Franklin Coombs. Gallegher, Falconer, and Hoyle were to stay with McLeod upon the Quintufue and set up what many thought might be a death watch.

The next day, August 31, they dried some meat over slow fires for the trip; they shod horses, molded bullets, and examined rifles and pistols. In the late afternoon they were ready to start. At that moment Lieutenant Hann returned, with no success. He had found no road the wagons could travel.

An hour before sundown the hundred men of Sutton and Cooke filled their gourds and canteens, mounted their horses, and set out soberly to the west. They made six or eight miles and camped at the foot of the Llano below the Caprock. They did not know how far it was to Santa Fé.

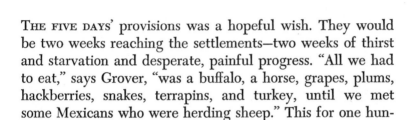

5. SUTTON AND COOKE ACROSS

THE LLANO

THE FIVE DAYS' provisions was a hopeful wish. They would be two weeks reaching the settlements—two weeks of thirst and starvation and desperate, painful progress. "All we had to eat," says Grover, "was a buffalo, a horse, grapes, plums, hackberries, snakes, terrapins, and turkey, until we met some Mexicans who were herding sheep." This for one hundred men.

They were unshaven; their hats were knocked out of shape by rain and wind and by use as pillows; their clothing was scanty and ragged, filled with sand and soaked with water, for almost immediately on mounting the Llano they ran into a norther with rain.

Each man was well armed with a pair of heavy belt pistols, a Colt revolver, and knives. Kendall had also a heavy Harper's Ferry dragoon pistol and a bell-muzzled pistol loaded with two or three balls and a handful of buckshot.

They made their way up the Caprock that first day and camped at the edge of Quitaque Canyon, east of what is now Plainview. They ate no supper that night, and saddled up at two o'clock in the morning. The decision had been to travel northwest, and they crossed the canyon, although it would have been easier, they found out later, to go around it.

[67]

One man killed an antelope, and Sutton, having ordered that none fire without permission (to save their powder and lead), arrested him and sent him to the rear. This may well have been the first real discipline during the entire expedition.

On September 3 they crossed another canyon, the Tule. It was three to five hundred yards wide and eight hundred to one thousand feet deep, and the descent and ascent were hazardous.

On September 4 their supplies were almost gone, but they continued northwest. They spotted an old buffalo bull on the prairie and chased him for miles, firing everything they had into him without bringing him down. They went through a rainstorm that night, and the norther with it was cold, but the next morning they went to look for the buffalo and found him down. They killed him and brought the tough meat back to camp. They made a pretense of cooking it over buffalo chips, but Kendall says they were so hungry they barely took time to warm it.

They kept on northwest, hearing wolves howl around them every night. The old-timers said this meant Indians or white people; if whites, it meant an end to the vast prairies. They had been making thirty miles a day, but many began to despair, for the great plains stretched on and on without apparent end.

On September 7, however, they descended from the Llano near the present town of Glenrio, New Mexico, some distance east of Tucumcari. They found prickly pears,[1] plums, and grapes. Water was no more plentiful than it had been. Game was still scarce. The country was rough, and some of the horses' shoes were torn off; their feet became tender, making it difficult for them to move.

Still going northwest, they struck the Canadian River near the present town of Logan, New Mexico. They found an old cart road on September 9 and were overjoyed, but the road ended abruptly in the sand. They saw, at last, three moun-

[1] Prickly pear was not found on the Llano. Haley, *Charles Goodnight*, 43.

tains, which undoubtedly were the Cuervos that Carlos had anticipated.

By that time the men were driven almost desperate by hunger. Let Kendall tell it:

Little or no order could be preserved by the officers, the volunteers scattering about in every direction, hunting for plums, grapes, and such game as might fall in their way. Few deer or antelope were seen, and they were so shy that it was impossible to shoot them; but in place of them every tortoise and snake, every living and creeping thing was seized upon and swallowed by our famishing men with a rapacity that nothing but the direst hunger could induce. Occasionally a skunk or polecat[2] would reward some one more fortunate than the rest; but seven out of every ten of us were compelled to journey on without a morsel of anything.

It is now apparent that McLeod is not required to shoulder the entire blame for the lack of discipline, for even under Sutton, who was an "excellent officer," the same conditions prevailed.

They flushed a flock of wild turkeys near the bed of a dry stream, and fifty rifles were fired, but only two or three turkeys were killed. They were facing starvation, and Kendall's despairing cry is most eloquent: "To go further without something to eat was now deemed impossible—the wild and haggard expression, the sunken eyes, the sallow, fleshless faces of the men too plainly showed that some means of sustenance must be provided."

A horse that had belonged to Howland, which had been one of the best animals on the expedition, was found to be so badly broken down that they shot him and divided his flesh among the men. "It was tough as Indian rubber," Kendall says, "and the more a piece of it was masticated the larger it became in the mouth. Poor as it was, however, and hard to

2 Despite colloquial usage of the words, a skunk and a polecat are two different animals. Apparently Kendall knew that. This passage is in the *Narrative*, I, 253.

swallow, I am confident that many a man in the party ate four or five pounds of it, half cooked and without salt."

That night there was a biting northeast wind, and they got no sleep.

They went southwest six or eight miles, but found themselves at a dead end and had to return. After a conference, dejected but refusing to give up, they decided to cross the mountains ahead of them. They found themselves again on the Canadian, in a deep valley. At this point, at the bottom of the valley, "it was now discovered that two of our men were missing, unable, probably, from their own weakness and the jaded condition of their horses, to keep up with the main body. We could only hope that they might be able to follow our trail and overtake us at our encampment—it was impossible, so weak and lame were all our horses, to go back in search of them." Kendall does not name these two men and he does not again mention them. No doubt the Indians got them.

Thomas W. Hunt, the surveyor who was acting as a guide, set out with Sutton to find a passage through the mountains and along the river. They found a Mexican cart road. Stunted pines and cedars were the principal vegetation. The rocky walls rose high on both sides, and they realized that they were at last in the Narrows, a canyon through which the Canadian River flows, about fifteen miles northwest of what is now Tucumcari, New Mexico. They had traveled a long and arduous way since Carlos had first talked about the Narrows.

From around a bend, Hunt shouted back: "People! Mexicans!"

Those in advance forced their weary horses into a tired gallop. They rounded the bend and burst upon a small camp of Mexicans who were sitting around a campfire.

The Mexicans were astonished to see this large party of gaunt-faced men, riding horses whose ribs protruded through their sides. The Mexicans were cautious at first, but when

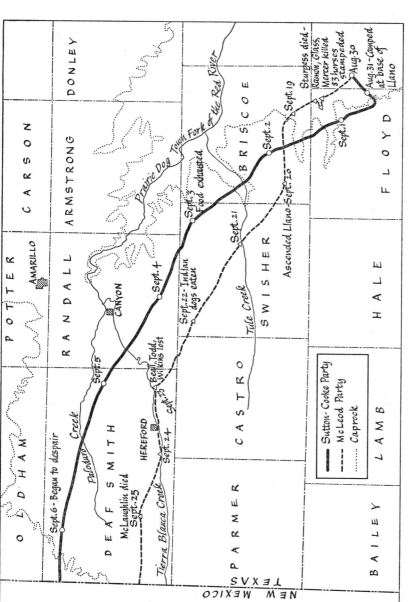

Across the Llano in two parties: Sutton-Cooke, August 30–September 6, 1841; and McLeod, August 30–September 25, 1841.

they realized the desperate condition of the Texans and saw they intended no harm to them, they invited them down and asked where they had come from.

Van Ness, Captain Lewis, and probably William Hunt and others, as well as some Mexican servants with the expedition, acted as interpreters. They told the Mexicans they had been on the Llano[3] for thirteen days, and the Mexicans could hardly believe it. They could have made it in four days, they said.

But the Sutton-Cooke men's condition attested to their ordeal, and the Mexicans[4] did not question their truthfulness. The Mexicans themselves, unfortunately, had very little to eat, and no food to spare but a small quantity of barley meal—barely enough to make a taste apiece for the ninety-seven men.

The first important town, said the Mexicans, was San Miguel, but that was still eighty miles away. However, first they would come across large herds of sheep and the village of Anton Chico, where they would be able to get *tortillas* and *atole*.[5]

Cooke hired three of the Mexicans to go back to McLeod with Matías, a servant of Major Howard, who now appears for the very first time. Matías was disguised so he would not be recognized by the Indians and linked with the *Tejanos*— automatic enemies of all wild Indians. The four men were given the best mules and a package of letters for McLeod, telling him what they had found and instructing him to leave all surplus baggage and equipment and come on to San Miguel. Then the main body, still without food but buoyed up by renewed hope, continued west and camped supperless on the Conchas River.

[3] The old-timers called it "Yarner." The "ll" in Southwestern Spanish is treated as a single letter and is pronounced "y."

[4] Kendall says these Mexicans had been trading with Kiowas and Comanches. In other words, they were *comancheros*.

[5] *Atole* was a thin mush made of corn meal and goat's milk; its use probably was not as widespread as some other items of Mexican food, but it was a standard dish for that part of the country.

[72]

The next morning Sutton sent four men ahead to buy provisions. Kendall and Fitzgerald found half a hatful of wild parsley and ate it raw. Then one of the advance men returned with the glad news that they had come upon a herd of seventeen thousand sheep and had bought enough for everybody. Half an hour later they camped on the Gallinas River and forgot everything but eating. Twenty fat sheep had been bought and dressed, and every ramrod and every stick in the area was soon supporting mutton ribs, shoulders, livers, and hearts over many fires. The Mexicans had supplied plenty of salt, and Kendall says that is the thing that saved many from death by overeating.

The shepherds were friendly, but there was a feeling of reservation—more than the typical Mexican caution. The shepherds seemed afraid of them in spite of their obvious friendliness.

Finally it came out: the country was in arms against the Texans. The Howland party—which had left them over a month before on the Wichita River—was in prison in Santa Fé, and other Americans in the region had been arrested by order of Armijo, governor of New Mexico. Troops were being recruited at that moment, and at Armijo's instigation some of the priests were warning the people that the *Tejanos* were coming to kill and steal and despoil their women.

This news should have stopped the Texans in their tracks, and a message should have been sent immediately to McLeod, but neither of these things happened. With their bellies full for the first time in some months and with awareness of the Mexican propensity for exaggeration, the officers did not accept this information at face value.

They were now about one hundred miles west of the present New Mexico state line and about forty miles east of San Miguel, and they celebrated the next morning with another big meal of broiled sheep and *atole*.

After breakfast a measure of caution returned, however, and the officers decided to send George Van Ness and Captain Lewis on to San Miguel. These men, both of whom were able to speak Spanish, were to contact the authorities, sound out the general feeling of the people toward the Texans, and buy provisions to send back to McLeod. Major Howard, Archibald Fitzgerald, Kendall, and a Mexican servant named Manuel from San Antonio, who also now appears for the first time,[6] were to go with them.

These six men of the Van Ness detachment went ahead rapidly and approached the village of Anton Chico, southeast of San Miguel, at 2:00 P.M. and had a dinner of *tortillas*,[7] boiled eggs, and *miel*[8] with a Mexican who lived there. That day the daughters of the same Mexican signified they were not averse to fraternization by giving each of the Texans a bundle of *cigarritos* (which Ruxton insists were called *cigarros* in Mexico—cigars being called *puros*).[9] The tobacco was *punche*.[10] They stayed that night with the Mexican but did not sleep, for there were thirty others of the Mexican family sleeping in the same room, and most of the thirty had whooping cough.

At 1:00 A.M. on the morning of September 15 a Mexican awoke them and told them they were about to be attacked

[6] Kendall, *Narrative*, I, 271, presents a footnote on Manuel and says he was shot shortly after "in mere wantonness" by a drummer.

[7] *Tortillas* were and are thin cakes of corn meal. They were standard fare all the way to the City of Mexico. Somewhat tough and tasteless to the uninitiated, they have great staying power.

[8] Kendall says *miel* was molasses and water; some say honey; others say a honey made from cornstalks.

[9] The use of *puros* and *cigarros* is confirmed by Ignaz Pfefferkorn, *Description of the Province of Sonora* (trans. and annotated by Theodore E. Treutlein), 178. Undoubtedly Kendall used the words as he heard them from the Texans around him, since he did not speak Spanish.

[10] *Punche*, the black tobacco of the common people in New Mexico, is a plant of some mystery. It is thought by some to have been an inferior tobacco plant, by others a different plant entirely. At any rate, as a product it was distinguished from "real tobacco," and thus the people could smoke freely and still avoid the heavy tax on tobacco, the industry of which in all phases was a government monopoly; its cultivation was permitted only in certain coastal areas of Mexico. (Ruxton says in parts of Oajaca, Veracruz, and Puebla.) See Leslie A. White, "Punche: Tobacco in New Mexico History," *New Mexico Historical Review*, Vol. XVIII, No. 4 (October, 1943).

and most certainly executed. They were annoyed and went back to bed, but Kendall was cautious enough to hide part of his gold pieces under the buttons on the sides of his riding pantaloons; the rest he kept in his linen moneybelt and put that in his pocket. He concealed a valuable breastpin under a waistband button, and two or three items of jewelry in the folds of his shirt bosom;[11] a gold watch and chain were secreted "as safely as possible."

That morning, Kendall, in his still unsatisfied hunger for bread, bought all of that food he could stow in his saddlebags, and they took up the road to San Miguel.

They reached the village of Cuesta, and suddenly, without any previous warning—or at least without any warning that they had paid any serious attention to—they found themselves surrounded by one hundred soldiers armed with "lances, swords, bows and arrows, and miserable *escopetas*, or old-fashioned carbines."

The leader, Captain Dámaso Salazar,[12] greeted them in a friendly manner and requested that they place their rifles and pistols in his care—each labeled, of course, with the owner's name. It seemed the course of prudence to do as Salazar requested, and, as a matter of fact, they were so completely outnumbered that it was the only sensible thing to do, so they turned their arms over to the Mexicans, hoping that it was indeed a formality.[13]

But men without arms, they discovered, are men without authority, for as soon as Salazar had control of their rifles and

[11] It rather seems that Kendall had saved some dress-up clothes for this occasion.

[12] Throughout the *Narrative*, Kendall speaks of him as Dimasio Salezar, but in Vol. II, 403, footnote, he says the correct spelling is "Damasio Salazar." However, material from the Museum of New Mexico spells it Dámaso Salazar, as does correspondence from the *Secretaria de la Defensa Nacional* in Mexico, D. F. Pages 201–14, Bolton Transcriptions, in the archives of the library of the University of Texas, refer to him as Dámaso Salazar.

[13] It would take a predetermined mind to hold that this naïve surrender was the act of a party bent on conquest.

[75]

pistols, he ordered their pockets turned inside out and their bodies thoroughly searched.

It was an indignity, but the search could not have been very thorough, for neither Kendall's money nor his jewelry was discovered. Salazar did, however, take his papers, note-book, penknife, and everything else in his pockets except the moneybelt, which still contained almost one hundred dollars. A soldier pulled the end of the moneybelt from Kendall's pocket, but seeing that it was soiled and dirty, assumed it was nothing valuable and did not take it.

Salazar went into conference with his officers, and while they were waiting, Kendall fed his horse, Jim the Butcher, some of the bread he had bought at Anton Chico, and the six men speculated on what was to happen next.

The conference of the Mexicans ended. Salazar and his officers returned. Salazar barked an order, and twelve men, all armed with rifles, marched in front of the Texans. For an instant they were puzzled, then thunderstruck. Fitzgerald swore and clenched his fists.

"They're going to shoot us!" he cried. "Let's pitch into 'em!"

Kendall looked around and saw that the crowd of curious Mexicans behind them was falling away to leave an open path—obviously to get out of the way of stray bullets. Kendall spotted two Colt pistols, just taken away from one of the Texans and now stuck into a Mexican's waistband, and glanced at Fitzgerald for a signal to start a fight.

But an argument arose between Salazar and another Mex-ican named Vigil,[14] and, from Van Ness and Lewis, Kendall learned that the argument was over the execution of the Texans! Vigil won the argument by his contention that the power of life and death rested with the governor, Armijo.

Salazar then ordered Don Jesús (Kendall does not further identify him) to take the prisoners to San Miguel.[15] Their

[14] Gregorio Vigil, a prominent rancher near San Miguel.
[15] In the vicinity of the present Las Vegas, New Mexico. In Santa Fé Trail days San Miguel was the point at which the caravans turned west toward

horses were kept by Salazar, and they were left on foot. In Cuesta they were imprisoned for half an hour, during which time women and children visited them, bringing bread, cheese, and stewed pumpkins, and sympathizing with them intensely because Armijo was a brutal tyrant who undoubtedly would execute them all immediately.[16]

Don Jesús brought lariats to bind the Texans, but they refused this attention, guaranteeing that they would walk to San Miguel without giving trouble. Jesús finally accepted their promise, and they started off, guarded by Jesús on horseback with an American rifle and his barefoot soldiers with bows and arrows.

This seems to be the most incomprehensible aspect of the entire trip. These five men could have escaped with probably no loss to themselves, but they did not try. Kendall says they could have disarmed the guards, but they had no way of rejoining their own men, and as they knew that recapture would mean death, they did not consider escape. For men who only a few weeks before had launched themselves into hostile Indian country as a lark, they showed remarkably little initiative. Perhaps they still were not convinced that they were prisoners of the Mexicans.

An hour's march brought them to Puertecito, the home town of both Salazar and Jesús, and there Kendall first heard an expression that would come to his ears many times before his departure from Mexico—and always with pleasure, for it came from the Mexican women as they gave the prisoners bread, cheese, and whatever food they had.

"¡Pobrecitos!" is the word, and Kendall's note on its meaning is expressive: "Poor fellows! I believe is a literal translation, although it means much more. Nothing can be more touchingly sweet than the pronunciation of this word by a

Santa Fé. Hiram M. Chittenden, *The American Fur Trade of the Far West*, II, 503. Becknell went through San Miguel on his first wagon-train trip by the Cimarron route. Ray Allen Billington, *The Far Western Frontier*, 39.

16 It must be about this time that Manuel was separated from them, for Kendall, although he describes this part of the trip at length, does not mention Manuel at all.

Spanish or Mexican woman. The tones come fresh and warm from the heart when an object worthy of compassion presents itself."[17]

They were now about twelve miles from San Miguel and were forced to wade the Pecos River, which was about two feet deep. Kendall's lame ankle had started to swell, and he was afraid to take off his boots for fear he could not get them on again; so he waded the river and continued the march in wet boots.

They reached San Miguel at sundown, and once again were subjected to the curious stares of the villagers.[18] The five were imprisoned in a tiny room that served as a *calabozo*,[19] and they were given a poor meal of *tortillas* and thin mutton broth. The village priest, however, sent each one a large bowl of hot coffee.

They had not a single blanket among them, but the *alcalde*,[20] who appeared to be in charge of them for the night, shrugged his shoulders and said he could do nothing. Then a woman sent them a buffalo hide and a blanket, and Kendall bought another blanket from a man "in the crowd." With these they made a bed for five persons on the hard earth that served as a floor.[21]

But there was no sleep for them that night. The food they had had that day—to which their stomachs were not accustomed, either in quantity or in seasoning—gave them trouble; Kendall says the bread caused him to have a severe attack of colic. The next morning he was weak and tired.

On the morning of September 16 they bought a sheep

[17] Kendall, *Narrative*, I, 289n.

[18] Both Kendall in 1841–42 and Ruxton in 1846 (among many) were much annoyed at the staring to which they were subjected all through Mexico.

[19] From whence "calaboose" in the Southwest. The Spanish word for "jail" is not *juzgado* as freely used by Southwesterners. *Juzgado* means judged or sentenced, and a sentence to a Mexican peon was equivalent to jail, for he had no money to pay a fine; from this came the American word "hoosegow." H. L. Mencken, *The American Language*, 221.

[20] In a small Mexican town, a combination of mayor and justice of the peace.

[21] More than one traveler in Mexico has remarked on the fact that earth packed by bare human feet feels harder than stone when one sleeps on it.

through an intermediary, Tomás Bustamante, and ate a part of it for breakfast. This illustrates another peculiar facet of Mexican imprisonment. The men bought a blanket which they paid for with an English sovereign, and later a whole sheep, but Jesús did not think it strange that they should have money and did not order them searched again. It seems that the fact that they had been searched officially was the end of it.

It was sixty miles to Santa Fé, and again they were paraded before the start. This time a woman ran to give them a bottle of "the country whisky,"[22] which they drank upon the spot, although they were guarded by eight men.

They started for Santa Fé, and during the morning they met two hundred soldiers under a "piratical-visaged scoundrel" who cursed them and said that they should have been shot. The two hundred men were going to join Salazar to act against the Sutton-Cooke party.

Jesús, upbraided by the officer for not having the prisoners tied, as soon as the officer left brought out lariats and fastened them around the wrists of Van Ness, Fitzgerald, and Lewis, with the other ends held by the guards. Major Howard and Kendall both being lame, Jesús desisted from tying them, on condition that they fold their hands on their breasts as a token of submission whenever they met another party of troops.

"Never shall I forget this Don Jesús,"[23] says Kendall. "He had a coarse, dark, hang-dog face, a black but vicious eye, . . . and if he had a heart at all, it legitimately belonged to a hyena or a prairie wolf."[24]

Jesús drove them until midafternoon, during which time they passed nearly one thousand troops, most of them, as be-

[22] Either *aguardiente* (water with teeth) from Paso or perhaps the far-famed Taos lightning.

[23] Kendall invariably refers to him only as "Don Jesús." If he had known the word *don* was a mark of respect and affection, he probably would have ascertained Jesús's surname.

[24] Actually, nothing appears in the *Narrative* or anywhere else to explain this derogatory opinion. As far as Kendall relates it, Jesús's conduct would seem to have been considerate. (*Narrative*, I, 294.)

fore, armed with bows and arrows or worn-out muskets. Then a trumpet blast announced that Armijo and his party were approaching from Santa Fé.

Armijo was a fine-looking, portly man, mounted on an immense mule, and richly uniformed. Without dismounting, the Governor shook hands with them and asked their names. Lewis said they were merchants from the United States. Van Ness started to correct him, but Armijo seized the collar of Lewis's jacket and pulled him near his mule. He pointed to the buttons and the word "Texas" and a single star on each, and triumphantly pronounced the word "Texas."

He asked questions about the other parties and read Kendall's passport, signed by the Mexican consul at New Orleans,[25] but turned it back to Jesús and said that Kendall, being in company with enemies of New Mexico, would have to be detained.

Kendall says he was not much disappointed in this treatment but happy that he was not going to be summarily shot. He was getting the spirit.

Armijo then asked which one best understood Spanish, as he wanted an interpreter, and Lewis quickly offered his services. Armijo ordered a mule for him to ride and had his hands untied. Then he ordered Jesús to take them back to San Miguel that night, for he wanted to talk to them in the morning.

Jesús said they had already walked thirty miles that day, but Armijo pooh-poohed the very thought that they could not walk another thirty miles. "The Texans are active and untiring people—I know them. If one of them *pretends* to be sick or tired on the road, *shoot him down and bring me his ears!*"[26] It was a command that would be obeyed literally more than once before they reached Paso del Norte.

[25] There was a great deal of controversy over this passport, the Mexicans maintaining that Kendall never had one. Kendall himself and a number of other Americans or Texans were very positive about it. The Mexican Vice-Consul at New Orleans said it was never issued, but at least two Texans asserted under oath that it was and that they had read it, and they repeated the wording. There is other evidence which will be discussed later.

[26] Kendall, *Narrative,* I, 298.

6. SURRENDER OF THE

SUTTON-COOKE PARTY

LEWIS RODE OFF with Armijo, leaving the four prisoners with Jesús. They had to wait until Armijo's entire party passed them and then Jesús took them back toward San Miguel.

Kendall's ankle was in bad shape, and he hired a seat on the donkey of one of the Mexicans "at an exorbitant rate." The donkey was not more than eight hands high, Kendall thought, but the owner started to mount the animal behind Kendall. The donkey kicked skyward, and Kendall went off. He says that a second kickup sent him again into the air, but he was not hurt, and they all laughed. It is a little hard to believe that he took two kicks from a donkey without being hurt, for a jackass can whip a stallion twice as big as itself. However, that was Kendall's story a year later.

Within six miles of San Miguel a thunderstorm came up, and it was impossible to see the way; therefore, they all lay down on the bare ground and slept soundly till morning, although it was raining a deluge.

The morning of September 17 they were taken on to San Miguel and put in a small room that had a single window facing on the public square. Minutes later, watching through the window, they saw a man led across the square by a small guard of soldiers. His hands were tied behind his back and

[81]

his eyes were blindfolded. They could not see him well enough to identify him, but his dress was Texan, and a priest, coming into their cell, said that this man had been taken prisoner, had attempted to escape, and had been captured again.

This man was taken to a spot about twenty yards from the prison room. The sergeant pushed him to his knees, with his head against a wall. Six of the soldiers stepped back about ten feet, and at the corporal's "*¡Fuego!*" they shot the prisoner in the back. He was wounded but not killed, and lay writhing and moaning on the ground. The corporal stepped up with a pistol and shot him through the heart. The shot was so close that the man's shirt was set on fire by the powder flash, and it continued to burn, says Kendall, until it was quenched by his blood.

Kendall and his fellow prisoners watched through the small window, horrified, helpless to give assistance, and unable to determine who the man was. They had no doubt he was one of the three men in the Howland party that had left on August 11 from the Wichita River, about halfway between the Cross Timbers and the Llano. Those men had been Howland, Baker, and Rosenberry. Which one was lying dead on the ground before them?

The four prisoners were taken from their cell and led outside into the square. The dead Texan's body was at one side. Nothing was said to them, and they had learned how useless it was to ask questions. They waited and watched, fearful, for the next move.

A squad of Mexican soldiers came across the ground with a prisoner, and they recognized him with horror—Samuel Howland. They stared at the ghastly sight he made. When he had left the Wichita River, he had been hale and hearty, but now he was a terrible sight. His hands were tied behind him; his left ear and cheek were cut off entirely, and his left arm was cut up as by a sword. Within ten feet of them he

[82]

looked at them and smiled, but the smile was ghastly. He tried to say something, but was not allowed to finish.

He was made to stand beside the body of Alexander Baker, which they now recognized, still where it had fallen. He was blindfolded and pushed to his knees, face toward the wall. Six guards then shot him in the back from a distance of a few paces. His head fell over and his body slumped; he collapsed suddenly and fell beside Baker.[1]

The four Texans were returned to their cell, sick at the stomach and weak in the knees from the double execution of their friends. While they talked in low tones, through their small window they saw one detachment after another of mounted Mexicans leave the square in the direction of Anton Chico, and they were told that Sutton and Cooke were camped near that town. Two pieces of cannon left San Miguel, pulled by oxen. Most of the Mexican soldiers were rural militia or *rurales,* made up of nondescript Indians and Mexicans.

In the meantime, Armijo, with his best men, remained safe in San Miguel—waiting for news, Kendall says, for if the ninety Texans should defeat the Mexicans, Armijo planned to escape to Albuquerque and then to Mexico.[2] So close were the Texans to the success of their original plan.

Kendall learned that Howland, Baker, and Rosenberry had been captured three weeks before but had escaped from Santa Fé and had traveled through the mountains, moving by night, sleeping by day, trying to reach the Sutton-Cooke command, of whose approach they had news, to warn of the hostility of Armijo.

But Armijo, equally aware of the importance of this information to the Sutton-Cooke party, combed the mountains to

[1] Carlos María Bustamante says the Howland party arrived in Santa Fé as prisoners September 4; that they were detained, but were armed by others and escaped; that they were discovered by three young men, who with darts (or arrows), killed one and imprisoned the other two. *Gabinete Mexicano,* II, 217–20; Brief, 498–500.

[2] *Narrative,* I, 308. Kendall does not say where he got this information, but it seems consistent with Armijo's practices; this is just what he did five years later when Kearny invaded New Mexico.

find them. They were discovered, and put up a fight. Rosenberry was killed, but Baker and Howland were taken alive and saved for the firing squad. Armijo offered Howland his life and liberty if he would join the Mexicans and help persuade the Sutton-Cooke men to surrender without a fight, but Howland turned down the offer without hesitation.

The bodies of the two men were not moved until almost night. In the meantime, the many dogs that were part of every Mexican village gathered around them, licking their blood and tearing their clothes. The bodies were finally taken to a prairie near San Miguel and thrown on the ground without burial. They were eaten by the wolves.

All that afternoon Mexican officers and soldiers came and went. More than one thousand men, the Mexicans repeated, had surrounded Sutton and Cooke, but the four prisoners were not impressed. They felt confident that the Sutton-Cooke party would fight and that they would defeat the Mexicans, because the report was that the Texans were well entrenched.

Couriers came and went constantly. The tension of expectancy mounted in the village, and the square was thronged with ragged but fierce-looking soldiers. Rumors spread first that a great battle was in progress, and second that Cooke had surrendered. The four prisoners speculated anxiously but helplessly. They did not think Cooke would surrender while he was in a defensible position, but if he did, said one, it would be by treachery. And if there was treachery, said another, it would come from William P. Lewis.

And while they watched and awaited the conclusion of the affair, they had of necessity to keep eating the food brought them by Mexican women. The women arrived one after the other, says Kendall, and he took occasion to observe their small feet, their finely turned ankles, their *rebosos* and their well-developed busts, their small and classically formed hands, their dark and lustrous eyes, their teeth of beautiful shape and dazzling whiteness, and their hair of rich and jetty blackness.[3]

[84]

Kendall relates that they were forced to eat a dozen meals a day and were nearly killed by kindness in the form of *chile guisado, olla podrida* or hash of stewed mutton, *atole* and *miel,* milk, eggs, and *tortillas* or bread. He says they were forced to keep eating so as not to give offense, for the worst insult a man could offer a Mexican *señorita* was to refuse food from her. It was a far cry from the thirteen days on the Llano.

And so Kendall and his three companions were imprisoned in their small cell with one tiny window. They had plenty to eat and many worries, but between eating and worrying there was nothing to do but speculate on the friendliness of the Mexican girls who brought them food and who lingered by their window with smiles and soft words.

In the meantime, a few miles away, Cooke was having his own troubles. On September 16, following the departure of the Van Ness detachment, the Sutton-Cooke party moved on west to the village of Anton Chico, where the Van Ness detachment had spent a sleepless night that was destined to be their last night as free men for a long time. Sutton and Cooke camped across the river from the town, on the edge of a ravine, with running water at their feet. Cooke sent four Texans across the stream and into the town to buy provisions, but they were immediately arrested by Salazar, who had gone to Anton Chico after turning the Van Ness men over to Don Jesús.

Salazar sent one of the four back, requesting that Cooke and Brenham come to the village to talk to him. Cooke and Brenham returned word that Salazar could come to their camp if he wanted to talk—and where were their three other men? Salazar came to meet them, and the three men were turned over to Cooke. Cooke asked about the Van Ness detachment, and Salazar said they had been treated as friends and sent to meet the governor.

At ten o'clock the next morning (September 17) Salazar sent a messenger to say that Armijo would soon arrive and to advise them that he, Salazar, would cross the river and camp

³ *Narrative,* I, 321.

near them to show his friendliness. However, his men marched around them, and Salazar, with four hundred men, camped within two hundred yards.

Sutton had the Texans drop their rifles, which they had been holding at present arms, but told them to be ready to start firing on short notice.

Fifteen minutes later two hundred men advanced to their right rear, and Cooke told Sutton to form the men for battle. Then someone said that Captain Lewis was leading the Mexican party, and the men were told to stand at ease. The two parties of Mexicans joined, and the combined force was about six hundred.

Lewis and a Mexican rode out toward the Texan party. The Mexican was Manuel Chaves, nephew of Governor Armijo. Lewis told Cooke that the people of New Mexico were aroused at the Texan invasion and in arms against them.

Cooke reminded Lewis with some indignation that it was not in any sense an invasion: in the first place, this was Texan territory; in the second place, they were instructed to take over Santa Fé only if the people wanted it so.

Lewis paid no attention to this protest. He went on to say that Armijo was within a few hours' march; that he had four thousand of the best-equipped men Lewis had ever seen, and that five thousand more were coming from Chihuahua and were expected at any time.

Cooke looked around at his ninety ragged and starving Texans, and the odds were not very promising, even though Texans were used to being outnumbered five to one or ten to one by Mexicans. It was not the prospect of fighting an overwhelmingly superior force that made him hesitate, but the question of what to do if they should defeat the Mexican force.

They had just spent two very arduous weeks almost without food; their horses were in poor shape; they had only forty or fifty rounds of ammunition apiece. If they won the battle, they still would be in a hazardous spot, for they had no provisions, and they did not dare penetrate farther into an aroused countryside with huge forces of enemy soldiers harassing every move. The only logical move was to go back across the Llano and try to join McLeod.[4]

Lewis kept up his persuasion. "The Governor has commissioned me," he said, "to offer you the right to trade in New Mexico if you will give up your arms."

"We will not surrender our arms," said Cooke.

"It is not a question of surrender," Lewis told him. "All you have to do is deposit your arms, and you will be allowed to trade for eight days; then your arms and horses will be returned to you."

Captain Sutton shook his head. "We'd have no defense whatever if we gave up our arms and our horses," he said.

"I *know* this is the custom of the traders from St. Louis," said the artillery captain. "No possible harm can come from this proposition."

"How do we know," asked Thomas Lubbock, "that you are telling the truth?"

"Every word I have spoken is the truth," Lewis insisted. "I swear it on my honor."

"I don't like it," said Sutton, "You keep talking about us but you don't include yourself with us. Why are you in any different position from the rest of us?"

Lieutenant Munson said, "I propose that we return to McLeod by the same route by which we left him; if we can do no better, we will walk, and live on the horses that are left."

Chaves became articulate. "That would never do, *señores*. My uncle, the governor, knows that Americans are gentlemen, and he would never permit such indignities."

Sutton insisted. "We can't give up our arms."[5]

---

[4] It is hardly necessary to point out that a would-be conqueror would have gambled to win the battle (that is, if he thought, as Cooke did, that he had a good chance) and to enforce his will on the country, taking supplies and food, either capturing the governor or chasing him out of the country. Cooke's attitude was not that of a man conditioned to think in terms of conquest.

[5] This conversation is given as Lubbock reported it; he did not give the authors of all statements, however, and where that information is missing, speculation has been indulged in.

[87]

Lewis and Chaves, seeing the Texans were in no mood to give up their rifles, started back to Salazar's camp, and the Texan officers—Cooke, Doctor Brenham, Captain Sutton, Lieutenant Brown, Lieutenant Munson, and, most likely, William W. Alsbury, the interpreter—went into immediate consultation.

One of the officers wanted to know why Lewis was acting as a confidant to Salazar. Why had he turned and gone back to the Mexican lines instead of staying with them? Cooke said that was only natural; inasmuch as Lewis had come to negotiate between the two parties, he would have to go back to Salazar to report the attitude of the Texans and possibly secure some concessions from Salazar.

One of the officers repeated that Lewis had talked as if he did not belong to the expedition; another pointed out that the man was evasive and did not look them straight in the eye; a third said he acted like a man of evil.

Many agreed, and yet, as Cooke pointed out, if they fought the Mexicans, there would be the tremendous problem of making their way back across the Llano bearing wounded (the inevitable result of a battle), and he called attention to the men—gaunt, starving, unshaven, and broken out in ulcerous sores on their hands and faces for lack of proper food. Sutton admitted that the men were in bad shape, mentally as well as physically. What should they do?

They looked at one another questioningly. Lewis had held out the offer of hope—safety, food, the end of their trials. Was it fair to suspect him of deceit?

Each man thought back over his association with Lewis. Had the man done anything to make them think he was untrustworthy? Nobody could say that he had. Nor could they honestly say there was anything wrong in his acting as a negotiator between them and the Mexicans. It was only that he asked them to give up their rifles—and that was a hard thing for a Texan to do. And there was Lewis's manner.

Finally Cooke spoke up. "I have sat in lodge with Lewis

[88]

as a Mason," he said. "I can find out if he is telling the truth or not." Many of those around Cooke were Masons, and they began to nod in agreement. This could be the solution, and they were relieved to see a way out.

Masonry was a strong factor in early Texas, a majority of the Republic's public figures being members of the lodge— and, as they well knew, it was hardly conceivable that any Mason, put to the test of truth as only another Mason could put him, would hold to a lie. Yes, they agreed. Cooke, who knew Lewis better than did anybody else, who had seen Lewis take the degrees, who had been one of those to congratulate him on passing the tests, would certainly be able to find out if Lewis was telling the truth.[6]

It could have been, one suggested, that Lewis was under pressure, that some of Salazar's men had their rifle sights trained on his back. Another, not a Mason, was skeptic enough to insist that Lewis was trying to betray them for his own profit. Nevertheless, all recognized the seriousness of their position and the desirability of a peaceful settlement, and they agreed that Cooke should talk privately to Lewis and try to find out the truth.

Cooke went out; Lewis came from the Mexican lines to meet him. They held a private conversation, with Cooke demanding, across the Masonic handshake, to know the truth. And after a moment or two he came back to the Texan lines.

"You must be wrong," he told the suspicious ones. "Lewis pledged his Masonic faith to me for the truth of every word."

"If you're satisfied," said Sutton, "we'll abide by your judgment."

Cooke drew a deep breath. It was a heavy decision for a man of thirty-three; the lives and safety of ninety men depended on it. If they fought, he knew that many of those around him would be dead by morning, and many more would die as they toiled back across the grand prairie under the scorching sun,

---

[6] A discussion of the verifiable data on this phase of the expedition will be found in Chapter XI below.

without food, without water, without medicine, without horses, possibly without ammunition—and with Mexicans and Indians harassing their flanks at every step.

Cooke compressed his lips and shook his head. Honorable treatment by the Mexicans would save much suffering and many deaths. He looked back east toward the dreadful Llano, and his hope that Lewis was telling the truth overcame his doubts. He turned to Sutton. "Tell the men we shall not fight."

Salazar and a small squad came from the Mexican camp, followed by Lewis and Chaves. Salazar told them to discharge their rifles and lay them on the ground.[7]

Sutton gave the order. They fired their rifles into the air and laid them on the ground. The pistols followed. Shortly before dark, Salazar gave orders for them to form in line. Salazar's manner was changing; he was becoming peremptory.

"We are not prisoners," Cooke reminded him.

Salazar said coldly, "You have nothing to fight with. Have your men stay in line until they are searched."

"*Searched!*" shouted Cooke, for no Texan would ever willingly submit to such an indignity.

"You may have other weapons," Salazar pointed out.

Cooke walked off and called to Lewis. "You said we would be treated as friends."

Lewis opened his mouth but said nothing. He looked away.

As Salazar's men began to go through the pockets of the Texans, Cooke started after Lewis. Two Mexican soldiers pushed him back into line. He resisted indignantly, but, with their rifles centered on his chest, he kept his place. But the realization grew on him that Lewis had betrayed them.

He shouted at Lewis in futile anger: "You lied to me!"

Lewis did not answer.

A barefoot Mexican soldier led Cooke's half-starved horse away.

[7] Most of these probably were muzzleloaders, for muzzleloaders were still the predominant shoulder arm twenty years later in the Civil War. They had to be loaded by hand and fired one shot at a time; therefore, in close quarters a discharged rifle was useless.

"You betrayed us!" Cooke cried, but still he could hardly believe it.

Lewis stayed back out of reach, watching Cooke warily.

The Mexican soldiers took knives, watches, money, all clothing except shoes, hats, shirts, stockings, and pants, and all blankets except one for each Texan.

Cooke watched his men being stripped, and the incredible but undeniable fact of Lewis' treason came over him in all its shocking unbelievability. He walked out a little from his men, and his scathing voice, filled with outrage and helpless fury, penetrated the entire area.

Before the Texans whom Lewis had betrayed and before the Mexicans with whom he had conspired, Cooke denounced him. He excoriated him for his pledged honor which had been forgotten, for his plighted Masonic faith which had been broken, and for his unjustifiable conduct as a man. "But for your perfidy," Cooke said bitterly, "we would have died fighting." But these were only words, and there was no gunpowder on the Texan side to back them up.

The men, all their belongings taken away except essential clothes and one blanket apiece, were formed double file and marched closer to Anton Chico, where they were camped for the night, surrounded by hundreds of armed guards.

That night the men huddled around their campfires, no longer able to cook their few pieces of mutton on their ramrods, for they had no rifles, but warming them over the flickering fires by hanging them from sticks of cottonwood, which they could not even sharpen because the Mexicans had their knives.

They were frightened men, dazed men. One disaster after another had stricken them. And they were not sure that some further tragedy was not in the offing. Yet they were hungry.

The Mexican soldiers dumped some hard bread on the ground, and they snatched at it, cautiously but greedily. It did not go very far, for it was a small amount. They had some mutton, and they half-cooked it and ate it wolfishly, and

[91]

gnawed at the hard bread while they watched the darkness warily, for all around them were Mexicans—armed, mounted, well fed.

The Texans were only ninety men in a strange country where most of them could not understand the language, where their bodies could not even legally be buried in a cemetery, for most of them were Protestants.[8]

Cooke sat apart, shaking his head at all efforts of his associates to talk to him. He warmed his meat at the fire and ate it without tasting it. From time to time he got to his feet and walked through the camp, punishing himself with the sight of every ragged man in his party, staring into the darkness, hearing the horses nicker, watching the yellow fires of the Mexicans and seeing an occasional *rural* officer making the rounds to inspect the guard, hearing the monotonous *"¡Centinela alerta!"* and wondering over and over what would next happen to his ninety men who had already been through hell.

There was no sleep for Cooke that night. When their small fires died and the men huddled up in their thin blankets, Cooke sat alone by the ashes, humiliated by the enormity of his own mistake—for now, too late, he realized the harsh truth: that neither the man Lewis nor the Mexicans had any compunction; their purpose was to get the Texans in their power, and one way had been as good as another; the only requirement had been that it work. And this time it had worked. The advance detachment of the Texan army had surrendered without firing a shot. No reflection could have been more crucifying as Cooke sat with bowed head awaiting the dawn.

On the next day Armijo arrived, and was exasperated because the prisoners were not tied. At his orders, lariats were brought forth and the prisoners were bound—four, six, or eight in a group—as many as each lariat would hold, while Armijo's sycophants kept up cries of "Kill them! Kill them! Death to the *Tejanos!*"

[8] This feature of Mexican law was corrected a few years later.

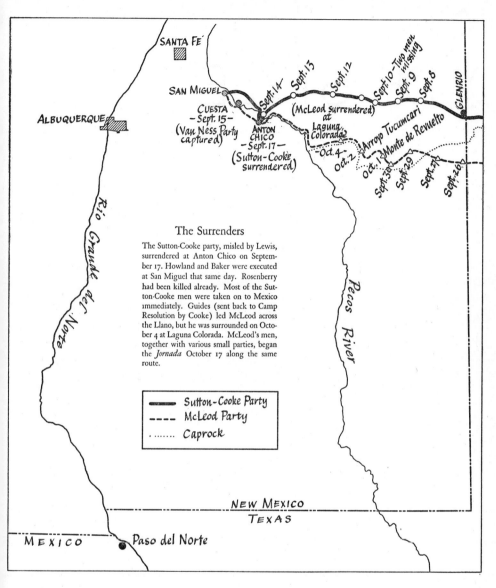

The Surrenders

The Sutton-Cooke party, misled by Lewis, surrendered at Anton Chico on September 17. Howland and Baker were executed at San Miguel that same day. Rosenberry had been killed already. Most of the Sutton-Cooke men were taken on to Mexico immediately. Guides (sent back to Camp Resolution by Cooke) led McLeod across the Llano, but he was surrounded on October 4 at Laguna Colorada. McLeod's men, together with various small parties, began the *Jornada* October 17 along the same route.

	Sutton-Cooke Party
	McLeod Party
	Caprock

*West to the descent of the Llano; capture and imprisonment
at San Miguel*

All day the Texans were surrounded by hundreds of scurrying soldiers, marching and countermarching, and shortly after nightfall Armijo called a conference of his principal officers, within hearing of the Texans. It did not take long for Cooke to find out the subject of the meeting: Armijo proposed to execute on the spot the entire party of ninety men.

Some of the Mexican officers objected, however, and one suggested sending the prisoners to the City of Mexico to demonstrate the great valor and military prowess of General Armijo. The governor, plainly disappointed but not quite willing to risk a charge of mass murder so openly, finally compromised by ordering a vote taken among the officers.

Again we can imagine Cooke, already aged far beyond his thirty-three years, standing by the fire, his eyes on the Mexican officers, waiting for the result, bitter at Lewis and sick at heart with himself. Cooke must have died a thousand deaths as he watched the endless deliberation and waited for the fate of his ninety men to be decided by the vote of a handful of Mexican officers.

Great must have been his relief when the officer who counted the ballots announced that by a majority of *one vote* they had decided not to shoot the Texans but to send them on to the City of Mexico.[9]

On the morning of September 20, therefore, the Sutton-Cooke party marched through San Miguel, tied up with lariats to demonstrate the power of the great Armijo.[10] They were not allowed to stop. They heard it said among the soldiers that Howland, Baker and Rosenberry were dead, and they

---

[9] Lubbock is not the only one who mentions this vote on execution of the entire Sutton-Cooke party. Franklin Coombs' report, published in Folsom, *Mexico in 1842*, 238, and in *Niles' National Register*, Vol. LXII, No. 1 (March 5, 1842), 2, says also that they escaped execution by one vote, and further that Armijo was enraged because of the vote, cursing and raving like a madman. The wonder is that a man of Armijo's temperament submitted the decision to a vote in the first place. Perhaps he felt sure the vote would be for execution.

[10] There is a discrepancy concerning dates in the narrative of Kendall and that of the Sutton-Cooke party.

Head Quarters Santa Fé Pioneers.
General Order 9
(No. 20)
Camp Resolution,
Head Waters of Red River, Sept. 1st 1841.
Comrades of ????

Comrades.—

Our march thro' a
wilderness hitherto unknown, except to the
savage, has never been surpassed, and per=
haps seldom equalled, in Military annals,
by the obstacles you have encountered, and
the courage with which you have surmounted
them.— The rugged steeps and yawning chasms
over which you have toiled, and constructed
roads, and the fortitude and energy you have
displayed, under the most adverse circumstances,
extort the warmest thanks of your Commanding
Officer, and, merit the gratitude of your Country.

A period has arrived, which calls for a
higher sacrifice, and bolder exertion. Our
situation is known to you all. We are hemmed
in by mountains and ravines.— Our subsistence
is reduced to a few beeves— without Coffee,
bread, or scarcely Salt.— The teams employed
in the transportation of the Merchandize goods
which we pledged our honor to escort in safety,
and the loss of which would ruin them,— these
teams are jaded and worn down; and to in=
crease our annoyance, our hunting parties, who
made too large to kill game, are overwhelmed
by hundreds of Comanches, who hover at a
most provoking distance, and prance around
us, in defiance of our jaded steeds.

To continue our march under such

General Order at Camp Resolution

[continued overleaf]

Circumstances, would only prolong our difficulty for a few days. — And to abandon the property of the Merchants would be a violation of our faith and honor — This is our dilemma

I propose, after a conference with the Commissioners and the Company officers, to adopt the only honorable remedy in our power. I have ordered a special detail of one hundred men (including the Commissioners and their attendants) with the best horses, to proceed under the command of Captain Sutton, to the Settlements, which we are all aware, are within one hundred miles, to procure guides, subsistence and transportation, and immediately return to our relief.

Col. Wm. G. Cooke has volunteered to accompany the Detachment, and will employ every means to accomplish that end.

The Commanding officer will remain with the command and share their fortune.

If necessary, we must subsist upon our teams, but he hopes they will endure with Cheerfulness privations which are unavoidable, realize the hopes of friends, and disappoint the Malice of enemies, and redeem of our pledged honor, to surmount privations, toil and danger, by marching successfully to our claimed Territory of Santa Fé.

(Signed) H. McLeod
Bvt. Brig. Genl.
Comg. Santa Fé Pioneers.

assumed that Kendall, Howard, Fitzgerald, and Van Ness also had been executed. Apparently only the traitor was still alive.

But there were other worries. Cooke and Sutton talked it over as they shuffled along, tied up like animals, at the beginning of their two-thousand-mile trip. What would happen to McLeod, they wondered. Matías had carried letters telling McLeod to come to New Mexico as fast as possible. McLeod was heading into a trap, Cooke pointed out, perhaps with Lewis again acting as bait.

Sutton said they ought to try to send him a warning, but as he scrutinized the men under his command, he shook his head slowly. A lone, half-starved man without arms would have no chance to escape from their present guards, much less to make the long trip across the Llano.

7. McLEOD CROSSES THE LLANO

THE SUTTON-COOKE party had left Camp Resolution, just below the eastern Caprock, on the evening of August 31. Immediately after their departure, McLeod ordered the wagons formed into a square, with the cattle herded inside. The men would sleep outside; the horses would be hobbled and staked out.

There was little said that night as they ate their scant portions of half-cooked beef. Now that the first enthusiasm over the prospect of relief had passed, a great feeling of hopelessness settled over the rank and file. These were tired, hungry men, beset with uncertainty, lost in the wilderness, constantly under peril from the Kiowas. They got to thinking about Sutton and Cooke and their five days' rations, and despair came over them. The opinion was openly expressed that Sutton and Cooke had little chance to get across the Llano, that it was a desperation gamble. Others remembered that their own party also had only a few days' rations. What were they to live on when that was gone?

Members of the expedition were following their own whims rather than any sort of discipline. Small parties went off hunting game whenever they felt like it. As a matter of fact, three men—Donovan, J. Kenyon, and Klein, as previously reported —had disappeared the day before the Sutton-Cooke party left. None of them ever returned.

On the night Donovan's party left, Captain Caldwell's horse was stolen, and the next day Donovan's horse was found dead. No Indians had been seen, but hope for the missing Donovan was not very high.

On September 1, Private Willis of Company C was charged with stealing meat from a commissary wagon. He was court-martialed but acquitted. Apparently they found out more about the sword that Pisarzewski was supposed to have sold, for he was ordered to return to duty, the charge against him having proved unfounded. (He had already been acquitted, according to Special Order No. 16, but it now appears that the acquittal was reached with reservations.) Musician Willis (C. C. Willis) was convicted of selling the sword, but his punishment is not recorded in the Bancroft Papers.[1]

Glass and his companion, who had gone out to scout or hunt food on August 28, returned September 2. They had been northeast thirty miles. They had found Indian trails and hastily abandoned Indian villages, but no Indians. One might almost think the Indians did not trust the whites.

Glass had crossed several streams—some fresh, some salty. But the salt streams of the red land of that area, says Falconer, were nowhere near as bitter, nauseous, and unpalatable as the gypsum waters they had come through.

The next day they moved a short distance upstream to get fresh grazing for the animals. They set guard fires at an edge of high ground to the south; the river protected them on the north. In the afternoon McLeod issued an order for a daily drill, but when this got to the men there was something of a ruckus. The men gathered in groups, crying, "Beef, beef! No drill!" while Caldwell and other officers talked it over with McLeod.

The general was adamant. They were going to drill for an hour after sunset every day, so they would be able to act in concert and assist one another in emergencies. "Return to

[1] The disciplinary events of September 1 are listed in Special Orders No. 18 and 19, related in the Bancroft Papers, 802.

[97]

your commands," McLeod ordered his officers, "and arrest the first man who shall utter these cries."

There probably would have been more courts-martial if it had not been for an unexpected tragedy the next day. At 8:30 in the morning, in broad daylight, the Indians stampeded and drove off all the cattle and eighty-three horses.

The sentries could not have been very alert, for the animals were grazing about two hundred yards from camp when thirty Indians came out from behind a hill and charged the horses, yelling and whooping. The Texans ran out from camp with arms and stopped the Indians, but the horses and cattle stampeded toward the camp. The animals, as tired and gaunt as the men, were not too rambunctious; they slowed down and began to mill. Then some excited amateur fired his musket, and the horses and oxen took off anew and raced down the valley. The Indians took advantage of this assistance and fell in behind the animals with shouts and lance thrusts to keep them going.

The few horses not stampeded were saddled immediately, and all who had mounts—including General McLeod—took off after the Indians. They were unable to catch either the Indians or the horses, but they recovered the cattle and drove them back to camp. They still had their beef, but eighty-three men were afoot.

But that was not the whole story. The Kiowas were as eager for scalps as for horses, and while most of the 180 men of the expedition concentrated on the stampeded animals and the Indians driving them, a few other Indians, awaiting their turn, caught a Mexican named Ramón, who probably was engaged in some menial task near camp, and killed him and scalped him. His body was found about four hundred yards from camp.[2]

Now the men complained of their campground, saying that if they had camped on the high ground, it would not have happened, but Falconer says that if they had camped on the

[2] Ramón must have been one of the "4 Mexican servants" listed by Folsom.

high ground, the men would still have complained. One truism of the plains had been well demonstrated: "After rain, look out for Indians."[3] They had had a heavy thunderstorm and a bitter norther the night before.

On September 5 they moved upstream and camped on the edge of the prairie, with the animals grazing below along the river. That day they killed seven oxen with the idea of drying the meat in case there was another stampede.

The order was to kill the oxen and dry the meat, but, when the animals were killed, the men paid no attention to the order. They cut the meat and started to dry it over their fires, but they gave way to hunger and began to eat it.

Once started, there was no stopping. Hours passed as they ate the beef, and yet there is no recorded statement, even by Falconer, whose sympathies were with McLeod, that any of the officers made any attempt to stop the eating, which might very well have meant starvation for them all. Were the officers so hungry themselves that they did not try to control the men? It is a repetitious question.

McLeod had made strenuous efforts to conserve the beef herd, and this new development—the butchering and eating of seven oxen—must have been a serious blow. It is a safe guess that not over seven oxen were left.[4] The food supply was very low.

[3] Because sticks, leaves, and vegetation, being wet, do not make much sound, and the Indians took advantage of that fact to add to their natural stealthiness.

[4] This incident provides an enlightening bit of information on the condition of the oxen. Starving men eat incredible amounts of food. See Haley, *Charles Goodnight*, 89, where fourteen men ate three old buck deer in one night. Assuming around ninety pounds of edible meat per deer, this means that the men ate close to twenty pounds of meat each during the night. This agrees with accounts of Indians' eating after several days without food. (It was not eaten at one sitting; they would eat until they were full, then give it a couple of hours to digest, and go back for more.) If we allow the pioneers fifteen pounds to a man, we can figure the oxen dressed out about 430 pounds each of edible meat—which, though little enough, is an improvement over our previous calculation. The animals had been on good grass for a while and had a chance to put on weight.

Also, we may now wonder about Grover's report that on August 31 the

Later the same day, hope was abandoned for Donovan, Kenyon, and Klein. It was as well. Their bleached skeletons probably were picked up forty years later and tossed into a wagonful of buffalo bones.

On the night of September 6 the Indian dogs that had been with them about a month were barking continually, and the frontiersmen were sure that Indians lurked around the camp in the dark.

The next day it rained steadily. Caldwell was sent with twenty-five men to look for Indians. A facetious person might think they had enough Indians as it was. Caldwell returned and said he had reached the head of the river at a fine spring in a canyon in the Caprock. He had ascended to the edge of the Llano and had viewed a vast level prairie without a tree or a shrub as far as a man could see.

On September 8 there were light showers, and there were two courts-martial. Private Westgate of Company C was convicted of gross neglect of duty and sentenced to fatigue duty for the remainder of the march, for absenting himself from guard duty without permission.

Private Hamrich of Company B was charged with mutinous conduct; he had tried to persuade the second relief not to turn out, and had said he would be damned if *he* would. He pleaded guilty to this charge but not guilty to the charge of telling Sergeant Haines he did not know his business. He was sentenced to stand guard for two hours off and two hours on for one month, and to pay stoppage for the same period.

---

expedition had only four days' rations. At one and one-half pounds per man per day, McLeod's men would have had left only about two beef animals— for both the McLeod party and the Sutton-Cooke party seem to have divided the beef about evenly, with perhaps a fraction extra going to Cooke. However, we now have a situation where the men ate seven beeves, and there were still six or eight left, for later they used them to pull three wagons across the Llano. Grover's figures are supported by both Falconer and Kendall, and on the whole we have a situation difficult to explain. We may assume the six or eight remaining were classified as draft animals, but this does not explain the seven cattle they ate—unless they too were draft oxen not counted in Grover's calculation.

McLeod received these proceedings "with unqualified surprise. How a Court Martial . . . could treat the crime of mutinous conduct, . . . with the lenity due to an act of mere remissness, he is at a loss to comprehend. He calls boldly upon the officers of his command to do their duty; and demands in the Name of the Laws—their own honor, and the safety of the command; and in the name of the gallant Troops, who have to do the duty of delinquents, that penalties shall be inflicted [as] prescribed by the articles of war." Captain Hudson was president of this court-martial.[5]

The next day they had a cold wind from the north, and those familiar with Texas weather talked about the blue northers that would soon be upon them.

On the night of September 10, Major Sturgess, the paymaster, died of consumption. "We buried him where no mark that I can mention could designate the spot," says Falconer. "Gen. McLeod read the funeral service excellently well, and when the grave was closed, he made a short address, speaking of the major as an honorable gentleman, faithful in his engagements, and high minded even in his quarrels."[6]

According to Gallegher's figures, the expedition had traveled, up to Camp Resolution, 214 miles north and 320 miles west. Presumably this is the distance represented by the shortest route between camps—much less than the actual mileage traveled.

On September 12, after serious muttering among the men and anxious conferences among the officers, McLeod announced that if no news arrived from Cooke by September 20, Captain Caldwell would return to Texas. Almost the entire company was ready to go with him.

Around midday Glass, a man named Mercer, and an unnamed German went out to pick mesquite beans and were attacked by Kiowas. The German threw away his rifle and galloped into camp for help. The Indians retreated, but Glass

[5] General Order No. 21, Bancroft Papers, 734-35.
[6] Falconer, *Letters and Notes*, 108.

was found dead and scalped and Mercer had a lance wound in the breast and two wounds in his back. They carried Mercer into camp for treatment. Glass's body was put "astride a horse, and held on, and was thus brought into camp, his face hanging down, and his bloody head nodding as he came along. We buried him close to the camp."[7]

Mercer said he had cried, "¡Amigo—no americano!" and that an old Indian had tried to stop the Kiowas, but too late.

The next day a rifle fired "accidentally" sent a ball through the arm of Dr. Beall. The ball had come across the camp and passed near McLeod. ("Accidentally" is Falconer's word; one wonders how much design there was in such an "accident.") The men were greatly dissatisfied; there was growing dissension and renewed demand to return home.

On the next day there were weighty conferences. Navarro said it was almost bound to be fatal that they had no friendly Indians along to combat the Kiowas; only Indians could cope with Indians, and he reminded McLeod that he had urged the hiring of some Lipans before the start.[8] Other officers noted growing signs of unrest.

McLeod asked various ones privately if they would stand by him. Falconer assured him that he would, and it is reasonably certain that Navarro and the other officers and influential persons agreed.

On September 15 the camp was moved again, and, prob-

[7] Ibid.

[8] This unquestionably implies that those in charge of the expedition had not considered Indian guides necessary. The statement about Navarro is from Falconer's Diary, in Letters and Notes, 108. In Papers of Lamar, III, 544, appears a fascinating sidelight. Samuel A. Roberts, writing on July 14, 1841, says: "For a wonder we have had no messenger from the Santa Fé expedition —yes, we have." It then appears that one Powhatan Archer had just appeared to take a Mexican prisoner captured by Captain Chandler to guide the Pioneers to "the Indian village." Chandler refused. Archer raised "12 or 15 men" and returned by way of Franklin for the prisoner. Archer must have left the expedition about the time McLeod returned to it. On McLeod's return, there must have been considerable pressure brought to secure a guide. As to the availability of guides, it is worth noting that the Austin City Gazette of June 30, 1841, reported that a "party of Tonkawa spies" had gone to join Burleson, who was hunting Comanches.

ably at Navarro's suggestion, the horses were herded by the Mexican system, with a mounted guard, so that every man with a horse left would not run out after it whenever there was an alarm.[9] It was almost like locking the barn after the stampede. Many of the men were bitter against the order; there was rising discontent, and a proposition arose to burn everything and go back to Texas.

The next day the prairie dog telegraph was that Cooke had lost his way or had been cut off by the Mexicans, and the resolution to go back with Caldwell became almost unanimous. (The gossip about Cooke could have been nothing but speculation.) There had been a severe norther all night, and the day was unusually cold.

At one o'clock the sentries closed up the cattle and began to drive them in. A sentinel named Griffith, a Welshman, galloped in from his post on the hill, followed by an Indian who shot at him and wounded him. He was rescued from scalping, however, and brought to camp. The men complained that if Griffith had not run away, the Indian would have communicated with him! Griffith's comments are not recorded.

A lad named Clark went out and tried to talk to the Indians, but the only thing he could remember of their conversation was the Spanish word *tonto* (stupid). The Gallegher-Hoyle *Journal* adds to the foregoing (which is Falconer's relation) by saying that the Indian told Clark in Spanish that they did not know where they were going and that their captain was a fool. And one of the men commented, "He guesses damned well for a savage."

The Indians refused to give information about the country or directions to anywhere. They well knew that if the Texans got through to New Mexico, there would be more Texans following them.

September 17: the situation of the camp was desperate.

[9] Special Order No. 20, Bolton Papers, 1014: "Hereafter the horses belonging to the command will be turned over to the guard hobbled—they will be herded with the cattle, and the Teamsters who have heretofore acted as cattle guard on foot will be mounted by a detail from Companies."

[103]

The men were feeble and languid; a scratch on a man's hand would ulcerate, and scurvy seemed imminent.

Now it seemed that time itself was against the Pioneers. There had been talk of returning home, and it had been almost agreed upon, but lassitude, illness, and feebleness had held them at Camp Resolution until it was almost too late.

But at eleven o'clock four men were seen coming toward camp at a gallop. One of the four raised a small flag, and the men shouted in relief. Matías was recognized, and "so shrill and singular a cry was made that a shout of laughter immediately followed. The men ran up to Matías, pulled him, shook him, and then he, like a true Mexican courier, commenced exhibiting the devices he had employed to secure his despatches, which at last appeared."[10]

McLeod tore open the letters, read them, and looked up, tremendous relief on his face.

"Cooke is sending provisions from San Miguel," he announced, "and they should be here within another four or five days. We are to destroy all baggage and wagons except those absolutely necessary for our existence, ascend the Caprock, and follow the guides to Santa Fé. The way is much shorter and easier than Cooke's route."

Some of the merchants began to object. They had thousands of dollars invested in trade goods, they said; many of them had put every penny they had in the goods; they had been invited to go by the Republic of Texas, and the Republic had promised to protect them.

"Gentlemen!" said McLeod, "I am aware of your position—but you must remember that the lives of 180 men are at stake. We are forced to do the best we can. Further," he said, undoubtedly remembering protocol, "Cooke has authority over the military. We must obey his command."

The camp was suddenly a beehive of activity, and McLeod, in his great relief and high hopes, issued the following statement: "Comrades: Our anxieties and Suspense is at length

10 Falconer, *Letters and Notes*, 109.

agreeably terminated, by the reception of intelligence from our Detachment; and the prospect of a glorious close to our arduous campaign dawns brightly upon us.

"The privations we have encountered will add a lustre to our success. And the cheerfulness with which you have borne them, will be the willing theme of your Commander. . . . Energy, promptness and determination, will in a few days end our privations and reward our exertions with an abundance of bread, salt, and every necessary of life."[11]

The wagons were unloaded and some supplies repacked, for the guides said they would show them a place where they could take wagons up the Caprock. But McLeod insisted that everything not absolutely necessary be destroyed, for a long trip was still ahead of them. They were to have two freight wagons and the Jersey carryall, to be used as a sick-wagon. The merchant Golpin even then was unable to ride a horse, and he would have to be carried in the sick-wagon. They left a large quantity of tobacco and a cask of copper medals of the Virgin of Oaxaca—both of which they might well have taken with them, as it turned out, for tobacco and those particular medals had more influence than did money with the Mexicans.[12]

On the morning of September 19 they were ready to start. At that time Mercer died of his wounds, and they delayed

[11] Bancroft Papers, 1012; Brief, 154.

[12] No list of goods carried by the merchants has turned up, as far as this writer knows, but James Josiah Webb, outfitting for Santa Fé three years later, should give us a fair idea of the items carried. His merchandise was largely clothing, hardware, dry goods, jewelry, and notions, including mourning prints, sheeting, muslin, drilling, zebra cloth, alpaca, flannel, cambric, cashmere, domestics, lawns, linens, edgings, cotton flags, bandannas, shawls, hose, hickory shirts, blue denims (the word "denim" does not appear in Webster's *Unabridged Dictionary* for 1847, but in the 1864 edition it is defined as "a coarse cotton drilling used for overalls"), leather gloves, black silk ties, suspenders, shoe thread, ivory combs, beads, necklaces, gold rings, fancy hair pins, pearl shirt buttons, gilded buttons, needles, scissors, razors, coffee mills, sad irons, log chains, shovels, spades, hoes, axes, cork inkstands, shaving soap, and candlewick. *Adventures in the Santa Fé Trade 1844–1847*, 128–29n. A much longer and very interesting list appears in Ralph P. Bieber, *The Papers of James J. Webb*, 300–302.

long enough to bury him. They burned six wagons, according to most accounts, and they were taking three with them. They had started with twenty-three and added one. Therefore they must have lost fifteen en route—most of them in the Cross Timbers. Judging by the one that burned in the prairie fire August 13, if twelve of those were merchants' wagons, then $86,000 worth of goods already had been left behind—and the amount was about to be increased by $40,000 more.[13]

The guides took the expedition northwest to the foot of the Caprock near the Arroyo Atuley (west of the present town of Quitaque). They reached this spot on September 19, and Carroll says they camped at what later became Cottonwood Springs. At eight o'clock the next morning, in about an hour's time, they ascended the Caprock at a spot about one mile south of the present highway between Quitaque and Silverton.[14]

The found themselves on the grand prairie, where they proceeded over grassy plains and camped at a small lagoon. Gallegher's Diary says there was no wood. The Gallegher-Hoyle *Journal* notes that the prairie was perfectly level without a tree, and with round basins for water holes, not discernible at a distance of four hundred yards.[15] From the edge of the Caprock the entire panorama of the tableland below was like a map, with a white line marking the sandy bed of the river and green clumps showing the mesquite trees. It was now obvious that on the Caprock the Kiowas had had a perfect observation post and undoubtedly had known every time a party, small or large, had left the camp.

Up on the Llano, fortunately, the grass was still green; this was grama grass that cured well in the hot sun, and it made

[13] Ninety-six years later Carroll found scraps of old wagon irons at the junction of Quitaque and Los Lingos creeks, and located older residents who remembered having seen the complete circle of irons. *The Texan Santa Fé Trail,* 146.

[14] Carroll, *The Texan Santa Fé Trail,* 147. Carroll says this is the only *puerta* for a considerable distance by which the wagons could have ascended the Caprock.

[15] Buffalo wallows.

fine pasture. But there was not a tree or a shrub. The only fuel was buffalo chips—which seemed plentiful, but perhaps Mc-Leod and Navarro and some others were wondering what to feed 180 men for a week or more, for no wild game appeared anywhere.

They made about fifteen miles a day on the Llano. The Sutton-Cooke men had made thirty miles a day, but McLeod's party was held back by three wagons and eighty men on foot. For two days they progressed. The food supply was severely short, and the men complained. One man pointed to the Indian dogs still following them, and asked why not. Others agreed with him—but some did not.

Falconer says: "A remarkable and painful sight. The Indian dogs had remained with us a long time, and had become attached to different companies; . . . the first one or two were shot, the others ran far away howling; . . . if I had been starving I could not have destroyed the faithful animals. But then others suffered more than I did; and it is not when free from the pangs of starvation that we can reason with those who feel them."[16] The only game that appeared anywhere on the Llano was antelope, and they were very shy.

On September 23 they noticed that the days were becoming colder. They camped on Escarbada Creek, in the dry bed of which, the guides said, water could be obtained by digging holes.[17] The stream or stream-course lay in a broad chasm about one hundred feet below the level of the prairie. They went down into it, but there was no running water. The animals drank from the few water holes, while the men dug into the sand for better water. They were about ten miles east of the present town of Hereford, having passed about twenty-five miles southwest of what is now Amarillo.

[16] Falconer, *Letters and Notes*, 111.
[17] Carroll identifies this as the present Tierra Blanca Creek. Probably there were various rivers or creeks or sand-courses in the vicinity of the Llano called something similar, for *Las Escarbadas* means "the scrapings," and most of the dry streams on the Llano would yield water by scraping unless the conditions were unusual.

[107]

Captain Caldwell was dispatched with nine men and one of the guides who had come with Matías, to reach San Miguel, buy provisions, contact Cooke, and return as soon as possible. The guide said it was three days' travel on horseback to San Miguel. Caldwell left, taking also his son Curtis.

The party had descended into the bed of the Escarbada by means of a well-worn road, for the stream was a principal thoroughfare of Indians traveling between the Red River and the Pecos, and they found the remains of a Mexican camp, with frames for drying meat, and a broken-down *carreta* or two-wheeled cart.

"Thanks be to God," Navarro said fervently. "Behold the signs of a Christian people."[18]

But the Kiowas, following precepts of their own, were still watching them. That day three men—Dr. Beall, who had been accidentally shot in the arm, Robert C. Todd, and a man named Wilkins—followed a small canyon to the north, picking plums and small grapes that were sweet and almost like currants. The three men did not come back. Although guns were fired and men went to search for them, they were never found. There was still one physician, Dr. Whitaker, with the Pioneers.

On September 25 they continued west, and a man named McLaughlin died, the cause not specified. They passed some small lagoons, and suddenly, on the next day, extreme depression struck the entire company. It appeared abruptly and inexplicably, says Falconer, noting that it did not affect himself or Navarro. When they camped that evening, there was no loud talking and no laughing. Once again the guides were suspected of treachery,[19] and Falconer says "the most painful silence prevailed in camp."

The next day they crossed the Texas–New Mexico boundary and camped about thirty miles north of the present town of Clovis. They were still on the Llano, and it seemed endless.

[18] Falconer, *Letters and Notes*, 112.
[19] This has reference to Juan Carlos back on the Wichita River.

The guides warned them that on September 27 they would have to make a dry camp—and they did. Without food and without water, with the boundless Llano still before them, the men were about ready to give up. They had been nine days on the Llano and had traveled 170 miles. But there was hope. The guides assured them they would descend from the Llano the next day.

They had been two days under the burning sun without water when on September 28 they reached the edge of the plains. To the west it looked like the view from the eastern Caprock, with numbers of isolated hills rising from the breaks below. These hills were flat on top and level with the plains. The expedition did not find the *puerta* until after dark, and took the wagons down with great difficulty. A cold wind blew steadily, but they found a water hole to camp by.

The next day they made five miles. The following day, September 30, the guides did not want to go ahead. No explanation for this is offered, so it may be that the guides, who were Mexican, were getting nervous at their proximity to Armijo's domain. They had reason to know the tenor of Armijo's hospitality toward any Mexican who would guide Texans to New Mexico. But even though the guides were reluctant, the officers insisted that the expedition proceed.

McLeod was far in the lead at five o'clock that afternoon, and Captain Houghton ordered a halt without water. It was a rocky, uneven country, filled with cactus. The general feeling in camp was very low.

On the morning of October 1 they found two fine springs only 150 yards from their camp. Falconer says that no little abuse fell on the guides, but it would seem that plenty fell on Houghton too, for in a communication addressed to McLeod that day, Houghton requested that a court-martial be assembled the next morning for his trial.[20] There is no record that it was ever held.

The question arises how this event could happen. It is char-

[20] Bancroft Papers, 796.

acteristic of Mexicans to keep their own counsel around *anglos,* and this was especially true where Texans were involved, so quite likely the guides, having been repulsed in their wish not to proceed west, had kept still and allowed Houghton to camp where he would.[21]

On his side, Houghton committed one more in the long list of errors that had plagued the expedition from the beginning. It seems rather obvious that he sent out no scouts of his own.

On October 2 they remained in camp all day at the Monte de Revuelto or Mixed Woods. Since no word had come from Caldwell and no further word from Cooke, McLeod dispatched still a third party under command of Lieutenant Burgess and including the merchants or "amateurs" Robert Scott and John Howard (a younger brother of Major Howard), Matías, and one of the guides who had come from Cooke. By this time the men's hair was long and matted, their faces browned and toughened by sun and wind, their hunting shirts torn and greasy. Burgess was not to go into San Miguel and contact the Mexican authorities, but to try to find out what had happened to Cooke and Caldwell and feel out the sentiment of the Mexican populace toward the expedition.

On October 3, following the general direction taken by Burgess, McLeod reached the Arroyo Tucumcari. There he found fresh sign of many horsemen, along with plenty of moccasin tracks. The Mexican guide was disturbed, but made no attempt to explain the sign—a typical Mexican reaction. They camped in a grove of cottonwoods near a stream, and saw horsemen on the distant ridges.

On October 4 they advanced west toward the Laguna Colorada.[22] About midday they were met by two well-armed Mexicans who told them Colonel Juan Andrés Archuleta was camped at the lake with a force of soldiers, but that the Texans

[21] The Mexicans were known to be excellent guides, and it was already obvious that they knew that area well.

[22] Kendall says this spot was thirty or forty miles south of the Angosturas. *Narrative,* I, 340.

Where the Pioneers Descended the Caprock

Photograph by C. Boone McClure
Courtesy Panhandle-Plains Historical Society

General Manuel Armijo

Courtesy Museum of New Mexico

would not be bothered if they would give up their rifles. McLeod refused and took his men on to the lake.[23]

They had traveled a route generally south of that of the Sutton-Cooke party. In the sandy bed of the lake were dead cedar trees that made sweet-smelling fires, but they had no flour, no bread, no salt, coffee, or sugar. Scurvy was common among them and caused great debility. On some it caused festers and pustules on the hands; others were so feeble they had difficulty getting to their feet.

McLeod, Navarro, Dr. Whitaker, and a "poor interpreter" went to meet Archuleta and his officers. Archuleta demanded their arms. He promised good treatment, but would give no information about the other parties. McLeod did not want to give up the arms, but finally agreed to deliver an answer at nine o'clock the next morning, and the Texans went back to their camp.

"I believe," said McLeod, "the Mexicans should be opposed. I say we go ahead with the wagons and not fire until we are fired on."

"Be reasonable," said one. "What would we fight with? Most of the men without horses have thrown away their rifles, and of those that are left, we have only fifty rounds of ammunition made up. We have only a few cattle left—just enough to pull the wagons—and they are all draft animals—poor bull."

Dr. Whitaker said they had about ninety men able to fight; the other ninety were sick and had to be cared for.

They stayed up most of the night making that hard decision. It was out of the question to try to fight their way on to Santa Fé through a hostile country, and in their condition they knew they could not make their way back across the Llano under any circumstances. They were confident they could whip Archuleta, but what then? They would be subject to constant harassment and the possibility of losing all their horses and cattle by stampede.

[23] Carroll places this important camp opposite the mouth of Bull Canyon, four miles southeast of Newkirk, N. M.

On the other hand, Navarro pointed out, Archuleta promised the security of their lives, the distribution of sheep for food, and the safety of their supplies as far as San Miguel.[24]

Besides, asked the younger officers, what had become of Cooke? It was an ominous question. Cooke had had some one hundred picked men and the best horses, and had left Camp Resolution in full health. He must have been captured, and if the Sutton-Cooke party had not been able to oppose the Mexicans, how could this miserable remnant under McLeod hope to do so?

McLeod finally gave in. If Archuleta would guarantee fair treatment, he would surrender. What else could he do?

On the morning of October 5, McLeod, Navarro, and other officers met Archuleta, but he still refused to give them any information about Cooke. It made no difference. They had no choice but surrender. A written agreement was drawn up and signed by officers on both sides. The life of Navarro was specifically guaranteed; the Pioneers agreed to lay down their arms, and were insured life and liberty and protection of their property to San Miguel,[25] and treatment as prisoners of war.[26]

In the afternoon the Texan officers called their men together and ordered them to discharge their rifles into the air and lay them on the ground. The rifles and the six pounder were put in a wagon. The baggage and merchandise of the Pioneers were hauled away by Mexicans.[27] The horses and mules were taken over.[28]

[24] It is a little difficult to determine exactly what was promised; it seems certain their lives were assured, and something else as far as San Miguel—which must have been their possessions.

[25] Gallegher-Hoyle *Journal*, Brief 323: "1st. To lay down our arms. 2nd. We were ensured life & liberty and protection of our property to San Miguel."

[26] Falconer, *Letters and Notes*, 44: "A written agreement . . . was drawn up, and every formality which should entitle the men to the privileges of war was observed." P. 91: "The terms, securing to the party the treatment of prisoners of war, were signed by the officers on both sides." This agreement, rather well documented it seems, never has come to light.

[27] It was standard practice in New Mexico to confiscate the property of a man arrested. In 1819 David Meriweather, working for the American Fur Company, was thrown into prison for alleged espionage. He was released

McLeod watched glumly as his force was rendered defenseless. What an inglorious ending to such a promising venture. He remembered the fine words spoken at Brushy Creek and could hardly believe it had come to this—a handful of ragged, dirty, starving men, stripped of all their possessions, now prisoners of war.[29]

Now that he was able to see the disposition of Archuleta's troops, McLeod realized that the Pioneers' position had been even more hopeless than they had known. Archuleta's main body was opposite them, intrenched among large boulders, with its center on high ground commanding the road. Some cavalry had been stationed across the lake, among which were many Indians, to harass McLeod's rear if he tried to move forward. About that time also a large body of additional troops arrived, and McLeod knew beyond question that to surrender was the most intelligent decision that had been made since June 20.

He saw Falconer come back from the Mexican camp. Falconer was a slight man with light hair and blue eyes, and, although he showed the effects of the trip, he did not seem hurt as much as some of the others. He had an armload of biscuits, and gave some to McLeod.

"At least we shall have bread," he said. McLeod did not answer.

later, but his fine horses and good rifles were taken from him. He later became governor of New Mexico. W. W. H. Davis, *El Gringo*, 240. In 1817, Auguste P. Chouteau's party was arrested on the Arkansas and kept in prison forty-eight days; all their property was taken. Pedro María de Allande was governor then. Ralph E. Twitchell, *The Leading Facts of New Mexican History*, I, 482.

[28] In Archuleta's report of the surrender, he says he took thirty-four horses and three mules; he does not mention any cattle. Archuleta's report is not too clear, being partly illegible, and at every place where he seems about to give the number of men captured, the report is disappointing. Brief, 511 (a photostat).

[29] The question of whether or not they were prisoners of war under international law or common criminals under domestic law was debated later at some length, but it seems even the Mexican officials eventually conceded that the surrender had been made with no less than the guarantee of life. A "copy" of the guarantee was sent from Santa Fé October 1, 1842, signed by Donasio Vigil, marked "Approved" (presumably by the governor). It noted that all lives were guaranteed "without exception."

8. LA JORNADA DEL MUERTE

On october 7 the McLeod men marched under guard ten miles west to Pajarito Creek, and there McLeod, Navarro, Falconer, Gallegher, and all the officers were separated from the men and sent on to San Miguel in advance.

At this time Cooke and Sutton, with their ninety men, were in the area of Chihuahua, marching south to the prisons in and near Mexico City; Kendall, Van Ness, Howard, and Fitzgerald were still in jail in San Miguel; Lieutenant Burgess and his men were quartered as prisoners on the Baca ranch; Captain Caldwell and his party were quartered as prisoners on the Vigil ranch.

At this point, Kendall sums up the reasons for failure: (1) late departure; (2) lack of Indian guides; (3) not enough wagons and oxen for goods; (4) not enough cattle; (5) a greater distance than anticipated; (6) the Indians' antagonism; (7) Armijo's resistance.[1]

"Poor planning" would seem to cover most of these points, and there might be added these reasons: absence of discipline, failure to use scouts, failure of one party to communi-

[1] Walter Prescott Webb, *The Great Plains*, 194ff., discusses the art of war on the Great Plains and the army's failure; he points out that Jefferson Davis had expressed decided opinions on the inadequacy of traditional army methods such as McLeod tried to utilize. Colonel Randolph B. Marcy, *Army Life on the Border*, 67, says, "The old system [is] almost wholly impotent."

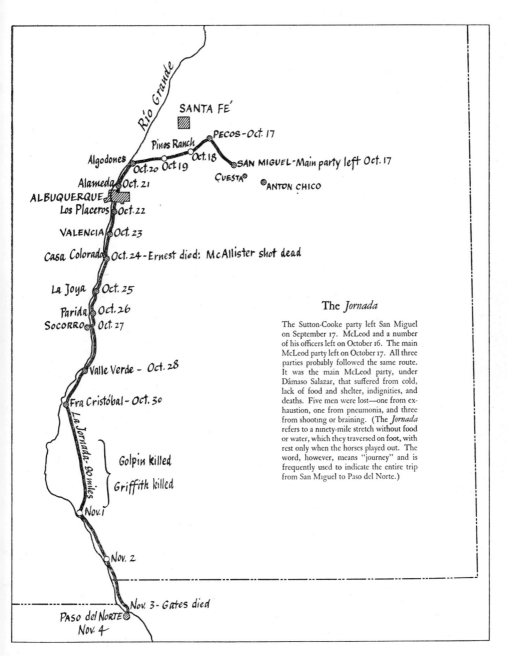

The *Jornada*

The Sutton-Cooke party left San Miguel on September 17. McLeod and a number of his officers left on October 16. The main McLeod party left on October 17. All three parties probably followed the same route. It was the main McLeod party, under Dámaso Salazar, that suffered from cold, lack of food and shelter, indignities, and deaths. Five men were lost—one from exhaustion, one from pneumonia, and three from shooting or braining. (The *Jornada* refers to a ninety-mile stretch without food or water, which they traversed on foot, with rest only when the horses played out. The word, however, means "journey" and is frequently used to indicate the entire trip from San Miguel to Paso del Norte.)

Route of the main McLeod party south to Paso del Norte as prisoners. Also route of Sutton-Cooke party earlier.

cate with another, and utter failure to recognize the signs of resistance.

The expedition had followed the familiar steps of disintegration of every party on the Great Plains: lack of water, grass, and food; harassment by Indians; loss of control; and separation of the command.

Kendall says that on October 12 McLeod's men were marched into the plaza, worn down and emaciated, pale and haggard, showing that they had suffered dreadfully; many had but shirt and pantaloons and a single blanket. At the same time, Lewis was in San Miguel, "well mounted and well dressed." He did not talk to the prisoners.

McLeod's wagons were lined up on the plaza and the goods divided by the Governor; a large share went to Lewis.

On October 16, McLeod, at the head of thirteen men, left San Miguel for El Paso del Norte in charge of Lieutenant Teodoro Quintana.

The next day—October 17—Kendall and his four companions[2] were taken to the main body. The Burgess party came in from the Baca ranch, and one of Baca's daughters, in love with a prisoner (Kendall, of course, does not say which one), wept touchingly.

"Old Paint" Caldwell and his men were brought in, and such was the affection in which he was held that the lines broke and men surged forward to shake his hand.

Guarded by two hundred men, armed mostly with bows and arrows and lances, the main body set out; the guards rode single file on both sides. Accompanied by two of their own wagons and a herd of nineteen beef oxen, they headed south under Captain Salazar.

Kendall says it was a journey of over two thousand miles on foot.[3] Kendall's feet were so badly swollen and blistered

---

[2] This may be Kendall's error; there should have been only three.

[3] Kendall overstates it, although it is hard to determine just what the distance really was. James Josiah Webb says it was 1,750 miles; Ruxton supports this; Folsom cuts it down to 1,335; Ruxton says it is 1,250 miles from Mexico City to Chihuahua, and Wislizenus shows 684 from Chihuahua to Santa Fé.

that he had to take off his boots and march with no protection on his feet but stockings. Many of the prisoners' feet, he says, were bleeding at every step, and that night they were driven one by one into a cowpen and counted like sheep. They received a pint of meal each. It got so cold toward morning that they were glad to get up, and then they found frost on the blankets.

Salazar warned them that if a single man should be missing, the entire expedition would be executed.

Kendall's biggest trouble at first was with his feet. He had been in jail for a month, and his skin was tender. Great blisters formed on his heels, and when he would take off his stockings the skin would stick to them and pull off. Gravel worked into his stockings, but he had to keep them on to avoid pulling off more skin.

They would get up in the morning with their toes frostbitten, and for two or three hours they were tortured by severe leg pains; these would wear off, but the toes and feet swelled and hurt intensely. On October 19 it was a great relief to bathe their feet in the cold water of the Río Grande. That night they were issued a piece of barley bread too hard to eat without boiling. The night was bitingly cold, and the men, sleeping in the open, nestled close together to keep warm.

Rations were issued by Salazar about once a day in very small quantity; in the meantime, the prisoners lived on food given them by women along the way. Dry ears of corn were prized by all.

Toenails began to come off from frostbite, but Salazar told them he would drive them so hard they would have no ambition or strength to attempt escape. They were making thirty and forty miles a day on foot.

At Algodones occurred the episode of the two small rooms that has been made infamous by many stories. Van Ness

Perhaps Kendall was not far off. Road maps for 1955 show more than 1,600 miles.

[117]

pleaded for some kind of shelter, and Salazar and his men drove the entire group into two small rooms and locked a heavy wooden door. There was no window in the rear room, and they were too crowded to sit down. Presently some felt suffocated, and they began to shout for air. They tried to break down the door but could not. The door opened inward, and they could not push back hard enough to open it. Finally, a guard unlocked the door and allowed fifty to go outside. Kendall went to a cowyard and crawled against a low mud wall, still reeking, he says, with perspiration from the torture of heat and fear of suffocation. A cold wind chilled them through, but it was better than suffocating.

Another hard ear of corn on October 21. That night Kendall tried to crawl into an outdoor oven, but found it already occupied.

At Albuquerque, Kendall saw a "perfect specimen of female loveliness," holding a pumpkin on her head; she was not more than fifteen, "yet her loose and flowing dress, but half concealing a bust of surpassing beauty and loveliness, disclosed that she was just entering womanhood."[4] Kendall was still the journalist.

It was good that they had such a pleasant momentary divertissement, for grim events were in the offing. One of the men named Gates (there were two on the expedition) was fighting off illness, running a fever. There was no physician with this party, Dr. Whitaker having gone with the first McLeod party, but it was apparent from the phlegm that Gates exhibited and from the tightness of his chest and the difficulty of his breathing that he was suffering from a "congestion of the lungs." But there was little they could do for him. Every man was weak and miserable and fighting for existence, and there was only the one thin blanket apiece against the chill winds of approaching winter. Undoubtedly the stronger ones helped him walk and gave him tiny portions of their pittance of food, but they had no way to provide the warmth which he

[4] *Narrative*, I, 383.

[118]

obviously needed. It was by this time a struggle to stay alive on the part of every man on the march.

A small, quiet man named Ernest began to lag behind, and some of the stronger ones went back and, with their arms around him, helped him to walk faster and keep up with the main party, for Salazar had repeatedly beaten laggards with his sword and had said he would kill any who fell behind. The Pioneers, exhausted by starvation and the endless cold nights, were thoroughly beaten down. There was no thought of fighting back—only the desperate will to stay alive somehow, anyhow.

Two days later, near a village called Valencia, they camped as usual in the open. The men slept on the ground, jammed against one another to conserve body warmth. They began waking up at 2:00 or 3:00 A. M. because of the cold, and presently all were awake and on their feet but one. That was Ernest.

The man who had slept next to Ernest went back and put his hand on Ernest's shoulder and said, "Come on, man. We're making a fire." But Ernest did not move. The man rolled him over. Ernest's body was stiff and cold, and the man stared in horror. He had been sleeping next to a dead man.

Salazar came back presently. With his skinning knife he cut off Ernest's ears, pierced them, and strung them on a rawhide thong which he hung about his neck. The guards stripped off Ernest's pitiful clothes and left the naked body by the side of the road.

There was bitter resentment among the Pioneers, but the guards gave them no chance to do anything about it. With the flats of swords and with doubled rope ends they got the men under way. But more trouble developed, and tragedy piled on tragedy.

John McAllister of Tennessee, who had had one lame ankle from childhood, sprained his other ankle. Salazar allowed him to sit in a Mexican *carreta* at the start. The two wagons taken from the Pioneers were still with them, but these were used

[119]

to transport personal effects of Salazar and the food he was supposed to ration out. The *alcalde* of Valencia, however, pitying the prisoners for their very bad condition, had provided a cart so that the worst of them could be transported. But within a mile it was too heavily loaded and broke down. The main body of prisoners marched on and was a quarter of a mile ahead. Salazar ordered McAllister to catch up with them. McAllister said he was completely unable to walk. Salazar drew his sword and ordered him on. At that point, says Kendall, Salazar had half a dozen mules without riders, any one of which McAllister could have ridden.

McAllister pointed to his swollen ankle and insisted he could not walk. Half a dozen of the Pioneers who had been with him in the cart now sensed tragedy and gathered around McAllister, hoping by their presence to dissuade Salazar from violence. But Salazar was not a man sensitive to such things. Again he ordered McAllister to catch up. Again McAllister said he could not. Salazar said, "*Adelante*—or I'll shoot."

McAllister must really have been unable to walk. He threw off his blanket and exposed his chest. "Then shoot!" he said. "And the quicker the better."

They all hoped that if this point ever came, Salazar would back down. But his black eyes showed a glint. He drew his Texan pistol and shot McAllister in the heart. He cut off his ears. His clothes were stripped off and given to the guards, and his body left for the wolves.

No longer was there any doubt that theirs was a desperate situation and that their very lives were subject to Salazar's cruel whims. The march became truly a trail of desperation and doggedness.

They passed a long train of wagons belonging to James Wiley Magoffin of Chihuahua. Kendall notes that the drivers "were all brown, healthy-looking Americans." They were forbidden to talk to them.

At that time, Kendall's moccasins had no soles in them, and he was walking on gravel, but at Parrida he bought a pair of walking shoes.

They did not like the town of Socorro. Kendall says the "inhabitants were a pack of scoundrels," but he does not say what contributed to such a conclusion.

On October 29 they were watched by an Apache chief. Kendall says he was dignified, about middle height (but mounted on a large and powerful gray horse), strong, sixty-five or seventy years old, white haired, dressed in old fashioned military clothes and a hat from the revolution. They made forty miles that day.

On October 30 they reached Fray Cristóval, but it could not have been much, for there was no house or settlement there; it must have been a campground—and it was the last stopping place before setting out on the *Jornada*.[5] They slept out at Fray Cristóval and awoke with three inches of snow on their blankets. In the afternoon they were told to fill their water gourds, for the *Jornada* was ninety miles long and there would be no water on it; the march would be made continuously; there would be no stop for sleep or rest.

The *Jornada*, was a sterile, desolate plain with a few scattered cacti, and was especially noted for the beargrass, whose root or trunk grows up six or seven feet, with the leaves branching out at the top. At Fray Cristóval, Salazar had one ox killed for food. Everybody had colds. There was a lake in the middle of the *Jornada*, but at that time of year it was dry. Salazar told them no more food would be issued until they finished the crossing. A raw wind was blowing down from the snow-clad mountains, and Kendall's fingers were so numb

[5] Any trip may be a *jornada*, but in this case the word refers to a section of the route near Paso, which is usually called *the Jornada*. It is a ninety-mile stretch of waterless desert, variously called *La Jornada del Muerto* (Journey of the Dead), Way of Death, and Road of Death. Cleve Hallenbeck and Juanita H. Williams, *Legends of the Spanish Southwest*, 61, say that the original name probably was *La Jornada del Muerte* (the Journey of Death).

that after he got his water gourd filled (it held about two quarts), it slipped from his hands, fell on the ground, and was broken.

They set out in the afternoon. It was too cold for the soldiers to ride their animals.

Kendall's description of the march is expressive: "The sufferings of that dreadful night cannot be forgotten. With sore and blistered feet . . . it was nothing to the biting cold and the helpless drowsiness. Toward daylight many of us were walking in our sleep and staggering from one side of the road to another."

At daylight they stopped for an hour to bring up the stragglers and count the prisoners. They marched all day and passed the dry lake. Toward sunset the merchant named Golpin, "a small, inoffensive man" who had a crippled right hand, felt that he could not walk much farther and made a bargain with one of the guards to trade his shirt for a ride on a mule. He was in the act of taking off his shirt when Salazar ordered him shot. The first ball wounded him; the second killed him instantly, and he died with the shirt still up about his face. Salazar took his ears, and the guards took his ragged clothing.

At ten o'clock that night they had to stop for three hours because the horses and mules could go no farther without rest. Then they were driven on.

They met Colonel Muñoz's Durango dragoons, on their way north to fight the Texans. The dragoons too were freezing; they would run from one tuft of creosote bush to another and light each to get warm by the brief fire. Many women were with them, and the Texans could not understand how the women, always thinly clad, could endure the cold. A dragoon, standing by a burning clump, would wrap his great blue cloak about himself and a woman, and they would get a moment of warmth.

That whole terrible march was an unbelievable nightmare. At dawn of the second day the man Griffith, who had been wounded by the Kiowas at Camp Resolution, became so paralyzed from cold that he could no longer ride the mule for which he must have paid. He jumped off and tried to walk, but, weak and lame and numb, he sank to the ground. A soldier told him to get up or he would kill him. Griffith tried, but his legs gave way, and the soldier knocked out his brains with the musket.

The only thing that saved many of them on this latter part of the trip was the fact that Salazar was riding in one of the wagons, asleep under plenty of blankets, and did not know how straggling the body of prisoners became.

After the killing of Griffith, Salazar had another ox killed,[6] and for some unexplained reason administered a severe beating to one of the prisoners with the flat of his sword across the man's shoulders.

The prisoners were giving up shirts and shoes and blankets for a ride of a few miles. After forty hours on the *Jornada* they saw the water of the Río Grande, but they were not allowed to stop until pitch dark that night, some fourteen hours later.

Salazar left the remaining oxen on the road, along with thirty horses and mules—obviously to make it appear that these animals were used or lost, so that later he could sell them for his own benefit.

Somebody said Gates was in bad shape. His eyes were glassy, and there was a rattling in his throat. He asked for water. A young Mexican snapped an empty musket in his face. Gates raised his hands convulsively and shrank back. The Mexican again pointed the gun and snapped it. Gates shuddered and went limp. The Mexicans looked at him and found he was dead. They dragged the body to the roadside and cut off the ears.

The next day the long march of horror came to an end. They went into El Paso del Norte,[7] saw the advance McLeod party,

[6] Kendall, *Narrative*, II, 18, says this ox had traveled all the way from Austin.

who were clean shaved and neatly dressed, and were turned over to Colonel Elías, who treated them kindly. He and the priest, Father Ramón Ortiz, fed the prisoners, gave them facilities for bathing and shaving, and put them to sleep in clean sheets.

The next day, Salazar came to see Elías and threw down the five pairs of ears. Elías accused him of murder and of trying to steal sixteen head of cattle left back on the road. He ordered an investigation, which resulted in an order for Salazar's court-martial.[8]

A few days later—November 9—they left Paso for Chihuahua. A man named Neal or Neil was left behind, supposedly ill, though Kendall did not think he was ill. The road to Chihuahua was over desert, but they had a big train and were well treated. Colonel Elías and Father Ramón had given them money, along with horses for the sick and lame.

They changed commanders at Chihuahua, at Cerro Gordo, at Cuencamé, Zacatecas, San Luis Potosí, Guanajuato, and Querétaro. Some commanders were good; some were very bad.

One night they would be hovered around tiny fires in a rocky, sterile mountain region; the next they might be released on parole and entertained and fed by wives of prominent Mexicans or wives (invariably Mexican) of Americans in Mexico. Kendall said it was hardly believable how their situation could change.

They thought of escape but did not try it. At Saucillo, below Chihuahua, they woke up one morning to find Larrabee cold and stiff in one of the carts, and Captain Ochoa, one of their most thoughtful commanders, requested that Dr. Whitaker see if he was "dead enough to bury" (Kendall's words).

At Ojo Caliente below Zacatecas they were allowed to bathe in the warm springs, and it was there that the Mexican girls

[7] Not the present El Paso, but a village near what is now Ciudad Juárez. There was no settlement on the left bank until Magoffinsville was established in 1849.

[8] More details of this affair will be given in a later chapter.

*South from Paso del Norte to Cuencamé. McLeod party, No-
vember 9–December 20, 1841; Sutton-Cooke party
about two months earlier.*

[125]

divested themselves of their clothing and went in to bathe with them. No objections have been anywhere recorded.[9]

With their feet sometimes dragging the ground, they willingly rode the donkeys occasionally provided, and called themselves the "Texas heavy light cavalry."

They got into the heights of the Sierra Madres—deep, dark, dreary mountain passes sometimes only fifty feet wide, rugged precipices, huge prickly pear, cedar trees, and the great *órgano* cactus. The trail was rocky and steep, and little towns and sometimes good-sized cities were crowded into pockets in the mountains. Some were mining towns only; Querétaro was known for soap and cigars. They began to get into the tropics, and saw orange trees blooming in January, although they were still at a high altitude.

In all the long trip they were insulted openly once—at Querétaro, where they were stoned on the streets.[10] The populace in general was very kind to them—especially *anglos*, Europeans, and Mexicans of high position.

The kind treatment started with Elías and Father Ramón in Paso, and a Mrs. Stevenson in that town, the Mexican wife of an *anglo*. In Chihuahua, Mrs. Magoffin saw that they were generously fed. Henry Connelly[11] had already advanced Sutton and Cooke $1,339 against the credit of the Texas government, and he probably advanced more to the McLeod party. A "young merchant from Massachusetts" offered help of clothing and small amounts of money; Dr. Jennison, director of the mint at Chihuahua, gave each of the McLeod party a pair of shoes and a tin cup. At Durango, José Heredia, Mexican governor, gave the McLeod party $500.

The foreigners and wealthy Mexicans in San Luis Potosí

[9] Ruxton, *Adventures in Mexico,* 59, tells how, when strangers stared too openly at the girls bathing in the canals of Querétaro, the girls would laugh and call them *sinvergüenzas* (shameless ones) and splash water in their faces. A fitting punishment.

[10] Kendall, *Narrative,* II, 189.

[11] The same man who had led the Connelly Expedition in 1839–40—whose trail they had found west of the Cross Timbers.

made up a purse for them. In Zacatecas they were given $1,000, says one report, while another says $1.00 was given to each man, along with new clothing, six horses with saddles and bridles, and two wagons. At Guanajuato they gave $10.00 to each officer and merchant, $1.00 to each man, and shoes and shirts to those who needed them. In April some Mexicans gave them $500, and two men from Boston, one a Mr. Talbot, gave eight doubloons ($128) each.

On the day of San Lázaro—March 11—at the prison of San Lázaro, the Mexican people brought gifts for all inmates, and, Kendall says, a Mexican lady sent in sumptuous dinners, and by the end of the day he had "enough stuff to load a handcar, a hatful of cigars and cigarettes, and several dollars worth of money."

On their release, even the poor *léperos* gave them clothes. Powhatan Ellis, the first American envoy with whom they dealt, gave the prisoners $1,000, then when he left Mexico, sold his library, table service, and furniture, and gave them the proceeds. L. S. Hargous, American vice-consul in Vera Cruz, advanced them $6,253.66 to get back home, and Waddy Thompson, the new American minister, advanced about $5,000 more. (Four years later, Thompson noted that Mr. Hargous had not been repaid.) Nathan Gilliland of New York offered $200, and the American stage drivers between Vera Cruz and Mexico City gave from $500 to $1,000 apiece.

And, of course, the Mexican women of all classes constantly brought them food, tobacco, and clothing, did their washing, cared for them when they were ill, hid them when they escaped, helped disguise them, told them the roads, and gave them money to travel on.

But there were other complications by the time they reached San Luis Potosí, about two-thirds of the distance from Chihuahua to Mexico City. The men had been complaining of headaches and cramps, and at that town they left three men in the hospital, suspected of having smallpox. By the time they reached Guanajuato some men were delirious, and seventeen were left in the hospital there. (Two Sutton-Cooke men had been left at Silao.) Three were left at Tula, and finally, on February 1, they reached the prison of San Cristóbal. Falconer and Van Ness were set at liberty. Franklin Coombs, with the Sutton-Cooke party, had been released a few days before at Santiago. Fitzgerald was released at Guanajuato February 28.

Some individual escapes had been made. North of Paso, Alsbury, Hancock, Adams, and Sheldon of the Sutton-Cooke party escaped, but were recaptured by Pueblo Indians. Lubbock and Mazur escaped from Santiago and returned to Texas. "Comanche" escaped before reaching Mexico, but was recaptured. McJunkins and a partner (unidentified) escaped about the same time, but were recaptured. Howard and Hudson would escape from Puebla in April and return to Texas. Two unidentified Pioneers, Thomas Stosoases and Radulfo Studion (these are Mexican spellings), escaped from Puebla.

Tom Lubbock gives an interesting note: "We once or twice [not far south of Chihuahua] determined amongst ourselves to make a united effort at escaping; but though the black-hearted Lewis was behind, another traitor was amongst us. Our purposes were disclosed, and of course defeated."[12]

The preliminary releases and the escapes, however, had little significance for the main body of prisoners. The Sutton-Cooke men had been largely imprisoned at Santiago, just north of Mexico City, and most of them were still there. San Cristóbal, then, became the distribution center for the McLeod men. On February 9 about 125 men, including McLeod, went on to the prison at Puebla, eighty miles east of Mexico City. Of these, 52, still including McLeod, were sent on ninety miles farther east to Perote.

In the meantime, those considered too sick to travel were sent to San Lázaro, on the eastern outskirts of Mexico City. This group included Kendall. So many of the Texan prisoners had smallpox or symptoms of the disease that the authorities

[12] Brief, 463.

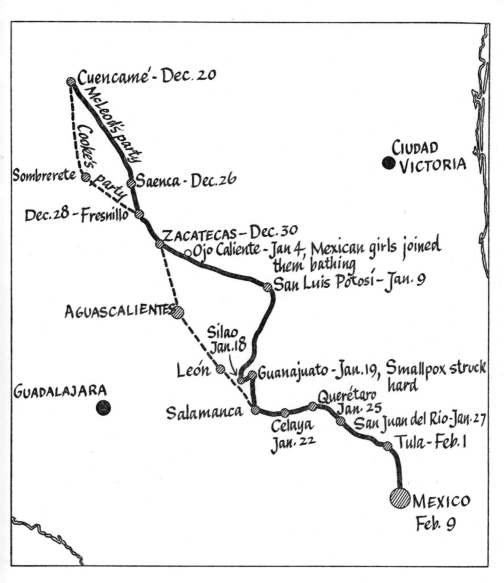

South and east from Cuencamé to Mexico [City]. McLeod party, December 20, 1841–February 9, 1842; Sutton-Cooke party about two months earlier.

decided not to take them to a regular smallpox hospital, but sent them instead to San Lázaro, which Kendall discovered, to his horror, was a lepers' prison. There they were mixed with the lepers, and the surroundings of maimed and horribly diseased persons in all stages of dying were so upsetting that many of the Texans could not eat the first day. They found they were being offered the eating utensils of the lepers, and rebelled.

Kendall, still believing he would be released any day, at first was patient. Then he became disheartened and began seriously to plan escape. Prisoners came and went from San Lázaro. They moved Kendall and some of his companions to another place, infested with bedbugs, then moved them back. Meanwhile, Powhatan Ellis and, in April, Waddy Thompson, labored with Bocanegra, the minister of foreign relations, Tornel, the minister of war, and Santa Anna, the provisional president.

It rather seems that the initial treatment of the Texans put the Mexican officials into a bad spot from which they would have been happy to extricate themselves if they could do so without losing face. Bocanegra's arguments were rather weak, and this was not becoming to Bocanegra, for he was a capable jurist. Daniel Webster's arguments and Waddy Thompson's arguments were rather well thought out and forceful, on the other hand, since they had considerable right and justice on their side.

Santa Anna's real complaint, Thompson said, was over United States recognition of Texas as a republic. Thompson pointed out that the same complaint could be made against England, France, Holland, and Belgium, all of whom had recognized Texas by the end of 1840. He also pointed out that the United States had recognized the independence of Mexico long before Spain had done so.

In the meantime, Kendall was trying to accustom himself to his surroundings. He describes the disease of leprosy:

It makes its first appearance by scaly eruptions on different parts of the face and body . . . The limbs of many, and more especially the hands, at first appear to be drawn and twisted out of all shape. Gradually the nose or parts of the feet are carried away, while the features become distorted and hideous. The voice assumes, at times, a husky and unnatural tone, and again the doomed patient is unable to articulate except in a shrill, piping treble. . . . Death steps in at last to relieve the poor creatures of their sufferings. . . . Whether the leprosy of Mexico is contagious I am unable to say.[13]

The prisoners at Santiago were in chains and were made to work on the public roads. All prisoners were more or less confined with—sometimes chained to—hardened and depraved criminals. Beatings apparently were frequent. Food was often insufficient. Sometimes the men were packed into a room so tightly that there was no space to lie down to sleep, and they were forced to sit or stand all night.

The ministers of England, France, Prussia, Switzerland, and the Vatican tried to intervene. Some were successful, and between April 21 and April 28 twenty-six prisoners were released on various pretexts. Kendall was one of these. On May 12, fourteen of the released prisoners sailed from Vera Cruz on the United States revenue cutter *Woodbury*.

Large numbers of the Texans became ill with smallpox and yellow fever. Many were in hospitals. Some of those released in April were too sick to go home.

At long last, on June 13, Santa Anna ordered a general release. It was not, as has been said, Santa Anna's birthday. Santa Anna's patron saint was St. Anthony, and the ostensible reason for the Texans' release was St. Anthony's day.[14] At that time 2 were released from the *Acordada*, the most dreaded

---

[13] *Narrative*, II, 222–23.

[14] Suggested by a priest at the Dominican Library, Minneapolis, Minn., in March, 1955. Verified by Waddy Thompson, who says Santa Anna's saint was Saint Antonio.

of all Mexican prisons, 47 were released from Perote, 65 were released from Puebla, and 119 from Santiago. A total of 185 men prepared to embark on the *Rosa Alvina* on July 27, but the ship was quarantined because of yellow fever; they did not sail until August 12, and at that time about 40 stayed in Mexico—some by choice, some because of illness. On September 13 "the rest" sailed for Texas on the *Woodbury*. Navarro, however, was still in the *Acordada,* and did not escape until 1845. His case will be treated separately.

For the Texans the long ordeal was over, but for some there were other ordeals to come. All of them had taken an oath not to bear arms against Mexico, but either this promise was forgotten in the confusion of invasions and counterinvasions that followed, or some of the Texans declared it null and void, as Santa Anna himself had declared his promises at San Jacinto null and void. Three of the Pioneers, Fitzgerald, Brenham, and Hancock, were taken in a surprise attack on San Antonio—in Texas territory—and subjected to the consequences of their oath, but later their death sentences were commuted to ten years' imprisonment.

From this distance it seems that the Mexican government was repeatedly in the position of taking harsh action against the Texans, but did not consider the consequences of its deeds and was not prepared to back them up.

But the episode of the Pioneers marked only the beginning of Mexico's troubles. For the *anglos* were on the march. They would come on and on, and with all their incredible stupidity and waste they had a quality that Santa Anna could not meet: their stubborn persistence. They never quit and blundered through until they won. It was a mystery how they did it, but the final result was undeniable.

But let us go back to June 16, 1842. Waddy Thompson describes the scene, although he does not tell where it occurred. Santa Anna, with 10,000 troops and 40,000 spectators, reviewed that ragged band of half-starved Texans as they stumbled out of their prisons, blinking in the bright sunlight.

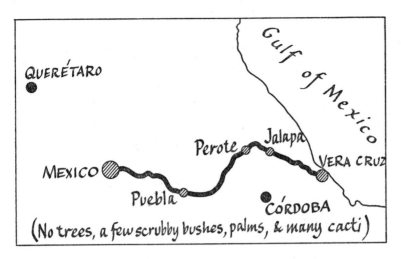

From Mexico [City] to Vera Cruz.

When the order of liberation was given, it was received with acclamation and shouts by the Mexican troops. The officers and others threw pieces of money to the Americans, and as they [the Pioneers] passed through the crowd, instead of jeers and insults, every Mexican had a word of kindness for them, running up to them and shaking hands and exclaiming, "*Amigo, amigo—*" "My friend, my friend." I saw one poor *lépero* pull off his blanket and offer it to a Texian who was more ragged than he was himself. As they passed along the streets, men and women would run out from the shops and offer them bread and other articles. Remember they had been taught to regard the Texians as born enemies, the *tejanos* having all the associations that the word *moros* had with the Spanish.[15]

Which indicates that when one side gets more than its share of misery and privation, all of us are brothers under the skin.

[15] *Recollections,* 92.

[133]

9. SALAZAR, ARMIJO, SANTA ANNA, CARLOS

THERE IS AVAILABLE almost no biographical information on Salazar. Colonel Elías ordered an investigation at Paso of his actions. There were a number of witnesses, and their testimony was substantially the same: that only two or three oxen had been killed for food; that fifteen or sixteen were left; that Salazar had drawn various supplies of bread and wheat, and also had sold wheat, bread, corn, and beans. Most of the witnesses agreed that two men were killed. Salazar himself said one had been shot because of having spoken many offensive words; he did not know that there had been another killed by arms because no one had told him about it; he admitted that one prisoner had a rotted and stinking arm, but denied that he insisted that prisoner keep the general pace, although he did say that he would not let the man ride in the cart. He said the prisoners did not eat all of the food furnished because, by his economy and the help of some friends, he still had one hundred pesos and nine head of cattle.[1]

Either the Minister of War or the President on December 17, 1841, ordered Salazar "tried and sentenced according to law."[2] On April 6, 1842, Armijo wrote the Minister of War: "There is in my possession an order of Dec. 17 of last year

[1] Bolton Transcriptions, Brief 104A–104N.
[2] Bolton Transcriptions, Brief 104B.

[134]

ordering summary prosecution against Capt. Domico Salazar
. . . for which I have already taken the necessary steps."

This writer has not been able to find any record of the
court-martial. The *New Mexico Historical Review* says he
was sent back to New Mexico in disgrace.[3] He appears again
in Colonel John C. Hughes' diary: "Monday, August 17, 1846.
Today we expect to have an engagement with the Spanish
general Salasar. . . . Among the prisoners is the son of the
Spanish Gen. Salasar. He reports that there are disputes between his father and Governor Armijo for the command."[4]
Bancroft says this son was captured at San Miguel.

Salazar did not flee New Mexico with Armijo, but did not
fight Kearny's forces.

W. W. H. Davis describes Salazar in February, 1854, as
dark and swarthy. Salazar was asking $5,000 damages for his
son, who had been killed by Indians. The Indian Intercourse
Act did not recognize such claims, says Davis.[5] Captain James
Hobbs says a "General Salazar" was executed in 1865, along
with several hundred military prisoners, under the "black flag
decree" of Maximilian.[6]

There is not a great deal to be said about Armijo. He was
shrewd and an opportunist and clever in the use of all methods
of waging war, except fighting. A reading of his many long
letters to the Minister of War describing the great need for
money and troops becomes somewhat monotonous, especially
since in the next breath he usually says that he is surrounded
by disloyal people who are eagerly awaiting the Texans.

He captured the Texans without a shot being fired—an excellent performance.

He was not a man to ride the river with. One of his letters
to the Minister of War, dated May 1, 1840, says: "Although
this Spaniard charged me with secrecy as I have said and I

3 Vol. XXV, No. 4 (October, 1950), 278.
4 William E. Connelley, *Doniphan's Expedition*, 60.
5 *El Gringo*, 293.
6 *Wild Life in the Far West*, 299.

promised to maintain it, being a matter which concerns the
national interest, I have not been able to do less than communicate to persons of my confidence and principally the
priest Juan Felipe Ortiz."[7]

On February 8, 1842, it appears that Armijo was too much
even for his fellow-governor Conde of Chihuahua, for Conde
wrote a long letter to the Minister of War protesting against
Armijo's complaint that Conde had exhibited great indolence
in coming to Armijo's rescue. Conde denies the charge of
indolence, then suggests that Armijo's attitude has changed
for the worse since he has been made a general.

This writer's impression is that Armijo was one of the most
self-contradictory men in American history.

But perhaps the most revealing fact of all is that when
Kearny invaded New Mexico five years later, Armijo left
Albuquerque with seven wagonloads of cotton goods (a very
precious commodity in that country). Ruxton met him traveling in company with Adolph Speyer's wagon train.[8]

Armijo was court-martialed in Mexico for cowardice, but
was acquitted. He died in 1853 near Socorro.

Santa Anna has been given considerable unfavorable attention by Henry Stuart Foote, William Preston Stapp, and
others. He was born in or near Jalapa February 21, probably
in 1796, and was a revolutionist and opportunist and finally
a dictator.

The *Papers of Lamar* speak of his career of forgery and
seduction,[9] and also say that Santa Anna courted Navarro's
sister, but was rejected because of forgery.[10]

At the Battle of San Jacinto he was captured in disguise,
trying to escape, and subsequently signed the secret treaty
that suggested the Río Grande might be acceptable as the
boundary of Texas.

[7] Bancroft Papers, 883.
[8] *Adventures in Mexico*, 110.
[9] Vol. VI, 338.
[10] Vol. VI, 219.

When Navarro's death sentence was commuted by the supreme court-martial, Santa Anna rebuked that decision "with great acrimony."[11]

He was six times president or emperor of Mexico, and was exiled three times. He died in 1876 in Mexico City, poverty stricken and unnoticed.

Juan Carlos deserves more attention. Early in this study the question of Carlos' motivations became an intriguing one. Many writers seem to feel that Carlos was a spy and that he led the Pioneers into trouble intentionally, and at first glance it seems so, but a careful study reveals factors inconsistent with this conclusion.

Carlos had been a trapper around Taos, but for several years before the expedition he had carried mail between Austin and San Antonio and had been regarded as trustworthy by *anglos* of both towns. He spoke the Comanche language to some extent.

Early in August, Carlos, who had been attached to one of the companies as a volunteer, said he recognized the river they were following (which was the Wichita); he said also that the country around it was the same as the Red River on which he had trapped.

It seems more likely that he had trapped on the Canadian River than the Red River of Natchitoches, which they were hoping to follow west to New Mexico, because the Canadian at that time was often called the Colorado (Red) in its upper portion. Nobody, however, noticed that, and all were so relieved to find somebody who knew where they were that, for a few days, all were happy.

Kendall says in two places that the water of the Red River of Natchitoches and that of the Wichita were similar: brown-looking and brackish-tasting,[12] and that the surrounding country was very similar.

11 Bustamante, *Gabinete Mexicano*, II, 221; Brief, 502.
12 *Narrative*, I, 127, 185.

If Carlos was right, they were not far from the New Mexican settlements. Days went by, however, and the men began to grumble and express suspicion of Carlos. Then Caldwell, scouting as he should have scouted around the Cross Timbers, roamed to the south and discovered a river that, because of its much lighter color and more saline taste, could have been none other than the Brazos. They realized that this meant that they were not on the Red at all and that Carlos was wrong.

They must have landed on Carlos with muttering and threats, for Carlos was a Mexican, and these were tired, hungry, thirsty, and disgruntled men.

Carlos and an Italian, Francisco Brignoli, with whom Carlos had been prospecting for gold or silver ore, deserted that night. At this point most writers have been satisfied to drop Carlos and pick him up again after the surrender. Falconer, for instance, says Carlos and Brignoli found the means to reach San Miguel first and to give exaggerated and injurious accounts of the purpose of the expedition. Falconer, of course, was not there.

We must concede that when Carlos finally came in contact with Armijo, he probably told a big story about the expedition. It seems unlikely that he knew even that the Texans wanted to extend their sovereignty to the Río Grande, but he very likely multiplied the number of soldiers and cannon, because that was the habit at that time.

Niles' National Register[13] reports that Carlos and Brignoli, who were with the expedition, but who "fled from it in advance for that purpose," informed Armijo of the Texans' advance. The *Register,* however, says its information came from the Mexican paper, *Diario del Gobierno,* of October 16, 1841. Likewise, the *Diario's* information must have come secondhand, probably from the Minister of War, who must have received it from Conde, who in turn had received it from Armijo.

William C. Crane is quoted as saying (in *Life and Select*

13 Vol. LXI, No. 21 (Jan. 22, 1842), 321.

Literary Remains of Sam Houston, 134) that he thought Carlos was in the pay of the Mexican government; that a letter from Armijo to Conde, dated September 22, 1841, says that Carlos was "connected with the expedition for the laudable purpose of giving information."[14]

This letter to Conde does not appear in the Bancroft Papers, but a very similar letter of October 22, addressed to the Minister of War, does not mention Carlos.[15]

The letter to Conde appears in the Bolton Transcriptions,[16] however, and H. Bailey Carroll's translation reads: "I secured this information from an Italian and a New Mexican who had been in Béxar three years and escaped from the expedition in order to report the hostile intentions of the Texans."

Not even Carlos María Bustamante, who dedicated himself to the glorification of Armijo,[17] claims they joined the expedition *for the purpose* of acting as spies. His words are: "A Mexican from Taos and . . . an italian . . . informed him that they had become separated from the expedition of Texans which marched to invade the department and both came with the object of delivering this news."[18]

Unless more evidence comes to hand, it appears that a misinterpretation has falsely labeled Carlos and that the greatest crime of which he can be accused is leaving the expedition for the purpose of informing Armijo (not the same as deliberate spying). But this is also subject to examination.

If Carlos had left the expedition to inform Armijo, he would have gone to Armijo as fast as possible. Howland left the expedition August 11 and was in Santa Fé on September 4. Carlos left August 15, and on September 12 was still east of San Miguel.

He and Brignoli were first seen by two of the Sutton-Cooke

---

[14] *The Southwestern Historical Quarterly,* Vol. XXVII, No. 2 (October, 1923), 103.
[15] Bancroft Papers, 1025.
[16] Vol. II, 136.
[17] Bustamante, *Gabinete Mexicano,* II (Dedication).
[18] *Ibid.,* II, 218; Brief, 498.

men on September 9; they were in bad shape, worn and half-starved, and begged for provisions; they promised to join the camp that night, but did not.[19] On September 12 they were seen by the first Mexicans encountered by Sutton and Cooke.[20] Had they been lost, here were men of Carlos' own race; all he had to do was inquire. But he did not. It seems obvious that Carlos and Brignoli, afraid and undecided, wandered around in the area east of San Miguel for some time. They were afraid of the Texans behind them, but at the same time Carlos did not want to encounter Armijo's men, for he knew he would have to tell the whole story if he did.

Finally, near starvation, they went into the settlements and were taken to Santa Fé. Even there it appears that their first stories were not very convincing—certainly not those of either hired or self-appointed spies, for when Carlos was next seen, on September 16, his arms and breast were bandaged; he had been stabbed by Armijo's nephew for his close connection with the expedition.[21]

Bustamante says that Armijo gave them the one hundred pesos he had offered as a reward for first news of the expedition, but this again is evidence after the fact.

In conclusion, most of the available evidence against Carlos appears to be based on the one letter of Armijo, which was misinterpreted, while the facts seem to justify the conclusion that Carlos was not a spy and did not want to be an informer.

[19] Kendall, *Narrative*, I, 252.
[20] *Ibid.*, 263.
[21] *Ibid.*, 298.

10. NAVARRO; KENDALL'S PASSPORT

José ANTONIO NAVARRO was early singled out by Santa Anna for punishment. He was taken from the McLeod party near Cuautitlán on January 31 and sent to the hellhole known as the *Acordada*. It must have been well known to the officers of the Pioneers that Santa Anna would seek that kind of vengeance, for several accounts mention specifically that Navarro's life was guaranteed. Perhaps the story of Santa Anna's rejection by Navarro's sister because of his forgery has a basis in fact.

Kendall describes his meeting with Navarro in the *Acordada* in April, 1842: "[There were] terrible changes in the appearance of my old companion—his unshaved face was pale and haggard, his hair long and uncombed, his vestments ragged and much soiled. . . . his fellow-prisoners, composed of the most loathsome and abandoned wretches, had robbed him not only of his money but his clothing." Kendall surreptitiously gave him money.

Santa Anna insisted that Navarro be tried for high treason because of his acceptance of the Texan government, and perhaps because Navarro had signed the Texas Declaration of Independence.

It was an old story to Navarro. His father had come from Corsica and had died in 1808; his mother was from Saltillo;

his family had been persecuted by the Spanish king's officers in 1813. But it made it no easier to bear. Navarro had a wife and seven children at home.

He was tried and convicted and sentenced to death, but appealed. The appeal was upheld on two grounds: lack of jurisdiction and the fact that all prisoners were guaranteed their lives if they would surrender; this was confirmed by Armijo, as noted previously.

Santa Anna did not like this; he "rebuked their conduct with great acrimony." The judges stuck to their decision, however; the sentence was commuted on September 24, 1842, to imprisonment for life, and he was sent to San Juan de Ulúa on a small island in the harbor of Vera Cruz. There he was held until January, 1845, when he was paroled to Vera Cruz and escaped, and, almost at the same time, was pardoned.

There are eighty documents relating to this matter, but they are repetitious. It is hard to dispute the fact that Santa Anna personally wanted Navarro punished.

Navarro eventually reached San Antonio and his big family again. Cooke married his niece before Navarro returned. Navarro died in 1871—five years before Santa Anna.

Kendall's life is well covered in *Kendall of the Picayune*, by Fayette Copeland; an interesting article about him appears in *The Louisiana Historical Quarterly*, Vol. XI, No. 2 (April, 1928), 261–85.

The question of his passport on the expedition is interesting. It was not customary in 1841 to have a passport from Independence to Santa Fé, but in 1840 the Mexican Congress passed a law that prohibited entry into Mexico from Texas without permission. The permission would normally be a passport, which could be issued by a consul or a governor; however, a consul had authority to issue a passport only to the next port, where it had to be endorsed.

No penalty was provided by the Mexican law of 1840 for violation of its entry requirements; presumably, the only action to be taken by the Mexican government was the return of the violator to Texas.

Kendall did not understand Spanish and took an interpreter with him to the Mexican consulate when he applied for the passport. He says that James H. Brewer was with him;[1] Brewer himself said later that he was with Kendall;[2] Francis Lumsden said he had seen the passport (he was Kendall's partner); others said they saw it frequently on the trip to San Miguel. Kendall says he showed it to Salazar, who could not read it and turned it over to Don Jesús, who read it and returned it; Kendall showed it then to Armijo, he says, but Armijo said he could not honor it and did not return it. He did not destroy it in Kendall's presence.

Kendall thought for several months that his passport would procure his release, but presently he found himself in San Lázaro, still without the passport. He related the details to Powhatan Ellis; Ellis went to Bocanegra, who said that Kendall would have to produce his passport before they could honor it. This was a very unhappy state of affairs, and Kendall wasted no time saying so. How was he to prove his legal entry when the very evidence was held by the Mexicans?

Tornel wrote Armijo about the passport, and Armijo answered that Kendall's statement "that an official destroyed his passport in my presence [Kendall insisted he never made that statement at all] . . . and as such pretense touches the extremity of falsehood, I assure you that it is false and untrue, although there were condemned to the fires some papers of those who brought them, it was only the proclamations, constitutions, and laws which they wished to set up here as conquerors."[3]

Manuel Álvarez, the American consul at Santa Fé, said the passport was burned, but Kendall stubbornly believed that

[1] Kendall, *Narrative*, I, 19.

[2] *The Southwestern Historical Quarterly*, Vol. XXXVI, No. 4 (April, 1933), 294n.

[3] Jacinto G. Torres, *Mexico, Memorias Relaciones 1841–1843*, xxviii; Brief, 494; Bancroft Papers, 759.

Armijo had sent it to Mexico and that the officials had it all the time. They may have had it and not known it; bureaucracy was at one of its depths under the Mexican government of that period.

The argument was complicated by the discovery by Bocanegra that a New Orleans newspaper—not the *Picayune*—had referred to Kendall as an avant-courier of the expedition. Kendall, Thompson, and Webster all argued that this was not incriminating evidence and that, at any rate, an avant-courier was not a commissioner, as Bocanegra had argued.[4]

A great public meeting at the Bank Arcade in New Orleans in February, 1842, expressed the indignation of the *anglos*, and Mexican Vice-Consul Salvador Prats felt called on to write a letter to the papers, saying that he had been vice-consul there from September, 1837, to September, 1841, and that Kendall never obtained a passport from the Mexican consulate.[5]

Kendall still insisted, and finally Bocanegra admitted the consular returns from New Orleans had not been received.[6] This was in February, 1842; the passport was said to have been issued in May, 1841.

Finally, on March 21, 1842, Francisco de Arrangoíz, of the consulate, issued a statement that the name of Kendall did not appear in the book of passports.[7]

A few days later, George Van Ness, on oath before John Black, American vice-consul in Mexico, declared that he had seen Kendall present his passport to Salazar and then to Armijo, and that Armijo had said he could not respect it because Kendall was associated with enemies of Mexico.[8]

Then both Van Ness and Thomas Falconer appeared under

[4] In 1844, Kendall said that the man who wrote the Chihuahua letter and used the words *"avant couriers"* was dead. *Narrative*, II, 302n. It is possible he was referring to John Jennison, director of the mint at Chihuahua, who was in New Orleans in April, 1840, and spoke about an expedition then.
[5] 27 Cong., 2 sess., *Senate Doc. No.* 325, 75.
[6] *Ibid.*, 31.
[7] Torres, *Mexico, Memorias Relaciones*, xxv; Brief, 494.
[8] *Senate Doc. No.* 325, 33.

oath and described the passport, giving the wording on it as follows:

El Ciudadano Salvador Prats, Vice Consul de la República Mexicana en Nueva Orleans, concedo passporte á George Wilkins Kendall, *natural de los Estados Unidos, de profession* [blank] *para que pase á qualquiera puerta en* [blank] *Firma del interesado. Dado en Nueva Orleans á de 1841.* George Wilkins Kendall.

Salvador Prats.

They did not recollect the date; they thought the fact that the line commencing *"en"* was blank contemplated his entering Mexico by an inland port. They said it bore a stamp with the emblem of an eagle and the words *"Consulado Mexicano en Nueva Orleans."*[9]

On consideration of the above facts, it appears that never did anyone but Salvador Prats claim that Kendall did *not* have a passport; Armijo merely said that he had not destroyed the passport in Kendall's presence. On the other hand, the statements of Lumsden, Brewer, Van Ness, and Falconer would seem to be worthy of considerable weight.

Kendall provides one more interesting subject for discussion; his use of the phrase, "I have seen the elephant."

In the *Narrative* (I, 108) he writes, "There is a cant expression, *'I've seen the elephant'* [italic Kendall's], in very common use in Texas, although I never heard it until we entered the Cross Timbers. . . . When a man is disappointed in anything he undertakes, when he has seen enough, when he gets sick and tired of any job he may have set himself about, he has *'seen the elephant.'* "

Likewise, Milo Milton Quaife, in his historical introduction to Reuben Cole Shaw, *Across the Plains in Forty-Nine,* accepts this definition.[10] Mitford M. Mathews also partially

[9] *Ibid.,* 49–50.
[10] Page *xxvii,* n. 4.

adopts this definition in *A Dictionary of Americanisms.*

But there is another interpretation of the phrase. The first elephant of modern times reached the United States in 1796.[11] It was exhibited in New York, and seeing the huge and strange beast was, to speak in the vernacular of 1955, *real George.*

Eric Partridge, in *A Dictionary of Slang and Unconventional English* (and nobody knows better than Partridge just how unconventional English can be!), gives this definition: "to gain worldly experience. c. 1840." John Camden Hotten (*The Slang Dictionary*) and John Russell Bartlett (*Dictionary of Americanisms*) agree. So does *The Century Dictionary* (1889).

A large group of theater books exhibit the phrase, and so do Elisabeth Margo, *Taming the Forty-Niner,* 3, and Carl I. Wheat, *The Shirley Letters,* 174. Wheat says the term signifies "that one had experienced the ultimate possibilities of a situation."

Archer Butler Hulbert, in his epic *Forty-Niners,* 41: "It comes from circus talk . . . 'did you see the elephant?' . . . Did you see the thing you started on through to the end?" Page 222: "Get there, and you . . . [have] eaten the 'Elephant's ears,' . . . whether the god, Luck, will give you gold or not is another question and out of your control." Grant Foreman agrees with Hulbert.

Kendall became acquainted with the term after that terribly hard day in the Cross Timbers, and he naturally associated it with disappointment. His definition, however, is too restrictive. Fundamentally, the phrase involves the action of the participant, regardless of his emotional reaction.

As a clincher (and there *is* a clincher), Kendall says (I, 163): "I was particularly anxious to hasten forward . . . the season was becoming far advanced, and I was in no little anxiety to prosecute my journey. . . . I had passed about time enough . . . on weak coffee without sugar, and a rather short

11 Joseph Nathan Kane, *Famous First Facts,* 24.

allowance of beef. . . . To sum up all, *'I had seen the ele-phant.'* "

This latter statement was made about two weeks after they had left the Cross Timbers, and there is no implication of disappointment or of being fed up. He was hungry and he was undoubtedly tired, but he wanted to get on with his journey.

Actually, he was anticipating himself again, for the elephant in the case was Santa Fé.

The ironic fact is that when he made this last statement on August 11, he was soon to see far more of the elephant than he had any presentiment. There was still ahead of him, not Santa Fé at all, but purgative water, starvation, the deadly Kiowas, eight months in Mexican prisons, more hunger, small-pox, yellow fever, lepers, chains, indignity, and despair.

There is one indisputable fact: by the time George Wilkins Kendall would go again down Camp Street and walk into the front door of the *Picayune* office, he would have seen the elephant and eaten both its ears.

11. WAS WILLIAM P. LEWIS A TRAITOR?

"It is painful to denounce one with whom I have associated as a brother officer and . . . looked upon as a man . . . but the facts are too conclusive—William P. Lewis betrayed his associates to a cruel and inhuman enemy. He has the mark upon his forehead, and will yet be found, recognised, and punished as the Judas of the nineteenth century."[1] These are the words of Lieutenant Thomas Lubbock, who watched the entire betrayal of the Sutton-Cooke party. Is Lubbock's appraisal correct? Was Lewis actually guilty of treason? If so, what was the reason for his conduct—the motivation for his treachery? Finally, guilty or not, what eventually became of him?

Texas researchers do not seem to have looked into the life of William P. Lewis and put their findings into available form. Lewis does not seem to be treated in *The Southwestern Historical Quarterly,* nor is he listed at all in *The Handbook of Texas;* he is not treated by Johnson and Barker, or by Kennedy, and is only mentioned in passing by Yoakum.

It is not difficult to understand the reasons for ignoring Lewis, for from all accounts he seems to have been a thoroughgoing scoundrel. Yet it is the business of historians to treat scoundrels as well as heroes. Sometimes the distinction is not accurately made, but the writer has a responsibility to try.

[1] "Lubbock's Narrative," Brief, 461.

To begin with, who was Lewis? Not much background is offered by the various accounts. Kendall, who gives the most details, has a disconcerting way of tossing out information after the fact, with the assumption that we know all he has omitted; likewise, while free with general statements, he is (after the fashion of those times among newspaper writers) negligent in giving specific details that would offer a chance for verification, and almost wholly lacking in identification of sources.

Lewis is referred to by Kendall as a young man,[2] and Grover gives his "native place" as Pennsylvania,[3] but lists no place of residence in Texas. There are reasons, to appear later, for believing his home town in 1841 was Austin.

He had lived in Chihuahua and possibly in Santa Fé[4] and about 1835 had left Chihuahua with Samuel Howland to fight in the Texas Revolution.[5] He had been a clerk in Chihuahua. A year and a half before the expedition started, Major George T. Howard, in reporting his famous fight with the Comanches,[6] mentions "Lieut. Lewis," who may be the same man.[7]

Falconer says that Lewis was "an American [that is, a citizen of the United States], who had lived some years at Chihuahua."[8] Under international conditions of 1955 it is not easy to reconcile the word "American" with a captaincy in the Texas artillery, but this situation was not unusual in 1841. The agitation for statehood arose about the time the smoke drifted away from the battleground of San Jacinto, and both in the public mind and in protocol there was not too much distinction made between Texas and the United States.

None of the biographical registers of officers of the United States Army or of graduates of West Point that have been

[2] *Narrative*, I, 270.
[3] Grand Reference Sheet.
[4] Kendall, *Narrative*, I, 297.
[5] *Ibid.*, II, 82.
[6] For a narrative account of this fight, see Kendall, *Narrative*, I, 74–75.
[7] DeShields, *Border Wars of Texas*, 306.
[8] *Letters and Notes*, 86.

examined list Lewis; thus it does not seem that he had had experience as an army officer before going to Texas.

In 1841, however, Lewis's background begins to take shape, for in that year he joined the Masonic Lodge in Austin. This was to be a tragic step for the expedition, as has been related, for the surrender of the Sutton-Cooke party (and subsequently of the McLeod party) hinged to a large extent on Cooke's reliance on Lewis's word, and particularly on his word as a Mason.

The Masonic Order was influential in early Texas because of the heterogeneous population and the need for a common bond. It was all the more important because of the known fact that many settlers had private reasons for leaving the United States. Some of the reasons were not dishonorable, others were—and Masonic membership was used as a quick preliminary way to separate the sheep from the goats.

Thus the importance of Freemasonry in early Texas is undeniable. Stephen F. Austin, Anson Jones, J. P. Caldwell, Sam Houston, Antonio Navarro (who was also a Roman Catholic), and Mirabeau B. Lamar all were members of the lodge. Twenty of the fifty-nine who signed the Texan Declaration of Independence, seven of the nine speakers of the House during the Republic, eight of the fourteen chief justices, each of the four presidents, and each of the five vice presidents were members.[9] Under these circumstances it is not astonishing that Cooke used this test of Lewis's faith.

The Sutton-Cooke men, emaciated and starved by two terrible weeks on the Llano, were surrounded by superior Mexican forces who demanded their arms. The Texans, however, were in a strong position, and Cooke ordered Sutton to prepare for battle.[10] Then Lewis came up with the Mexicans and started to persuade Cooke to give up his arms; he said that Armijo was advancing, that within twenty-four hours the

[9] Joseph W. Hale, "Masonry in the Early Days of Texas," *The Southwestern Historical Quarterly*, Vol. XLIX, No. 3 (January, 1946).

[10] Kendall, *Narrative*, I, 324.

ninety Texans would have to fight four thousand well-equipped soldiers. He told Cooke also that it was the usual custom for Santa Fé traders to surrender their arms on entering New Mexico, and assured him that no harm could possibly result.

As far as Cooke could see, the alternative to giving up their arms was fighting an overwhelmingly superior force, with his own men in poor shape physically and mentally, and, in addition, poorly mounted and not too well supplied with ammunition (forty or fifty rounds apiece). Afterward, win or lose, they would have to retreat across the terrible Llano, with the Kiowas ahead of them and the Mexicans behind.[11] Yet he was determined to fight rather than surrender in ignominy.

However, if the statements by Lewis were true, no real surrender was involved—merely the deposit of their arms for a few days while they traded in New Mexico. But some of the officers told Cooke they thought Lewis was lying. They did not like his looks. And so, with ninety Texans watching, Cooke went off to one side with Lewis and held a private conversation with him.

Falconer says Lewis "went through the form of a masonic oath with some freemasons of the company to secure confidence in his statement."[12] Falconer, of course, was not with Cooke but back at Camp Resolution, and is repeating hearsay information.

Lieutenant Lubbock, in his statement of events at the surrender,[13] said that Cooke "held a private conversation with

[11] Again, this obviously was not the attitude of a would-be conqueror.
[12] *Letters and Notes*, 87.
[13] This statement of Thomas S. Lubbock, lieutenant in Company C, is quoted at length by Kendall in his *Narrative*, I, 323–26, but Kendall does not identify it except as coming from Lubbock. An inquiry directed to the archives of the library of the University of Texas brought this reply, dated June 1, 1955: "Kendall quotes much from Tom Lubbock but his manuscript must have been destroyed together with a wagonload of Kendall's material after his death." The original publication of Lubbock's report, however, eventually was located in the *Colorado Gazette*, as told in the bibliography. Lubbock was a brother of Francis R. Lubbock, who was to be elected governor of Texas in 1861. Lubbock County was named after Tom.

him [Lewis] and that Lewis had pledged his masonic faith to the correctness of what he had stated."[14] Lubbock was an officer of the Sutton-Cooke party and must have been present. He was also a Mason, presumably at that time.

A member of the Masonic Lodge can visualize the "private" conversation Cooke held with Lewis. Masonic rituals stress truth, and a very impressive oath is provided for testing another member's veracity. Among Masons this oath carries great significance, for the ceremony in which it is first communicated is most dramatic. Therefore, Cooke was putting Lewis to the most severe test he knew.

The facts suggest that Cooke had known Lewis *as a Mason* —that he had sat in lodge with him. Lewis was initiated by Austin Lodge No. 12 in 1841.[15] Cooke probably witnessed his initiation, perhaps took part as a visiting member,[16] and perhaps even "raised" Lewis, which might have created closeness.

At any rate, Cooke, under great pressure, accepted Lewis's word on the two important points: the forces opposing him and the good treatment promised, and surrendered the arms of his command. Then came the tremendous denouement. Cooke looked on in incredible disbelief while his men were made prisoners and their goods, personal possessions, and even their clothing and extra blankets were taken from them. He saw them humiliated by being searched, and he stared at Lewis, who showed some embarrassment but little else.

The full enormity of Lewis's crime came over Cooke, and he turned on Lewis bitterly and, before them all—the betrayed Texans and the Mexican officers with whom Lewis had conspired—denounced him as a Mason, as a Texan, and

---

[14] Kendall, *Narrative*, I, 325; Brief, 460.

[15] Letter from the Grand Lodge of Texas, A.F.&A.M., March 22, 1955. (All records of Austin Lodge No. 12 were destroyed by fire in 1866.)

[16] Cooke was not a member of any Blue Lodge in Texas during 1841, according to a check of the records by Harvey C. Byrd, Grand Secretary of the Grand Lodge of Texas. However, Bolton, *Guide*, 283, lists a certificate to the effect that Cooke had received the degree of Royal Arch from Austin Lone Star Royal Arch Lodge, May 27, 1841. Obviously, Cooke's Blue Lodge membership was outside Texas.

as a man. Lubbock says that Cooke "in the hearing of his betrayed and [of the surrounding Mexicans] denounced him . . . his pledged honour . . . his plighted masonic faith."[17]

Cooke's wrought-up emotions must have been terrifying as he excoriated the traitor who had sold his ragged and starving men into captivity, but there is no record of Lewis's reaction—if he had one.

A remarkable unanimity of opinion exists on the point of Lewis's guilt. It is so unanimous that one might feel that the opinions of many were influenced by the opinion of one (expressed in the dramatic denunciation by Cooke), except that there appears no evidence in Lewis's favor. During the days following the surrender, there must have been many opportunities for Lewis to give assistance, large or small, to the captives, but there is no record that he did so, although he was around San Miguel for several days.

Kendall says: "Treachery had done the work, and . . . Lewis was the instrument; but such was our confidence in the man that a majority of us could not believe he had turned traitor."[18] Again: "The blackest piece of treachery to be found on record."[19]

Kendall speaks what is perhaps the only good word for Lewis when he tells of Salazar's abortive attempt to execute the five members of the Van Ness party (including Kendall and Lewis). This was two days before the Sutton-Cooke party surrendered, and Kendall, speaking a year later, says, "I will give Lewis the credit of acting, in that moment of extreme peril, as became a man."[20] He does not describe Lewis's actions, but we may assume Lewis exhibited fortitude and resolution. Kendall has many more remarks to make about Lewis, but none of them are complimentary.[21]

[17] Kendall, *Narrative,* I, 326; Brief, 461.
[18] *Narrative,* I, 311.
[19] *Ibid.,* I, 313.
[20] *Ibid.,* I, 285.
[21] Kendall also was a Mason, although he later married a Roman Catholic girl from France.

The Gallegher-Hoyle *Journal* states that, on October 7, Captain Lewis and the Governor's secretary demanded the commissions and the belts of the officers of the McLeod party.[22] By that time the Sutton-Cooke party had been on the prisoners' march to Chihuahua for three weeks, but the McLeod party had just been captured and was still in and near San Miguel.

Both Falconer and Gallegher speak of seeing Lewis with Armijo in October (almost a month after Sutton and Cooke surrendered); Kendall also says that on October 13, "the wagons [of General McLeod's party] were drawn up in line . . . and preparations made for dividing the goods . . . Lewis . . . frequently pointing out a box or bale of goods, which was placed in a large pile, apparently for him. . . . he . . . was plainly seen and heard laughing and joking with [the governor and the Mexican officers]. How the abandoned man could . . . act thus . . . is a mystery to me."[23]

Later, Kendall relates, "Lewis frequently passed our window . . . but not once did he offer to speak to us."[24] Later still, however, Lewis favored them with a visit: "For the first and only time, Lewis entered our room. There was a hang-dog expression, if I may so call it, about him."[25] Kendall probably called it more pungent things than that when he discussed it with his fellow prisoners.

Kendall speculates on the singular fact that Lewis fooled them: "It is hard to suspect one . . . whose life has been unstained by a single bad act, of the blackest crime in the catalogue."[26] Upon reflection, it seems doubtful that Lewis had always been above reproach, but rather that he had been careful.

A little later, however, Kendall becomes thoroughly realistic: "Not a doubt exists that to Lewis [we] were indebted

22 Carroll, *The Texan Santa Fé Trail*, 178.
23 *Narrative*, I, 342-43.
24 *Ibid.*, I, 343.
25 *Ibid.*, I, 343-44.
26 *Ibid.*, I, 344.

for months of suffering . . . the traitor probably thought that we . . . would make his treachery known to the Americans at Santa Fé, and . . . the same cowardly impulse . . . now caused him . . . to save himself from his own countrymen [by seeing that the prisoners were kept locked up and not allowed to communicate with the Americans at Santa Fé]."[27]

Kendall also relates the damning story of Lewis's deception of his friend Farley and of Houghtaling, who had secreted valuable watches. Lewis told them to give the watches to him and he would sell them for large sums, which they would need in Mexico. They gave him the watches—but never got the money.[28]

With the exception of Falconer's description, most of this evidence is given by men on the spot. There was also an official opinion given by Brenham and Cooke, the would-be commissioners of Santa Fé. Brenham was thirty-one, Cooke thirty-three; Brenham had a college education and had practiced medicine in Texas until he joined the expedition; Cooke had been in business, had been quartermaster general of the Republic, and had laid out the military road from the Brazos to the Red River under severe difficulties. None of these facts has any bearing on their intelligence or integrity, but they do indicate that the two were men of experience. They were not quick to point the finger of guilt. Their combined opinions appear in a document known as the Brenham-Cooke Report,[29] dated November 9, 1841, at Allende,[30] Chihuahua.

It is addressed to Samuel A. Roberts, secretary of state of the Republic of Texas, and reads: "Capt. Lewis stated that the people of the country were all arrayed in arms and greatly exasperated against us,[31] . . . [he was] guilty of falsehood in

[27] *Ibid.*, I, 364.

[28] *Ibid.*, I, 345.

[29] Garrison, *Texan Diplomatic Correspondence*, II, 780–81.

[30] This is not San Miguel Allende, between Guanajuato and Querétaro, but a village just east of Parral, in the southern part of the state of Chihuahua.

[31] It is obvious that the people could not have been "in arms," but it appears that Armijo and his men had done a good propaganda job, for the native Mexicans did seem to be in fear of the Texans. See Kendall, *Narrative*, I, 270ff.

his representation of the condition of the country and the character and number of the governor's troops.[32] . . . We had been duped by a *traitor* [italic theirs], and . . . Lewis had purchased his own safety at the expense of our liberty, his country's interest and his own honor. . . . His treachery is now made manifest and placed beyond a doubt."[33]

Interest now turns to motivation. Kendall indirectly gives his opinion—that Lewis betrayed them for his own life and liberty—when he says, "The governor offered [Howland] his life and liberty—the same terms Lewis accepted—if he would betray his companions and assist him in capturing them."[34] Howland, of course, was executed.

Beginning at page 294 (Vol. I) of the *Narrative*, it is not difficult to follow Lewis's thought processes. At that point the five men of the Van Ness party, including Lewis, were in their second day of captivity and were on the march afoot to Santa Fé; Lewis was "tied and led along like a dog." They met Armijo, who, it appears from Kendall's relation of this scene and of a later scene in San Miguel, must have been able to understand and speak some English. Armijo questioned them. Lewis said he was an American merchant, but Armijo took hold of one of the buttons on his dragoon (or artillery jacket) and pointed out the word "Texas" with a scathing comment. After a parley, during which Armijo read Kendall's

[32] As to arms, not even the Mexican soldiers were well armed. See Kendall, *Narrative*, I, 293, 280: "miserably-armed Mexicans"; "armed with lances, swords, bows and arrows, and miserable *escopetas*, or old-fashioned carbines." As to numbers, Lewis said they would have to fight altogether 9,000 men, while Kendall's account indicates about 1,000 were present; Lubbock accounts for 400 to 600; the Brenham-Cooke Report says "near one thousand." The Mexicans were well mounted, but poorly armed.

[33] So far there are three counts against Lewis: that he overstated the number of Mexican troops, that he lied about the condition of their arms, and that he misrepresented the treatment the Texans would receive. This writer has looked, without conclusive results, for evidence of a fourth count: namely, that he told the Sutton-Cooke party that Van Ness and his men and the Howland party were being well cared for. Many writings imply that Lewis lied on this count, but only Falconer supports his claim, and Falconer's statements in this matter are hearsay.

[34] *Narrative*, I, 309.

American passport aloud, Armijo asked for the one who best spoke Spanish to act as interpreter, and Lewis "eagerly pressed forward," although Van Ness, secretary to the commissioners, could also speak Spanish and might have seemed the logical choice.

The rest came naturally. Armijo gave him a sample of what it would be like on the Mexican side; he untied Lewis's hands and assigned him a mule to ride. Then Lewis, having taken the first step, was an easy conquest for Armijo (who was a master at this sort of thing anyway), and Armijo apparently offered him not only life and liberty, but also concrete rewards, if Lewis would co-operate fully. Perhaps Lewis was ambitious for money, although he does not seem to have taken advantage of his subsequent rewards. Perhaps he was only a little man who was afraid to be hurt.

Armijo himself said only that he had given Lewis permission to travel throughout all Mexico without restraint,[35] but Kendall has already described how Lewis chose a portion of the spoils for himself, and he says also that "At Chihuahua I saw a copy of *La Luna,* a small paper, with a letter from Armijo to García Conde, which stated: 'In consideration of the great service rendered by Capt. W. P. Lewis, in assisting me to capture these Texans, I have given him his liberty and his goods, and earnestly recommend him to the notice of the Central Government.' "[36]

Kendall adds: "We all knew that all the goods Lewis had with him he could carry in his hat." Obviously, then, the goods referred to were those given to Lewis by Armijo at San Miguel. These would have been personal possessions—clothing, jewelry, and such items, and supplies for the troops, for all the merchants' goods had been destroyed at Camp Resolution.

Niles' National Register has this to add: "From an *official*

---

[35] Bancroft Papers, 1025; Brief, 62a.

[36] *Narrative,* I, 346. This is not the same as the letter appearing in Bolton Transcriptions, II, 136.

[157]

document": (italic theirs) Lewis and Chaves arrived and persuaded them to surrender. "Captain Lewis obtained his liberty and the privilege of importing goods duty free to New Mexico as a reward for his treachery."[37]

The *Register* does not identify the source. It may have been the Brenham-Cooke Report, which was dated November 9, 1841, and which says Lewis "had been released from all restraint with a passport to travel where he pleased in the country, and a license from his Excellency to introduce any amount of goods into N. Mexico."[38]

Kendall's *Narrative* was published in book form in 1844, two years after Kendall was released from prison, at a time when the events of the expedition must still have been fresh in many minds. If any disputed his facts about Lewis's deceptions, such disagreements do not seem to have appeared in print.

Then, too, Kendall and Falconer formed a strong friendship,[39] as is obvious from Kendall's many references to Falconer. It was Lumsden, Kendall and Company which printed Falconer's *Account* in New Orleans in 1842.[40] Kendall conferred with Falconer and other survivors after returning to Texas;[41] in 1855, Kendall visited Falconer in London, at which time Falconer gave him the Diary of events at Camp Resolution, which Kendall included in the seventh edition of his *Narrative;*[42] in 1856, Kendall wrote a personal and chatty letter to Falconer and spoke of Howard, Van Ness, and Navarro.[43] It rather seems that any important discrepancy would have come to light.

There remains little to be told but Lewis's fate, which Kendall gives without reference to the source of his information.[44]

[37] Vol. LXI, No. 24 (February 12, 1842), 369.
[38] Garrison, *Texan Diplomatic Correspondence*, II, 781.
[39] Falconer, *Letters and Notes*, 11.
[40] *Ibid.*, 31 (a reproduction of the title page of the *Account*).
[41] *Narrative*, I, i.
[42] Falconer, *Letters and Notes*, 104–105.
[43] *Ibid.*, 142–44.
[44] *Narrative*, II, 81. Kendall learned this in the summer of 1843.

H. R. Buchanan

From a drawing by H. D. Bugbee in H. Bailey Carroll,
The Texan Santa Fé Trail
Reproduced by permission of the Panhandle-Plains Historical Society

Passing through Guanajuato

From George Wilkins Kendall, *Narrative of the Texan Santa Fé Expedition*

(Lubbock also mentions it briefly.) In spite of Lewis's care, his treachery became known in Santa Fé, where there were a number of Americans, and he found it advisable to go to Chihuahua. But in Chihuahua, too, there were Americans and others who had no use for a traitor. Lewis went on to Guaymas, a Pacific Coast town in Mexico, but "He met the same cool reception there" and sailed for the Sandwich Islands,[45] from where, "under an assumed name," he went to Valparaíso or some other South American port, and presumably nothing more has ever been heard from him.[46]

Perhaps some day someone will come forth with information about the further career of William P. Lewis. It seems unlikely that he ever tried to return to Texas, for he must have known that men were sometimes hanged for treason.[47] Did he die young or did he live long? Did he found an illustrious family in some foreign country or did he die without sons or daughters to carry on his name? Kendall says he changed his name—and perhaps his weakness got him into further trouble that brought him to a quick end. ¿Quien sabe?

[45] Hawaiian Islands.

[46] Webb, *Adventures in the Santa Fé Trade 1844–1847*, 88, makes a remark that appears to throw some doubt on Kendall's summary: "The arrest and execution of the persons executed as spies of the Texas expedition was in consequence of information given by an American who resided in the territory several years before and for many years after, who was very clever and tolerably well liked by Americans and Mexicans, but such an inveterate babbler that we could seldom trust him; always, like others of his class, ready to tell all he knew, and generally a good deal more." Webb does not identify Lewis by name.

It seems obvious that Lewis did not carry through his betrayal to gratify a propensity for babbling. Most important, Webb wrote his *Adventures* in 1888 at the age of seventy, forty years afterward. It rather seems that in Webb's memory Lewis became merged with some other person.

[47] Miss Louise Weakley, in "The Story of Treason in the Republic of Texas," a thesis in the library of Sul Ross State College, Alpine, Tex., examines the constitution of the Republic as it refers to treason. The constitution, she says, defines treason as "giving aid and support" to the enemies of the Republic, and it may be performed by a person who is not a citizen of the Republic. Every person convicted shall suffer death, but two credible witnesses are necessary to convict. On p. 7, Miss Weakley says that high treason is the worst crime that can be committed; this is treason directed against the supreme authority of the state, and presumably does not apply to Lewis's actions.

There is one last word—though Lewis didn't have it. In this day when a man with money and a clever lawyer can seemingly get by with a great many things, Lewis's last punishment in Texas, though he may not have known about it and possibly would not have cared, is peculiarly fitting. The fact is stark and bare: on October 1, 1842, shortly after Cooke's return from Mexico, Lewis was expelled from Austin Lodge No. 12. No other lodge records beyond the cold facts of admittance and expulsion are in existence.

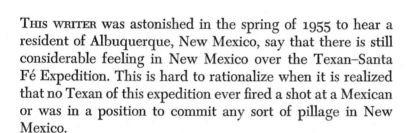

12. WAS A MILITARY CONQUEST

INTENDED?

THIS WRITER was astonished in the spring of 1955 to hear a resident of Albuquerque, New Mexico, say that there is still considerable feeling in New Mexico over the Texan–Santa Fé Expedition. This is hard to rationalize when it is realized that no Texan of this expedition ever fired a shot at a Mexican or was in a position to commit any sort of pillage in New Mexico.

It becomes important, then, to root out the basis of this feeling. If it is justified, surely enough time has gone by to erase the deep-seated hostility that resulted from the expedition. If not justified, then it is indeed time to determine how it came into being, with the object of abating the still-existing hostility.

This writer suggests that the entire structure of fear and hatred was manufactured by Armijo and his sycophants. It was not an unusual thing to do then and is not now. Propaganda is still a powerful weapon. But it seems unusual for the antagonism to persist. Perhaps that has happened because no one has sifted the facts and examined the accusations.

Hubert Howe Bancroft seems disposed to accept Armijo's implied version of the affair, and Bancroft's judgment is, to say the least, hasty. Ralph E. Twitchell accepts Bancroft's verdict, and others have followed.

[161]

Even the master of all writers on New Mexico, Harvey Fergusson, apparently accepts the situation when he says: "Between Texans and Mexicans there was a traditional hostility, going back to the Alamo and, even more, to the ill-fated Texan invasion of New Mexico in 1841."[1]

It was Elliott Arnold who suggested that Armijo used certain priests to implant a deadly fear of the Texans as murderers, rapists, and destroyers.[2]

The following arguments are commonly proposed as reflecting against Lamar's judgment and against his intentions:

1. There was no legal basis for Texas to claim all the territory as far as the Río Grande, and, therefore, the expedition was nothing but a filibuster or an attempt at outright conquest.

2. There was not enough trading possibility in dollar volume to justify opening a route.

3. Lamar should have known the New Mexicans would resist.

4. The only reason for sending such a large force was military conquest.

Legal Status of the Texan Claim

Bancroft says: "The Texans had a theory, without foundation in fact or justice, that their territory extended to the Río Grande."[3] That seems to be a hasty statement.

It is fairly well known that when Santa Anna was captured, he signed two agreements, one public and one secret. These were known as the Treaty of Velasco. There has been much pedantic discussion regarding whether or not the secret agreement was legal, but it is something like ruling out a touchdown made last year. The agreements were made, and Santa Anna signed them, and after he returned to Mexico he ordered them complied with.

[1] *The Conquest of Don Pedro,* 140.
[2] *The Time of the Gringo.*
[3] Hubert Howe Bancroft, *The History of Arizona and New Mexico,* 320.

On May 14, 1836, at Velasco, Santa Anna signed the two agreements. His argument for a secret agreement was that it would give him time to return to Mexico and soothe the public animosity that undoubtedly would result if the terms were made public immediately. It would also give him time to rebuild his political fences and overcome the loss of prestige he had suffered.

The public agreement was composed of ten articles, providing that Santa Anna would not again fight against Texas during the war; that hostilities should cease and the Mexican troops go beyond the Río Grande; for indemnification of damages caused by the Mexicans; for a neutral zone of five leagues; for notification to the two opposing military commanders; for release of prisoners; and for return of Santa Anna to Vera Cruz.[4] It was signed by Santa Anna as president and general-in-chief of the Mexican Army.

The secret agreement, of six articles, is substantially the same, except for two articles. Article 3 reads as follows: "He [Santa Anna] will so prepare matters . . . that all differences may be settled, *and the independence that has been declared by the convention may be acknowledged*" (italic supplied). Article 4 provides: "A treaty of commerce, amity, and limits, will be established between Mexico and Texas, the territory of the latter not to extend beyond the Río Bravo del Norte."[5] It is hardly necessary to point out that "treaties" are negotiated between or among nations—not between a nation and a rebel against that nation. Santa Anna signed the secret agreement as "General-in-Chief of the Army of Operations, and President of the Republic of Mexico."

Article 3, acknowledging Texas' independence, would seem to indicate future Texan captives would be prisoners of war; this was a question which was to come up many times during the negotiations over the release of the Pioneers.

On November 5, 1836, Santa Anna wrote a letter to Hous-

---

[4] Yoakum, *History of Texas*, II, 526–27.
[5] *Ibid.*, 528.

ton which apparently affirms the secret agreement, for he says the boundary "may be fixed at the Nueces, del Norte, or any other boundary, as may be decided on at Washington."[6] At the time of this letter Santa Anna was in Mexico.

In 1837 he issued a lengthy *manifiesto* to the Mexican people,[7] for he was under fire; he explained that as a captive he had no power to sign such papers and the Texans should have known it; anyway, they had been nasty to him, in that 130 men, enraged over the Goliad massacre, had tried to kill him. This is the old double-talk policy all over again.

John Quincy Adams asserted in debate in the United States Congress[8] that Texas had never declared her boundaries, but he was talking either in ignorance or with oratorical license.[9]

In November, 1836, Stephen F. Austin, Texan secretary of state, wrote to H. H. Wharton, Texan minister at Washington, and outlined Texas' claim to the Río Grande;[10] this was in connection with the proposed annexation of Texas to the United States. On September 30, 1836, the Texan Secretary of War had said Santa Fé was twelve miles east of the Río Grande and therefore within the statutory limits of Texas, and he proposed the construction of a military road from Austin to Santa Fé. On December 19, 1836, the western boundary was set at the Río Grande by act of the Texan Congress, and approved by President Houston.[11] It would seem that the entire world—including John Quincy Adams and Santa Anna—had ample notice of Texas' claim.

The chances are that Santa Anna thought it good riddance in 1836, for New Mexico was little more than an annoying liability at that time. It should be noted that at no time was the

---

[6] *Ibid.*, 530–31.

[7] Carlos E. Castañeda, *The Mexican Side of the Texan Revolution*, 5ff., especially 39–41.

[8] Folsom, *Mexico in 1842*, 205n.

[9] F. A. Wislizenus, *Memoir of a Tour to Northern Mexico*, 21n, holds that the "revolutionary title" of Texas to the Río Grande was superior to the right acquired from Santa Anna, and that such right included the right of conquest.

[10] Garrison, *Texan Diplomatic Correspondence*, I, 132.

[11] *The Southwestern Historical Quarterly*, Vol. XXIV, No. 2 (October, 1920), 88.

Río Grande actually agreed on as the boundary. On the other hand, for five years Santa Anna did nothing to protest against it, and it would seem there was ample reason for Texas to feel a legitimate claim to that area.

It was not a passing thing as far as Texas was concerned, for in the fall of 1848 Texas sent Spruce M. Baird into the area as a judge, to form the county of Santa Fé and extend Texan laws over it; the people of New Mexico refused. Once again, in 1850, Texas sent Robert S. Neighbors, with instructions to divide the country into counties and hold elections; nobody went to the polls, and the plan was not carried out.[12]

Kearny recognized the Río Grande as the boundary in Order No. 13, Headquarters, Army of the West, August 17, 1846: "1. By the annexation of Texas, the Río Grande from its mouth to its source has become the boundary between the United States and Mexico."[13] The United States paid Texas ten million dollars for her claim to that territory, and former President Grant notes that Texas organized a state from the Sabine to the Río Grande.[14]

These various items do not prove the legality of the boundary, but they do emphasize the fact that Texas had reason to believe she had a legitimate claim, and she proceeded on that assumption. The United States must have felt the claim reasonably justified or this country would not have paid a large sum for territory that might well have been claimed as a result of the Mexican War.

Notice should be taken of Houston's opposition to Lamar, for this undoubtedly played a part in the tradition built up around the Santa Fé Expedition. Lamar was a flamboyant personality; he went to Texas just in time to lead a charge at San Jacinto and vault into Texan fame; he was alternately a planner, a poet and philosopher, and an Indian fighter. It is hard to say that Houston offered Texas any more than did

[12] *Ibid.*, Vol. XXIV, No. 1 (July, 1920), 7, 24.

[13] George Rutledge Gibson, *Journal of a Soldier Under Kearny and Doniphan, 1846–1847* (ed. by Ralph P. Bieber), 370.

[14] Frank W. Johnson, *A History of Texas and Texans*, I, 497–498.

Lamar; Houston was narrow of vision and extremely personal in his actions. Either you adored Houston or you hated him.

Houston was the first elected president of the Texas Republic, and it was his theory that treaties could be made with the Indians. The plan undoubtedly worked with the Cherokees, among whom he had lived, but there were thirty other tribes in Texas—especially the Apaches, Kiowas, and Comanches—to whom Houston was just another name, and the abundance of Indian fights during his administration does not indicate that he had any better control of the situation than anybody else. He was president until December 10, 1838. In that year of 1838 there was the bloody Surveyors' Fight with the Kickapoos; Henderson and Sparks had men killed by Indians; the William Smith family had a notable fight on the Brazos; Indians entered Bastrop several times and killed citizens; Henry Carnes had a fight on the Arroyo Seco; Matilda Lockhart and the Putnam children were captured; Rusk fought the Kickapoos; Colonel Neil fought the Comanches; Rusk fought the Caddos. So the idea that Houston had exceptional ability to get along with Indians begins to take on the tinge of myth. Likewise, Texas money was down to fifteen or twenty cents on the dollar by the time Lamar took office.[15]

---

[15] His adherents usually maintain that Houston, by economy and frugality, kept Texas' finances from going on the rocks, but an interesting commentary on this matter occurs in E. W. Winkler, *Manuscripts, Letters and Documents of Early Texians,* 251. This is a letter from James Webb to James H. Starr, December 13, 1841, just after Houston's second inauguration: "He [Houston] asserted in his speech that at the close of his former administration, the whole amt. of public debt including liabilities contracted during the war, was only $670,000—when I have before me at this moment, the comptroller's report, showing that the debt at that time was $3,759,571.01 exclusive of the debt contracted for the purchase of the Navy, which at this time including interest amts. to upwards of one million. Instead therefore of its being only $670,000 as he asserted, it was nearly five millions. He also asserted that Congress had made an appropriation of only $50,000 for the defence of the country during his whole administration, when the statute book shows that there was appropriated under his administration, *and the laws approved by him,* one million and twenty thousand dollars for military purposes alone, and $250,000 for Naval purposes!!" So it would seem that in order to clear away the mists from the Texan–Santa Fé Expedition, we must also consider those thrown up by Houston's coterie.

All in all, then, Texas' fortunes did not differ greatly under the two men. Nevertheless, Houston opposed Lamar in every way, and the extent of his personal feeling is shown by a letter to Anthony Butler, on February 2, 1841, saying that the "sole object of Lamar is to insure his re-election." This in face of the Texas constitution, which prohibited any president from succeeding himself.

Possibilities of Trade

In 1839 the Santa Fé Trail trade, measured in cost of goods in St. Louis and Independence, was $250,000;[16] the value was doubled or tripled by the time the goods reached Santa Fé. In 1843 it was $450,000, and Josiah Gregg says the duties alone at Santa Fé amounted to as much as $80,000 a year.[17] He estimated the total North Mexican trade at perhaps $5,000,000 a year; this included goods from Independence and goods brought in by the British through Matamoros, Vera Cruz, and Tampico, through Mazatlán on the Pacific Coast, via Durango, and from Guaymas on the Pacific Coast to Chihuahua. All of these goods were funneled into New Mexico, Chihuahua, Durango, Sonora, and Zacatecas. The value of imported merchandise in 1855 was $750,000 in New Mexico alone.[18]

There was a considerable contraband Mexican trade on the Presidio road, which had gone on for many years between Béxar and Chihuahua. Falconer says that several times he saw upwards of fifty pack mules leave Béxar for the Río Grande, laden with manufactured goods.[19]

Chihuahua was getting a substantial quantity of goods from San Antonio in 1846,[20] and only two years after that Major

[16] *Falconer, Letters and Notes,* 36n.
[17] *Commerce of the Prairies* (ed. Moorhead), 336.
[18] *Ibid.,* 334. See also Bancroft, *History of Arizona and New Mexico,* 644.
[19] Falconer, *Letters and Notes,* 74.
[20] John Russell Bartlett, *Personal Narrative of Explorations and Incidents,* II, 435–36.

Howard organized the Chihuahua–El Paso Pioneer Expedition. In 1852, Julius Froebel, writing from Weyne City, near Independence, Missouri, spoke of the trade to Chihuahua in these words: "The North Americans have begun to prefer the much shorter journey by Texas to the Missouri route."[21]

The evidence seems to support the idea, then, that the attempt to establish a trade route across Texas was a good, hard-headed business venture that might have meant a great deal to Texas.

Receptivity of the Inhabitants

W. Jefferson Jones, in 1839, urged the Santa Fé trade on Lamar; he estimated the possibility at $30,000,000 a year, and said that the people of New Mexico were determined to throw off the yoke of their government.[22] William G. Dryden, a resident merchant of Santa Fé, wrote on March 10, 1841, that all the Americans and two-thirds of the Mexicans would welcome the Texans.[23]

Finally, though we accept anything Armijo says with reservations, we have some significant phrases from his letters: To the Minister of War: "The great affection that I note among the people for the foreigners."[24] To Conde: "I am really noticing much discontent among the settlers, many of whom are much in favor of the Texans."[25] To the Minister of the Interior: "The majority of settlers in this town are very much inclined to revolt."[26] To the Minister of War: "Most of the lower country is in favor of the invaders."[27]

Considering the fluid state of political affairs at that time, even in the national government of Mexico itself, it rather

[21] *Seven Years' Travel in Central America*, 204.
[22] *Papers of Lamar*, II, 439–40.
[23] *The Southwestern Historical Quarterly*, Vol. XXIV, No. 2 (October, 1920), 111.
[24] Bolton Transcriptions, I, 194.
[25] *Ibid.*, I, 215.
[26] *Ibid.*, I, 72.
[27] Bancroft Papers, 894; Brief, 42a.

appears that there is not too much justification for saying that Lamar should have known the inhabitants would oppose Texan sovereignty.

Intent as Shown by Lamar's Instructions

Lamar's own words are, of course, self-serving and cannot be taken as proof, and yet in the absence of any contradictory matter they carry some weight.

It is noteworthy that a letter from Mariano Arista, dated at Monterrey August 12, 1841, at a time when most of the volunteers declared they knew nothing about the "real" objects of the expedition, indicates his belief that the object of the expedition was known to him exactly as it has been preserved in official documents. "If they [the inhabitants] refuse to receive them [the Texans] peacefully," he said, "they will return without antagonizing anybody."[28] Arista might have been the object of deceit, but apparently he was convinced of the good faith of the president's instruction.

Included in the instructions is this passage: "Upon entering the city of Santa fé, your first object will be, to endeavor to get into your hands all the public property. . . . you will try all gentle means before resorting to force. . . . The President anxious as he is to have our National flag acknowledged in Santa fé, does not consider it expedient at this time to force it upon that portion of the Republic. If the Mexican authorities are prepared to defend the place with arms, and *if you can satisfy yourselves that they will be supported by the mass of the people* . . . you will not be authorized to risk a battle."[29] (Italic supplied.)

Two paragraphs later the instructions say: "This military detachment will be left subordinate to the civil authority of this government." These instructions were signed in Lamar's absence by Samuel A. Roberts, acting secretary of state.

[28] Bancroft Papers, 925; Brief, 45a.
[29] Garrison, *Texan Diplomatic Correspondence*, II, 738ff.

"If they [the people of Santa Fé] can be brought with their own free will and consent . . . but if they are awed into submission by threats, or . . . application of military power, the disastrous consequences . . . cannot well be foreseen."

These are the instructions to the commissioners intended to take charge of the government immediately, and a considerable section deals with the various rights which will be guaranteed to the inhabitants: life, liberty, property, due process, freedom of speech, and so on. At the same time, Roberts issued separate instructions to Cooke as resident commissioner —none of which contradict the above.[30]

It appears that until new evidence to the contrary appears, we are justified in assuming the expedition's intention was not military conquest. Undoubtedly, Lamar anticipated that Armijo would not give up his lush position without a token resistance, for Armijo at Santa Fé was practically an independent monarch. Lamar contemplated some action against Armijo and the government officials, but not against the people.

The Size of the Military Force

This argument has been belabored at times, but is not firmly enough structured to hold up. Assuming that the Pioneers had 400 men on the expedition, it must be remembered that New Mexico in 1842 had 57,000 inhabitants,[31] and, in McLeod's words, it was quixotic to contemplate the conquest of that many persons and that big an area with a few hundred men—all of whom were not soldiers.

There is more substantial evidence, however. In 1841 the danger from marauding Indians was real and immediate. It was customary for trains on the Santa Fé Trail to be large and to have many fighting men. As a matter of fact, in 1829 the United States sent 70 dragoons to protect a group of

30 *Ibid.*, II, 743.
31 Wislizenus, *Memoir of a Tour to Northern Mexico,* 26.

wagons; in 1834 the United States sent 40; in 1843 the United States sent 200.[32] Nor was this the entire story. Josiah Gregg himself says that in 1831 his company had two hundred fighting men, although none of these were United States soldiers.[33]

Reports of Mexican Agents

Arista, general-in-chief of Mexico's Army of the North, had agents in San Antonio and Austin, and none of them seem to have thought the expedition was anything more than commercial.

Antonio de la Garza, reporting May 6, 1841, says that a commercial expedition was being organized by Lamar.[34] Antonio Cortasar wrote, on May 11, that the expedition would leave soon with the purpose of opening a road. He may or may not imply that Texas will try to introduce its goods without paying duties; the sentence is confused.[35]

It would seem that Arista, who was close to the situation, believed the expedition primarily commercial. On the other hand, in justice to Armijo we must say he acted to protect his sovereignty. A point to remember is that he was a man who talked loudly and repetitiously and in whatever direction seemed to serve his purposes at the moment; perhaps the only kind of evidence from Armijo that we can rely on is that which is self-convicting.

Is the Evidence of Intent Upheld by the Actions?

The fact, as noted frequently throughout this narrative, that

[32] Gregg, *Commerce of the Prairies* (ed. Thwaites), I, 185, says that in 1829 "four companies" of soldiers escorted a caravan; another source says seventy dragoons. Gregg says in 1834 (p. 187) there were sixty dragoons. In 1843 there were two hundred soldiers. Chittenden, *The American Fur Trade of the Far West*, lists these in the table on p. 519, Vol. II, but does not give the numbers. Kennedy, *Texas*, says two hundred dragoons escorted a Santa Fé train in 1839.
[33] *Commerce of the Prairies* (ed. Thwaites), I, 199.
[34] Bolton Transcriptions, I, 98; Brief, 7b.
[35] Bancroft Papers, 366.

the Texans did not act like would-be conquerors; the fact that they had given notice more than a year before; the fact that they did not fire a single shot in New Mexico or, as far as it is known, cause harm to a single person—all these facts challenge the validity of any charge of conquest. It would rather appear that, in the absence of any objection from Santa Anna, the time had come for Texas to assert her right to the Río Grande.

Lamar's view of Armijo was realistic enough. He knew that Armijo had been fattening on the people for a number of years and that he would be reluctant to give up his berth. It appears that Lamar's attitude was too broad, too trusting, and too democratic. His most serious mistake, perhaps, was in *not* sending a force intended for conquest.

What Caused Mexican Fear of the Texans?

Since the Texans actually did no harm, one is led to inquire why such a legend has persisted for over one hundred years. Elliott Arnold seems to have the answer to that question, as stated above. W. W. H. Davis describes the process of spreading misinformation among the uneducated peons,[36] starting in 1837 when Armijo was among those who convinced the common people that the government of Mexico was going to compel husbands to pay a tax for sleeping with their wives. "The leaders dispatched secret agents into all parts of the country to excite the populace and induce them to resist the law." In 1846 "a number of priests joined in the conspiracy, and some even preached rebellion in the pulpit." A close reading of the Bancroft Papers bears out the fact that Armijo was an astute propagandist.[37]

[36] *El Gringo*, 87ff.
[37] A letter from Armijo, dated October 22, 1841, to the Minister of War: "I recommend in particular one Felipe Ortis who with his exhortations and circulars which he directed to his parish assisted me in solidifying opinion, and drew the faithful to the just path from which they appeared to be faltering." Bancroft Papers, 1025.

13. TREATMENT OF THE PRISONERS

THE SAD ASPECT of this entire situation is that Armijo's very effective propaganda, topped by Salazar's brutality and some harsh and cruel treatment in Mexican prisons, has served to build up and perpetuate a hostility that never should have existed. Later writers, beginning with Bancroft, should have been careful in their judgments, and some reflection might have cast the affair in an entirely different light. In an effort to dispose of all questions arising, the statement has frequently been made that the Pioneers got no more than they deserved. This writer proposes to examine this platitude more closely.

If, for the last 115 years, a myth has been perpetuated that the Texans were treated badly when actually they were treated as well as might have been expected, then it is time for Texans to face the fact. On the other hand, if their treatment was bad, it is time for all Mexicans who have, up to now, shrugged it off, to make a mental confession and start over.

Needless to say, this writer has an opinion. I had none when I started. Having lived as a boy in both New Mexico and Texas, I was intrigued with finding the answer to the question. This can be done objectively, and even a final conviction may be objective.

[173]

Did the Pioneers Surrender at Discretion?

To surrender at discretion means to throw oneself on the discretion of the victor. The phrase is used a great deal in the many papers dealing with this matter, but it seems now undeniable that the Pioneers' lives were guaranteed. Their property in some cases was supposed to be returned to them; in others—Archuleta's acceptance of McLeod's surrender—it seems doubtful that possessions were guaranteed. Archuleta himself said, "I am obligated to them only for the security of their lives."[1] Armijo endorsed this report. Most Texan journalists say that Navarro's life was specifically guaranteed, and most of them say that articles of capitulation were drawn up and signed by officers on both sides, but no copy of this document has turned up in the Bancroft Papers, the Bolton Transcriptions, the archives of the Museum of New Mexico, or the archives in Mexico City.

Bustamante, who is necessarily taking his information largely from Armijo's reports and is very favorable to Armijo, implies that the Sutton-Cooke party surrendered with guarantee of their lives.[2] Andrade verified this when he was judge in the court-martial which sentenced Navarro to death.[3] Armijo verified it again on October 1, 1842, and enclosed a copy of the surrender document to the Minister of War.[4] There are many other confirmations.

Were They Rebels or Prisoners of War?

If Texas was still a part of Mexico, then the Pioneers were rebels, subject to the internal laws of Mexico. If, however, Texas was a republic in its own right, then the prisoners were entitled to the rights of prisoners of war, which were rather well defined.

[1] Bancroft Papers, 983; Brief, 56a.
[2] Bustamante, *Gabinete Mexicano*, I, 219; Brief, 499.
[3] Bancroft Papers, 1051; Brief, 68a.
[4] Bancroft Papers, 985; Brief, 56a.

Peter Gallegher

From H. Bailey Carroll, *The Texan Santa Fé Trail*
Reproduced by permission of the Panhandle-Plains Historical Society

This day attended the Llano
Estacado,
water at a basin like impression in the
llano, the Bufalo cliffs

and the water was running in
the Creek, This is a great
thoroughfare for the Indians
in crossing the Llano Estacado
as there was at least 20
Horse Trails cut in the
solid lime stone Rock
as we advanced up the creek
we had high lime stone that
cliffs on each side 100 feet
higer, the Creek forked the first
day we took the right hand
fork which had gradually
gave out away with the
remaining level, the Indian
Trail in this valley is the
largest Trail we found on
the Plains.

Page from the Gallegher Diary

From H. Bailey Carroll, *The Texan Santa Fé Trail*
Reproduced by permission of the Panhandle-Plains Historical Society

Daniel Webster pointed out that for six years there had been no attempt to retake Texas, that the independence of Texas had been recognized by the United States, England, Belgium, and France, and that by neglect alone, if by no other way, Mexico had implicitly acknowledged that Texas was a separate nation.

Armijo told Archuleta to treat the general, officers, and troops "according to the rules and ordinances."[5] Later, Santa Anna said that they "have been treated according to the usages in cases of prisoners of war."[6]

Daniel Webster pointed out the rights of prisoners of war: "Compacts between enemies, such as truces and capitulations, shall be faithfully adhered to."[7] "The law of war forbids the wounding, killing, impressment into the troops of the country, or the enslaving or otherwise maltreating of prisoners of war, unless they have been guilty of some grave crime."[8] He further admonished Waddy Thompson to demand explicitly of the Mexican government that the prisoners "be not confined in loathsome dungeons, with malefactors and persons diseased; that they be not chained, or subjected to ignominy, or to any particular rigor in their detention; that they be not obliged to labor on the public works, or put to any other hardship."[9]

Some modern writers have been discriminating. Rev. Lansing Bloom, a New Mexican writer, is quite objective in his chapter, "Texas Aggressions, 1841–1843."[10] Ray Allen Billington calls it a trading expedition.[11] On the other hand, a Texas writer, Frank Bryan, referred to it in a Texas newspaper recently as "the war of 1841."

In a 1956 edition of Rufus B. Sage, LeRoy R. Hafen refers

[5] Falconer, *Letters and Notes*, 45.
[6] *Ibid.*, 61.
[7] 27 Cong., 2 sess., *House Doc. No. 266*, 32.
[8] *Ibid.*
[9] *Ibid.*, 33.
[10] *Old Santa Fé*, Vol. II, No. 6 (October, 1914).
[11] *The Far Western Frontier*, 39.

to the Snively expedition of 1843 as a "second attempt to sub-jugate the province of Santa Fé to the government of the new-born Republic of Texas."[12] Actually, Sage himself does not say that; he says they were to "annoy the Mexican frontier, intercept their trade, and force them, if possible, to some terms by which a peace might be secured between the two countries."[13] But a misconception so deeply rooted is difficult to destroy.

It is hard to know what gave Bancroft his original bias in this matter. Santa Anna had said, in the *Niles' Register*[14] and other places, "Our agreement [with the Texans] lost its valid-ity as soon as they commenced to treat me" as a slave. This would seem to be a sort of flexible one-way agreement, by which a man who has given his word later decides that he does not want to abide by it.

Bancroft says: "If the promises alleged to have been broken were given in good faith to the Texans as peaceful traders, Armijo was fully justified in breaking them on learning, through Lewis' treachery and Lamar's proclamation, how he had been deceived."[15]

Twitchell seems to have read Bancroft: "Even if it be ad-mitted that Armijo did break his promises, still, when he ascertained from an inspection of the Lamar proclamations, just what were the intentions of the invading party, he was justified in disregarding any promise which he had made."[16]

But both these eminent writers overlooked one important fact: some copies of the Lamar proclamation were burned at San Miguel after the surrender of Cooke on September 17, and Armijo must have been well aware of its contents before Archuleta accepted McLeod's surrender on October 5.

Bancroft says further: "Waddy Thompson, U. S. minister in Mex., in his *Recollections*, 5, 50, 92–3, 155–6, mentions this

---

[12] *Rufus B. Sage: His Letters and Papers, 1836–1847* (ed. Hafen), II, 252.
[13] Rufus B. Sage, *Rocky Mountain Life*, 300.
[14] *Niles' National Register*, Vol. LXII, No. 4 (March 26, 1842), 51.
[15] Bancroft, *History of Arizona and New Mexico*, 326.
[16] Twitchell, *Leading Facts*, II, 81.

affair, and states, what indeed is practically admitted by all, that the prisoners were well enough treated in Mexico."[17]

Twitchell says: "Waddy Thompson, United States minister to Mexico at the time, mentions this affair in his *Recollections*, and states, what indeed is practically admitted by all, that the prisoners were well enough treated while in Mexico."[18]

What Thompson actually said was not in his *Recollections* at all, but in a letter to Daniel Webster, dated April 29, 1842: "I found their condition and treatment as good as is usual with prisoners of war, *except that they were chained and subjected to labor on the public streets. These things I regarded as a violation of the well established usages of civilized war and without excuse or apology.*"[19] (Italic supplied.)

Now that we have observed the birth and maturity of these opinions, it is time to examine the facts and decide whether the prisoners actually were treated badly or whether the complaints were based primarily on technicalities. If the latter, it is much ado about nothing. If the former, once again the history books will stand some correction.[20]

Franklin Coombs said that, on the march, they were tied six or eight together; a man would have a rope on his waist, neck, or arms, with the other end fast to the saddle of a Mexican soldier, and the soldiers would gallop.

Lubbock tells that in Chihuahua "the men were wretchedly treated by the soldiery. A great many of them were cruelly whipped, and made to work in the streets . . . undergoing privations and sufferings, continual outrage and insult from the soldiery."

The story of the *Jornada* has already been told, except for Kendall's later narration that Salazar severely beat lame and

[17] Bancroft, *History of Arizona and New Mexico*, 324.
[18] Twitchell, *Leading Facts*, II, 81.
[19] *House Doc. No. 266*, 34.
[20] Bancroft, *History of Arizona and New Mexico*, 326, strengthens the charge of bias against him when he says: "Active preparations [for "vengeance"] began as soon as the captives of 1841 had returned." Bancroft should have known that Texas had been invaded twice by Mexicans before the *Rosa Alvina* sailed from Vera Cruz.

sick prisoners with a sword. As it occurred he describes it only once; the other times are told in a summary.

Kendall says that at San Cristóbal, the Mexican government sent them fifty cents each for five days' food. Brantz Mayer visited San Cristóbal and reported that the prisoners were in rags, were covered with filth and vermin, and had a disease resembling varioloid.[21]

Also at San Cristóbal, Adolph Hegewick, doctor of medicine and surgery and public professor in Mexico, examined the prisoners on February 6, 1842, and said that nine of them were afflicted with varioloid and several others were also ill— one of them nearly dead. Four had an eruption of "ecrantenca," one appeared to have typhoid fever, and three others dysentery. The 145 prisoners were crowded into a space so small that they touched one another, and there was no roof over them. "The entire nakedness of the greater part of those sick induces me to predict a fatal result from the disease with which they are afflicted."[22]

Conditions at San Lázaro have been described. The food was satisfactory, once they learned to eat it surrounded by lepers; their restraints were not too onerous. At Santiago, as related, they were confined over the cemetery. The food was good. They were appointed to do some "debasing" work, but refused. At Santiago they were chained a large part of the time. The chains were described as log chains, and Thomas Green said they weighed about twenty pounds each.

At Puebla conditions were worse. V. Ostrander reported: "We have been in a space of 50 yards square with 300 criminals. We are chained and heavily ironed. We are compelled to perform the most laborious work in company with the aforenamed villains, from amongst whom are chosen the most worthless to act as drivers over us. Many of our companions in a state of nakedness are compelled to work under a scorching sun."[23]

[21] *Senate Doc. No. 325*, 51–52. [22] *Ibid.*, 56.
[23] Bancroft Papers, 630–31; Brief, 358–59.

Also at Puebla: "[We] are chained to Mexican felons whose crimes are of the most degrading and revolting nature. By day we are hurried into the streets to perform the most laborious work, such as carrying heavy loads of stone a distance of half a mile on our heads. Inability calls down the most severe chastisement. At night we are driven into a room inadequate to contain half of our number and are compelled to sleep in a sitting posture. . . . Since writing the foregoing, our means of subsistence have been reduced to one rial[24] per diem, which is positively insufficient to obtain one meal of victuals. Previous to the 21st, we have always received two rials."[25] (Signed by eleven men, including several officers and H. R. Buchanan.)

From Perote there seems to be no specific complaint, although it had a reputation as one of the bad prisons of Mexico. The horrible conditions at the *Acordada* have been described.

The situation of the prisoners is thus described by a non-American observer, Madame Calderón de la Barca, a Scotswoman married to the Spanish minister to Mexico: "Their situation is represented to be very miserable, and as it is said that they have been stripped of their hats, shoes, and coats; some of the Mexican families . . . regardless of political enmity, have subscribed to send them a supply of linen and other necessary articles" (*Life in Mexico*, 519).

Daniel Webster said: "If these facts be not disproved, they constitute an outrage by the local authorities of Mexico, for which there can be no apology. The privations and indignities to which they were subjected during their march of 2,000 miles to the City of Mexico, at the most inclement season of the year, were horrible, and, if they were not well authenticated, it would have been incredible."[26]

[24] A *rial* was worth at that time about nineteen cents. J. Villasana Haggard, *Handbook for Translators of Spanish Historical Documents* (Archives Collections, University of Texas, 1941), 107.
[25] *Senate Doc. No. 325*, 61–62.
[26] *House Doc. No. 266*, 30–31.

One may well ask: "If conditions were so bad, why didn't the prisoners try to escape?" Apparently there were two or three reasons. One was their naïve belief that as soon as the Mexican authorities found out their designs were not militaristic, they would be released. Another was their poor physical and mental condition and their fear of the hazards of the country. A third was the fact that many of them were boys from sixteen years to twenty, with no particular tradition behind them to make them pull together. The United States was young, Texas was barely a nation, and to many the whole thing was a lark. When the need for sternness came, the lack of tradition and background was a big handicap.

Actually there were many discussions concerning escape, but at the times when they could have accomplished it, escape seems to have been farthest from their minds. Four men did escape from the Sutton-Cooke party north of Paso, but were recaptured; Comanche escaped, but was recaptured; McJunkins and his partner were recaptured. There were either four or six successful escapes, but the astonishing thing is that there was no wholesale breakout. It was talked of south of Chihuahua, but Navarro persuaded them that they were in a very bad position to get out of the country—which they were. That was the McLeod party. It must have been at about the same place a month earlier that the Sutton-Cooke party formed serious plans to escape, but was betrayed.

The fact remains that these were frontiersmen, skilled at fighting, experienced in making their way through the country, and with supposed contempt for the fighting ability of the Mexican guards, who seldom had adequate arms—but they did not take advantage of the situation. Kendall says that at one time they would have rebelled if their guards had had better arms.[27] This was north of Paso.

It would seem to this writer, from an examination of all material available to him, that the above facts concerning

[27] *Narrative*, I, 394.

the treatment of the prisoners do not present a distorted picture, and the conclusion is obvious.[28]

[28] Opinions on reliability of writers vary considerably. J. Manuel Espinosa, translator, *First Expedition of Vargas into New Mexico, 1692* (Vol. X, Coronado Quarto Centennial Publications, 1540–1940), 30, considers W. W. H. Davis' account of the reconquest of New Mexico "absolutely unreliable," but says H. H. Bancroft laid the ground work for a serious study. Twitchell, on the other hand (*Leading Facts*, II), relies on Davis for many facts concerning New Mexico at the time Davis was there. Many quote Carlos María Bustamante, *Gabinete Mexicano*, but a very little reading will show that Bustamante is not a mature writer. His Vol. II is dedicated to Armijo. Its language and the acknowledgment of his sources are revealing: "On reading so much in official quarters and in the notes which have been sent to me . . . an eternal and indisputable honor in our history, and at the same time . . . there are warriors and patriots who know enough to defend their independence, their religion and their homes." It is difficult for any writer to escape preformed judgments, and the seriously interested reader should examine each author's work and determine that author's competence, frankness, and presence or absence of bias for himself. This also applies, naturally, to the work of the present writer.

14. REPERCUSSIONS

In MARCH, 1842, General Rafael Vásquez invaded San Antonio; Mexican detachments took Goliad and other places; on July 7, General Canales fought Davis on the Nueces; on September 11, Woll invaded San Antonio again and took many prisoners; Dawson's men were massacred; Caldwell defeated Woll on the Salado.

In October the Somervell Expedition was organized to Laredo; in December it broke up, and a great many dissatisfied Texans organized the Mier Expedition; they captured Mier and then surrendered to Ampudia in an action that never will be fully understood. Three months later they were drawing the black beans at Hacienda Salado, and seventeen men were executed.

In the meantime other things were happening. The Mexican newspaper *El Siglo XIX* (*The Nineteenth Century*), on December 14, 1841, published the following statement: "We have the pain to announce to the public an act of barbarism committed by Captain D. Dámaso Salazar ... had the iniquity to kill three of these prisoners in cold blood, because they had become wearied. It was reserved for Salazar to eclipse the triumphs of Señor Armijo by this cruel and brutal action. Every one is indignant at such an atrocious act, peculiar only to a cannibal. . . . We hope that such a scandalous act will be punished with all the severity of the law."[1]

But information of the capture of the Texans did not reach the United States or Texas for more than another month. Houston was elected president to succeed Lamar, and went into office not knowing the fate of the Pioneers. The first definite word was from Manuel Álvarez, United States consul at Santa Fé, on January 18, 1842. The news was stunning, and the Texan Congress, then in session, promptly passed a resolution to annex to Texas all of Chihuahua, Sonora, New Mexico, Baja California, and Alta California, and parts of Tamaulipas, Coahuila, Durango, and Sinaloa. Houston vetoed the act, pointing out that it might be regarded as a legislative jest; Congress promptly passed it over his veto and adjourned.[2]

There was nothing left but to prepare for war—without an army, without equipment, without money. Houston pulled in his belt. He sent word to New Orleans that volunteers would be welcome, but only if they were self-equipped. On March 6, following Vásquez' invasion of San Antonio, Houston declared a naval blockade against Mexico.

Public meetings were held across the United States, to raise funds and recruit volunteers. Kendall says several state legislatures passed resolutions condemning the barbarous actions of Mexico.[3] These referred, of course, to Salazar's conduct, but Salazar was a captain in the Mexican armed forces, and the only step which might have redeemed Mexico's national reputation—punishment and offer of indemnities—was not taken. In such matters as these, Santa Anna was still a child.

A letter from Arrangoíz at New Orleans, dated January 14, 1842, to the Minister of Foreign Relations of Mexico, informs him "of the hostile intentions of the legislature of Kentucky against the republic. . . . I believe that it will not be the only legislature which will express itself in these terms."[4] There were public meetings at New Orleans, Mobile, Savannah,

---

[1] *Niles' National Register*, Vol. LXI, No. 22 (January 29, 1842), 343.

[2] Yoakum, *History of Texas*, II, 343.

[3] *Narrative*, II, 264.

[4] Bancroft Papers, 853; Brief, 36a.

Augusta, Georgia, New York, and Philadelphia, and at Augusta $1,000 was subscribed.[5]

Arrangoíz describes the meeting at New Orleans, where some five thousand persons met in the Bank Arcade in that hot-blooded town, traditional seat of revolution, counterrevolution, and filibuster. "It appears now that the legislature of Louisiana also has asked resolutions because of the news and also because of personal injuries to the American consul in Santa Fé. . . . Never has there been seen a greater assemblage in the city nor one more mob-like. Three deputies of the legislature of the state figured in that meeting, and one of them expressed himself in the most severe terms against us."[6]

The situation did not improve. On March 24 a company of seventy volunteers left Mobile for Galveston, and three days later three hundred left New Orleans.[7]

There were, of course, many dissident opinions on the affair. On the whole there were many sympathizers in the United States, for Texas was settled by men from this country. But very often a personal or regional bias influenced the attitude of some in the opposite direction. Mississippi, for instance, wanted Texas in the Union because it would make another Southern state,[8] while Georgia (or at least one newspaper there) wanted no part of the Republic. They had little sympathy for Texas, the newspaper intimated, because Texas would be too much of a competitor in the raising and marketing of cotton. The editor added, "The people of the United States are already too much embarrassed, besides being threatened with still greater evils, to think of extending aid to foreigners."[9] The argument seems to have a familiar ring.

On April 6, Washington D. Miller wrote a letter to Ashbel Smith, saying: "Troops are arriving from the United States.

[5] *Niles' National Register*, Vol. LXII, No. 6 (April 9, 1842), 83.
[6] Bancroft Papers, 856; Brief, 37a.
[7] *Niles' National Register*, Vol. LXII, No. 6 (April 9, 1842), 83.
[8] *The Southwestern Historical Quarterly*, Vol. XXIII, No. 1 (July, 1919), 9–10.
[9] *Niles' National Register*, Vol. LXII, No. 6 (April 9, 1842), 83.

The times are auspicious."[10] But on May 25 there was another reaction. Andrew Jackson, former president of the United States, wrote to President Houston: "The wild-goose campaign to Santa Fé was an ill-judged affair."[11]

Only two weeks before, the old war horse, John Quincy Adams, also former president of the United States and a bitter foe of Jackson (and therefore without any feeling of friendliness toward Houston, who was a protégé of Jackson), said in the House of Representatives, at a meeting of the Civil Appropriations Committee: "Were they not taken *flagrante bello*, actually engaged in a war . . . got up by the president of the republic of Texas for conquest within the Mexican territory."[12] It might seem that Adams spoke with more vehemence than considered judgment—as he did on many occasions.[13]

It was a sore point with Adams. Again, on September 17, when he returned home to Massachusetts after the Congressional session, he made a public talk about Texas: "The president of Texas is a native of Tennessee, and neighbor of Gen. Jackson. . . . Referring solely to the year 1841, we see the expedition of Santa Fé of which so much has been spoken; it was an invasion of adventurers, hostile, projected, recruited and undertaken by the citizens of the United States. . . . Fortunately it had a bad end; they did not even treat of saving their lives but surrendered at discretion. If they had been triumphant, the consequences would have been most disastrous."[14] It would seem that an "elder statesman" might be more judicious in his utterances. The press of Mexico, however, was pleased to quote Adams—for which they could hardly be blamed.

By the first of May the prisoners were beginning to arrive

---

[10] Winkler, *Manuscripts, Letters and Documents*, 262.
[11] Yoakum, *History of Texas*, II, 329.
[12] *Niles' National Register*, Vol. LXII, No. 9 (April 30, 1842), 137.
[13] Read Adams' speeches in the house during the year 1842. Many are reproduced in *Niles' National Register*.
[14] Bustamante, *Gabinete Mexicano*, II, 224; Brief, 504.

in New Orleans and Galveston. Kendall was one, and when he wrote his *Narrative* he included several pages on the Roman Catholic religion in Mexico—or more particularly, as he explained it, about the priesthood in Mexico. He says: "The faults of the holy brotherhood I shall allude to with reluctance, for from one and all I never received other than the kindest and most benevolent treatment."[15] He speaks of their eating and drinking, their lack of celibacy, and their intolerance, which he says was calculated, because of its effect at keeping the population under their control. He mentions the fact that they controlled a great part of the wealth of Mexico. On the whole his remarks are quite well mannered and certainly without meanness. Apparently it was an unbiased expression, for later he married a Roman Catholic girl against his Protestant mother's wishes.

Others were not as tempered in their remarks. Bustamante says of Kendall: "Freedom was extended to all the Texan prisoners. Then Kendall renewed his attack with double fury against the Mexicans. This is littleness in all its ugliness. To use clemency with this type of immoral people is to cast pearls before swine."[16]

It is doubtful that Bustamante represents any substantial portion of Mexican thought at that time; Bustamante's sweetish dedication to Armijo and his juvenile writing make it an unfair comparison.

It seems likely that DeShields gives a fairly accurate summary when he says the Santa Fé Expedition "made Texas' claim to its 'northwestern territory' sufficiently good for the state to obtain for its relinquishment in 1850, $10,000,000 from the United States government. The financial cost of the expedition was less than $80,000. The greatest cost was the loss of so many noble lives."[17]

When it came time for the release, all prisoners were re-

[15] *Narrative*, II, 341–45.
[16] Bustamante, *Gabinete Mexicano*, II, 220; Brief, 500.
[17] *Border Wars of Texas*, 370–71.

quired to take an oath that they would not again take up arms against Mexico, and they were warned that violation of this oath would mean death.[18] Nevertheless, there were many who took up the rifle before many months had passed. Whether they, like Santa Anna, considered that subsequent acts released them from the oath is hard to know, but at least twenty of the Pioneers were involved in the affairs that started with Woll's capture of San Antonio, went into the Somervell and Mier expeditions and the Black Bean executions, and ended back in Puebla, Perote, and the *Acordada*.

Men involved in both affairs were D. Allen, Alsbury (imprisoned), Beidler, Bennet, Bonnell (killed), Bray, Brenham (killed), Burke, Mathew Caldwell, Cummings (killed), Fitzgerald (killed), Hancock (imprisoned), Howard, Jackson (killed), John E. Jones (killed), Kuykendall, Lyons (killed), Morgan (imprisoned), Van Ness (imprisoned), Lubbock, John S. Sutton, and William Wallace.

Howard, among many others, took part in the Mexican War; Texas furnished six thousand troops for that affair. Howard also was with Kearny when the Army of the West took New Mexico. He took an active part in the Civil War on the side of the Confederacy, as did many other Pioneers.

George Grover's son lives today in Galveston, and there were others on the expedition who may have living sons or daughters, for Grover was about a median age in 1841.

[18] A very curious item appears in this connection in Bancroft Papers, 558; Brief, 18a:

Commandancia General del Departamento de Puebla. E. S. Quedo impuesto por la nota de V. E. fha 15 del que cursa de la que en el mismo dia se sirvió dirijir ál E. S. Comandante gral de Veracruz a fin de que remita la acta del Juramento que hicieron los priocioneros Tejanos al ponerlos en libertad; y por lo que respecta a la que subscribieron en esta Ciudad el dia 13 del citado, ya tube el honor de elevarla á V. E. ayer.

    Dios y L.   Puebla.   Junio 17 de 1842.

                        Valentín Canalizo (rúbrica)

E. S. Mtro de la grra.

    Junio 18/42.

        Enterado.

This seems to imply that the Minister of War ordered the oath remitted. No supporting evidence has been found.

Santa Anna is a man of whom much has been written, a good deal of it uncomplimentary. Like Armijo, he could talk on both sides of the fence. Like Armijo, he was in and out of Mexican politics, but for much longer. It was a little hard to know who was president of Mexico, with the considerable turnover experienced in that government. It was convenient for Santa Anna; if he needed an alibi, as he frequently did, he could always plead—as he did concerning the treaties of Velasco—that he had acted as an individual and not as an official.

But one of his finest gestures probably was one of the least noticed: the granting of a special insignia to those Mexican troops who had taken part in the victory over the Texans. (For it was a victory; a conquest made by connivance is every bit as final as one made with arms.) Those soldiers who took part were directed to wear a shield on their left arms, with a green ground and a national eagle with outstretched wings, with gold cord for officers, yellow silk for troops.[19] One wonders if any of Armijo's soldiers ever wore this shield.

The murderous cruelties of Salazar inflamed the United States as well as Texas. The feeling was intensified by the subsequent indignities in Mexican prisons—for to a civilized man there are few things more precious than his dignity. Santa Anna overestimated the efficiency of his fighting forces when he ordered counterinvasions of Texas. Within four years the Mexican War broke out.

What if the Pioneers had been successful in establishing a trade route and in extending their jurisdiction to the Río Grande, and there had been no Mexican War? What effect would that have had on the present territorial limits of the United States?

By the time of the Mexican War, Texas had already been annexed to the United States partly as a result of her own necessity for protection against Mexico; Kearny took the Southwest, and Mexico ceded a great area to the United

19 *Niles' National Register*, Vol. LXI, No. 21 (January 22, 1842), 322.

States. The entire acquisition included (together with the area then still claimed by Texas) all of Texas, Utah, Nevada, California, Arizona, and New Mexico, half of Colorado, part of Wyoming, and part of Oklahoma and Kansas. Add the Gadsden Purchase, and altogether the final outcome of the Texas-Mexican trouble added to the United States almost one million square miles.

The Louisiana Purchase added to this nation 921,495 square miles; the Mexican trouble added 947,570 square miles.[20] Who is to say that the juvenile, blundering efforts of the Texan–Santa Fé Pioneers were wasted?

[20] Edward M. Douglas, *Boundaries, Areas, Geographic Centers, and Altitudes of the United States and the Several States,* 247–48.

APPENDICES

APPENDIX A

*Preliminary Biographical Roster of
the Texan–Santa Fé Pioneers*

This list can hardly be more than suggestive. Inevitably it will contain errors of fact, for it has been distilled from a considerable mass of data. There will be errors of conclusion too—though it is hoped not many. Every effort has been made to avoid padding the list, and often several names that on the surface show little resemblance, on closer examination have been telescoped into one. At the same time it is desirable to include every name that seems to represent an individual.

The big question is: how many started on the trip? No complete official list exists. If McLeod had a muster roll it was taken by the Mexicans. As a matter of fact, on Oct. 12, 1841, McLeod said in a letter to Armijo: "If the trunk containing my official . . . papers is allowed to me I can furnish your excellency with complete rolls of the troops and of all persons connected with this expedition." (Falconer, *Letters and Notes*, 49; Brief, 224.27.)

Grover seems to have made up the list with the earliest date: his Grand Reference Sheet, showing, at Camp Resolution on Aug. 31, 1841, 95 names in the Sutton-Cooke party and 153 in the McLeod party. Some of these are too faded to read, but this is the total number of names. This total, plus 47 casualties on his Reference Sheet, makes a grand total of 295, but we know that a number of names are omitted. Both of these documents were prepared some months later in Mexico, however, as Grover says his original journal was lost.

In the archives of the Texas State Library there is a second

THE TEXAN-SANTA FÉ PIONEERS

Reference Sheet, also apparently in Grover's handwriting. To judge from the lack of ornamentation on this second sheet, it is a copy of the one in the Rosenberg Library, made by Grover himself. Data-wise, it is not exactly the same as the Rosenberg Reference Sheet.

To judge by Kendall's figure of 90 in the Sutton-Cooke party when it left San Miguel (original total of 95, less 5 captured by Salazar) and his figure of 187 in the McLeod party when it left San Miguel, it would seem simple to add those previously lost—about 30—and get the total at the start: 307. But Kendall gives no information concerning the source of these figures and no list of names.

(For the record, Heredia, governor of Durango, reported to the Minister of War July 24, 1841, that "a person of known faithfulness and patriotism" advised him that 1,000 men and 200 carts had taken the road to Santa Fé. Bancroft Papers, 525.)

It is entirely possible, by choosing one's figures, to get totals of men starting and of men lost along the way to support the figure of 320. Any such process, however, must be arbitrary, and a careful study will find real flaws in it. This compiler suggests that the original figure of 320 sprang from one source— the bulk figure quoted by the *Austin City Gazette*—and that others who never saw a copy of the paper to add the editor's own sub-totals accepted this figure and agreed with it.

In adding various components, it was notable that on occasions when the totals matched the sub-totals, it would be discovered that one set of figures was being balanced against another set, both of which had the same source.

Brenham and Cooke, who were not present, said McLeod surrendered with 182 men; Kendall, who also was not present, supports this by saying that 187 men left San Miguel (or did he include the 13 McLeod officers and merchants who already had gone to Paso?). Kendall says 187 started and one was left in Paso, but Conde says a month later that 175 left Chihuahua. At least 11 men (perhaps 24) had vanished.

Trenco said the 175 arrived at Zacatecas, but only 139 reached San Cristóbal. We know of 25 left in various hospitals, and perhaps McJunkins and his comrade were not yet recaptured. Also, Navarro had been separated from them. This accounts for 167; again we have a shrinkage of 8 human lives— 19 between Paso and San Cristóbal. This is hard to accept.

Thompson, in his *Recollections,* says that only one man died of yellow fever in Vera Cruz; Grover lists six; Bollaert says 14 died. Bollaert also says 183 came in the "brig," which is hardly possible, for only 139 men were physically able to sail.

Grover lists 47 men who were lost in various ways; this compiler lists 60; Falconer says "above 60" were lost.

These contradictory figures give an idea of what the compiler faces. The roster can be built up or trimmed down if one wishes. This compiler has accepted whatever grist has come to hand and has processed it as intelligently as possible—a qualification imposed by nature.

There are a number of lists, as explained in the bibliography. None of these is complete. They arise from different sources, and it must be remembered that much of the spelling is phonetic, that somewhere along the line every name was handwritten, and that some of the lists have never been printed and are now somewhat faded and illegible. The Mexican lists present some very strange spellings.

One list is printed in *Mexico in 1842,* taken from the list in the *Austin City Gazette,* January 5, 1842; there are two in *Senate Doc. No. 325.* Sergeant Doran of the Pioneers is identified with two lists. Grover made some new lists—one as the released men waited for clearance from Vera Cruz—and he included various bits of information. But nowhere, except in the Reference Sheet and Grand Reference Sheet, did anyone attempt to list every man in the expedition and his fate. In any list available we can find positive omissions, and it is not unreasonable to think that there may be other omissions—possibly extensive, because the expedition was poorly organized.

What is more, Grover left Camp Resolution with the Sutton-

Cooke party. This decision to split the command was made quickly, and it seems doubtful that Grover had time or opportunity to make an actual roll of members. Nor would any reason have appeared at that time for his doing so (he was a private in the artillery). At best, then, his Reference Sheet and Grand Reference Sheet are reconstructions at Santiago, long after the fact, from his own memory and that of others.

The figure of 320 has been accepted as a good approximation by most writers until now, but no attempt appears to have been made to put all the lists in one central file. And, if Kendall's or Grover's figures appear final, what about those in the *Austin City Gazette* for June 23, 1841, printed only three days after the expedition started? The figure given is 321, but addition of its "Recapitulation" gives 361, while addition of its more extended detail gives 362. And it adds that they expected to receive 121 volunteers on the Brazos. Where did G. K. Teulon get those figures?

He is specific concerning the officers and the number of men in each company, plus 77 "merchants, amateurs, servants, drivers, etc." He changed this to 37 in a later issue of the paper.

After compilation of this roster, through an obscure note in a report of the Mexican vice-consul at New Orleans, a list of the entire personnel was located in the New Orleans *Commercial Bulletin* for January 27, 1842. This led back to the *Austin City Gazette* for January 5, 1842. These lists are practically identical, and Folsom's list appears to have been taken from the *Gazette*, although Folsom added a few surnames and a few Christian names. All lists have been incorporated in the roster.

It is interesting to note that H. Bailey Carroll's six major lists have been added to until we now have nineteen major lists, fourteen minor lists, and eleven mentions of numbers and dates, as "Thirteen men arrived at San Lázaro this morning." In many cases it has been possible to identify men referred to by numbers only.

In the *Austin City Gazette* for September 8, 1841, it is said that General Tarrant found "one of the muster rolls" of the expedition near the Brazos. Did Teulon get his January list from this muster roll? Probably not, for he says "one" of the rolls was found—perhaps the roll of one company. If so, it is an intriguing question, since there was extremely scanty communication from the Pioneers up to that time: where did Teulon get his January list? So far the muster roll itself remains hidden.

An additional factor of uncertainty is injected by McLeod's statement at San Miguel in October that he had a complete list of the personnel in his official trunk (Falconer, *Letters and Notes*, 49).

Did Teulon's compilation possibly come from the long missing list of McLeod? Ordinarily, that should have been the source for a newspaperman, although there is no proof that it was. If one adds Teulon's figures of 362 and 121 one gets a fantastic total of 483. We do not, however, have any direct figures on the Brazos volunteers after the fact, except an indirect statement some time later that Spooner and Mercer joined there. We do have a statement by Spooner almost a year later that the expected reinforcements did not appear, but he does not say that none of them appeared.

In view of the somewhat startling results of the compilation of this roster, which indicates a total of 377 Pioneers out of 417 entries, it is now desirable to give some explanation of the process used to compile it. Every scrap of information that seemed likely to assist in identification was entered on 3x5 cards (these were too small for some names), and these were studied and compared to reach conclusions regarding which should be put down separately and which should be combined. If a name appeared on Grover's list as being in the City of Mexico on Jan. 1, 1842, while a similar name was given as arriving with McLeod at San Cristóbal Feb. 4, 1842, then in most cases it would be assumed that these were two different men. Initials, given names, nativity, and position with the expedition (including the company) were not as a

[197]

rule given much weight. Initials varied greatly; nativity also; position with the company was changeable, although company designations were quite consistent.

In some cases a man's first appearance on any list occurs at his death. In this connection a highly significant sentence appears in a letter written by Powhatan Ellis to Daniel Webster, April 9, 1842. He names eleven men who were lost or killed by the Kiowas, and adds: "Others besides these were lost or killed, but their names are not now recollected by the surviving officers" (*Senate Doc. No. 325, 76*).

At the time he was talking about—that is, as the expedition finished its trip across the Llano and approached San Miguel—the expedition had already lost at least twenty-eight men. *But the officers' memories six months later did not recall the other seventeen names.*

From various surprises encountered in making up this tentative list, it seems reasonable to assume that names were omitted as well as duplicated. On several occasions the compiler was ready to combine names when he discovered important facts that were incompatible.

A name like "Kuykendall" may not be expected to be duplicated; therefore every similar name, unless accompanied by fairly positive information that differentiates it, is assumed to be a variant spelling. However, "Kellett" appears twice consistently; perhaps they were brothers. A name like "Johnson," with eleven different sets of initials, gives trouble—and it appears there were two "Thomas Johnsons." On two or three names, such as "Smith," the information available makes a reasonable conclusion hopeless; in such a case—there were not very many—the names were combined where it seemed justified, but put down separately where there was no legitimate reason for combining. As an example of combining, the name "Hosey" appears in one list, but eventually was deemed to be the same as "Antonio José Jímerez."

Alternate spellings and initials (except some more distorted Mexican variants) have been included in brackets in this list

[198]

for the aid of future checkers, as well as some other items that seem important to identification. Determination of the name for entry has followed preponderance of evidence, considering frequency and weight of every item. Most of the Mexican documents were transcribed into typewriting by Dr. Bolton or his staff, and we allow for errors in that process, as we shall be forced to allow for errors if we ourselves do the transcribing. Scrutiny of the Grover lists will show the difficulty of complete accuracy. Remembering that, a man's name signed at the bottom of a letter to Thompson will generally be given preference over a name appearing in a list. It is obvious, therefore, that this roster must be used as a guide rather than, as was once hoped, an authority.

A number of men captured by the Mexicans during the fighting of early 1842 along the Río Grande got mixed with the prisoners, and, especially in Mexican records, they were not distinguished. It is believed, however, that these have been eliminated from this roster.

It should be noted that designations of nationality or origin vary confusingly. All those mentioned are given under each name, together with the town of residence if available.

Our knowledge of the movements of men in the expedition is pegged largely to the various lists, and it may be helpful to summarize these:

The list in the *Austin City Gazette*, on June 23, 1841, does not give names of enlisted men.

One of the first long lists of names appears in *Senate Doc. No. 325,* 52–53, and reports men of the Sutton-Cooke party "in the city of Mexico," Dec. 30, 1841. It should be noted that any designation of Mexico City is not specific, for San Cristóbal, Santiago, San Lázaro, Tacubaya, the *Acordada,* and another unnamed prison inhabited by the Texans all were in or near Mexico City, and frequently a letter written from one of them is dated "Mexico" or "City of Mexico."

Since the list of Dec. 30 is secondhand, the Jan. 1, 1842 "list of Texas prisoners in the city of Mexico," is used as a

[199]

point of reference. This was a list compiled by Grover, probably on the spot. The two lists are not identical. A second date is Feb. 4, taken from *Senate Doc. No. 325*, when the McLeod party was at San Cristóbal.

The first general list of names appeared in the *Austin City Gazette* for January 5, 1842. Its source is unknown. This list was reprinted in the New Orleans *Commercial Bulletin* for January 27, 1842. It was also used by Charles J. Folsom (whose real name was George Folsom) in *Mexico in 1842;* it is fairly obvious that in this latter case the list somewhere was transmitted orally, for there are a number of obvious aural mistakes.

There is a Mexican list (so referred to here) of Feb. 11—being primarily the Sutton-Cooke men at Santiago. This appears to be a copy of a list signed by John Doran, but the original list is not in evidence.

As of Feb. 28 we have a Mexican list of prisoners at Santiago —primarily the Sutton-Cooke party.

There is a list of noncommissioned officers and privates, headed by John Doran, which is called here the Doran list, being primarily of members of the McLeod party at Santiago between Apr. 25 and Apr. 28. A very fortunate circumstance enables us to date this list; otherwise it would be of little value. A man named William Bissett was left ill with smallpox at Guanajuato; he arrived at Santiago Apr. 25 and was released Apr. 28; his name is on the Doran list. After that discovery, every name on the Doran list was checked to see if any conflict would develop on dates. None did; therefore it seems safe to date the Doran list Apr. 25–28.

There is a Mexican list of prisoners released from Puebla on June 13. We have a Mexican list of "119" (actually 122 are shown) prisoners released from Santiago June 14.

Finally, there is Grover's list of 139 men who (apparently) sailed from Vera Cruz on Aug. 12. Identification of this list is not positive. He shows also more than thirty men who remained at that time in Mexico, for illness or other reasons.

The *Gazette* list of January 5, 1842, seems to have been

[200]

used as the basis for a list of 120 names, entitled "Late Republic To the following persons: To services on the Santa Fé Expedition from the date of enrollment to the 13th July 1842 and for losses." This list, in the archives of the Texas State Library, obviously was compiled after Texas was admitted to the union in 1845. It is accompanied in the archives by an old payroll, now in fragments, which offers a hint regarding where Teulon might have gotten the list of January 5.

The *Gazette* list also is the basis for a list of 199 persons who Thomas S. Lubbock and John Tardif swore, on August 25, 1851, had been taken prisoner. The derivation of both these lists is evident from the fact that the order of names is practically identical with that of the *Gazette*.

Since these latter two lists turned up just before the galley proofs on this book were received, and since they were compiled some time after the events of the expedition, not all the information in them appears in the roster here printed. There are many apparent errors in these two lists, and only where additional information of importance and seeming reliability occurs has that been included in the printed roster, although all is shown on the compiler's card file.

It should be noted that servants and Mexicans frequently were not listed by name; also, in arriving at a total, it might be noted that there are fifteen names on Grover's Grand Reference Sheet too faded to be read; these have not been counted separately in the grand total.

It may be noted here that the compiler doubts that more than—at most—twenty-five names can be trimmed with justice from this roster, in the absence of a large quantity of more definite information—which seems unlikely to appear.

Where only a fragmentary reference exists, and that occurs in only one place, the source is given.

Sergeant Doran's list comes through Mexican channels and was taken from the Bancroft Papers; Folsom's list appears in *Mexico of 1842;* Green's list is in his *Mier Expedition,* and most of the references to Mier prisoners are taken from Green;

Senate Doc. No. 325 has been described; the Bolton Transcriptions, as noted are at the University of Texas Library, and the Bancroft Papers are at the Bancroft Library. Most references to Masonic affiliation are to Carter, *Masonry in Texas. The Handbook of Texas* and *The Southwestern Historical Quarterly* have been used freely. Grover's lists are from his unpublished papers at the Rosenberg Library.

This roster has been compiled for identification; a statistical study of the expedition would deal with different factors and should be conducted from the original records. For instance, Grover shows 139 men who left Vera Cruz Aug. 12, but from deduction and scattered sources this roster will show 145.

There will be those who are uncomfortable over the rather large total derived from the compiler's card file. For them one bit of advice. A certain Indian agent once explained to Quanah Parker that his several wives were against the law, that he would have to dispose of all but one. Old Quanah said, "Fine, fine! You tell 'em which ones have to leave."

Members of the Pioneers
(Dates refer to 1842 unless specified.)

ACKLAN [Aclin, H. Ackland]. Tennessee. Blacksmith, Co. E. [Newton Acklen, Co. D]. At San Cristóbal Feb. 4; at Santiago Apr. 25–28; left Vera Cruz Aug. 12.

ADAMS, ALLENSWORTH [A., Alexander]. Lancaster, Ky. Brother in Texas; wife and two children. Co. E. At Mexico City Jan. 1; released from Santiago Apr. 27; certificate of service given Apr. 28; left Vera Cruz May 12.

ADAMS, THOS. W. [T. W., Jas. M.]. Tennessee. 2nd corp., Co. E. At Mexico City Jan. 1; at Santiago Feb. 28; released from Santiago June 14; left Vera Cruz Aug. 12.

AHART, A. At Santiago Feb. 25–28 (Doran's list).

AHART, C. At Santiago Feb. 25–28 (Doran's list).

AKLES. Co. A (*Gazette* list of 1842. Payroll list says "deserted.")

ALEXANDER, J. M. [J. N.]. Lieut., assistant quartermaster. At

San Cristóbal Feb. 4; to Puebla Feb. 9; released from Puebla June 13. Complained of very bad treatment at Puebla; restricted communication and confinement with depraved criminals in a small area, laborious work, naked under a hot sun, in irons, and the lash without mercy.

ALEXANDER, ROBERT F. [F., F.H.]. Tennessee. Co. E. At San Cristóbal Feb. 4; to San Lázaro Feb. 9; at Santiago Feb. 28; released from Santiago June 14; left Vera Cruz Aug. 12.

ALLEN, D. Connecticut. Pvt., artillery. At San Cristóbal Feb. 4; left Vera Cruz Aug. 12. (David Allen, of Harris, Tex., origin Virginia, was on the Mier Expedition.)

ALLEN, H. A. [Allan; A. H.]. Kentucky. Hospital steward. At Mexico City Jan. 1; at Santiago Feb. 28; released from Santiago June 14; left Vera Cruz Aug. 12.

ALLISON. Co. B. Left Vera Cruz Aug. 12. (Grover's list.)

ALLYN, SAML. [Allen; S. J., S. T.]. Artillery. At Santiago Feb. 25–28; released from Puebla June 13. (May be D. Allen.)

ALSBURY, WM. M. [Allsberry, Allsbury]. San Antonio. Interpreter for the commissioners. At Mexico City Jan. 1; at Santiago Feb. 28; released from Santiago June 14; left Vera Cruz Aug. 12. (A. H. Asbarry was released from a prison in Mexico in 1844 as a member of the Béxar prisoners. Green's list.)

APACHE. See Chavis, Antonio.

ARCHER, POWHATAN. A confused but definite reference to this man occurs in *The Papers of Mirabeau Bonaparte Lamar*, III, 544. Samuel A. Roberts, in a letter written July 14, 1841, says Archer arrived from the Pioneers to get a Mexican prisoner to act as guide. He raised "12 or 15 men" and returned by way of Franklin for the prisoner. Did Archer and his twelve or fifteen men join the Pioneers? He is not mentioned anywhere, nor is he listed by Folsom or Grover. Are these thirteen or sixteen men to be added to the long list of men unaccounted for? They have not been counted in the total by this compiler.

AYERS, GEORGE [Ayres]. Virginia. Pvt., Co. B. Left ill at Guana-juato; arrived at Santiago Apr. 25; released from Santiago June 14; left Vera Cruz Aug. 12.

BAKER, ALEXANDER. North Carolina. Artillery. Sent ahead Aug. 11, 1841, to New Mexico; captured Sept. 4; escaped from Santa Fé and recaptured; executed in the plaza at San Miguel Sept. 17.

BALLE, B. O. Co. D. (Probably an error by Folsom.)

BARCHATT, JOHN. Remained ill in Tula; died Mar. 7. (Letter from Juan José de Andrada to the Minister of War. Bar-chatt's name appears nowhere else.)

BARKER, H. Durham, England. Pvt., Co. E. At Mexico City Jan. 1; at Santiago Feb. 28; released from Santiago June 14; left Vera Cruz Aug. 12. (H. Bark—of Co. B. is listed by Grover.)

BARNARD, GEORGE [Bernard, Bernardo]. Born 1818 at Hartford, Conn.; arrived in Texas Nov. 12, 1839; an Indian trader with Torrey's Trading Houses (established the first one on the Navasota River); was sick in June, 1841, and joined the ex-pedition for his health. 3rd corp., artillery. At Mexico City Jan. 1; at Santiago Feb. 28; released from Santiago June 14; left Vera Cruz Aug. 12. Charter member of Bosque Masonic Lodge at Waco; died in Waco in 1883.

BASMAN, T. B. Co. E.

BEALL, H. [Bealle]. Young man. District of Columbia. Assist-ant surgeon. Accidentally shot in arm Sept. 13, 1841; wan-dered from McLeod party on Sept. 24, 1841, and never returned. (Robt. Beale of the District of Columbia was on the Mier Expedition.) (Listed as Pvt., Co. D, in Payroll list.)

BEARDSLEY, W. [Bardsle, Beardslee; L.]. Connecticut. Pvt., Co. C. At San Cristóbal Feb. 4; at Santiago Apr. 25–28; left Vera Cruz Aug. 12.

BEIDLER, JONAS [Beadley, Beadles, Bedlar]. Pennsylvania; home in San Antonio. Pvt. Co. C. At Mexico City Jan. 1; at Santiago Feb. 28; released from Santiago June 14; left Vera Cruz Aug. 12. (John Bideler, origin Pennsylvania, home Milam, Tex., was left wounded at Mier fight, and escaped.)

BELLS, N. J. Released from Santiago June 14. (Mexican list; probably a duplicate entry, but not yet identified.)

BENNET, VALENTINE. Sixty-one years old. Six feet tall, slender, erect, fine sense of humor; "a scripture-quoting Quaker," he said the plagues of Egypt were trifling compared to the *chinches* (bedbugs) of Mexican prisons; on entering the City of Mexico on a donkey, he was suffering with smallpox, but when the usual crowd of Mexican women lined the streets to watch the painful progress of the prisoners, Bennet pulled his donkey's head around by one ear, raised his hand and said impressively, "Weep not, daughters of Mexico; your rulers are coming, seated upon asses." He was born in Massachusetts in 1780, of Puritan descent; was a lieutenant in the War of 1812; his wife died, and he moved to Texas in 1825, living in Gonzales; he was wounded at the Battle of Velasco in 1832 in the face and hip; was in the Siege of Béxar, 1835, and the Battle of Concepción, 1835. Major; quartermaster of the Pioneers. Sick at San Cristóbal Feb. 7; to San Lázaro Feb. 9; returned to Santiago Feb. 25; back to San Lázaro Feb. 28; to Santiago Mar. 9; released from Santiago June 14. Reached Galveston "broken in health," but rejoined the army and commanded a regiment in the Somervell Expedition. Died at his daughter's home in Texas in the fall of 1843. A Mason.

BERNARD, J. [Benard]. Co. B. At Santiago Apr. 25–28. (This is not George Barnard; this man was with McLeod; George Barnard was with Sutton-Cooke.)

BESTWICK, WM. [Bertwick, Bostwick]. Terbershire [?], England. Co. D. At Mexico City Jan. 1; at Santiago Feb. 28; released from Santiago June 14; stayed in Jalapa (presumably ill) Aug. 12.

BICKFORD, P. [Rickford]. Boston. Had lived in Houston as a merchant for two years; intended to return via St. Louis. Court-martialed Aug. 2 for mutinous conduct and disobedience; pleaded guilty; sentenced to pay stoppage and fatigue duty. At Mexico City Jan. 1; at Santiago Feb. 28; released from Santiago June 14; left Vera Cruz Aug. 12. He was a townsman of the "Mr. Coolidge" of whom Kendall speaks.

BIGBY [H. Bigbee, Biglee]. English. Co. C. At San Cristóbal Feb. 4; at Santiago Apr. 25–28.

BINK, JAMES. New York. At San Cristóbal Feb. 4. (*Senate Doc. No. 325.*)

BISSETT, ROBERT P. [Bisset, Disset]. Scotland. Corp., artillery. At San Cristóbal Feb. 4; at Santiago Apr. 25–28; released from Puebla June 13.

BISSETT, WM. [W. M.] Ord. sgt., artillery. Left ill at Guanajuato; arrived at Santiago Apr. 25; released from Santiago Apr. 28; certificate of service given Apr. 28; left Vera Cruz Aug. 12. It is this man's stay of three days at Santiago that enables us to date the Doran list.

BITTLER, L. Pvt., Co. C. Left Vera Cruz Aug. 12. (Grover's list.)

BLACKWELL, CHAS. M. Born in Halifax County, Va.; went on the trip because of curiosity. Pvt., artillery; teamster. Left ill at Guanajuato; arrived at Santiago Apr. 25; [C. J. Bazqull —Mexican list] released from Santiago June 14; left Vera Cruz Aug. 12.

BLAKE, L. C. [probably same as L. W.]. Went from Mississippi to Texas in 1839; became ill; left Austin to return home, but became ill at Bastrop; roommate of James L. Mabry; joined the expedition for his health and was attached to a company for protection from the Indians. At Mexico City Jan. 1; at Santiago Feb. 28; released from Santiago June 14. L. W. Blake left Vera Cruz Aug. 12.

BOARDLEY, AKLES [M.] Co. A. At Santiago Apr. 25–28. (Probably the same as Akles, but a Bradley is listed on the Payroll and by Lubbock-Tardif.)

BONNELL, GEORGE W. [F. A.] Mississippi or South Carolina (*The Handbook of Texas* says he went to Texas from New York in 1836). Member of the artillery company; he had held the rank of major previously (Grover lists F. A. Bonnell as a private of artillery.) At Mexico City Jan. 1; at Santiago Feb. 28; released from Santiago June 14; left Vera Cruz Aug. 12. He was a first lieutenant of the navy in the Mier Expedition and was captured and shot by a Mexican soldier. A Mason.

BOOTH, JOSHUA [Boothe]. Kentucky. (But on Apr. 29 John Booth, sixteen years old, of Missouri, signed a letter to Thompson.) Pvt., Co. A. At San Cristóbal Feb. 4; at Santiago Apr. 25–28; at Puebla Apr. 29; released from Puebla June 13; left Vera Cruz Aug. 12. (A Mexican letter dated June 23 says that Joshua Booth asked to remain in Mexico but could not be found; perhaps he changed his mind.)

BOWEN, SMITH. A young man from Maine; home in Iowa. Went to Texas for his uncle. Pvt., artillery. At Mexico City Jan. 1; at Santiago Feb. 28; at San Lázaro Apr. 18 with smallpox, delirious and incoherent; released from Santiago June 14 but still in hospital; left Vera Cruz Aug. 12.

BOWMAN, THOS. Co. E. Left Vera Cruz Aug. 12. (Grover's list.)

BOYD, JAMES. Died July 27, 1842, at Vera Cruz, of smallpox. (Grover's list. Grover said in his second Reference Sheet that this man was not a Pioneer.)

BOYD, M. D. [M. B.] South Carolina. Pvt., Co. D. At Mexico City Jan. 1; at Santiago Feb. 28; released from Santiago June 14; left Vera Cruz Aug. 12. On Apr. 23 he wrote a letter to Waddy Thompson, reminding Thompson that he (Thompson) had been at Boyd's father's home in Laurance district, South Carolina. "We need tobacco most," he said.

BOZEMAN, THOS. [Borrsman, Bosmen; Jhas.]. Alabama. Corp., Co. E. At San Cristóbal Feb. 4; at Santiago Apr. 25–28; released from Puebla June 13; left Vera Cruz Aug. 12.

BRANNARD, JAS. Co. B. (*Gazette* list of 1842.)

BRASHEAR. Doctor. Died Aug. 16, 1841, of liver ailment (or consumption) at Sulphur Springs, a branch of the "Wichitau."

[207]

BRASHEAR, J. H. L. Co. E. (Folsom's list; this man is not starred to indicate a death, as are others on Folsom's list; this may not be the Doctor Brashear listed above.)

BRATTON, JOSEPH [Bracken]. 2nd Lieut., Co. B. At San Cristóbal Feb. 4.

BRAY, JOHN. Co. B. (Folsom's list.) (F. Bray, of German nationality, home Victoria, Tex., was on the Mier Expedition.)

BRENHAM, RICHARD F. Doctor. Born in 1810 in Kentucky; fought in the Texan Army in 1836; practiced medicine in Austin. One of the civil commissioners to Santa Fé and was to be collector of customs there. At Mexico City Jan. 1; at Santiago Feb. 28; released from Santiago June 14. In 1842 he joined the Somervell Expedition, then was surgeon with the Mier Expedition. He opposed the surrender to Ampudia, but was captured and was said to be of great help to the wounded. In the outbreak at Salado, Mexico, he killed two guards and wounded a third, then fell on the bayonet of the third and was killed. On Dec. 11, 1841, Kendall found his name written on a wall at Cerro Gordo, Mexico, along with those of Cooke and Coombs.

BRIGNOLI, FRANCISCO [Francis Brignall]. Italian. Artillery. Deserted with Carlos Aug. 15, 1841. Seen by Sutton-Cooke party Sept. 7 and Sept. 12, 1841; reached Taos in early September, 1841, according to *The Southwestern Historical Quarterly*, Vol. XXVII, No. 2 (October, 1923), 103. No further information.

BRINKLEY, WM. [Broadley; M.]. Maryland. Pvt., Co. E. Strayed Aug. 30, 1841, but returned. At San Cristóbal Feb. 4; at Santiago Apr. 25–28; released from Puebla June 13; left Vera Cruz Aug. 12.

BROCK. Pvt., Co. B or C. Left Vera Cruz Aug. 12. (Grover's list.)

BROWN, JOHN. English. Pvt., Co. B. At San Cristóbal Feb. 4; at Santiago Apr. 25–28; released from Santiago June 14; left Vera Cruz Aug. 12.

BROWN, JOHN M. [J. H. Browne]. English; New York. Co. D.

At Mexico City Jan. 1; at Santiago Feb. 28; released from Puebla June 13; remained at Vera Cruz, presumably ill, Aug. 12. (Apparently not the same as the John Brown above; the first was with the McLeod party, as shown by the Feb. 4 arrival date, and was released from Santiago; the second arrived with Sutton-Cooke Jan. 1 and was released from Puebla.)

BROWN, JOHN H. [Browne]. Victoria, Tex. 2nd Lieut., Co. D. At Mexico City Jan. 1; released from Santiago June 14; left Vera Cruz Aug. 12 (This man does not appear to be identifiable with either of the other John Brown's. This man was an officer; he was with Sutton-Cooke, and was released from Santiago.)

BROWN, S. Artillery. (*Gazette* list of 1842.)

BRYAN, JOHN. Pennsylvania. Co. E. At San Cristóbal Feb. 4; at Santiago Apr. 25–28; released from Puebla June 13; left Vera Cruz Aug. 12.

BUCHANAN, H. R. [Bucannon; T.]. Tennessee. Merchant with pack mule and servant; he visited Texas for the first time the day before the expedition started. At San Cristóbal Feb. 4; to Puebla Feb. 9; released from Puebla Apr. 21; left Vera Cruz May 12.

BULLOCK, J. C. [Bulluck; A. C.]. Connecticut. Pvt., Co. E. Left ill in Guanajuato; at Santiago April 25; released from Santiago June 14; left Vera Cruz Aug. 12.

BURGESS, CHARLES. 2nd Lieut., Co. A. At San Cristóbal Feb. 4; at San Lázaro Feb. 10. Later married a girl named Catalina Fonseca, whom he met at San Lázaro.

BURGESS, C. T. Artillery. (*Gazette* list of 1842.)

BURKE, JAMES [Burk]. Pvt., Co. B. At Santiago Apr. 25–28. Member of Masonic lodge, Austin. (James Burk from Ohio, living at Fort Bend, Tex., was in the Mier Expedition.)

BURNS, DAN. Released from Santiago June 14. (Mexican list; no other appearance; not in Green's list.)

BUTLER, LEVI. Lived in Albany, N. Y., for nine years; went to Texas in December, 1839, as a trader in Houston. Co. C.

At Mexico City Jan. 1; at Santiago Feb. 28; released from Santiago June 14. In a letter written April 27, he said: "My case is precisely similar to Mess. Houghtailing and Torry's who are already liberated [except] I done volunteer duty and they did not."

B - - - LY. Co. C. Left Vera Cruz Aug. 12. (Grover's list; illegible.)

C. ? German. Released from Santiago Apr. 28. (Grover's list.)

CALDWELL, CURTIS. Between twelve and fifteen years old. Son of Mathew Caldwell, who said he was twelve. His father was left at Guanajuato with smallpox, and a few days later Curtis developed the disease; the Mexican governor took care of him and returned him to his father Jan. 24. They were both released sometime after Apr. 25 (at which time they were still in Guanajuato) and returned to Texas via Vera Cruz, Key West, Pensacola, New Orleans, and Galveston. (New Orleans *Picayune*, Aug. 21, 1842; quoted in Copeland, *Kendall of the Picayune*.) Carter, *Masonry in Texas*, says that Curtis was a member of Lafayette Masonic Lodge No. 34, but this must have been later. A physician who examined him at Guanajuato said he had a cancerous ulcer on his right leg which would not permit travel, for he was in continual pain.

CALDWELL, MATHEW. About forty-three years old. Born in Kentucky; native of Nashville, Tenn.; home at Gonzales, Tex. Had a black beard spotted with white, and was called "Old Paint"; an experienced and capable frontiersman, well liked. Married two times and had at least three children. A signer of the Texan Declaration of Independence; in the Council House fight, where he was said to have thrown rocks at an Indian when temporarily disarmed; in Plum Creek fight against the Comanches; said he was a trapper and dealer in furs on the Mexican frontier. Capt., Co. D., of the Pioneers. Left ill with smallpox at Guanajuato Jan. 19; he said he was seventy years old, but this likely was a bid for sympathy, or perhaps he meant that he felt seventy years old. On Sept. 18, 1842, he defeated Woll in the Battle of the Salado, near San Antonio. At 7:00 P.M. on Sept. 17 he sent a report, which ended: "The enemy are all around me, on every side; but I fear them not. I will hold my position till I hear from reinforcements. Come and help me —it is the most favorable opportunity I have ever seen. [Caldwell had 300 men against Woll's 1,400.] I can whip them on my own ground without any help, but I cannot take prisoners. Why don't you come?" Nelson Lee, *Three Years Among the Camanches*, 74.

CAMPBELL, MICHAEL. Thirty-four years old. Tyrone County, Ireland. Co. A. At Mexico City Jan. 1; at Santiago Feb. 28; released from Santiago June 14; left Vera Cruz Aug. 12. Court-martialed July 5, 1841, for sleeping on post; pleaded not guilty, but was sentenced to fourteen days' fatigue duty and to lead his horse and pack his luggage for two days. He was still living in Bastrop County, Tex., in 1871.

CAMPBELL, WILLIAM. New York. Pvt., Co. B. At San Cristóbal Feb. 4; at Santiago Apr. 25–28; left Vera Cruz Aug. 12.

CARDMER [Cardwin]. Co. C. Left Vera Cruz Aug. 12. (Grover's list.)

CARLOS [probably "Juan Carlos" of Co. B. in *Gazette* list]. Blamed by many for betraying the expedition, but it now appears he made an honest mistake. Other than the fact that he was lost (by no means a condition peculiar to Carlos), there is no evidence of his guilt except evidence after the fact. Lived in San Antonio. Mail carrier, San Antonio to Austin; known to San Antonio men as trustworthy. He had been a trapper around Taos, and claimed he recognized the Red River bottoms as the Eutaw River and that it was only 140 miles to the outlying ranches of New Mexico. He was wrong, and when the Pioneers discovered it and began to make threats against him, he and Brignoli deserted on Aug. 15, 1841. He was seen by two men of the Sutton-Cooke party Sept. 7, 1841; seen by Mexicans with whom the Sutton-Cooke men talked Sept. 11, 1841; seen by Sutton-Cooke

[211]

men Sept. 12; he was in bad shape and was invited to come in and join the party, but did not. Stabbed by Armijo's nephew (probably Chaves) Sept. 16, 1841; arrived in Taos in early September, 1841 (?); Falconer says he was killed in Santa Fé, but this likely refers to the stabbing—after which he was seen riding after Armijo with his arm and side bandaged.

CARR. Ohio. At San Cristóbal Feb. 4. (*Senate Doc. No. 325.*)

CARRIGAN. See Corrigan.

CASE, JOEL T. 4th Sgt., artillery. At Santiago Apr. 25–28; released from Puebla June 13. A Mason; minister at Galveston.

CASEY, G. M. [G. G.] 1st Lieut., Co. E. At San Cristóbal Feb. 4; to Puebla Feb. 9; released from Puebla June 13. South of Chihuahua on the trail was recognized by the Mexican commander, Captain Ygnacio García, as one in whose home Captain García had been quartered after the Battle of San Jacinto.

CHAMBERLAIN, HENRY. Pennsylvania; lived in Victoria, Tex. 2nd Sgt., Co. D. At Mexico City Jan. 1; at Santiago Feb. 28; released from Santiago June 14; left Vera Cruz Aug. 12.

CHAVIS, ANTONIO [given in the Doran list as "Antonio Chavis Apache"; probably a nickname]. At Santiago Apr. 25–28; released from Puebla June 13.

CLARK, JAMES W. [The Clarks will give us some trouble; it seems there must have been two, but the given names are confused on the various lists.] Seventeen years old. Lexington, Ky. Teamster; pvt., Co. D. At Santiago Apr. 25–28; at Puebla Apr. 29; released from Puebla June 13; left Vera Cruz Aug. 12.

CLARK, RICHARD [Clarke; R. H.]. Fifteen years old. Lexington, Ky. Listed as pvt., Co. D, also as a servant. At San Cristóbal Feb. 4; at Puebla Apr. 29; released from Puebla June 13; left Vera Cruz Aug. 12. Talked to Indians Sept. 16, 1841; the only word he understood was a free use of the Spanish *tonto* (fool).

COLLIER, JOHN [Colier]. From Maryland. Pvt., Co. B. At San

Cristóbal Feb. 4; at Santiago Apr. 25–28; left Vera Cruz Aug. 12.

COMANCHE. See Jesús Cuellar and Frank Holmes.

CONN. Co. E. (Gazette list of 1842.)

COOKE, WILLIAM G. Thirty-three years old. Born in Virginia; home, San Antonio. Fought with Mexicans against the Royalists and was imprisoned by Iturbide; given a land grant in Texas in 1828; was in the fighting at Goliad, according to Bollaert; was in the Siege of Béxar; in 1837 went into the drug business; quartermaster general of the Republic; laid out the military road from the Brazos to Red River in 1840. Nominated for vice president of the Republic in February, 1841, but declined. One of the civil commissioners to Santa Fé, and in charge of the commission. It was he who finally accepted Lewis's oath as a Mason and surrendered the Texan arms. Arrived at Santiago Dec. 26, 1841; at Mexico City Jan. 1; in chains Jan. 27; at Santiago Feb. 28; released from Santiago June 14. Became Adjutant General of Texas State Militia in 1846; about 1842 married Angela Navarro, niece of Antonio Navarro. Died Dec. 24, 1847. A Royal Arch Mason. Cooke was noted as a frontiersman and was said to be superior to "old veteren Deaf Smith." At San Jacinto he saved Santa Anna's life from the enraged Texan soldiers, who wanted revenge for the Goliad massacre. In Mexico, Cooke declined to remind Santa Anna of this, and served his time in Santiago along with the others. An interesting sketch of Cooke appears in the *Texas State Historical Quarterly*, Vol. IX, No. 3 (January, 1906, 210–19.)

COOMBS, FRANKLIN S. [Combs; Francis; the *Cyclopædia of American Biography* gives "Coombs"]. Seventeen years old. His father was General Leslie Coombs, governor of Kentucky, who had assisted greatly in the Texas Revolution. Listed as a guest or tourist; once as a merchant. Not in good health and hard of hearing. At Mexico City Jan. 1; released from Santiago Jan. 25; the Mexican list places him at Mexico City Feb. 11, but this is an error as far as his

[213]

imprisonment is concerned. Coombs was the first man released. He was accused later, on April 15, of having entered
Texas with a force of soldiers to invade Mexico, but there
appears to be no substantiation whatever. He and Kendall
were good friends and bunked together on the prairie. Doc-
tors examined Coombs in Mexico and said he was "of a
scrofulous habit and is liable to cerebral congestion, indicated by vertigo, nervousness of the head, &c; besides this
he is inflicted with a chronic inflammation of the organs of
hearing which threatens an entire loss of that sense. . . .
imprisonment is dangerous to his life." This was not altogether from his treatment in Mexico, for Kendall said at
the beginning he was hard of hearing.

CORRIGAN, JOHN [Carrigan, Harrigan]. Of Cork, Ireland. Co.
D. In Mexico City Jan. 1; at Santiago Feb. 28; released from
Santiago June 14; left Vera Cruz Aug. 12.

COVINGTON, HAYS [Hayes]. Of Kentucky; Independence. Co.
B. At Mexico City Jan. 1; at Santiago Feb. 28; released
from Santiago June 14, but remained in hospital; died of
smallpox June 18.

COYLE, JAS. D. [T.D.] Of Dublin, Ireland. Artillery. At Mexico
City Jan. 1; at Santiago Feb. 28; given a certificate of service
Apr. 28, probably at Santiago; Aug. 12, remained in Mexi-
co "for the Pacific."

CROWDER, J. T. From Pennsylvania or Virginia. Co. B. At Mexico City Feb. 11; at Santiago Feb. 28; remained ill in Mexico
June 1; remained at Vera Cruz Aug. 12, presumably ill.

CUELLAR, JESÚS. Called "Comanche"; perhaps had some Co-
manche blood. As a captain in the Mexican Army had left
Santa Anna in 1836 to serve Texas; had a brother in the
Mexican Army. As a member of the Pioneers, Cuellar es-
caped from Santiago Jan. 24; recaptured near San Juan del
Río and returned to Santiago Feb. 15. See *The Southwestern
Historical Quarterly*, Vol. XXX, No. 1 (July, 1926), 56–62.

CUMMINGS, JOHN A. Pennsylvania. Pvt., Co. D. At Mexico City
Jan. 1; at Santiago Feb. 28; released from Santiago June 14;

left Vera Cruz Aug. 12. (A John Cummings was killed at the Salado in 1842.)

DAUGHERTY. Ireland. Died in January at Guanajuato, presumably of smallpox. (Grover's list; this name appears nowhere else.)

DAVIDSON, ABRAHAM [F.]. Tennessee. Pvt., Co. D. At San Cristóbal Feb. 4; at Santiago Apr. 25–28; released from Puebla June 13; left Vera Cruz Aug. 12.

DAVIDSON, P. Scottish. Pvt., Co. A. At Mexico City Jan. 1; at Santiago Feb. 28; released from Santiago June 14; left Vera Cruz Aug. 12.

DAVIS, ANDREW JACKSON. Virginia. Accidentally shot June 12, 1841, at Camp on Walnut Creek. A bulletin from H. Q. S. F. P. (Headquarters, Santa Fé Pioneers) and signed by "H. McLeod, Col. Comdg.," says: "The body will be interred with military honors so soon as a coffin can be obtained." Apparently had fought in the Texas Revolution.

DEMANS. Artillery. Left Vera Cruz Aug. 12. (Grover's list.)

DENNISON, JAMES [Denison]. Pennsylvania or Tennessee. Teamster. At San Cristóbal Feb. 4. At Santiago Apr. 25–28. Died at Vera Cruz before Aug. 12.

DENYER, SAMUEL I. [Denger; J. J., S. I.]. Sixteen years old. From Baltimore City. No father or mother. At Santiago Apr. 25–28; at Puebla Apr. 29; released from Puebla June 13; left Vera Cruz Aug. 12.

DIAMOND, JOHN. 2nd Sgt., Co. B. (*Gazette* list of 1842. Payroll list says "deserted.")

DIGGINS, CORNELIUS. English. Co. B. At San Cristóbal Feb. 4; at Santiago Apr. 25–28; released from Puebla June 13.

DONOVAN, A. A. STOUT [Donnavan, Donnovan]. Kentucky. Co. C. Missing from Camp Resolution Aug. 29, 1841; horse found dead with an Indian arrow in it, Sept. 1, 1841.

DORAN, JOHN. English. Sergeant major. At San Cristóbal Feb. 4; at Santiago Apr. 25–28. Apparently signed the "original" list (undiscovered) from which was copied the Mexican list of Feb. 11. Musician on some lists.

[215]

DORCHESEY, BURTON. A "Texas prisoner"; died at 1:00 A.M. Jan. 24 in the hospital of Belén at Guanajuato. (An official Mexican report; Dorchesey's only appearance in the records.)

DOUGHERTY, B. M. [Doughert]. Co. E. At Santiago Apr. 25–28.

DUNN, ROBERT [James]. Co. E. Frequently referred to as "captain." Killed by Kiowas Aug. 30, 1841.

DUTCHMAN [No name given]. A servant of Cooke. Shot at on June 25 but missed. No further identification. (He may have been one of the "Germans" listed, or he may never have been listed by name.)

DWYER. Pennsylvania. At San Cristóbal Feb. 4. (*Senate Doc. No. 325.*)

EBERLY, W. Baden, Germany. Co. A. At Mexico City Jan. 1; at Santiago Feb. 28; released from Santiago Apr. 28. (This probably is the W. or N. Easly who was given a certificate of service by Grover Apr. 28.)

EBNER, ADOLPHUS [W.]. German. Pvt., artillery. At San Cristóbal Feb. 4; at Santiago Apr. 25–28; left Vera Cruz Aug. 12.

EDGAR, JAMES M. [Pat]. From New Jersey; home in Houston. At Mexico City Jan. 1; at Santiago Feb. 28; released from Santiago June 14; left Vera Cruz Aug. 12.

ELLIOTT, JACOB [Eliot, Elliot]. Pvt., Co. D. Left at San Luis Potosí, probably ill; arrived at Santiago about Feb. 25; left Vera Cruz Aug. 12.

ELLISON, THEOPHILUS [Elesion; James]. From Kentucky; had been in Texas five or six months. Co. B; joined as a waggoner, not to bear arms. At San Cristóbal Feb. 4; at Santiago Apr. 25–28; at Puebla May 2; released from Puebla June 13.

ERHART, ANTONIO [Eckart]. German. Co. B. At San Cristóbal Feb. 4; at San Lázaro Feb. 9; at Santiago Feb. 28; given certificate of service Apr. 28; released from Santiago Apr. 28.

ERHART, K. [Ernard]. Co. E. (This appears to be a different man from A. Erhart, because Grover lists, in the party that stayed on the Palo Duro, Erhart in Co. B and Erhart in Co. E.)

ERNEST, FELIX [Earnest; F. B.]. Tennessee. Co. D. Died during the night of Oct. 24, 1841, of exhaustion, at Valencia in New Mexico.

ERWIN, EDWIN. Ireland. Corp., Co. B. At Mexico City Feb. 11; left Vera Cruz Aug. 12.

EVANS, JAMES M. [Evens]. Sixteen years old. New York. Co. A. At San Cristóbal Feb. 4; at Santiago Apr. 25–28; at Puebla Apr. 29; released from Puebla June 13; remained in Mexico Aug. 12, presumably ill. (In Grover's handwritten list, the word "died" referring to Hickey might possibly apply to Evans.)

EWING or EMORY. Co. C. Left Vera Cruz Aug. 12. (Grover's list; handwriting hard to make out. Not Evans, because Evans did not leave Vera Cruz Aug. 12.)

FALCONER, THOMAS. Thirty-six years old. High, wide forehead, light hair, deep eyes, small mouth, small goatee in later years; mild, agreeable, sociable; strong friendship with Kendall. London. Son of a preacher. An advocate by profession. A guest on the expedition; supported McLeod and commented on many occurrences with restraint. With the McLeod party; released from San Cristóbal Feb. 1; told Kendall goodby at San Lázaro Mar. 3; left Vera Cruz Mar. 9 (*Letters and Notes*, 141). Kendall saw him several years later in England, and Falconer's career was illustrious; he served for England on the Oregon boundary commission. He died in 1882. He wrote several items about the expedition—all reconstructed, as his original notes were taken. His Diary was published as an appendix to Vol. I of the seventh edition of Kendall's *Narrative;* he wrote also a Letter to the *New Orleans Bee*, some Notes, and an extended *Account*—all of which were gathered and published by Dauber & Pine in 1930, with editorial work by F. W. Hodge. This is one of the important sources for information about the early part of the expedition, especially as he was at Camp Resolution, along with Gallegher and Hoyle, while Kendall and Grover were crossing the Llano with Sutton-Cooke.

[217]

FARDOFF. Pvt., Co. C. Left Vera Cruz Aug. 12. (Grover's list.)

FARLEY, HORACE H. 4th Corp., artillery. A merchant, not a Texas citizen; expected to return via St. Louis. McLeod party. At Santiago Apr. 25–28; at Perote May 2. An intimate friend of William P. Lewis, but Lewis took his watch at San Miguel and neglected to deliver the money he was to get for it.

FERGUSON, JAMES. New York. Pvt., Co. D [C]. At San Cristóbal Feb. 4; at Santiago Apr. 25–28; released from Puebla June 13; left Vera Cruz Aug. 12.

FITZGERALD, ARCHIBALD. An Irish soldier of fortune, who had fought in Spain and other countries. Home, San Antonio. He was, says Kendall, "one of the best fellows that ever the sun shone upon." He was from a good family in Ireland, many members of which had been distinguished in government service. He was educated to be a priest, but refused to take the orders. At eighteen he went to Spain to fight under Isabella and received a captain's commission; he fought in the Persian Army (or tried to), went to the Cape of Good Hope, Van Diemen's Land, and Brazil. Spoke French and Spanish. Listed as a merchant, and Kendall says he had "considerable" merchandise. Jan. 19, left delirious in Guanajuato (with smallpox); almost died, but recovered; released from custody about Feb. 28. He was captured in San Antonio by General Woll Sept. 11, 1842, along with Hancock and Van Ness; sentenced to death and sent to Perote; sentence commuted to ten years; attached to the Mier prisoners when they arrived at Saltillo Feb. 5, 1843. Fitzgerald, Hancock, Van Ness, Brenham, and Patrick Lyons were in the breakout at Salado, when one hundred unarmed Texans, fighting with brickbats, overcame three hundred Mexicans and received their surrender, then turned them loose. Fitzgerald and Hancock were wounded; they were put in a rough cart and started to Mexico. Fitzgerald died the second day, and his body was thrown on the prairie.

FLEMING, R. R. Sgt., Co. C. McLeod party. Left ill at Silao; moved to Querétaro Apr. 23; at Santiago Apr. 25–28; released from Santiago June 14; left Vera Cruz Aug. 12.

FLENNER, SAMUEL [Flennert]. Pennsylvania. 3rd Sgt., Co. E. Killed by Kiowas Apr. 30, 1841.

FLINT, SAMUEL. New Hampshire. Died of colic on the Bosque River July 5, 1841. A Mason.

FLORES, JOHN [Flory]. Nineteen years old. Ohio. 3rd Sgt., Co. A. At San Cristóbal Feb. 4; at Santiago Apr. 25–28; at Puebla Apr. 29; released from Puebla June 13.

FLORES, NABOR. Released from Santiago June 14. (Mexican list.)

FONLY [Fpucky]. New York. Artillery. At San Cristóbal Feb. 4; left Vera Cruz Aug. 12. (This is not the same man as John Flores, for both appear on the same list, nor is it Stickney, who also appears on that list.)

FREEMAN, LUKE. Of Roscommon County, Ireland. Co. A. At Mexico City Jan. 1; at Santiago Feb. 28; released from Santiago June 14 but remained at Vera Cruz Aug. 12, probably ill.

GALLEGHER, PETER [Galiger; C.]. Twenty-nine years old. Born in Ireland. Stone mason and merchant; Kendall says he had "considerable" merchandise. At San Cristóbal Feb. 4; left San Cristóbal Feb. 9; to Perote from Puebla Feb. 15–Feb. 18; put in chains Mar. 1; chains removed Mar. 3; order for release from Perote May 1; left Vera Cruz May 12, arrived New Orleans May 23. Although a British subject when he left Austin, he died in Texas in 1878. He kept the only contemporary diary so far discovered.

GALTON [possibly Salton]. Co. C. (Grover's list of those who stayed on the Palo Duro.)

GATES. Co. A. New York. Died of pneumonia Nov. 1, 1841, eight miles north of El Paso del Norte.

GATES, THOS. [A. W.]. A Cornishman. Co. E. At San Cristóbal Feb. 4; at Santiago Apr. 25–28. Court-martialed about June 23, 1841, for taking bread; fined one-half month's pay.

GERLACH, CASPER [Garlach]. From the grand duchy of Mecklenburg-Schwerin, Germany; lived in Houston. At Mexico City Jan. 1; at Santiago Feb. 28; given certificate of service Apr. 28; released from Santiago Apr. 28.

GIBSON, GEO. N. Co. E. Left at Tula, probably ill; arrived Santiago about Feb. 25 (?); released from Santiago June 14. Left Vera Cruz Aug. 12.

GILMORE, P. W. Pennsylvania; lived in San Antonio. 3rd Sgt., Co. B. At Mexico City Jan. 1; at Santiago [J. W.] Feb. 28; released from Santiago June 14 but remained at Jalapa, probably ill, Aug. 12.

GLASS, THOS. [T. F.] Kentucky. Co. E. Seems to have been an experienced frontiersman. On July 1, 1841, he was court-martialed for taking sugar, but acquitted. On Sept. 12 he left Camp Resolution to pick mesquite beans for food and was killed and scalped by Kiowas.

GLENN. Co. A. (*Gazette* list of 1842.)

GOLDAP. Mississippi. Sutton-Cooke party. Released Apr. 23 at Mexico. Obviously not Golpin.

GOLPIN, AMOS A. [Gaulpin, Golphin]. Had a crippled or withered right hand; "inoffensive and harmless." Mississippi. A small merchant. In the sick wagon Sept. 18, 1841, and was there off and on until he was shot on the *Jornada* Nov. 1, 1841. Kendall, in the introduction to his *Narrative*, exhibits strong feeling when he accuses Captain Frank Marryat of impeaching Kendall's honesty in the description of Golpin's death; Kendall was referring to Marryat's *Adventures of . . . Monsieur Violet*, which is said by many to be freely plagiarized from Kendall and several others. In view of the circumstances, Marryat would have done better to continue plagiarizing when he described Golpin's death, for his relation of it is somewhat fantastic.

GOMPERS. Co. A. (From Grover's list of those who stayed on the Palo Duro; appears no other place.)

GORDON, J. L. [G. S., John, Nabg. L.]. Native of Connecticut; tailor in New York City; failed in 1840 and went to New

Orleans as an employee; not a citizen of Texas (from letter written from Puebla May 3). Corp., Co. C. At San Cristóbal Feb. 4; at Santiago Apr. 25–28; released from Puebla June 13, but remained in the hospital at Vera Cruz Aug. 12.

GOWEN, Pvt., Co. A. (Payroll list and Lubbock-Tardif list.)

GRAY, WM. [Grey]. Ireland. 1st Corp., Co. B. At San Cristóbal Feb. 4; ill Feb. 7; at Santiago Apr. 25–28; remained at Vera Cruz, probably ill, Aug. 12.

GREEN, ASA [Greene]. Born in South Carolina. Said to come from Alabama. Blacksmith, Co. C. At San Cristóbal Feb. 4; at Santiago Apr. 25–28; certified a citizen of Louisiana by McLeod at Perote May 1; left Vera Cruz Aug. 12. Likely a brother of Burwell Green.

GREEN, BURWELL. Born in South Carolina; certified by McLeod at Perote May 1 to be a resident of St. Clair County, Alabama. Had a wife and family in Alabama. Blackmith, Co. C. At San Cristóbal Feb. 4; at Santiago Apr. 25–28; left Vera Cruz Aug. 12.

GREEN, EDWARD. Kentucky. Corp., Co. D. At San Cristóbal Feb. 4; at Santiago Apr. 25–28; left Vera Cruz. Aug. 12. (Three Green's are listed within a space of two inches on Grover's list of Aug. 12.)

GRIFFITH, EDWARD. A Welshman; of Missouri. Wounded by a Kiowa shot Sept. 16, 1841; brains knocked out Nov. 2, 1841, on the *Jornada.*

GRISWOLD, S. P. [Gildmold, Greswold, Griswool; J. P.]. From New York. Ordnance sgt., quartermaster's clerk. At San Cristóbal Feb. 4; at San Lázaro Feb. 10; released from Santiago June 14, but in hospital; in hospital at Mexico City July 3; in hospital at Santiago July 7; remained in hospital at Vera Cruz Aug. 12.

GROVER, GEORGE W. Twenty-one years old. From Ohio. Artillery. Arrived at Santiago Dec. 26, 1841; chains removed because of illness Mar. 13; published a handwritten prison paper, *The True Blue*, under the pen name of Simon Pure, assisted by John Talk; released from Santiago June 14; left

Vera Cruz Aug. 12. Grover left many writings and easily the most extensive lists of names. For personnel of the expedition we are more indebted to Grover than any other source. Astonishingly enough a son of George Grover is now living in Galveston, Tex., at the age of 88, and from him has been obtained the following additional material on George Grover's life. Three Grovers emigrated from Wales before the Revolution. One of these, Nathan, settled in Sackett's Harbor, N. Y., where George was born. They moved to Cincinnati in 1824, where George was educated in private schools. He worked for the Cincinnati Type Foundry and Machine Co. as a bookkeeper. In 1840 he and his father went to Texas and settled seven miles below Austin. He fought in the Plum Creek Fight under Mathew Caldwell, while his father fought in another unit. When George was released from Santiago he and his companions were left on their own resources to get to Vera Cruz, and George felt the temper of the country so strongly against them that he and two companions traveled by night and hid during the day. A Mexican woman discovered them and showed them how to reach Vera Cruz without using the main road. They remained hidden until dusk, then finished their trip to the coast. He married in Cincinnati in 1844, but his wife died of tuberculosis. In 1849 he went via Chagres to California and returned in 1850. He married Eliza Ann Crane, daughter of a Revolutionary soldier. They had six children—five born in Galveston, one in New York; two died of yellow fever. He lived through the Civil War at Galveston and died there Dec. 21, 1902; buried in the Episcopal cemetery.

GRUSH, H. L. [N. D. Gring on a Mexican list.] From Maryland. Lived in Austin. Major, commissary of subsistence for the Pioneers. At Mexico City Jan. 1; at Santiago Feb. 28; released from Santiago June 14. On June 21, 1841, he went to Bryan's Settlement for one wagon, four yoke of oxen, and necessary chains; on June 27 he went back to Austin for beef cattle.

HADDON, G. [?]. Alabama. Co. D. (Grover's list.)

HAINES, EPHRAIM M. Native of Philadelphia; to Tennessee in 1833 as clerk; into dry goods business in 1836; failed in general panic, 1838; to New Orleans; took goods to Houston and Galveston for employers; in February, 1841, they offered to set him up in Santa Fé; otherwise he went from love of adventure and enterprise (from a letter written by him to Waddy Thompson). Ord. sgt., Co. C. At Santiago Apr. 25–28; at Puebla May 3; released from Puebla June 13; left Vera Cruz Aug. 12.

HAINES, JOHN M. [Hain]. Also from Pennsylvania; perhaps a brother of Ephraim. 3rd Sgt., Co. C. At San Cristóbal Feb. 4; at Santiago Apr. 25–28; released from Puebla June 13; left Vera Cruz Aug. 12. (The evidence is pretty definite in favor of two men named Haines.)

HALL, EDW. Co. E. McLeod party. Left ill at Guanajuato; arrived at Santiago Apr. 25; left Vera Cruz Aug. 12.

HAMMER, J. (Somewhat illegible.) Pvt., Co. B. Left Vera Cruz Aug. 12. (Grover's list.)

HAMMETT, JACOB. Kentucky. Had been in Texas five or six months. A teamster or waggoner; not to bear arms; Co. B. At San Cristóbal Feb. 4; at Santiago Apr. 25–28; at Puebla May 2; released from Puebla June 13; died at Vera Cruz. He had assumed the name of Jacob Lindley or Lindsey.

HAMRICH, JOHN [Hamenck, Hemrich]. Pennsylvania. Pvt., Co. B. At San Cristóbal Feb. 4. Court-martialed Sept. 8, 1841, for mutinous conduct; pleaded guilty; ordered to stand guard two hours off and two hours on for one month, and his pay was stopped for one month. McLeod received the proceedings "with unqualified surprise" at the leniency of the punishment.

HANCOCK, THOMAS. Illinois. Pvt., Co. D; also listed as a "merchant." An original, or what we might now call a character; had been a captive of the Winnebagoes at eight years of age for about eighteen months; captured by the Comanches in Texas; altogether was captured four times and escaped

[223]

twice; born in 1821; went to Texas in 1836, at fifteen (*William Bollaert's Texas*). Kendall says he was uncouth in appearance, but when his body straightened in excitement, he was wary, knotted, and active. He had a marvelous sense of observation. He had been in many frays with Mexicans and Indians. At Mexico City Jan. 1; at Santiago Feb. 28; released from Santiago June 14 but in the hospital; still in the hospital July 3, but left Vera Cruz Aug. 12. Captured Sept. 11, 1842, in San Antonio, by General Woll; wounded in attack on the Mexican guard at Hacienda de Salado Feb. 11, 1843; recovered and sent to Perote; condemned to death for violating his pledge not to bear arms against the Mexican government; this would seem to have been self-defense; commuted to ten years; escaped and was recaptured; released with Béxar prisoners Mar. 23, 1844. (See Archibald Fitzgerald, this list.)

HANN, JOHN W. [Hand]. 1st Lieut., artillery. At San Cristóbal Feb. 4; ill at San Cristóbal Feb. 7; at San Lázaro Feb. 10; at Santiago Feb. 25; released from Santiago June 14.

HARDING, T. [Hardin]. Ireland. Had been in Co. C, First Texas Infantry, in 1839. 1st Corp., Co. A of the Pioneers. At San Cristóbal Feb. 4; at Santiago Apr. 25–28; left Vera Cruz Aug. 12. (The Mexican list shows Thos. Hadeng released from Puebla June 13; probably the same.)

HARRIS. English. Released from Santiago Apr. 28. (Grover's list.)

HARRIS, ENOCH. Died at 8:00 A.M., Feb. 27, at Guanajuato, probably of smallpox.

HARRISON, WM. B. Co. C. Left at Guanajuato; arrived at Santiago Apr. 25. Given certificate of service Apr. 28.

HART, ANTONIO E. 2nd Corp., Co. B. At San Lázaro Feb. 10.

HASMANN, F. [Harman]. Of Bidefeld (Bideford, England?). At Mexico City Jan. 1 and Feb. 11.

HATCH (probably same as Hutch).

HAYES, HENRY [Hays]. English. Pvt., Co. A. At San Cristóbal

Feb. 4; at Santiago Apr. 25–28; released from Puebla June 13; left Vera Cruz Aug. 12.

HEMRIDGE, J. At Santiago Apr. 25–28.

HENRY, WILLIAM NELSON. 1st Lieut., Co. D. In San Cristóbal Feb. 4; to Perote Feb. 18; released from Puebla June 13.

HICKEY, JAMES. English. Co. A. McLeod party. At San Cristóbal Feb. 4; at Santiago Apr. 25–28; remained at Vera Cruz Aug. 12; died.

HOLLIDAY, JOHN J. Lieut., assistant commissary of subsistence. Escaped from the Goliad Massacre (according to *William Bollaert's Texas,* 180); carved his name on a tree near Wichita River. At San Cristóbal Feb. 4; to Perote Feb. 18; died of yellow fever on board the *Rosa Alvina* 3° south of Galveston Aug. 19.

HOME. Co. C. (Gazette list of 1842.)

HOLMES, FRANK [P. L. Jms on a Mexican list]. Also known as Comanche. Sutton-Cooke party. Released from Santiago June 14.

HOODEL, JACOB [Hirdel, Huoodle]. French. In Co. C, First Texas Infantry, 1839. Co. A, Pioneers. At Mexico City Jan. 1; at Santiago Feb. 28; given certificate of service Apr. 28; released from Santiago Apr. 28.

HORACE, BEALLE. Co. D. (*Gazette* list of Jan. 5, 1842.) Folsom lists two men, B. O. Balle and B. O. Horace, but it appears that Folsom took his list from the *Gazette* and either made errors in transcribing or found additional information.

HORN, ALEXANDER. English or Scottish. Co. C. At Mexico City Jan. 1; at Santiago Feb. 28; released from Santiago Apr. 28. Given certificate of service Apr. 28.

HORNSBY, C. C. 1st Lieut. of cavalry, Co. B. At San Cristóbal Feb. 4. Kendall says he was the best dressed of the entire party on the *Jornada,* but he was forced by an unprincipled Mexican *ranchero* to trade off his fine clothes and blanket for coarser ones, which Hornsby discovered actually were better because they were warmer.

[225]

HOTCHKISS, WM. Pvt., Co. B. McLeod party. At Santiago Apr. 25–28; released from Santiago June 14; left Vera Cruz Aug. 12.

HOUGHTALING, J. B. [Haftalin, Haughtelling, Houghtailing, Houghtalin; J. H.]. Merchant. At San Cristóbal Feb. 4; released from Puebla Apr. 21; left Vera Cruz May 12. Martin Van Buren (former president of the United States) intervened for him. (Houghtaling also lost a watch to Lewis.)

HOUGHTON, W. D. Capt., Co. B. Ordered a halt at night just short of water Sept. 30, 1841, and was severely criticized; requested a court-martial, but it was not held. (This was in New Mexico, just five days before they surrendered, half-starved.) At San Cristóbal Feb. 4; to Perote with McLeod party Feb. 18.

HOWARD, GEORGE THOMAS. Twenty-seven years old. Light, curly hair and florid complexion. An old Indian fighter of many exploits and a Texas Ranger; had several old wounds. Born in the District of Columbia. Sent to New Orleans by Lamar to buy supplies for the expedition, and there met George Wilkins Kendall and interested him in going. Howard was listed as a merchant or civilian, but started out as aide-de-camp to McLeod with the rank of major; he resigned after a meeting of officers in the Cross Timbers requested McLeod to resign. With the Sutton-Cooke party. Sick at San Cristóbal Feb. 7; to Puebla Feb. 9; escaped from Puebla Apr. 14 with Captain Hudson. He was lieutenant colonel in the Somervell Expedition; sheriff of Béxar County; in the Texas Volunteer Cavalry in the Mexican War. Was sent to Taos in connection with the Kearny Expedition. Helped organize and finance the Chihuahua–El Paso Pioneer Expedition in 1848. Married Mary Frances McCormick and settled in San Antonio. In 1856 Kendall wrote Falconer and said Major Tom Howard was fat as ever, and wealthy. In the Civil War he took a commission in the Confederacy; supplied cattle to the Confederacy and accepted cotton, which he traded to Mexican merchants. He died in Washington, D. C., in 1866. Member of a Masonic lodge at Houston.

HOWARD, JOHN C. [J. T.]. Washington, D. C. Younger brother of George T. Howard; had come to Texas but found the market dull. At San Cristóbal Feb. 4; at San Lázaro Feb. 10; at Santiago Feb. 25; released from Santiago Apr. 21; left Vera Cruz May 12. (Various confusing details are given about what seem at first to be three Howards, but a letter from Nathaniel Amory, secretary of the Texas legation in Washington, to the Secretary of State of the Texas Republic, dated Jan. 4, 1841 [1842], says: "A brother of Major G. Thomas Howard and John C. Howard requests I will enquire if they were in the Santa Fé Expedition" [*Texan Diplomatic Correspondence*, I, 523]. It seems fairly clear that there were only two Howard brothers with the Pioneers.) John became 1st Lieut. in United States infantry in 1847; in 1856 was a captain stationed in Oregon; resigned in 1861, probably to enter Confederate service; died in 1885.

HOWLAND, SAMUEL W. Native of New Bedford, Mass.; good family and a gentleman. Sent ahead on Aug. 11, 1841; was captured and imprisoned in Santa Fé; escaped but recaptured; on Sept. 4, with his left ear and cheek cut entirely off and his left arm hacked by a sword, he was led to the northeast corner of the plaza in San Miguel and executed before the eyes of Kendall and his party.

HOYLE, STEPHEN Z. [Howle; F. Z., James]. English. Hospital steward. At San Cristóbal Feb. 4; to Puebla Feb. 9 and to Perote on Feb. 18; probably released from Perote (but James Hoyle was released from Santiago June 14). Secretary of State of Texas in 1842. A Mason. (According to H. Bailey Carroll, Hoyle rewrote Gallegher's Diary after they reached Mexico; this document, the Gallegher-Hoyle *Journal,* is printed in the *Panhandle-Plains Historical Review* for 1951.)

HUDSON, JOSHUA [F.]. Of London. Co. A. At Mexico City Jan. 1; at Santiago Feb. 28; released from Santiago June 14; left Vera Cruz Aug. 12.

HUDSON, N. G. [A. G.] (Not Radcliffe Hudson.) Alabama. Pvt., Co. D. At Mexico City Jan. 1; at Santiago Feb. 28; released from Santiago June 14 but in hospital; still in hospital July 7, but left Vera Cruz Aug. 12.

HUDSON, RADCLIFFE [Ratcliffe]. Houston, Tex. Capt., Co. C. An original, a joker. Charged with bad singing in kangaroo court at San Cristóbal and fined $1.50. At San Cristóbal Feb. 4; to Puebla Feb. 9; he escaped from Puebla Apr. 14 with Major Howard; released May 1 by request of Governor of Connecticut, although he was still at large and busy carving his name in one of the towers of a cathedral of Mexico City—and added, "Of the Texan Santa Fé Pioneers." Kendall says "Capt. H." could not talk Spanish, but if this meant Hudson, Kendall was wrong, for Hudson cavorted around Mexico City for two weeks and was not detected. Kendall says "Capt. H." was dead by 1844, but the compiler has not been able to determine whether this is Hudson or Houghton. He may have meant the latter. In a letter to Ashbel Smith in 1839 Hudson said he had invested his money in land claims high on the Brazos, Colorado, or San Saba Rivers.

HUGHES, F. [T.]. Ireland. Pvt., Co. E. At Mexico City Jan. 1; at Santiago Feb. 28; released from Santiago June 14; left Vera Cruz Aug. 12.

HUGHES, JAMES H. Pennsylvania. Co. E. At San Cristóbal Feb. 4; at San Lázaro Feb. 10; at Santiago Apr. 25–28; released from Puebla June 13; left Vera Cruz Aug. 12. (F. Hughes and James H. Hughes are badly jumbled, but there seems no doubt they were separate men.)

HULL, G. R. English. Only child of Major General Trevor Hull; had himself held a captain's commission in the British navy; principal proprietor of the town of Lamar, Tex.; much respected and honorable. Lieut., Co. E. Killed by Kiowas at Camp Resolution Aug. 30, 1841.

HUNT, GEORGE. Georgia. At San Cristóbal Feb. 4. (Senate Doc. 325.)

HUNT, THOS. W. [Wm. H.; Thos. N. Huat]. New York. Pvt., Co. D; surveyor and guide. At Mexico City Jan. 1; at San Lázaro Feb. 10; at Santiago Feb. 28; released from Santiago June 14; left Vera Cruz Aug. 12. Had $1,000 or $1,200 worth of goods, "like Sheldon." A Mason.

HUNTER, SAMUEL P. Kentucky. Pvt., artillery. At Mexico City Jan. 1; at Santiago Feb. 28; left Vera Cruz Aug. 12.

HUTCH, JOSEPH T. [Hatch]. Eighteen years old. Davidson County, North Carolina. At San Cristóbal Feb. 4; at Santiago Apr. 25–28; at Puebla Apr. 29; released from Puebla June 13; left Vera Cruz Aug. 12.

IDGER, J. M. New Jersey. At Mexico City Dec. 30, 1841. (*Senate Doc. No. 325.*)

IMENS, JOSÉ MARÍA. Pvt., Co. B (Payroll and Lubbock-Tardif lists.) (Jimerez?)

INDAS, JOHN T. Alias of Plasmann. (From *The True Blue.*)

IRWIN, EDWARD [Irvin]. Co. B. Of Cork, Ireland. At Mexico City Jan. 1; at Santiago Feb. 28.

JACKSON, WM. H. Ireland. Corp., Co. A. At San Cristóbal Feb. 4; at Santiago Apr. 25–28; released from Puebla June 13; a letter from the commandant at Puebla dated June 23 says that he asked to remain in Mexico but cannot be found (perhaps he changed his mind along with Joshua Booth); left Vera Cruz Aug. 12. (J. Jackson of Ireland, said by Green to be a Pioneer, was killed at Mier.)

JAMES, WM. London. Co. D. At Mexico City Jan. 1; at Santiago Feb. 28; released from Santiago June 14 but in hospital; still in hospital July 7, and remained in Mexico Aug. 12 when the *Woodbury* sailed.

JIMEREZ, MARTIN JOSÉ [Jimnez, Hosey]. Co. B Court-martialed for sleeping on post July 30, 1841, at Five-Mile Creek. Pleaded not guilty; acquitted.

JOHNSON, CHARLES. New York. Artillery. At San Cristóbal Feb. 4; at Santiago Apr. 25–28; remained at Vera Cruz, probably ill, Aug. 12.

JOHNSON, THOMAS. Twenty years old. Hair and complexion

fair, eyes blue, no beard, long and massive nose, large forehead with temples, height five feet, six inches, bad health.
A merchant. Asked to remain in Mexico, and did remain
at Puebla Aug. 12. On June 23 he had asked the protection
of the United States. He said his father was a colonel in the
United States Army and his brother was also in that army.
Perhaps the family was descended from Thomas Johnson,
many of whose descendants were military men, according
to Appleton's *Cyclopædia of American Biography*. One of
the females of the family married John Quincy Adams.

JOHNSON, THOMAS. [T. J.]. 1st Lieut., Co. A. At San Cristóbal
Feb. 4; to Puebla Feb. 9; released from Puebla June 13.
(There are similarities and differences between the two men
named Thomas Johnson; it is a tossup whether they are
the same.)

JOHNSON, WM. J. Pennsylvania. Ordnance Sgt., Co. B. At San
Cristóbal Feb. 4; at Santiago Apr. 25–28; died in June at
Vera Cruz.

JONES. Servant. This name appears in an unidentified list. It
is the only Jones not identified with a company. (E. Juoin
was released from Santiago June 14—Mexican list.)

JONES, CALVIN [Chrs.]. Kentucky. Pvt., artillery. At San Cristóbal Feb. 4; at Santiago Apr. 25–28; released from Puebla
June 13; left Vera Cruz Aug. 12.

JONES, C. M. or C. W. Pvt., Co. A. Released from Puebla June
13; left Vera Cruz Aug. 12. (C. Jones and C. M. Jones appear
on the same Mexican list.)

JONES, JOHN E. Of Kildare County, Ireland. 2nd Sgt., artillery.
At Mexico City Jan. 1; at Santiago Feb. 28; released from
Santiago Apr. 28; given certificate of service Apr. 28; left
Vera Cruz May 12. (John E. Jones, English, a Pioneer,
living at Harris, Tex., was killed on the Mier Expedition,
Green, *Mier Expedition,* 87.)

JONES, MYERS FISHER. Listed by Carter as a Masonic member.
No other reference appears.

JUSTICE, MILTON M. North Carolina; home listed as San Antonio. 3rd Corp., Co. A. At Mexico City Jan. 1; at Santiago Feb. 28; released from Santiago June 14 but in hospital; still in hospital July 7, but left Vera Cruz Aug. 12.

KEENAN, FRANCIS. Wandered and lost on Aug. 27, 1841. (Gallegher-Hoyle *Journal*.)

KEENON, JOHN. Co. B. Probably the same as Francis Keenan, for the Reference Sheet says he wandered off and did not return. (*Gazette* list of 1842.)

KELLETT, E. Manchester, England. Pvt., Co. C. At Mexico City Jan. 1; at Santiago Feb. 28; released from Santiago June 14; left Vera Cruz Aug. 12. Court-martialed below the Cross Timbers for falling asleep on guard June 24, 1841; pleaded guilty; received a reprimand and pay stoppage for one month.

KELLETT, WM. J. Georgia. Pvt., Co. B. Left at Guanajuato with smallpox; arrived at Santiago Apr. 25; left Vera Cruz Aug. 12. Said he was attached to a company only to get rations.

KELLY, WM. [Kelley]. Pvt. Co. B. At San Cristóbal Feb. 4; at Santiago Apr. 25–28; left Vera Cruz Aug. 12.

KEMPER, A. German. Co. A. At San Cristóbal Feb. 4; at Santiago Apr. 25–28; left Vera Cruz Aug. 12.

KENDALL, AMOS F. (No relation to George W.) Arrived in Texas in December, 1840; stayed in Crockett, then Austin. First musician of the Pioneers (with three other musicians, he said). At San Cristóbal Feb. 4; sick at San Cristóbal Feb. 7; at San Lázaro Feb. 10; at Santiago Feb. 25; released from Santiago June 14; remained at Vera Cruz Aug. 12, probably ill. In a letter written Apr. 23, he said: "It was optionary with me to carry arms or not and I was not subject to any military duty. I of course carried arms but can truly assert that it was not with the intention of fighting Mexicans."

KENDALL, GEORGE WILKINS. Thirty-two years old. Born in New Hampshire; did newspaper work under Horace Greeley; with Francis Lumsden established the *Picayune* in New Orleans in 1837; an aggressive and imaginative editor; went to the scene; pioneered modern reporting. Went with

[231]

the Sutton-Cooke party, but made the *jornada* to Mexico with the McLeod party. At San Cristóbal Jan. 31; to San Lázaro Feb. 9; said to have measles but probably was varioloid, a mild form of smallpox; definitely had smallpox Feb. 14; moved to a new place, unnamed, Feb. 14, but encountered myriads of *chinches* (bedbugs) and he and his companions stayed awake at night and slept during the day; returned to San Lázaro (a leper's hospital which he describes graphically) Feb. 25; thought much of escaping, but a weak ankle (broken five days before the expedition left Austin) held him back; released from Santiago Apr. 25; left Vera Cruz May 12; arrived at the Mississippi Delta May 18. Kendall was highly indignant because Santa Anna released them as a personal favor and not as a right (*Narrative*, II, 312). Previously he had been disgusted because the demands of the British government carried more weight than those of the United States, and when Falconer was released on Feb. 1, Kendall wrote: "whose position [Falconer's] had certainly been more inimical [to the Mexican government] than mine" (*Narrative*, II, 212), but he does not say in what way. He saved a rivet from his leg chains as a memento of the trip (*Narrative*, II, 313). He wrote the two-volume work entitled *Narrative of the Texan Santa Fé Expedition*, which was published in seven editions in the United States by Harper & Brothers and in several editions in England by various publishers. It is literary in many places, but a monumental job of reporting also; if he had included more names it would have been superb. He was successful in later life and traveled abroad; although a Mason, he married a French girl who was a Catholic; he visited Falconer in London. He went to Mexico during the Mexican War and probably was the first war correspondent in the modern sense; he wrote a history of that war which is not easy to find today. He moved to Texas and raised sheep on a large scale. Henry Law Olmstead in 1856 visited Kendall on his sheep ranch five miles north of Neu-Braunfels, where he found Kendall had a good stock of mares, some cattle, and a large flock of sheep under charge of an imported Scotch shepherd. Olmstead asked him about visiting Mexico, and says: "In talking over our plans with him we found no particular encouragement toward entering" that country. "Certain circumstances in his first visit to Mexico, we thought, however, might have given him a permanently unfavorable impression." (*A Journey Through Texas,* 183.) During the Civil War he gave allegiance to the Confederacy; he died in Texas in 1867. A good biography of Kendall has been written by Fayette Copeland, *Kendall of the Picayune.* An interesting sketch appears in *The Louisiana Historical Quarterly,* Vol. 11, No. 2 (April, 1928). A wagonload of Kendall's original papers was burned after his death.

KENNEDY, ROBERT [Canedy]. Co. E. Pennsylvania. At San Cristóbal Feb. 4; at Santiago Apr. 25–28; released from Puebla June 13; left Vera Cruz Aug. 12.

KENNEDY, WM. H. Nineteen years old. Charleston, S. C. Pvt., Co. C. At San Cristóbal Feb. 4; at Santiago Apr. 25–28; at Puebla Apr. 29; released from Puebla June 13; left Vera Cruz Aug. 12.

KENNEYMORE, J. C. P. [Kennigmore, Kennymore; J. C. F., J. P. C.]. Pvt., artillery, McLeod party. At Santiago Apr. 25–28; released from Puebla June 13; left Vera Cruz Aug. 12. A Mason. He had been captain of Co. B, First Texas Infantry, in November, 1839.

KENYON, JOHN. Ireland. Missing from Camp Resolution Aug. 30, 1841.

KETHS, C. R. Co. D. (*Gazette* list of 1842.)

KILLETT or KISSELL (illegible). Pvt., Co. D. Left Vera Cruz Aug. 12. (Grover's list.)

KINSEY, HENRY M. [Kensie; L. C.]. Pennsylvania. Born in Philadelphia; left Jan. 20, 1841, for New Orleans; to Texas Apr. 9; went to Santa Fé to see the country, and intended to go home via St. Louis. He referred to James Buchanan, senator from Pennsylvania, and others, in a letter written Apr. 29 to Waddy Thompson. Pvt., ordnance sgt., Co. E. At San Cristóbal Feb. 4; at Santiago Apr. 25–28; at Puebla Apr. 29; released from Puebla June 13; left Vera Cruz Aug. 12.

KLEIN. Germany. Missing from Camp Resolution Aug. 30, 1841.

KORDELL, B. Mexican list shows him released from Santiago June 14. (Probably identifiable with some other name, but not yet placed.)

KUYKENDALL, HENRY A. [Hackendall, Key Kendall, Kuckenthal]. (Usually pronounced kirk-en-dawl within the compiler's knowledge.) London; lived in Houston. Pvt., Co. C. At Mexico City Jan. 1; at Santiago Feb. 28; released from Santiago June 14; left Vera Cruz Aug. 12. A Mason. (Hanks Kuykendall, Tennessee and Fort Bend, Tex., fought in the Mier Expedition.)

LAMB, JAMES. English. Co. A. At San Cristóbal Feb. 4; at Santiago Apr. 25–28.

LANDES, DAVID [Landers, Landis]. Ohio. A merchant; no military duty (but listed by *Gazette* as with the artillery). At San Cristóbal Feb. 4; at Santiago Apr. 25–28; certified by McLeod at Perote Apr. 30.

LANDERS, WM. Of V. (Vermont?). Merchant. McLeod party. Died at Vera Cruz. (This may have been the same man as David Landes.)

LARDNER, NICOLAS. [Laddner]. Switzerland. Co. C. San Cristóbal Feb. 4; at Santiago Apr. 25–28; at Perote May 12; Swiss consul asked release.

LARRABEE, JAMES B. A volunteer or servant. Died in a cart at Saucillo, and the Mexican Commander asked Dr. Whitaker to certify that he was "dead enough to bury." An interesting story about him is told in *The Southwestern Historical Quarterly*, Vol. IX, No. 3 (January, 1906),149–50.

LAUGHLIN. On several lists, but probably same as McLaughlin.

LEE, NELSON. Started on the expedition but became ill and returned. (Lee, *Three Years Among the Camanches*, 31.)

LEMON, JOHN [Lennon]. Pennsylvania. Carpenter. At San Cristóbal Feb. 4; at Santiago Apr. 25–28.

LEWIS, JOHN E. Ireland; New York. Co. A or artillery. At Mexico City Jan. 1; at Santiago Feb. 28; sick in Mexico City June 1; released from Santiago June 14 but remained in hospital until after Aug. 12. A Mason.

LEWIS, WILLIAM P. Pennsylvania. A "Lt. Lewis, a young man," is mentioned by Howard in 1839 (see DeShields, *Border Wars of Texas*, 306). There is little question that he betrayed the expedition to Armijo for the privilege of importing goods without paying duty. He had lived in Santa Fé and Chihuahua and left the latter city in 1835 with Samuel Howland to join the Texas Revolution. He was a Mason and Cooke knew him well, and this factor played a prominent part in the betrayal. He was damned by Kendall, Lubbock, Grover, Brenham, Cooke, and others. When last heard from he was on the way to Valparaíso, Chile. He was expelled from the Masonic lodge in 1842.

LEWISTON, JOSEPH [Levenston; C.]. Germany. Pvt., Co. B. At San Cristóbal Feb. 4; at Santiago Apr. 25–28; released from Puebla June 13; left Vera Cruz Aug. 12.

LIDDY, PATRICK. Of Clare County, Ireland. Pvt., Co. C. At Mexico City Jan. 1; at Santiago Feb. 28; released from Santiago June 14; left Vera Cruz Aug. 12.

LILLIE, G. [Lilly, Lily]. German. Co. C. At San Cristóbal Feb. 4; at Santiago Apr. 25–28.

LINDLEY, JACOB [Lindsey]. Assumed name of Jacob Hammett.

LITTLE, ROBERT P. [Robert B.]. English. Co. A. At San Cristóbal Feb. 4; at Santiago Apr. 25–28; released from Puebla June 13; left Vera Cruz Aug. 12. On Aug. 3, 1841, he was court-martialed for contumacy, general disobedience of orders, and refusal to observe silence; pleaded not guilty; sentenced to loss of pay for two months, fatigue duty, and to deprivation of his horse.

LOCKHART, DAVID. Pennsylvania. Pvt., Co. A. At San Cristóbal

Feb. 4; at San Lázaro Feb. 10; at Santiago Apr. 25–28; released from Santiago June 14; left Vera Cruz Aug. 12.

LOCKRIDGE, E. B. Louisiana. A lawyer; formerly of means. Shot and killed himself on Little River June 25, 1841, either accidentally or purposefully.

LONG, F. Remained at Vera Cruz Aug. 12. (Grover's list.)

LONGCOPE, CHARLES L. [Longcape]. New York. Pvt., Co. C. At San Cristóbal Feb. 4; at Santiago Apr. 25–28; released from Puebla June 13; left Vera Cruz Aug. 12.

LOVEY, F. 3rd Sgt. (Lubbock-Tardif list.)

LOWTER, RALPH. Artillery. (*Gazette* list of 1842.)

LUBBOCK, THOMAS S. Twenty-four years old. Born in South Carolina; lived in Houston. 1st Lieut., Co. C. Reached Santiago Dec. 26, 1841; escaped from Santiago with Mazur Jan. 21, 1842; left Vera Cruz Mar. 15; reached New Orleans before May 21. In 1842 he wrote a long account of the expedition, which was published in the *Colorado Gazette and Advertiser* at Matagorda, Tex., June 4, 1842. Kendall quotes part of this account in his *Narrative*. After Kendall's death the original report was burned with Kendall's papers. Took part in the Mier fighting. A Mason; brother of a future governor of Texas. Died as a Confederate officer Jan. 23, 1863, probably in Kentucky.

LYONS, PATRICK [Lyon]. Of Limerick County, Ireland; lived in San Antonio. 2nd Sgt., Co. A. At Mexico City Jan. 1; at Santiago Feb. 28; left Vera Cruz Aug. 12. (Patrick Lyons, of Ireland, home at Milam, Tex., was in the Mier Expedition and was shot down at Salado Feb. 11, 1843.)

MABEE, WILLIAM [Mabee, Maby, Maybee, Maybury, Mayby]. New Hampshire. Co. E. Killed by Kiowas at Camp Resolution Aug. 30, 1841.

MABRY, JAMES L. [Mabery, Maybury]. North Carolina or New York. Pvt., artillery. At Mexico City Jan. 1; at Santiago Feb. 28; helped Grover edit *The True Blue*; released June 14 (from Santiago, presumably); left Vera Cruz Aug. 12. He had been a roommate of L. C. Blake; Lewis had invited him to go with the expedition. Soon after his release, Mabry was lost on the Texan war schooner *San Antonio*.

MANUEL. A servant from Béxar. Went with the Sutton-Cooke party and then with Kendall and the Van Ness party; sent back to Cooke to warn of possible danger; shot by a Mexican drummer Oct. 9, 1841, or soon afterward—Kendall says "wantonly."

MARDILLE. French. Released from Santiago Apr. 28. (Grover's list. This may be Maryatte.)

MARGUERAT, L. F. [Margaret, Marguret; D. F.]. He lived at Austin. 1st Sgt., artillery. At Santiago Apr. 25–28. He carried from Austin a certificate authorizing him to establish a Masonic lodge in Santa Fé.

MARYATTE, CHARLES [Mariette, Marryate, Mayatte]. Co. A. At Mexico City Jan. 1; at Santiago Feb. 28; released from Santiago Apr. 28. (On Dec. 31, 1841, the Commandant at Santiago was ordered to present Charles Mariette de Wandille, a Texan prisoner, to the Minister of War. Bancroft Papers, 519; Brief, 14. This leads to the conclusion that Mardille, shown above, is identical with Maryatte.)

MATÍAS. Servant of Major Howard. Sent to guide Mexican traders to Camp Resolution to transmit orders from Cooke; quartered with Burgess at the Baca ranch near San Miguel, but not mentioned again.

MAZUR, LOUIS [Mazre, Mazieur]. France; home in San Antonio. Co. B. At Mexico City Jan. 1; escaped from Santiago Jan. 21 with Lubbock.

MC ALLISTER, JOHN D. Tennessee. A volunteer in artillery. Shot on the *Jornada* Oct. 24, 1841. His sister married a son of Chief Justice Marshall.

MCCLANAHAN, JOHN. [McClannahan]. Kentucky. Pvt., Co. D. He saw Hull and his party killed. At Mexico City Jan. 1; at Santiago Feb. 28; released from Santiago June 14; left Vera Cruz Aug. 12.

MC DONALD, JOHN [MacDonald]. English. Pvt., Co. B. At San Cristóbal Feb. 9; at Santiago Apr. 25–28; left Vera Cruz Aug. 12.

MC ELYEA, J. B. [Edyron, McElge, McEly, McElyra, McIlyea].
Kentucky. Co. E. At San Cristóbal Feb. 4; at Santiago Apr.
25–28; left Vera Cruz Aug. 12. (The Mexican list shows
M. C. Macyer released from Puebla June 13.)

MC GUIRE, THOMAS [Maguire]. Pennsylvania. Pvt., Co. A. At
San Cristóbal Feb. 4; at San Lázaro Feb. 10; at Santiago
Mar. 13; released from Santiago June 14; left Vera Cruz
Aug. 12.

MC JUNKINS, WILLIAM H. [McJenkins]. Native of Laurens, S.
C. Pvt., Co. C. At Santiago Apr. 25–28, according to the
Doran list; in the *Acordada* in April "with twenty-two other
Texans," only two of which (Navarro and one still unidentified) were Pioneers; left Vera Cruz Aug. 12. He and H. B.
Sutton had lived together in Texas. This offers a possible
test of Doran's list. Kendall says that two men escaped Jan.
28, were recaptured and taken to the *Acordada;* we have
the names of other Texan prisoners in the *Acordada,* but
they were not Pioneers. McJunkins wrote a letter to Thompson from the *Acordada,* dated only "April, 1842." This is a
long span of time. However, these two (McJunkins and
his partner) might have evaded capture for a long time,
or they might have gone to the *Acordada* by stages. Also,
Kendall, writing a year later, may be inserting as contemporary news, events which occurred later or about which
he learned later—which he often does without regard for
chronology. (He tells of the escape and subsequent imprisonment in the *Acordada* in the *Narrative,* II, 193.)

MC KAINE, WM. [McCain, McKain]. From Ohio. A teamster
in Co. B. At San Cristóbal Feb. 4; at Santiago Apr. 25–28;
released from Puebla June 13.

MC KEAN, Pvt., Co. A. Left Vera Cruz Aug. 12 (Grover's list.)
(Probably McKaine.)

MCKENNON, M. [McKenan, McKinnon, McKinow; W.] North
Carolina. Pvt., Co. D. At San Cristóbal Feb. 4; at Santiago
Apr. 25–28; released from Puebla June 13; left Vera Cruz
Aug. 12.

MCLAUGHLIN, JOHN [Laughlin]. Ireland. Died Sept. 25, 1841, on the way across the Llano with McLeod. (Loughlin, Co. A, Folsom's list, probably is the same man, although he is not starred as dead.)

MCLEOD, HUGH. Twenty-seven years old. Born in New York City. Graduated from United States Military Academy. Went to Texas 1836; studied and practiced law; was in several Indian fights, including the Council House Fight. Brigadier general, commander of the military section of the Pioneers. Surrendered to Colonel Archuleta Oct. 5, 1841; he told Armijo that Archuleta had his records. Reached San Cristóbal Feb. 4; to Puebla Feb. 9 (Kendall, *Narrative*); to Perote Feb. 18 (Gallegher-Hoyle *Journal*). These two dates are important because they are the only ones that mark the general movement of prisoners to those two prisons; it seems that 123 or 126 of the McLeod party went almost at once from San Cristóbal to Puebla, and that of that number, 52 went on to Perote. McLeod was at Perote Apr. 30. Among the documents at hand there is no record of his release. During the Mexican War he was Adjutant General of Texas; during the Civil War he became a Colonel in the Confederate forces, and died in camp Jan. 3, 1862. A Mason. He married a cousin of Lamar in 1842. Her maiden name was Rebecca Lamar.

MCMILLEN, JOHN [MacMillen]. Kentucky. Corp., Co. A. At Mexico City Jan. 1; at Santiago Feb. 28; released from Santiago June 14; left Vera Cruz Aug. 12.

MCNABB, JOHN [McKnabb]. English. Artillery. At San Cristóbal Feb. 4; at Santiago Apr. 25–28; released from Puebla June 13; left Vera Cruz Aug. 12.

MCWILLIAM. Co. A (*Gazette* list of 1842.)

MEALY, C. [Maulg, Menly, Mewly, Mihly; G.]. Swiss. In Mexico City Jan. 1; at Santiago Feb. 28; released from Santiago June 14. The Swiss consul intervened. (The Mexican list shows E. Nalle released from Santiago June 14.)

MERCER. New York. Joined from the falls of the Brazos.

Wounded by Kiowas Sept. 12, 1841; speared in breast and twice in the back; died Sept. 18, 1841.

MET, J. C. The Mexican list says he was released from Santiago June 14; probably a duplicate listing, but not yet placed.

MIGGINS, C. D. Pvt. (Lubbock-Tardif list.)

MILLER, A. Of Württemberg, Germany. Carpenter, Co. E. At Mexico City Jan. 1; at Santiago Feb. 28; released from Santiago Apr. 28; given certificate of service Apr. 28.

MILLER, GEORGE D. Pennsylvania or Virginia; lived in Gonzales, Tex. Ordnance sgt., Co. B or D. At Mexico City Jan. 1; at Santiago Feb. 28; released from Santiago June 14; left Vera Cruz Aug. 12.

MILLER, JOHN M. [H.]. Co. E. Released from Santiago, June 14. (H. Miller is in the *Gazette,* Payroll, and Lubbock-Tardif lists.)

MIMMS, DIGNID. [Mimmis, Mimons, Mims; Dignis, Wm.]. Twenty-four years old. Hair and complexion fair, eyes blue, nose sharp, large forehead with temples, height five feet, six inches; by occupation a printer. Pennsylvania or Virginia. 2nd Corp., artillery. At San Cristóbal Feb. 4; at Santiago Apr. 25–28; released from Puebla June 13, but asked to remain in Mexico and did not leave Vera Cruz Aug. 12. This must be the man mentioned on p. 88 of Copeland, *Kendall of the Picayune,* as telling the story of Morris, a "brother typo" who was troubled with rheumatism and was saved from Salazar's bullets when Kendall bought a ride for him on the *Jornada.* The story was printed in a Louisiana newspaper after Kendall's death, and on the side of the clipping is written: "Mr. Mims of this city says." It appears that the three printers, Kendall, Morris, and Mimms, became well acquainted, for Morris later visited Kendall at his ranch. On p. 289 of *Kendall of the Picayune,* the "brother typo" is further identified from Kendall's diary as G. W. Morris.

MITCHELL, A. S. 2nd Sgt., Co. E. At Santiago Apr. 25–28; left Vera Cruz Aug. 12.

MITCHELL, WM. North Carolina. Died on the road across the prairie in October, 1841. (This probably is Mitchell of Co. A in the *Gazette* list of 1842.)

MOFFITT, SPENCER [Moffatt]. Co. E. Tennessee. At San Cristóbal Feb. 4; at Santiago Apr. 25–28; released from Puebla June 13; left Vera Cruz Aug. 12. He was court-martialed for mutinous conduct and gross disobedience of orders Aug. 1, 1841; pay stopped one month, fatigue duty two months; sentence remitted.

MODOS, M. Mexican list says he was released from Santiago June 14; probably a duplication, although not yet identified.

MOORE, J. W. [S.]. Ohio. Pvt., Co. C. At San Cristóbal Feb. 4; at Santiago Apr. 25–28; left Vera Cruz Aug. 12. Court-martialed for fighting and disorderly conduct Aug. 17, 1841. The fighting probably was with Watkins who received the same punishment: fatigue duty and loss of two months' pay.

MORE, KENNEDY. Georgia. At San Cristóbal Feb. 4. (*Senate Doc. No. 325.*)

MORGAN, JOHN D. London. Pvt., artillery. At Mexico City Jan. 1; at Santiago Feb. 28; released from Santiago June 14; left Vera Cruz Aug. 12. (John Morgan, English, living at Bastrop, Tex., was captured on the Mier Expedition and later escaped from Mexico City. Green, *Mier Expedition,* 440, 446.)

MORLEY. Co. C. (*Gazette* list of 1842.)

MORRIS, GEORGE W. 1st Corp., artillery. At Santiago Apr. 25–28; given a certificate of service; left Vera Cruz Aug. 12. (This is the printer who, Mimms said after Kendall's death, was saved by Kendall.)

MORRIS, ISAAC. Georgia. Co. B. In San Cristóbal Feb. 4.

MORTON, JS. W. Irish. Artillery. At Mexico City Dec. 30.

MUNSON, IRA. New York; lived in Austin. 2nd Lieut., artillery. At Mexico City Jan. 1; at Santiago Feb. 28; released from Santiago June 14. A Mason.

MURPHY, DANL. Irish. Pvt., Co. C. At Mexico City Dec. 30,

[241]

1841; at Santiago Feb. 28; released from Santiago June 14; left Vera Cruz Aug. 12.

NAUGHTON, J. W. Ireland; Houston, Tex. 2nd Sgt., artillery. Sutton-Cooke party. (Grover, Grand Reference Sheet.) This may be the Sam Nanten or Nauten given in the Mexican list as having been released from Santiago June 14.

NAVARRO, JOSÉ ANTONIO. Forty-six years old. Born in Béxar (San Antonio) 1795. Had a wife and seven children. He took part in the revolt against Spain, and later signed the Texan Declaration of Independence. One of the civil commissioners to Santa Fé. His punishment was most severe; there is a suggestion that Santa Anna especially disliked Navarro because Navarro had discouraged Santa Anna's attentions to his sister because of Santa Anna's record as a forger. Whatever the reason, his feeling toward Navarro was recognized early, for several reports mention that at the surrender of McLeod, specific guarantees were made of Navarro's life. He was very lame and often could not even ride horseback, but he stayed with the McLeod party until Jan. 31, near Cuautitlán; to San Lázaro; to the *Acordada,* where Kendall saw him Apr. 27. He had been robbed of money and clothing, and was unshaved, pale and haggard, with hair long and uncombed and clothes ragged and soiled. Kendall gave him money. Santa Anna demanded that Navarro be tried for high treason; he was sentenced to death, but on review by a high court the sentence was commuted to ten years' imprisonment at San Juan de Ulúa, on an island in Vera Cruz harbor. Santa Anna was intensely displeased. Van Ness visited him on Feb. 1, 1844, and found Navarro afraid to leave his small "apartment" for fear of the commission of sodomy against him by the depraved criminals among whom he was confined. He had broken his leg as a child, and it had always been periodically infected, and on the trip was inflamed with cold. Navarro had been elected senator from Monclova, a city or other geographical division in what is now Coahuila, in 1835 or 1836 (Bolton, *Guide,* 322). His sentence at Ulúa was solitary confinement but was not enforced, although, as noted, the conditions were such that solitary confinement was self-imposed. Jan. 27, 1845, the President gave an order for his release, but he had already been paroled and allowed in Vera Cruz, and it was found he had escaped. He arrived in New Orleans by Mar. 3, 1845. He had four sons in the Confederate Army; died in 1871. He was a Roman Catholic and a Mason.

NEIL, A. [Neal]. Co. E. Wagonmaster and gunsmith. McLeod party. Left in Paso del Norte because of illness.

NELDES, S. G. The Mexican list says he was released from Santiago June 14; probably a duplication of some name in this list, but not yet identified.

NEWMAN, P. Co. A. Left at San Luis Potosí; arrived at Santiago about Feb. 25; released from Santiago June 14; remained at Vera Cruz Aug. 12.

NORRIS, J. Pvt., Co. B. Left in Guanajuato; arrived at Santiago Apr. 25; released from Santiago June 14; left Vera Cruz Aug. 12.

NORTON, JAS. W. Kilkenny, Ireland. Sgt., artillery. At Mexico City Jan. 1; at Santiago Feb. 28; released from Santiago June 14; left Vera Cruz Aug. 12.

O'CONNOR, JOHN [J. O. Conner]. Nineteen years old [or 36]. Hair and complexion fair, eyes blue, nose long with a scar on the right side, broad forehead with temples, height five feet, three inches; a laborer. Ireland. Co. D. At San Cristóbal Feb. 4; at Santiago Apr. 25–28; released from Puebla June 13, but remained there Aug. 12; he had asked permission to stay in Mexico.

OSTRANDER, V. 2nd Lieut., Co. C. At San Cristóbal Feb. 4; to Puebla Feb. 9; at Puebla Apr. 27; released from Puebla June 13. (The *Gazette* of Jan. 5, 1842, lists Oshander, Co. C. The Lubbock-Tardif list gives the first name as Volney.)

[243]

OWENS, B. W. [Owen]. Pennsylvania. Pvt., Co. E. Teamster. McLeod party. At San Cristóbal Feb. 4; at San Lázaro Feb. 10; at Santiago Mar. 10; left Vera Cruz Aug. 12.

PALMER, D. D. [Palmers]. Virginia. Co. D. Saw Hull killed Aug. 30, 1841. At San Cristóbal Feb. 4; at San Lázaro Feb. 10; released from Santiago June 14; left Vera Cruz Aug. 12.

PALMER, WM. [Walker]. Massachusetts. Pvt., Co. B. At San Cristóbal Feb. 4; at Santiago Apr. 25–28; left Vera Cruz Aug. 12.

PARKER, MILTON [J. M.]. Georgia. Teamster, quartermaster's department. At San Cristóbal Feb. 4; at Santiago Apr. 25–28; released from Puebla June 13; left Vera Cruz Aug. 12.

PAYNE, LEVI [Paine]. Tennessee. Pvt., Co. A or artillery. At Mexico City Jan. 1; at Santiago Feb. 28; released from Santiago June 14; left Vera Cruz Aug. 12.

PERKINS, F. R. [F. K.]. Tennessee. Co. E. At San Cristóbal Feb. 4; at Santiago Apr. 25–28; released from Puebla June 13; left Vera Cruz Aug. 12.

PHILLIPS, ROBERT D. [R. J.]. Sixteen years old. Hair and complexion chestnut, eyes olive-colored, nose regular, no beard, many freckles on his face, small forehead, height five feet. New York. 1st Corp., Co. C or D. Saw Hull killed Aug. 30, 1841. At San Cristóbal Feb. 4; at Santiago Apr. 25–28; at Puebla by Apr. 29; released from Puebla June 13, but asked to remain in Mexico and stayed at Puebla Aug. 12.

PHILPOT, J. Co. E (*Gazette* list of 1842.)

PIENT. Co. A. (*Gazette* list of 1842.)

PINDER, DANIEL [Pindar; B.]. English. Artillery. At San Cristóbal Feb. 4; at San Lázaro Feb. 10; released from Santiago June 14; remained in hospital at Vera Cruz Aug. 12.

PISARZEWSKI, ALPHONSE. [Pisarski, Pisowisky]. Musician. Court-martialed Aug. 25, 1841, for selling a sword, but acquitted. Musician Willis was found guilty of selling the sword. At San Cristóbal Feb. 7; at San Lázaro Feb. 10; at Santiago Apr. 25–28; remained in Mexico City Aug. 12, presumably ill.

PITTS, J. G. [Pitt; J. T., R.]. English. Pvt., Co. D. At San Cristóbal Feb. 4; at Santiago Apr. 25–28; released from Puebla June 13; left Vera Cruz Aug. 12.

PLASMANN, FREDERICK [Plasman]. Prussian by birth but naturalized in the United States, and lived at Columbus, Ga.; had been in Texas four months; naturalization papers in Russell County, Alabama. Co. B. At Mexico City Dec. 30, 1841; at Santiago Feb. 28; released at Mexico City Apr. 25.

QUINLAN, JOHN [Quinham, Quinlen, Quinlin]. Seventeen years old. New York City. Corp., Co. C. At San Cristóbal Feb. 4; at Santiago Apr. 25–28; at Puebla Apr. 29; released from Puebla June 13; left Vera Cruz Aug. 12.

RAEZER, WESTLUS. Eighteen years old. Virginia. At Puebla Apr. 29. (This is a name that appears in no other place, and yet he signed a letter to Waddy Thompson saying that he had joined the expedition and asking for the protection of the United States.)

RAHM, JOHN [Rahn]. Switzerland. At Mexico City Jan. 1; at Santiago Feb. 28; released from Santiago June 14. The Swiss consul attempted to intervene May 12.

RALPH, SAMUEL. Wedford (Ireland?); living at Trinity, Tex. Pvt., Co. B or C. At Mexico City Jan. 1; at Santiago Feb. 28; released from Santiago June 14; left Vera Cruz Aug. 12.

RAMÓN. Mexican. Killed and scalped by Kiowas Sept. 4, 1841.

RATS, JACOB. Co. D. McLeod party. Released from Puebla June 13.

REACH, T. [Roach, Roche, Rosch]. Blacksmith, Co. A. McLeod party. At San Cristóbal Feb. 4; at Santiago Apr. 25–28.

ROBERTSON, THOMPSON [Robinson; Howard T.]. English. Merchant. At San Cristóbal Feb. 4; at San Lázaro Feb. 10; at Santiago Feb. 25; released from Santiago Apr. 27; left Vera Cruz May 12.

ROCHE. See Reach.

RODNEY (partly illegible). Co. D. McLeod party. Grand Reference Sheet.)

ROGER, WESLEY [Rager, Ragun]. Virginia. Teamster, Co. B.

At San Cristóbal Feb. 4; at Santiago Apr. 25–28; released from Puebla June 13.

ROGERS, JOSEPH H. [Rodgers]. Tennessee. Wagonmaster, quartermaster's staff. At Mexico City Jan. 1; at Santiago Feb. 28; released from Santiago June 14. One issue of *The True Blue* announces that the subject for the fourth in Rogers' series of lectures will be "The State of Morality That at Present Exists Among the Men. 1. Moral. 2. Pretending to but not following morality. 3. Neither pretending to nor following it." A more compelling subject must have been "The Physical Formation of the Ears of Fannie's Puppies," at which *The True Blue* promised "a wet nurse will be in attendance to see that none [illegible]." He left Vera Cruz Aug. 12.

ROSENBERRY, WM. [Rosenberg]. Maryland. Artillery. One of the three men sent in advance Aug. 11, 1841. Captured and sent to Santa Fé; escaped and was killed resisting capture about September 16, 1841.

ROUSETTE, ADOLF [Rosette, Rousete, Rozet]. Louisiana, Teamster, Co. A. (Also listed as a servant.) At San Cristóbal Feb. 4; released from Puebla June 13. Remained in Mexico Aug. 12, presumably ill.

RUDGE, FRED. Gloucestershire, England. Co. A. At Mexico City Jan. 1; at Santiago Feb. 28; given certificate of service Apr. 28; released from Santiago June 14; remained in Mexico City Aug. 12 with Coyle, to go to the Pacific Coast.

SACSTEE, GEO. Mexican list; probably a duplication, but not identified so far.

SCARBOROUGH, PAUL D. [Scarbrough, Seartranel]. North Carolina. Corp. (?), Co. D. At Mexico City Jan. 1; at Santiago Feb. 28; released from Santiago June 14; left Vera Cruz Aug. 12.

SCOTT, ROBERT. Guest or amateur. At San Cristóbal Feb. 4.

SEVEY, THEODORE [Seavey]. Maine. Adjutant. At Mexico City Jan. 1; at Santiago Feb. 28; released from Santiago June 14; died of yellow fever at Puente Nacional Aug. 30. He refused to profess the Roman Catholic religion, and Thompson says his friends paid a priest $150 to secure his burial in a cemetery. (*Recollections*, 215.)

SHAW, J. D. At Santiago Apr. 25–28.

SHAW, J. G. F. [J. D. F., J. T. F.]. Alabama. Co. E. Died in January at Tula. (Unless Doran's list is in error, this is another Shaw.)

SHELDON, S. B. [A B., L. B., S. D., S. E.]. Mississippi. A trader with a mule, Co. D. At Mexico City Jan. 1; at Santiago Feb. 28; released from Santiago Apr. 28; given certificate of service Apr. 28; left Vera Cruz May 12.

SHORT, WARD. Left at San Luis Potosí; arrived at Santiago about Feb. 25. (Grover's list.)

SMITH, DANIEL B. Rhode Island. Musician. At San Cristóbal Feb. 4; at Santiago Apr. 25–28; left Vera Cruz Aug. 12.

SMITH, J. At Santiago Apr. 25–28. (Doran's list; appears immediately under Daniel B. Smith.)

SMITH, RISDEN. Co. B. (*Gazette* list of 1842 and the roster of Co. B of Oct., 1841.)

SNIVELY, DAVID H. Ohio. Had some merchandise. Released Apr. 21; left Vera Cruz May 12. (Not the same man as Jacob Snively; see the *Cumulative Index* of *The Southwestern Historical Quarterly*.)

SNIVELY, JACOB. Thirty-two years old. Maryland (*Senate Doc. No. 325*), or Pennsylvania (*The Handbook of Texas*); home in Nacogdoches. Surveyor, engineer, colonist. To Puebla Feb. 9; released from Puebla Apr. 21–28. He is the man who led the ill-starred Snively Expedition to raid Mexican shipping on the Santa Fé trail in 1843. Killed by Apaches in Arizona in 1871, but not buried until 1878.

SNOW, JOHN C. [S. C.]. Tennessee. Of Strain's Co. E. Accidentally shot in May, 1841, by a sentinel. He was "a brave man, and one who had fought for his country, when she needed the aid of every son," McLeod said in General Order No. 3, dated June 3, 1841. The implication is that he fought in the Texas Revolution.

SOWTER, RALPH. Artillery. McLeod party. (Grover's list. This name is partly illegible, but is distinct from that of Strouther, being separated from it by only one name.)

SPOONER, THOS. H. [J. F., L. H.]. Virginia. Joined at the falls of the Brazos "to attack an Indian village." At San Cristóbal Feb. 4; at Santiago Apr. 25–28; at Perote May 1; died in June at Vera Cruz. He says the expected reinforcements from the Brazos did not arrive.

STEGEE, WM. [Steger]. Mississippi. Co. A. At Mexico City Jan. 1; at Santiago Feb. 28; released from Santiago June 14.

STICKNEY, CHRISTIAN R. [Stickey, Stuckey, Stuke, Stukey]. Switzerland. Artillery. At San Cristóbal Feb. 4; at Santiago Apr. 25–28; released from Puebla June 13; the Swiss consul tried to intervene May 12. (This name gave a great deal of trouble, and probably is listed incorrectly, but a person of similar name undoubtedly was with the Pioneers.)

STOKES, FREDERIC. London. 3rd Sgt., Co. C. At Mexico City Jan. 1; at Santiago Feb. 28; released from Santiago Apr. 28; given certificate of service Apr. 28; left Vera Cruz May 12.

STORY, ALONZO [Storey]. New York. Pvt., Co. A. At Mexico City Jan. 1; at Santiago Feb. 28; released from Santiago June 14; left Vera Cruz Aug. 12. (*Gazette* of Jan. 5, 1842, lists Stoney, Co. A.)

STOSOASES, THOS. Escaped from hospital at Puebla Apr. 5. (This name so far is not otherwise identifiable. A Mexican report says that this man and Radulfo Studion, "Texan prisoners," escaped. These are obviously Mexican spellings of names difficult for them. The compiler likewise has been unable to identify them with any of the Mier prisoners.)

STRAIN, G. H. [J. H.]. Eastern Tennessee. Capt., Co. E. At San Cristóbal Feb. 4; to Perote Feb. 18. He had gone to visit in Texas in February, 1840, was ill for eleven months, and loaned money which he could not collect; he wanted to travel for his health and to see the country; he "was unanimously elected Capt. by my company without seeking for that office, or even desiring it."

STREET, CHARLES. Left at Guanajuato; arrived at Santiago Apr. 25. (Grover's list.)

STROUD, CHARLES. English. Pvt., Co. B. At Santiago Apr. 25–28; released from Santiago June 14; left Vera Cruz Aug. 12. (B. Strount, Mexican list, released from Puebla June 14.)

STROUTHER, JAMES [Enonder, Strosher, Strother; J. S.]. Artillery. At San Cristóbal Feb. 4; at Santiago Apr. 25–28; released from Santiago June 14.

STUDION, RADULFO. Escaped from hospital at Puebla Apr. 5. (Another Mexican spelling difficult to place; see Stosoases.)

STUMP, JOHN S. Pvt., Co. D. Left in Guanajuato; arrived at Santiago Apr. 25; released from Santiago June 14; left Vera Cruz Aug. 12. Kendall says that on the *Jornada* Stump was carried in the sick cart until McAllister was shot; then he immediately became the best walker in the outfit and led the column.

STURGES. Pvt., Co. A. Left Vera Cruz Aug. 12. (This could hardly be Sturgess, for he died at Camp Resolution.)

STURGESS, BENJAMIN B. [Sturgis]. Georgia. Major; paymaster. Died of consumption at Camp Resolution Sept. 10, 1841.

SUARES, D. W. [Sonres, Suaress, Suaris, Swarens; D. M., Guillermo]. South Carolina. Pvt., artillery; interpreter. At San Cristóbal Feb. 4; at Santiago Apr. 25–28; at Puebla by Apr. 27; released from Puebla June 13; left Vera Cruz Aug. 12.

SULLY, THEODORICK A. [C. A., P. A.]. Florida; San Antonio. A merchant; "young Sully spoke Spanish and was an interpreter." At Mexico City Jan. 1; at Santiago Feb. 28; released from Santiago Apr. 21; left Vera Cruz May 12.

SUTHERLAND, J. Mexican list; released from Santiago June 14.

SUTTON, H. B. or H. P. New York. At San Cristóbal Feb. 4; at Santiago Apr. 25–28; at Puebla May 3; released from Puebla June 13. He had arrived in Texas Apr. 8, 1841, from Mobile; had left May 28 for Santa Fé to take some provisions to a friend who lived there (Santa Fé?) and joined the expedition. Was compelled to join Co. C, but expected to be discharged in Santa Fé and to return via St. Louis. He was court-martialed Aug. 11, 1841, for lying down and sleeping on post; pleaded guilty; sentenced to wear ball and chain for one month, to give up his horse, and to serve on permanent fatigue and police duty; McLeod said "the sentence is too mild for the offense"; the ball-and-chain part was remitted; the rest was ordered to be carried out. In May, 1842, he said McJunkins could vouch for him, but apparently he is not the one who escaped with McJunkins. Sutton—as did most of those trying to get released—said he was not a Texas citizen. He wrote: "I have know earthly Claim in Texas."

SUTTON, JOHN S. Twenty years old. Born in New Castle, Del.; appointed to West Point; went to Texas in 1840 and lived at Austin or San Antonio. Capt., Co. A; senior captain of the expedition. At Mexico City Jan. 1; at Santiago Feb. 28; released from Santiago June 14, but remained at Jalapa, presumably ill, Aug. 12. In the Mier Expedition; fought Indians during Mexican War; went to California; returned to Port Lavaca; Lieut. Col. in Confederate Army, wounded fatally at Battle of Val Verde in 1862.

SWEED, JAS. Co. A. Released from Santiago June 14.

SWEEZY, JOHN [Sweeney, Sweesy; W.]. Ohio. Pvt., Co. C. At San Cristóbal Feb. 4; at San Lázaro Feb. 10; at Santiago Apr. 25–28; left Vera Cruz Aug. 12.

TALK, JOHN. New York. Pvt., artillery. At Mexico City Jan. 1; at Santiago Feb. 28; released from Santiago June 14; left Vera Cruz Aug. 12. Helped Grover edit *The True Blue* at Santiago.

TANLER, D. J. Mexican list; released from Santiago June 14. The compiler tried to combine this with Towler, but two Tanler's are given in the same list.

TANLER, JAS. Mexican list; released from Santiago June 14.

TARDIF, JOHN [Tarcliff, Tardy]. English. Co. C. At San Cristóbal Feb. 4; at Santiago Apr. 25–28; released from Puebla June 13.

THICKSTONE, LOUIS [Pickstun, Shickston, Thickston, Thickstun, Thrickstone; Lewis]. He said he was a citizen of Indiana; listed from New York or Independence. Co. B. At

Mexico City Jan. 1; at Santiago Feb. 28; released from Santiago June 14; left Vera Cruz Aug. 12. He had been in Texas as a traveler and had a few goods.

THOMAS, DANIEL. Mississippi. Co. D. At Santiago Apr. 25–28; certified by McLeod at Perote May 1.

THOMAS, JOHN [Tomam; J. S.]. Co. B. At San Cristóbal Feb. 4; released from Santiago June 14, but still in the hospital there July 7.

THOMPKINS, JOHN [W.]. Illinois; Victoria, Tex. A saddler with merchandise. At Mexico City Jan. 1; at Santiago Feb. 28; released from Santiago Apr. 28; given certificate of service Apr. 28; left Vera Cruz May 12. He was court-martialed Aug. 19, 1841, for lying down and sleeping on post; pleaded guilty; pay stopped for one month.

TODD, ROBERT C. Kentucky. Artillery. Missing on Sept. 4, 1841.

TOMPKINS, T. Artillery. (The listing in the *Gazette* of Jan. 5, 1842, makes it seem that T. Tompkins is not the same man as John Thompkins, about whom there was much confusion from the outset of this study. Most likely the court-martial should apply to Tompkins—and perhaps some of the other data, but the references are too confused for clarification at the present time.)

TORREY, THOS. J. [Thos. S.] Hartford, Conn. Merchant; intended to establish a regular business between the United States and Santa Fé. Hunted with Kendall in Texas before the expedition. At San Cristóbal Feb. 4; released from Puebla Apr. 21. (Jas. N. Torrey was executed at Salado. Green, *Mier Expedition*, 172, 444. This apparently is not the same man.) Thomas was a brother of John F. and David K. Torrey, and with them established the Torreys' trading houses on the Indian frontier of Texas.

TOWLER. English. At San Cristóbal Feb. 4. (*Senate Doc. No. 325.*) May be same as one of the Tanler's.

TRASKER, GEORGE L. Died Aug. 30 of smallpox at Vera Cruz. (Grover's list. Probably not a Pioneer.)

TROUTZ, C. [Proutz, Trouts]. Baden, Germany. Co. A. At Mexico City Jan. 1; at Santiago Feb. 28; released from Santiago Apr. 28; given certificate of service Apr. 28.

TUCKER, THOS. E. [C.]. New York. 1st Corp., Co. E. At Mexico City Jan. 1; at Santiago Feb. 28; released from Santiago June 14; left Vera Cruz Aug. 12.

TWEED, JAMES. Born in Ireland. Commissary sergeant, Co. A. A principal witness for the prosecution at the prisoners' kangaroo courts, at which he solemnly kissed a brickbat and testified against whoever was on trial; he taught them the "double compound action" at Puebla. (Kendall, *Narrative*, II, 295.) At San Cristóbal Feb. 4; at San Lázaro Feb. 10; moved from Santiago Feb. 14; returned Feb. 24; at Santiago Feb. 25; left Vera Cruz Aug. 12.

VAN NESS, GEORGE F. X. Nineteen years old. Talked Spanish. Born in Virginia; went to Texas in 1838; lived in San Antonio. Secretary of the civil commissioners to Santa Fé. Released from San Cristóbal Feb. 1. Was captured in San Antonio Sept. 11, 1842, by General Woll, along with Hancock and Fitzgerald; condemned to death, but sentence commuted to ten years' imprisonment. Released with Béxar prisoners from Perote Apr. 3, 1844. Kendall's letter to Falconer in 1856 says that Van Ness died at Eagle Pass, weighing three hundred pounds.

VASADO, JAS. At Mexico City Feb. 11. (Mexican list.)

WALDING, ELISHA [Walden, Waldon, Welling]. Seventeen years old. Listed from Alabama, but said he was from Warren County, Tenn. Co. E. At San Cristóbal Feb. 4; at Santiago Apr. 25–28; at Puebla Apr. 29; released from Puebla June 13; left Vera Cruz Aug. 12.

WALKER, J. L. Pennsylvania; lived in San Antonio. Ordnance Sgt. or 1st Sgt., Co. A. At Mexico City Jan. 1; at Santiago Feb. 28; released from Santiago June 14; left Vera Cruz Aug. 12.

WALKER, JOHN. Pennsylvania. Died at Belén hospital at Guanajuato, Feb. 4. (This name appears on the lists only at the time of his death.)

WALLACE, WM. Co. B. At Santiago Apr. 25–28. (Wm. A. Wallace, born in Virginia, home at Béxar, was in the Mier Expedition.)

WARD. Left at San Luis Potosí; arrived at Santiago about Feb. 25; remained at Vera Cruz Aug. 12.

WARD, D. S. Sgt., quartermaster's dept.; Co. E. At Santiago Apr. 25–28; released Santiago June 14; left Vera Cruz Aug. 12.

WARD, JAS. E. Born and raised in Chatham County, Ga.; went to Texas in December, 1840; joined the expedition for travel and profit. Corp., artillery or Co. A. At Mexico City Jan. 1; at Santiago Feb. 28; released from Santiago June 14; left Vera Cruz Aug. 12. (D. S. Ward was with the McLeod party; Jas. E. was with Sutton-Cooke. The third Ward remained at Vera Cruz Aug. 12.)

WARE, BEN. North Carolina. Corp., Co. A. At Mexico City Jan. 1; at Santiago Feb. 28; released from Santiago June 14; left Vera Cruz Aug. 12.

WARING, THOMAS [Warring]. Ireland. Pvt., artillery. At San Cristóbal Feb. 4; at Santiago Apr. 25–28; left Vera Cruz Aug. 12.

WATKINS, J. D. [Wadkins; J. T.]. Louisiana. Teamster; pvt., Co. C. At San Cristóbal Feb. 4; at Santiago Apr. 25–28; at Perote May 1; left Vera Cruz Aug. 12. He was court-martialed Aug. 17, 1841, for fighting and disorderly conduct; drew two months' pay stoppage and fatigue duty. (Probably fought with Moore.)

WEBSTER, J. English. Co. B. or E. At San Cristóbal Feb. 4; at Santiago Apr. 25–28.

WEEDER, JOHNSON [Weedes, Weever, Wilder]. Sgt., Co. B. At Santiago Apr. 25–28; remained at Vera Cruz, presumably ill, Aug. 12.

WESTGATE, E. C. or W. T. [Wescott]. Massachusetts. Joined as a volunteer to defend against the Indians. Pvt., Co. C. At San Cristóbal Feb. 4; at Santiago Apr. 25–28; at Perote May 2; left Vera Cruz Aug. 12. Court-martialed for gross neglect

[253]

of duty and being absent from post Sept. 5, 1841, at Camp Resolution; pleaded guilty; sentenced to stand cattle guard at that encampment and to fatigue duty for the rest of the march.

WHITAKER, FRANCIS Q. Surgeon. Pennsylvania. At Zacatecas Dec. 30, 1841, he knocked a sentinel sprawling into the mud for bawling *"¡Centinela alerta!"* every ten minutes and keeping the prisoners awake, but was not punished for it. At San Cristóbal Feb. 4; at San Lázaro Feb. 10; at Santiago Mar. 10; released from Santiago June 14, but died Aug. 29 at Puente Nacional of yellow fever. To secure a Christian burial he confessed to a Roman Catholic priest. (Thompson, *Recollections*, 215.)

WHITE, CHARLES. Louisiana. Co. B. At Mexico City Jan. 1; at Santiago Feb. 28; released from Santiago June 14, but remained at Vera Cruz Aug. 12. He was court-martialed Aug. 10, 1841, for disobedience of orders and conduct subversive of good order and military discipline, in refusing to help clear the road, spurring his horse and riding off; pleaded guilty; sentenced to fatigue duty all the way to Santa Fé.

WHITE, DANIEL. Louisiana. Pvt., Co. B [D]. At Mexico City Jan. 1; at Santiago Feb. 28; released from Santiago June 14; left Vera Cruz Aug. 12.

WILKINS, W. Virginia. Missing from camp Sept. 24, 1841, at Camp Resolution. Co. C.

WILLIS, CHAS. C. Musician, Co. C. New York. At San Cristóbal Feb. 4; at Santiago Apr. 25–28; released from Puebla June 13, but remained at Jalapa Aug. 12, probably ill. He was court-martialed Sept. 1, 1841, for selling a sword, public property, on the night of the fire (prairie fire?); convicted, but no record of sentence. Also court-martialed for theft of meat.

WINCHELL, JAMES H. Houston. A Mason. (Carter, *Masonry in Texas,* is the only authority for this name.)

WINKLER, WM. [Winklie]. Prussian. Co. A. At Mexico City

Jan. 1; at Santiago Feb. 28; released from Santiago Apr. 28; given certificate of service Apr. 28.

WOLF, C. Of Amsterdam. Co. A. At Mexico City Jan. 1; at Santiago Feb. 28; released from Santiago Apr. 28; given certificate of service Apr. 28.

WOODS, SAMUEL [Wood]. English. 3rd Corp., Co. B. At San Cristóbal Feb. 4; at Santiago Apr. 25–28.

WOODSON, FRANCIS B. [F. D., J. S., J. D.]. Georgia. Co. E. Killed Aug. 30, 1841, by Kiowas at Camp Resolution.

WOODWARD, JOHN. 1st. Sgt., Co. D [C]. At San Cristóbal Feb. 4; at Santiago Apr. 25–28; released from Puebla June 13; left Vera Cruz Aug. 12.

WRIGHT, JACOB. German. Co. D. At San Cristóbal Feb. 4; at Santiago Apr. 25–28.

WRINKLEY. Tennessee. At San Cristóbal Feb. 4. (*Senate Doc. No. 325.* This name was paired with "Winkler" until it was discovered Winkler was with Sutton-Cooke and this man with McLeod.)

YOUNG, WM. Ill at Silao Apr. 11; to Querétaro Apr. 23; released from Santiago June 14.

APPENDIX B

Transfers and Lists

(Page numbers of the Bancroft Papers refer to the compiler's microfilm copy; "Brief" refers to the compiler's reference brief on the expedition.)

June 23, 1841–362 men started; no enlisted men named. *Austin City Gazette;* Brief, 48. (Later reduced to 322 men.)

October, 1841–Roster of Co. B, 36 men. Source unknown. Bancroft Papers, 1002; Brief, 72.

As of Aug. 31, 1841–95 men in the Sutton-Cooke party, 153 men in the McLeod party at Camp Resolution. Grover, Grand Reference Sheet; Brief, 66–71.

[255]

Dec. 27, 1841—90 men at Mexico City. A Mexican list, said to be the same list as that of Feb. 11, 1842. Brief, 84.

Dec. 30, 1841—89 Sutton-Cooke men at Mexico City. *Senate Doc. No. 325.*

Jan. 1, 1842—90 Sutton-Cooke men at Mexico City. Grover's list; Brief, 58.

Jan. 5, 1842—305 men listed in *Austin City Gazette.*

Jan. 27, 1842—304 men listed in New Orleans *Commercial Bulletin.*

Feb. 4, 1842—139 McLeod men at San Cristóbal. *Senate Doc. No. 325.*

Feb. 7, 1842—19 men sick at San Cristóbal. A Mexican list. Bancroft Papers, 806; Brief, 86.

Feb. 9, 1842—123 went from San Cristóbal to Puebla. No list. Kendall, *Narrative,* II, 213; *Senate Doc. No. 325;* Brief, 480. Feb. 14: "126 Texans arrived." *Mexico in 1842,* 248; Bancroft Papers, 765; Brief, 28a.

Feb. 10, 1842—15 men at San Lázaro. A Mexican list. Bancroft Papers, 795; Brief, 92.

Feb. 11, 1842—90 Sutton-Cooke men at Santiago. A Mexican list. Bancroft Papers, 819–22; Brief, 80–83.

Feb. 11, 1842—18 McLeod men to San Lázaro (?). Grover; Brief, 52.

Feb. 14, 1842—11 left San Lázaro. No list. Kendall, *Narrative,* II, 227; Brief, 211.

Feb. 18, 1842—52 men from Puebla to Perote. "70 men left." No list. Gallegher-Hoyle *Journal; Niles' National Register,* May 7, 1842; *Mexico in 1842.*

Feb. 20, 1842—82 left at Puebla, 58 at Perote. *New Orleans Morning Advertiser,* Mar. 11, 1842; Bancroft Papers, 870; Brief 16. No list.

Feb. 25, 1842—6 men from San Lázaro to Santiago. Grover; Brief, 61.

Feb. 25, 1842—7 arrived at Santiago from San Lázaro, plus 4 who had been left on the road. Grover; Brief, 53.

Feb. 25, 1842—11 back to San Lázaro; 5 of these ordered on

(to Santiago?), plus 3 others at San Lázaro. No list. Kendall, *Narrative*, II, 232–33; Brief, 211.

Feb. 28, 1842—95 Sutton-Cooke men at Santiago. A Mexican list. Bancroft Papers, 785–88; Brief, 87–90.

Mar. 9, 1842—5 from San Lázaro to Santiago; 7 left in San Lázaro. No list. Kendall, *Narrative*, II, 241.

Mar. 13, 1842—4 men to Santiago (probably from San Lázaro). Grover; Brief, 54.

Mar. 28, 1842—78 men from Santiago to Tacubaya. No list. Grover; Brief, 54.

Apr. 11, 1842—78 men returned from Tacubaya to Santiago; 100 now at Santiago. No list. Grover; Brief, 54.

Apr. 21, 1842—13 men liberated at Mexico City, Apr. 21 to Apr. 28. Grover, Grand Reference Sheet.

Apr. 25, 1842—10 men arrived at Santiago from Guanajuato. Grover; Brief, 54.

Apr. 25–28, 1842—141 men at Santiago. Doran list; Bancroft Papers, 815–17; Brief, 77–79.

Apr. 28, 1842—19 men given certificates at Mexico City. Grover; Brief, 58.

Apr. 28, 1842—20 men released from Santiago. (7 duplicated on Grand Reference Sheet under Apr. 21.) Grover; Brief, 54.

May 12, 1842—14 men left Vera Cruz on United States revenue cutter *Woodbury. Niles' National Register*, Vol. LXII (June 4, 1842), 210.

June 1, 1842—8 men sick in Mexico City. Grover; Brief, 55.

June 13, 1842—65 men released from Puebla. A Mexican list. Bancroft Papers, 555–56; Brief, 96.

June 13, 1842—47 released from Perote, of whom 3 remained ill. No list. Bancroft Papers, 542; Brief, 17a.

June 14, 1842—119 released from Santiago, of whom 9 remained in a hospital. Bancroft Papers, 549–52; Brief, 93–95.

June 23, 1842—The 2 remaining prisoners released. A Mexican note; no list. Bancroft Papers, 565; Brief, 19a.

July 3, 1842—7 in hospital at Mexico. Bancroft Papers, 576; Brief, 19a.

[257]

July 27, 1842—185 ready to embark but detained by yellow fever quarantine of ship. Bancroft Papers, 311; Brief, 3a. 85 embarked: Bolton Transcriptions, II, 154; Brief, 11b.

Aug. 12, 1842—139 men left Vera Cruz on the *Rosa Alvina* (Bancroft Papers, 311); 36 stayed—3 in Mexico City (of whom 2 were going to the Pacific); 4 in Puebla; 4 in Jalapa (the town near Perote prison); 23 in Vera Cruz; 2 undesignated. In addition to the 8 who asked to remain in Mexico, probably most were ill in Vera Cruz, for an epidemic had swept the port. Grover; Brief, 55–57. A separate listing at Brief, 56, shows 4 more dead or left behind.

Sept. 13, 1842—40 men sailed on the *Woodbury*. No list. Bancroft Papers, 311; Brief, 3a. 14 men sailed: Bolton Transcriptions, II, 154; Brief, 11b.

1842—306 men listed in *Mexico in 1842*.

1845 or later—Payroll list, 120 names.

Aug. 25, 1851—Lubbock-Tardif prisoner list, 199 names.

Undated—47 casualties all told. Grover, Reference Sheet; Brief, 60–61.

Undated—38 officers and merchants. No source. Bancroft Papers, 1043; Brief, 97.

APPENDIX C

Commanders on the March to Mexico City

FLORES, SUB-LIEUT. FERNANDO. Conducted Sutton-Cooke party from Leon to Guanajuato, or possibly Querétaro.

GARCÍA, CAPT. YGNACIO. 3rd Cavalry. Conducted Sutton-Cooke party from Zacatecas to Leon. Also, it appears he conducted the McLeod party from San Luis Potosí to Guanajuato, although Kendall at several points says Roblado took them all the way to Guanajuato. Such a long trip would be unusual, because it involved two different states. Roblado was brutal, and undoubtedly stood out in Kendall's mind. But his identification of García is more positive, because he says García recognized Lieut. Casey as one in whose home he had been cared for after the battle of San Jacinto, and García was therefore very kind to them. Kendall refers to him as a "gentle officer of cavalry."

OCHOA, CAPT. Forty years old; good-humored. Conducted the McLeod party from Paso to Chihuahua and went on with them to Cerro Gordo. He had borrowed money from them, and on the morning of his leavetaking did not appear, and they were highly disillusioned, but in a few hours the money came by messenger, and Ochoa explained he did not like leavetaking.

ORTIZ, CAPT. FRANCISCO. Conducted the Sutton-Cooke party from Castle Coloran through Paso to Chihuahua. Excellent treatment.

ORTIZ, CAPT. PEDRO. Fifth Light Artillery. Conducted the Sutton-Cooke party from Durango to Fresnillo.

QUINTANA, LIEUT. TEODORO. Took the advance McLeod party from San Miguel to Paso. Good treatment.

ROBLADO, CAPT. Conducted the McLeod party from Cuencamé to San Luis Potosí. "A second Salazar."

ROCHA, CAPT. GERBACIO. Conducted the McLeod party from Guanajuato to Querétaro.

ROMERO, GEN. MANUEL. Seems to have gone hither and yon but conducted neither party, unless possibly the McLeod party from Zacatecas to Guanajuato; there is also an indication that he went to conduct the Sutton-Cooke party from Fresnillo to Zacatecas, but nowhere is there a positive, undisputed statement that he conducted either party.

SALAZAR, DÁMASO [Dimasio]. The villain of the whole affair. Conducted the McLeod party from San Miguel to Paso; he or his men killed three men and two others died; he starved and beat them and subjected them to indignities; he allowed them a very minimum of clothing and food; he would not allow the ill or lame to ride unless they could pay for it; he cut off the ears of the dead men and strung them on a rawhide thong; their bodies were not buried but

left by the roadside; their ragged garments were given to
the soldiers. At Paso, Col. Elías ordered an investigation,
and Salazar was found to have shot two of the prisoners
and to have withheld food; he had started with nineteen
oxen but had killed only two, and had left the rest on the
road outside of Paso. The President ordered Armijo to
court-martial and sentence him, but no record has been
uncovered to show that this was ever done. When Kearny
invaded New Mexico, Armijo fled, but Salazar did not agree
with him. The Americans expected an engagement with
"General Salazar," but it did not come. In January, 1847,
Colonel Price imprisoned Archuleta and Salazar to stop
the revolt in which Governor Bent was killed. Salazar's son
was taken prisoner. In February, 1854, Salazar demanded
$5,000 for his son, who had been killed by Indians, but
this claim was not allowable because there was no money
for such payment. (W. W. H. Davis, *El Gringo*, 293.) Davis
describes Salazar as dark and swarthy. Hobbs, *Wild Life
in the Far West*, 299, says Salazar was shot in 1865.

VASTIDA, CAPT. MIGUEL LA. Conducted the McLeod party from
Querétaro to Mexico City.

VELASCO, CAPT. Frontier Guard of Durango. Conducted the
McLeod party from Cerro Gordo to Cuencamé. A fierce-
looking old soldier who turned out to be a gentleman.

———. Conducted the Sutton-Cooke party from San Miguel
to Castle Coloran. Treatment bad.

———. Conducted the Sutton-Cooke party from Chihuahua
to Cerro Gordo; "a wretch."

———. Conducted the Sutton-Cooke party from Cerro Gordo
to Placquemine.

———. Conducted the Sutton-Cooke party from Placquemine
to Durango.

CAVALRY CAPTAIN. Conducted the Sutton-Cooke party from
Querétaro to Mexico City.

MAJOR ——— of the Chihuahua militia. Little, dapper, vain.
Conducted the McLeod party from Chihuahua to Cerro
Gordo.

[260]

APPENDIX D

Others Encountered in Study of the Expedition

ADALHABAKIA [MUPIKIOWA]. Kiowa chief killed in the massacre of the Hull party Aug. 30, 1841, at Camp Resolution.

ÁLVAREZ, MANUEL. United States consul in Santa Fé. He was attacked in his house in Santa Fé by a group led by Armijo's nephew. (Gregg, *Commerce of the Prairies* [ed. Thwaites], II, 26–27; the *Austin City Gazette*, Jan. 19, 1842. This nephew was not named Chaves as sometimes reported; Gregg says he was a nephew named Tomás Martin.) Álvarez went to Independence and sent letters to Daniel Webster and to the press, protesting Armijo's designation of the Pioneers as conquerors.

AMORY, NATHANIEL. Secretary of the Texas legation at Washington on Jan. 14, 1841.

ANDRADE, JUAN JOSÉ DE. Commandant general of Mexico June 6, 1842.

ARCHER, B. P. Texan Secretary of War and Navy June 5, 1841.

ARCHULETA, JUAN ANDRÉS. Secured the surrender of McLeod. He tried to get others to resist Kearny's invasion, but they would not. With others he organized the revolt of 1847, and after its failure he fled to California. He was readmitted to New Mexico on an oath of allegiance and made commander of the Territorial Militia in 1861, with the rank of brigadier general. He continued to live in Santa Fé as a white-haired old man, but died in 1884. At the time of the expedition he was prefect of the district of Santa Fé (sort of a county commissioner), and seems to have acted in military affairs with the rank of lieutenant colonel.

ARISTA, MARIANO. Had lived in Cincinnati. General-in-chief of Mexico's Army of the North, with headquarters at Monterrey. Later president of Mexico.

ARMIJO, AMBROSIO. Antonio Otero, later governor of New Mexico, says that Ambrosio was uncle by marriage to Otero.

(My Life on the Frontier, I, 175). In 1833 one Ambrosio Armijo was a deputy from New Mexico to the Congreso General in Mexico, but the man who became prominent under Manuel Armijo was only eleven years old in 1833. Keleher mentions that in 1864 Ambrosio Armijo had a wagon train plundered by the Kiowas and Apaches. He died at Albuquerque on Easter Sunday, Apr. 9, 1887, at sixty-five years of age. His official position under Manuel was treasurer, with the function of chief of hacienda. Ralph P. Bieber indicates Ambrosio was a brother of Manuel Armijo.

ARMIJO, MANUEL. Many things are said about him—mostly uncomplimentary and mostly agreed upon by historians. He was born to *peones* and worked up by aggressiveness, shrewdness, and lack of scruples. He was involved in the revolution of 1837 and apparently played all sides against one another and finally came out on top. He was covetous of women, especially young ones, and many tales are told of the lengths to which he would go to force a girl into his bed—even those from highly-placed families; his wife is said to have acted as his procuress. In spite of his many long and highly contradictory pronouncements of his great and undying loyalty to the fatherland, he always managed to come out on the profit side personally. After all his talk about defending New Mexico against the Pioneers, five years later he fled from New Mexico at the approach of Kearny without firing a shot. His flight was not so precipitous, however, as to prevent his taking seven wagonloads of cotton goods (one of the most precious products in Mexico); George Frederick Ruxton met him south of Chihuahua. He was court-martialed in Mexico City for cowardice and desertion concerning the loss of New Mexico (which led to the loss of the entire Southwest), but was acquitted. Josiah Webb is almost the only one who defends Armijo to any extent, but Webb's *Adventures in the Santa Fé Trade* was written in 1888, when Webb was seventy years old and when the Santa Fé Trail was over thirty years in the past;

it is possible that his memory of Armijo had been mellowed. Keleher says Armijo died Dec. 9, 1853. His *rancho* was at Limitar, N. M., and he was buried at Socorro.

ARRANGOÍZ, F. DE. Mexican consul at New Orleans Dec. 28, 1841.

BACA, ANTONIO. Rancher near San Miguel. One of his daughters fell in love with either Scott, Burgess, or John Howard. (Kendall, *Narrative*, I, 336.)

BARROETA, FRANCISCO. Administrator of a hospital in Mexico City July 3, 1842.

BEE, BARNARD ELLIOTT. Secretary of State of the Texas Republic; Texan chargé d'affaires at Washington, D. C., removed because of illness in the family Dec. 27, 1841.

BLACK, JOHN. American consul at Mexico City. He lived in Mexico forty years.

BLUNT, LIEUT. Of the United States Navy. He visited Kendall at San Lázaro. This may be James G. Blunt, who was a sailor at fifteen and who would have been sixteen in 1842.

BOCANEGRA, JOSÉ MARÍA DE. A distinguished lawyer in Mexico and one of the judges of the Supreme Court. In 1841 he became minister of foreign relations under Santa Anna. Characterized as a very able man.

BUSTAMANTE, ANASTASIO. President of Mexico until succeeded by Santa Anna in late 1841.

BUSTAMANTE, TOMÁS. Errand boy for Kendall and his three fellow prisoners at San Miguel. Tomás was somewhat tricky in his dealings.

CANALISO, VALENTÍN. Commandant general of the department of Puebla June 11, 1842.

CARRIÓN, LUIS. In charge of the hospital at Santiago June 6, 1842.

CHAVES, JOSÉ. Paid the expenses for the first New Mexico expedition (Archuleta's?) and for maintenance of the prisoners for a while.

CHAVES, MANUEL. Armijo's nephew. At the surrender of Cooke, Manuel was closely associated with Lewis.

CHAVES, MARIANO. One reference indicates he was Armijo's secretary and nephew, but Gregg says he was no relation. Very kind to the Pioneers. Brother of Antonio José Chaves, who was murdered by McDaniel in 1843 on the way to Independence.

CIRCUS PROPRIETOR. From Kentucky or Vermont. Kendall mentions him frequently. He went to Mexico from Jonesboro or Pecan Point, Ark., with Connelly's Expedition in 1840.

CLINE, HERR. At the Italian opera in Mexico City.

CONDE, GARCÍA. Governor of Chihuahua in 1841.

CONNELLY, DR. HENRY. An early trader on the Santa Fé trail; settled in Chihuahua. Organized the expeditions across Texas in 1839 and 1840. Advanced the Sutton-Cooke party $1,339. Later governor of New Mexico.

COOLIDGE, probably T. B. Apparently a resident of Mexico. On San Jacinto Day he sent the prisoners at Santiago six turkeys, wine, and liquor.

CORTASAR, ANTONIO. *Secretario interno* of northern Mexico; at Lampazos May 11, 1841.

CORTAZAR, PEDRO. "Gentlemanly governor of Guanajuato"; lived at Celaya.

CYPREY, BARON ALLEYE DE. French minister in Mexico.

DRYDEN, WILLIAM. Born near Richmond, Ky., in 1807. Became a Santa Fé trail trader in 1827; settled in Chihuahua, later in Santa Fé. Shipwrecked on the Texas coast in 1840, and visited Lamar; appointed confidential agent for Lamar in Santa Fé. Imprisoned at Chihuahua on suspicion of helping to organize a revolt, but finally was released. Went to California in 1850 and died there in 1869. In Chihuahua he testified that he was a Roman Catholic and that he had been a captain in the Mexican Army but never a naturalized citizen.

DORSEY. Arrived at Jalapa with dispatches for Thompson.

DUTCH BROOM GIRLS. They sold brooms on the street, according to Kendall, singing ballads, playing the tambourine and hurdy-gurdy; they had a monkey in their show. Kendall says: "One I well know, who was recognized in every street in the United States." Kendall casts some doubt on the quality of their brooms.

ELLIS, POWHATAN. United States envoy extraordinary and minister plenipotentiary to Mexico. He received criticism, particularly from Franklin Coombs, for not working hard enough to get the prisoners released. Apparently he was not as effective as his successor, Waddy Thompson, and he did not make much point of visiting the prisoners, but correspondence indicates that he worked very hard to free them, and he did get some released before he gave way to Thompson in April. Thompson says the mere fact that the United States appointed a new envoy gave him added prestige in the negotiations—which sounds reasonable.

EVE, JOSEPH. United States minister in Texas.

FOSTER, ROBERT. Wanted by the Mexican government when the McLeod party reached Zacatecas, but not a member of the expedition.

FRANCISCA. Grover, in his *True Blue*, says Francisca was one of the most comforting factors at Santiago. She and Spotted Pony, another Mexican girl, formed strong attachments for two of the Texan prisoners (*Kendall*, always discreet in such matters, gives no names), and waited on them, brought them food and soap, did their washing, and followed them when they were transferred. Francisca carried at least one note to Kendall from Santiago.

FRENCH WIDOW at Cerro Gordo. Entertained a number of the McLeod men.

FRENCH WOMAN at Chihuahua; wife of a German druggist. She was kind to the prisoners.

GARZA, ANTONIO DE LA. Was in Béxar Apr. 19, 1841, keeping an eye on things.

GEROLTE, FEDERICO. In charge of negotiations for Prussia in Mexico.

GONZALES, COL. JOSÉ MARÍA ELÍAS. Commandant of El Paso del Norte. Well bred, a liberal and gentlemanly officer. Ordered the investigation of Salazar.

GRAMONT. A French-Canadian with Falconer before the expedition left.

GUTIERRES, JOSÉ IGNACIO. Commandant at San Luis Potosí.

HARGOUS, L. S. [Hargoos, Hargos]. Acting American consul at Vera Cruz. Very helpful. Advanced $1,163.66 and $5,090.10 against the Texan government, which had no money to pay him.

HEREDIA, JOSÉ C. Commandant general of Durango.

ITURBIDE. Long political history in Mexico. Proclaimed emperor May 18, 1822. In 1823 Santa Anna, Echavari, and Victoria overthrew him.

JENNISON, JOHN. Director of the mint at Chihuahua. Very liberal with the prisoners.

DON JESÚS. Took the Van Ness party to meet Armijo. Kendall says he was mean to them, although it is not clear in what way. Don Jesús (no surname appears) was also with Salazar on the *Jornada*.

JONES. From Connecticut; director of the mint at Guanajuato. (Wise, *Los Gringos*, 243.)

JUVERO, JULIAN. Commandant general of Querétaro Dec. 21, 1841.

KADOGYATO. Kiowa chief or medicine man who was in the Camp Resolution area.

LAMAR, MIRABEAU BONAPARTE. Born in Georgia in 1798. Established the Columbus, Ga., *Enquirer*. Went to Texas in 1835; at the battle of San Jacinto; secretary of war; vice president; elected president in 1838; was succeeded by Houston in 1841. He died in 1859. A Mason. He was visionary but not practical; the things he wanted for Texas were things Texas should have had but possessed no means of getting. Houston was his bitter opponent. To do Lamar justice, it would appear that his illegal expedition to Santa Fé might actually have pulled Texas out of the hole created by the panic of

1837, a situation not improved by Houston and not helped by Lamar. Houston, on the other hand, was sometimes more practical than intelligent, and it was well known that he was strongly in favor of annexation anyway.

LAWRENCE, HENRY E. Brought dispatches from New Orleans to Ellis.

LICEAGA, JUAN. Commandant general of Guanajuato Dec. 31, 1841.

LIE, LUIS. A naturalized citizen of Taos, 1841.

LOVATO, BUENO VENTURA. At Taos May 31, 1841.

LUMSDEN, FRANCIS ASBURY. Co-owner of the *Picayune* with Kendall. He made a trip to Mexico to try to get Kendall released.

MAGOFFIN, JAMES WILEY. Born in Kentucky in 1799. On the Santa Fé Trail before 1825. Married María Gertrudes Valdez of a good San Antonio family and settled in Chihuahua; was first United States consul there. He and Mrs. Magoffin were very liberal with the Pioneers. Magoffin later played a key part in Kearny's conquest of New Mexico, but was imprisoned in Chihuahua for activities in connection with Doniphan's Expedition; the United States government eventually paid a bill for $30,000 for his losses; he was at one time sentenced to be executed, and was in jail for some three years. Founded Magoffinsville near what is now El Paso; was active in the Confederate Army. Died in San Antonio in 1868. Keleher (*Turmoil in New Mexico*), says Magoffin was imprisoned at Durango, and that Armijo, who then lived in Durango, was a relative of Magoffin's wife and intervened. Philip St. George Cooke says Magoffin obtained his release by the liberal use of champagne. Others say the fact that Father Ortiz was held as hostage was an important factor.

MARTIN, JUAN ANTONIO. Second judge of the second department of Taos.

MAYER, BRANTZ. Secretary of the United States legation in Mexico City. Took many things to the prisoners—news-

[267]

papers, food, clothing. Visited them and reserved rooms for those released on Apr. 21. Wrote a controversial book, *Mexico As It Was and As It is,* which does not seem at all distorted from this perspective.

MEADE, D. and R. They were merchants in Guanajuato who helped Caldwell a great deal while he was ill in the hospital there.

MILLARD, HENRY. Sought by the Mexican government at Guanajuato, but not with the Pioneers.

MIRANDA, GUADALUPE. Armijo's secretary.

MOORE, EDWIN WARD. Commander of the Texan Navy.

MORALES, COL. Provided mules for the officers from Paso to Chihuahua (McLeod party).

MORLET, GEN. MARIANO. Commandant general of Mexico Feb. 9, 1842, it appears from a letter from Andrade.

MEXICAN LADY. A concert singer at the Italian operas. Her husband was a Massachusetts man.

MUNOZ, COL. With his dragoons met the McLeod party on the *Jornada.* Muñoz was on his way north from Durango to fight the Texans.

NAIT. A naturalized citizen of New Mexico.

OLIVÉR, PEDRO PASCUELA. Apparently an envoy from the Vatican on Apr. 27, 1842.

ORTEGA, BLAS. A cripple who furnished information to Armijo.

ORTIZ, LIEUT. FRANCISCO BACA. Seems to have accompanied the Sutton-Cooke party from Santa Fé to Mexico City.

ORTIZ, JUAN RAPHAEL. A sycophant of Armijo. In one letter he said to Armijo: "I am a poor man and nobody likes me." He was one of the two men who assisted Armijo in propagandizing the general tax law of 1837 to foment a revolution, by telling the people, among other things, that men would be taxed for sleeping with their wives.

ORTIZ, RAMÓN. The priest at El Paso. Very kind to the prisoners; gave them food, money, beds to sleep in; furnished Kendall a horse. One of the reasons Magoffin was not shot at Chihuahua was that the *anglos* held Father Ortiz as hostage.

PAKENHAM, RICHARD. British minister to Mexico.

PAVÓN, FRANCISCO G. Acting governor of San Luis Potosí.

PERRIN, F. [Perin]. A young lawyer of standing and responsibility in Nuevo Leon.

PIEDRA, JOSÉ DE LA. In charge of Santiago June 13, 1842.

PINO, JUAN ESTEVÁN. He is the other man, besides Juan Raphael Ortiz, who helped Armijo foment the revolution in 1837.

PINO, MANUEL. Rode a beautiful black horse; Kendall describes him as pursy, bloated, sallow-faced. He was Captain of the Guard Oct. 9 with the McLeod party, and Gallegher-Hoyle say he was a great tyrant, cursing and making threats.

PINO, MIGUEL E. One of those who instigated the revolt of 1847.

PINO, NICOLAS. Another mover in the rebellion of 1847.

PINO. A brother of Manuel, at whose ranch the McLeod party stopped Oct. 18. Apparently a different man from Manuel.

PRATS, SALVADOR. Mexican vice-consul in New Orleans Feb. 9, 1842.

QUIJANO, BLASCO. Commandant general of the department of Vera Cruz Sept. 13, 1842.

RAMÓN. A guard who tortured Gates on the *Jornada* Nov. 3.

REYES, JOSÉ J. Commandant general of Puebla Apr. 6, 1842.

REILLY, JAMES. Texan minister in Washington.

ROBERTS, SAMUEL A. Acting Secretary of State of Texas when the expedition left.

ROWLAND, JOHN T. Merchant in San Miguel. Was arrested as a result of the Pioneers' approach, but later released and his goods restored.

ROWLAND, THOMAS. Brother of John Rowland. Also of San Miguel; also arrested and later released.

SALAZAR, FRANCISCO ANTONIO. A sergeant under Salazar on the *Jornada*.

SALAZAR, JOSÉ. Captain of *rurales* on the Río Abajo.

SANDOVAL, ANTONIO. Prefect of the district of Río Arriba.

SANDOVAL, JUAN. Ran errands for Kendall and his three fellow prisoners at San Miguel; especially efficient at supplying reeds which they needed to fashion pipes.

SANTA ANNA, ANTONIO LÓPEZ DE. Born in Jalapa June 13, 1792, says Wharton in *El Presidente,* but this is an error. June 13 was his saint's day; he was born Feb. 21, either 1795 or 1796. He had a turbulent political and military history; in his early days he had powerful support of the various Masonic lodges in Mexico. Six times either president or emperor; three times banished from Mexico. In 1842 he was fifty years old, five feet, ten inches tall, with olive skin, and striking looks. He had a spotty history in money affairs in his early years, and was said to be a great seducer of women. Perhaps one of the most revealing things about him is brought out by Thompson in his *Recollections,* 65: "The reader will, at least, agree that he is not the sanguinary monster which some have supposed him to be." Thompson also says Santa Anna never kept a political prisoner. If this is true, then he kept Navarro a prisoner for an even less worthy reason: because of personal animosity. Santa Anna lost one leg against the French at Vera Cruz, and Kendall, on seeing it borne through the streets like the figure of a saint, commented that it must have done him more good off than on. His wife was well liked by all, and is said to have wanted the Texan prisoners released. Santa Anna became provisional president Oct. 10, 1841, and remained in power until Dec. 6, 1844. Bollaert says (*William Bollaert's Texas,* 108n), that "Santana" lost the Battle of San Jacinto (which won the war for Texas) in 1836 because he was "closeted in the tent" with a mulatto girl named Emily and allowed himself to be detained too long to organize his troops. He died in 1876 in Mexico City at the age of eighty-four, poverty stricken and hardly noticed.

SASH-CE-ZINDA. "Surretaker" chief in 1840, to whom Lamar issued a passport. Hodge says "Sarritehca" is another word for "Arapaho," but it does not seem possible that any Arapahoes were in Texas in such a way as to need a passport in 1840.

SMALL, MATT. Kentucky. Was with Falconer shortly before the expedition left.

SPOTTED PONY. Grover, in *The True Blue*, says she was a small, pockmarked woman; apparently she was not as pretty as Francisca but just as affectionate and loyal. See Francisca.

SPYBUCK. A well-known Delaware or Shawnee scout who had been with Kirker in Mexico.

MRS. STEVENSON. A Mexican woman in Paso who gave the prisoners many necessities. No further identification.

SUGAR MILL OWNER. Passed them at Valencia with a wagon train. This man is also mentioned by Susan Shelby Magoffin, *Down the Santa Fé Trail.*

TARODI, LIEUT. COL. ANTONIO. In charge of Santiago June 14, 1842. This obviously is the Don Antonio who Kendall says allowed the fruit women to visit them at all times.

THOMPSON, WADDY. Born in South Carolina in 1798. Lawyer and politician. At one time elected Brigadier General of militia by the legislature. Sent as special minister to Mexico in 1842, and vigorously prosecuted release of the United States citizens. He says himself that the fact of his being sent was a strong weapon, but there is no doubt that his personal efforts were important. When the prisoners were released, Thompson contributed $1,000 toward a fund to get them home.

TIRRELL, CHARLEY. A Delaware scout with Kirker.

TORNEL, JOSÉ MARÍA DE. Minister of War. An able man; belligerent toward the United States.

TREAT, JAMES. Confidential agent and special commissioner of the government of Texas. On Sept. 29, 1840, he wrote A. S. Lipscomb, Secretary of State: "The fixing the Río Bravo del Norte for the military line of demarcation, they do not seem to like." (*Texan Diplomatic Correspondence*, II, 706.) Treat died Nov. 30, 1840, on the war schooner *San Antonio.*

TRENCO, FERNANDO. Commandant general of Zacatecas Dec. 10, 1841.

TRIQUEROS. Minister of finance. Forty years old.

ULIBARRI, ANTONIO JOSÉ. At the investigation of Salazar, testified that one of the Pioneers "was shot by the rear guard because he was very sick and filthy." Ulibarri was a sergeant under Salazar. At the investigation, Salazar himself brought up the fact that this prisoner had a "decomposing and stinking arm."

ULIBARRI, SANTIAGO. Prefect (?) of San Miguel.

VAN ZANDT, ISAAC. Texan chargé d'affaires at Washington, Mar. 23, 1843.

VASQUES, CIRIACO. General-in-chief of the canton of Jalapa June 12, 1842.

VEGA, J. IGNACIO. In charge of the presidio of Santiago Feb. 28, 1842. (The prisoners were confined in the convent, and this may or may not have been included within the presidio.)

VIDAURRI, SANTIAGO. Special agent in Béxar Apr. 23, 1841.

VIGIL, FRANCISCO. Captain of *rurales* in the Río Arriba.

VIGIL, GREGORIO. A rancher near San Miguel. He saved the Van Ness party from execution by Salazar. He was prominent in later Mexican politics, and Davis says in 1856 he was in reduced circumstances.

VRILLE. Unidentified. Wrote a letter to the *New York Herald* Nov. 1, 1841, saying: "It is reported, that several peaceable American citizens, who resided at Santa Fé, have been shot, and if true, 'Uncle Sam' may have work ahead."

WEBSTER, DANIEL. Secretary of state of the United States. He prosecuted the release of the "Americans" vigorously and firmly.

WEED, W. A. Vermont. Kendall met him in Mexico.

WILLETT. Director of the mint at Guanajuato; interceded for them and saved many lives of those sick with smallpox.

WISEMAN, PATRICK. Interpreter at Guanajuato.

WRIGHT, A. S. Secret agent of Texas government in Mexico in 1839.

YOUNG MERCHANT from Massachusetts whom Kendall met in Mexico.

ZAVALA, MANUEL. Commandant general at Durango Jan. 4, 1842.

APPENDIX E

Mexican Prisons

Acordada. Apparently the most dreaded prison in Mexico. It was in Mexico City, near the Alameda, a celebrated park in the western part of the city. Descriptions are given in Kendall, *Narrative*, II, 352; Green, *Mier Expedition*, 242ff.; Stapp, *Prisoners of Perote*, 149; Mayer, *Mexico As It Was and As It Is*, 268. It must have been frightful; there was a "show window" where every morning those murdered at the prison during the night were laid out for recognition by their relatives or friends. Only three of the Pioneers were sent there: Navarro, who was kept there for some two years, McJunkins, and one other unidentified man.

Perote. The treatment there was better than at Puebla, says Kendall. There was no hospital in the prison but one in the nearby town of Jalapa. Kendall gives a brief description in his *Narrative*, II, 384ff.; see also Stapp, *Prisoners of Perote*, 112ff., and Green, *Mier Expedition*, 238ff.; Wharton gives Perote's history in *El Presidente*, 107–108; a brief description with photos is in *The Southwestern Historical Quarterly*, Vol. XLVIII, No. 3 (January, 1945), 340ff. Green gives the ground plan in *Mier Expedition*, 238. It was east of Mexico City, between Puebla and Vera Cruz.

Puebla. Apparently the worst, next to the *Acordada*. At Puebla they were made to clean sewers, were fed meagerly and badly, clad poorly, afflicted with vermin, and made to associate with—sometimes were chained to—criminals of the worst class. East of Mexico City toward Vera Cruz.

Salón de los Distinguidos. At Chihuahua. A famous prison.

San Cristóbal [Cristóval] de Ecatepec. Between Lakes Cristóbal and Tezcuco, twelve or fourteen miles northeast of

Mexico City. "An old palace, crumbling in decay, desolate and gloomy."

San Lázaro. Not a regular smallpox hospital but a lepers' prison. North of the road as it comes from Vera Cruz into Mexico City. The first few days must have been difficult, for they were forced to mingle with the lepers, but apparently Kendall got used to even that. On the first day or so, some of the prisoners were unable to eat because of the surroundings.

———. Unnamed. Eleven men taken there Feb. 14. It was only three or four blocks from San Lázaro; they were bitten by myriads of bedbugs.

Santiago. On the great square of Tlaltelolco. "In a better part of the city," Kendall says, an hour's ride, probably west, from San Lázaro. Stapp in *Prisoners of Perote*, 82, says it was in the northern part of the city. In one part of the prison was a walled enclosure where thousands of cholera victims had been buried in 1833, and Coombs says the effluvium was extremely offensive.

Tacubaya. Some five miles from Santiago near the archbishop's palace. Thompson says three miles from Mexico; Stapp says six miles from Santiago and one mile from Chapultepec, in the western outskirts; Green says four miles southwest of Mexico City. The prisoners were not there very long.

Tula. Thirty miles north of Mexico City.

APPENDIX F

Ships

Atalantique. Falconer sailed on it from Vera Cruz Mar. 9, 1842.

Bainbridge. Carried the last prisoners released to Thompson, and he returned with them. This would place it about Feb. 1, 1844. These probably were Mier prisoners.

Boxer, United States brig. Brought Cooke and Houghton to Galveston Aug. 10, 1842, according to Bollaert.

San Antonio, Texas Navy schooner. *Niles' National Register* for May 7, 1842, says one Texan escaped and reached the *San Antonio,* but it does not give a name. In September, 1842, the *San Antonio* disappeared and was presumed lost in a storm. Mabry, who had been released with the Pioneers, was lost on her.

San Bernard, Texas Navy. Bollaert says Brenham arrived at Galveston Aug. 10, 1842, on it.

Solway. Falconer sailed on it from Havana to New Orleans.

Hermann, frigate. Navarro sailed on it to New Orleans Jan. 18, 1845.

Macedonian, United States frigate. Was off Vera Cruz Apr. 14, 1842.

Rosa Alvina. Apparently 185 Texans embarked July 27, but the ship was quarantined because yellow fever broke out on board, and it appears that 40 of the men were left in Vera Cruz when the quarantine was lifted and the ship sailed Aug. 12.

Water Witch. Lumsden sailed on this ship for Vera Cruz Dec. 27, 1841.

Wm. Bryan, schooner. Lumsden left Vera Cruz on her Mar. 9, 1842; Van Ness was with him.

Woodbury, United States revenue cutter. Left Vera Cruz May 12, 1842, with fourteen released prisoners; left Vera Cruz Sept. 13 with forty more.

APPENDIX G

Kendall's Itinerary

(Kendall's dates are not consistent. They differ from Falconer's, from Gallegher's, and from Gallegher-Hoyle's. Also, he often skips two or three days. But on the important dates he brings his chronology into accord with the other journalists.

This itinerary is not confined to Kendall's *Narrative* but is based on it.)

June 3—Snow killed accidentally by a sentinel.
June 12—Davis killed on Walnut Creek.
June 20—Left Brushy Creek Camp.
June 24—First buffalo.
June 25—Lockridge killed himself.
June 27—McLeod ill, left the command temporarily.
July 2—Camped dry.
July 5—Flint died of colic.
July 12—McLeod returned.
July 13—Prairie fire.
July 14—Camped dry.
July 21—Hit the Cross Timbers.
July 25—Howard resigned.
July 28—Camped without water.
July 29—Cleared the Cross Timbers.
Aug. 4—Carlos recognized (he thought) Red River. The Waco village.
Aug. 11—Howland, Baker, and Rosenberry sent ahead.
Aug. 12—Camped dry.
Aug. 13—Camped dry; prairie fire; Brazos discovered; mountains seen.
Aug. 15—Carlos and Brignoli deserted; camped dry.
Aug. 16—One-Minute Spring.
Aug. 17—Dr. Brashear died of consumption.
Aug. 21—Prairie dogs.
Aug. 23—First Indian trouble.
Aug. 27—Caprock in sight.
Aug. 28—Indians in evidence. Reached the Quintufue.
Aug. 29—Donovan missed from Camp Resolution.
Aug. 30—Hull, Mabee, Dunn, Flenner, Woodson massacred by Kiowas at Camp Resolution. Klein and Kenyon missed from Camp Resolution.
Aug. 31—Sutton-Cooke party left Camp Resolution. (Ken-

dall was with them; our knowledge of events at Camp Resolution comes from Falconer, Grover, Gallegher-Hoyle, and others.)

Sept. 4—Ramón killed by Kiowas at Camp Resolution. Indians stampeded and captured eighty-three horses.

Sept. 10—Sturgess died at Camp Resolution.

Sept. 12—Glass killed by Kiowas at Camp Resolution.

Sept. 13—Dr. Beall shot in arm.

Sept. 15—Men about to mutiny.

Sept. 16—Griffith lanced by Indians.

Sept. 18—Mercer died from Indian wounds at Camp Resolution.

Sutton-Cooke party to Oct. 17:

Sept. 7—Sutton finally descended from the Llano.

Sept. 10—Two men, unidentified, missing from Sutton-Cooke party.

Sept. 12—Having encountered Mexicans, Cooke sent Matías back to guide McLeod. That day the Sutton-Cooke party, close to starvation, encountered bands of sheep and had ample food for the first time in thirteen days.

Sept. 14—Van Ness party sent forward.

Sept. 15—Sutton-Cooke advance party captured.

Sept. 17—Sutton-Cooke surrendered; sent to Paso; Kendall's party stayed at San Miguel. Rosenberry killed; Howland and Baker executed at San Miguel.

Sept. 17—Matías reached McLeod. McLeod's party, also near starvation, prepared for immediate crossing of the Llano.

Sept. 20—McLeod ascended the Llano.

Sept. 24—Beall, Todd, and Wilkins missed.

Sept. 25—McLaughlin died.

Sept. 27—Camped dry.

Sept. 28—McLeod descended from the Llano.

Sept. 30—Camped dry.

Oct. ??—Mitchell missed.

Oct. 5—McLeod surrendered.

Oct. ??—Manuel killed by Mexicans.

Oct. 17—The McLeod party, joined by Kendall's group, left San Miguel for Paso del Norte.

Oct. 17—Spent the night at Pecos.

Oct. 18—Pino *rancho*.

Oct. 19—Camped.

Oct. 20—Algodones.

Oct. 21—Alameda.

Oct. 22—Los Placeres.

Oct. 23—Valencia; Ernest died at night; McAllister shot.

Oct. 24—Casa Colorada.

Oct. 25—Joya.

Oct. 26—Parrida.

Oct. 27—Socorro.

Oct. 29—Bosque de los Apaches.

Oct. 30—Fray Cristóbal. An ox killed for food.

Oct. 31—On the *Jornada;* they traveled all night.

Nov. 1 or 2—Golpin shot, Griffith brained. Another ox killed for food.

Nov. 3—Thirty miles from Paso.

Nov. 4—Gates died.

Nov. 5—Reached Paso.

Nov. 6—Left Paso.

Nov. 7—Camped.

Nov. 8—Camped dry.

Nov. 9—Ojo de San Malayuque.

Nov. 10—Same.

Nov. 11—Camped dry.

Nov. 12—Ojo del Lucero.

Nov. 13—Near Carazal.

Nov. 14—Near Carazal.

Nov. 15—Camped.

Nov. 16—Camped.

Nov. 18—Laguna Encinillos.

Nov. 19—Near Chihuahua.

Nov. 21—Reached Chihuahua.
Nov. 27—Camped dry.
Nov. 28—El Ojito.
Nov. 29—A *rancho.*
Nov. 30—San Pablo.
Dec. 1—Saucillo; Larrabee died.
Dec. 2—Near La Cruz.
Dec. 3—Santa Rosalia.
Dec. 4—A *rancho.*
Dec. 6—Guajuquilla (now Jiménez).
Dec. 7—Camped.
Dec. 8—Río Flórido.
Dec. 9—La Noria.
Dec. 10—Cerro Gordo.
Dec. 12—Camped.
Dec. 14—Palo Chino.
Dec. 15—El Gallo.
Dec. 16—A *rancho.*
Dec. 17—Dolores *hacienda.*
Dec. 18—Guadalupe *hacienda.*
Dec. 20—Cuencamé.
Dec. 22—A poor *rancho.*
Dec. 23—Juan Pérez *hacienda.*
Dec. 24—A village.
Dec. 25—San Sebastian.
Dec. 26—Saenea. Sutton-Cooke party reached Mexico City.
Dec. 27—Rancho Grande.
Dec. 28—Fresnillo.
Dec. 29—La Caleta; first sign of smallpox.
Dec. 30—Zacatecas.
Jan. 3—Refugio.
Jan. 4—Ojo Caliente; bathing.
Jan. 5—El Carro.
Jan. 6—Salina.
Jan. 7—Espíritu Santo.
Jan. 8—La Parada.

Jan. 9—San Luis Potosí; three left in hospital.

Jan. 12—Las Pilas.

Jan. 14—El Jaral.

Jan. 15—San Felipe.

Jan. 16—San Juan de los Llanos.

Jan. 17—Arparos.

Jan. 18—Silao; two left in hospital.

Jan. 19—Guanajuato; eighteen left in hospital.

Jan. 20—La Puerta.

Jan. 21—Salamanca.

Jan. 22—Celaya. Lubbock and Mazure escaped from Santiago.

Jan. 24—A *rancho* called Calera.

Jan. 25—Querétaro. Coombs released from Santiago.

Jan. 26—Camped.

Jan. 27—San Juan del Río. Comanche escaped from Santiago.

Jan. 28—McJunkins and one other escaped.

Feb. 1—Tula; three left in hospital.

Feb. 2—Arrived at San Cristóbal.

Feb. 3—Van Ness and Falconer released.

Feb. 9—Left for "Mexico."

Feb. 11—Comanche recaptured.

Feb. 28—Fitzgerald released.

Apr. 6—Studion and Stosoases escaped.

Apr. 14—Howard and Hudson escaped.

Apr. 21–28—Twenty released from Santiago.

May 12—Fourteen sailed on the *Woodbury*.

June 13—Sixty-five released from Puebla.

June 14—119 released from Santiago. Kendall was one of these.

June ??—Forty-seven released from Perote.

July 27—185 (?) embarked on the *Rosa Alvina*.

Aug. 12—The *Rosa Alvina* sailed from Vera Cruz with 139 men.

Sept. 13—The *Woodbury* sailed from Vera Cruz with the "rest" of the prisoners; some reports say 40, others 14.

February, 1845—Navarro escaped from Vera Cruz.

APPENDIX H

Advance Parties

Aug. 11—Howland, Baker, Rosenberry from McLeod.

Aug. 13—Caldwell went south and identified the Brazos.

Aug. 17—Caldwell sent north to find Red River.

Aug. 22—Caldwell returned.

Aug. 28—Capt. Strain sent out with about twenty-five men. Glass went to scout.

Aug. 29—Lieut. Hann (with Grover) and eight others went out from Camp Resolution.

Aug. 30—Capt. Strain returned.

Aug. 31—Sutton-Cooke party left, with Kendall and Grover.

Aug. 31—Lieut. Hann returned.

Sept. 2—Glass returned.

Sept. 4—Howland party captured.

Sept. 7—Caldwell and twenty-five men scouted and returned to Camp Resolution.

Sept. 14—Cooke sent ahead the Van Ness party, with Kendall.

Sept. 15—Van Ness party captured.

Sept. 16—Lewis deserted the party.

Sept. 17—Sutton-Cooke party captured.

Sept. 17—Matías with three guides reached McLeod. Howland and Baker executed; Rosenberry had been killed.

Sept. 20—Sutton-Cooke party to Mexico; Van Ness party remained in San Miguel.

Sept. 23—Caldwell and nine men dispatched by McLeod.

Oct. 2—Lieut. Burgess, with Scott, Howard, Matías and one guide dispatched by McLeod.

Oct. 3—Burgess party captured at Laguna Colorada and quartered at home of Antonio Baca.

Oct. 4—Caldwell party captured near San Miguel and quartered at home of Gregorio Vigil.

Oct. 5—McLeod party captured at Laguna Colorada.
Oct. 12—McLeod party to San Miguel.
Oct. 16—McLeod, Navarro, and a few officers to Paso.
Oct. 17—Main McLeod party, Van Ness party, Caldwell party, Burgess party to Paso.

BIBLIOGRAPHY

CONSIDERATION of the primary sources involves the movements of the several parties. The original party was under General McLeod. With it were George Wilkins Kendall, Thomas Falconer, George W. Grover, Peter Gallegher, and Stephen Hoyle, who left journals of various kinds. Other important materials were left by Thomas S. Lubbock, Dr. Richard F. Brenham and William G. Cooke, and General McLeod.

The original party left Brushy Creek in late June. By September 1 it was lost and starving, and on that date the Sutton-Cooke party of some 95 to 100 men was sent forward to make contact with the New Mexican settlements. Kendall, Grover, Brenham, and Lubbock went with the Sutton-Cooke party; Falconer, Gallegher and Hoyle remained with McLeod.

When the Sutton-Cooke party neared the settlements, an advance detachment of five men under Van Ness was sent forward. Kendall went with Van Ness; Grover stayed with Sutton and Cooke. The Van Ness men were put in jail; the rest of the Sutton-Cooke party was sent immediately toward the City of Mexico.

The McLeod party, arriving later at Laguna Colorada, was captured; the Van Ness party was added to it; and this detachment was started for the City of Mexico. With Sutton and Cooke were Grover, Brenham, and Lubbock. With McLeod were Kendall, Falconer, Gallegher, and Hoyle.

So much for the chroniclers; now for their chronicles. The most voluminous source of any account of the whole expedition must be Kendall's *Narrative of the Texan Santa Fé*

Expedition. Kendall's original notes were taken by Salazar, but after his release he consulted with many fellow survivors and rewrote the story from memory. (As a matter of fact, Falconer's notes and Grover's notes and all other papers were taken from the prisoners, except Gallegher's Diary, and so all of their journals except the Diary are reconstructions.)

Kendall journalizes frequently and is vague concerning dates; sometimes he scrambles dates and facts. Nevertheless, allowing for a few days' leeway in his recital, the *Narrative* stands up very well. It was published in two volumes; a seventh edition was printed in 1856, which brought the total United States sales to 40,000 copies. It was issued in several editions in England.

Kendall's accuracy and his attention to certain details and the lack of it in respect to others, are consistent from beginning to end. It is regrettable that his memory for names was not better employed.

The second narrative source is by Thomas Falconer, a London lawyer. He wrote four important items: his *Account,* his Notes, his Diary, and a Letter. As with Kendall, Falconer's original notes were taken by Mexican officials, and he also had to depend on memory. He and Kendall consulted after their release, and corresponded for a number of years. Falconer was released about Feb. 1, 1842, and the usefulness of his materials ends about the time the other members of the McLeod party began their imprisonment.

The *Account* was first published by Lumsden & Kendall in 1842. The Letter was published in the *New Orleans Bee,* one of Kendall's competing newspapers, on March 11, 1842. The Notes were published in the *Journal of the Royal Geographical Society of London* in 1844. The Diary was first published by Kendall in the 1856 edition of his *Narrative.*

All these materials of Falconer and the information about them have been brought together in a book entitled *Letters and Notes on the Texan Santa Fé Expedition 1841–1842,* with introduction and notes by F. W. Hodge.

The most fruitful source of names of members of the expedition and their different fates is in the various chronicles of George W. Grover, a young man of 21 who kept a record which was "lost." After he was imprisoned in the convent of Santiago, however, he rewrote his "Minutes of Adventure." He reached the City of Mexico with the Sutton-Cooke party Dec. 26, 1841, and his Minutes are dated Jan. 1, 1842. It is brief, and especially sketchy from the time of its date, but he gives a number of lists, including "List of Texas prisoners in the city of Mexico Jan. 1, 1842," and several smaller lists, as of men transferred from one prison to another, as well as a list of 139 men leaving on the *Rosa Alvina* Aug. 12, together with 36 men remaining in Mexico and 4 others dead or otherwise lost.

Grover also compiled a Reference Sheet "Exhibiting a list of the fatal casualities attending the Texan Santa Fe Pioneers 1841-2," showing 47 men lost. And, finally, there is his Grand Reference Sheet, showing a "List of the Detachment which left the main command upon the Palo Duro" (the Sutton-Cooke party), and "List of the Command, which remained upon the Palo Duro" (the McLeod party).

The Grover materials are in the Rosenberg Library at Galveston, Tex., and I am indebted to C. Lamar Wallis and Bill Holman, librarians, for their use. Their copy of the Grand Reference sheet is a photostat marked "Source unknown," but George Grover's son, Walter E. Grover, who lives in Galveston and who gave permission for the use of the Grover materials in this work, supplies the information that the original is in the Hall of State (Texas Building), at the Fair Grounds at Dallas, Tex.

The handwriting of several different persons appears on this very large sheet, but most of the names seem to have been written by Grover, and the distinctive typography—fancy hand lettering and ornamentation—of the heading are very similar to that of the Reference Sheet and also that on the cover of the "Farewell Sheet" of *The True Blue*, a prison paper edited by Grover at Santiago.

The handwriting on these documents is well executed and indicates a man of education, but the chirography is tricky, and in many places the writing, now 115 years old, is badly faded and indecipherable. H. Bailey Carroll prepared the Minutes for publication in the *Panhandle-Plains Historical Review* for 1936, but the various lists of names were not included. Altogether there are 101 unpublished pages of Grover materials in the Rosenberg Library. There is also the second Reference Sheet in the Texas State Library, as noted in Appendix A.

The only diary known to have been kept concurrently and to be still in existence is that of the merchant named Peter Gallegher. It is owned by H. Bailey Carroll of Austin, Texas.

At the Castle of Perote, Stephen Z. Hoyle took Gallegher's Diary, copied it in part and added some comments of his own, making up the Gallegher-Hoyle *Journal*. It was not until a few years ago that Carroll worked out the facts of these two chronicles and actually discovered the original documents; he tells about it in the *Panhandle-Plains Historical Review* for 1951. The text of the Gallegher-Hoyle *Journal* is there printed as an appendix to Carroll's *The Texan Santa Fé Trail*. The entire issue of the *Review* is comprised of this latter work, which deals primarily with the exact route and itinerary from Austin to San Miguel.

It is interesting to speculate on the present existence of some of those lost or confiscated journals—Kendall's, Falconer's, or Grover's. They may yet turn up in some Mexican deposit of official papers.

Tom Lubbock says "Doctor Richard F. Brenham kept a journal of the whole route." Needless to say, this compiler would be elated to see that journal turn up. Bollaert says (*William Bollaert's Texas*, 133) that Bonnell "intends to write a lengthened report." It is enough to make a historian's mouth water. If Bonnell wrote the report, it has not turned up.

The greatest accumulation of materials is an aggregation of some four thousand pages of microfilm, the bulk of which is of typed copies of Mexican documents and some American and Texan materials found in the Mexican archives and transcribed by Herbert E. Bolton. These are from the 150,000 pages or so of Bolton material now owned by the Bancroft Library at Berkeley, Calif. Much of this great accumulation is still being processed and will be for many years, for it is an enormous task, and I am greatly indebted to Mrs. Helen Harding Bretnor for selection of these items and for their availability to me. The material from the Bancroft Library is referred to herein as the Bancroft Papers.

Most of the material so furnished for this work is in Spanish but is typewritten—which facilitates its use. This writer's material is referred to herein by page number scratched on the microfilm with a tungsten carbide scriber. (It should be noted that the title, Bancroft Papers, includes some miscellaneous material not originating in Professor Bolton's work.)

In the Bancroft Papers are found the Order Book of the Texan Santa Fé Expedition, which includes the general military orders of the expedition. Also in the Bancroft Papers are found copies of the special military orders (source not noted). According to Carroll the originals of the general orders are in the Texas Archives, the originals of the special orders are in the General Archives of War and Navy at Mexico City, and typed copies of both sets are in the Archives at the Library of the University of Texas.

Mrs. Bretnor also furnished microfilm of Bustamante, *Gabinete Mexicano,* and Torres, *Mexico, Memorias Relaciones, 1841–1843.*

Included with the Bancroft Papers microfilm are a number of microfilmed items supplied by Miss Winnie Allen, archivist at the Eugene C. Barker Texas History Center in Austin. Photostats of the *Austin City Gazette* and other assistance were furnished by Mrs. B. Brandt, assistant archivist at the Texas State Library.

The Bancroft Papers are supplemented also by a micro-filmed copy, from the library of the University of Texas, of H. Bailey Carroll's translations of the Bolton Transcriptions. These are, as far as the writer has been able to determine, translations of many of the documents furnished me by the Bancroft Library. (Professor Bolton many years ago selected several hundred pages of documents and made copies for the library of the University of Texas, among others.)

Assistance and permissions have been given generously by Miss Gertrude Hill, chief librarian at the Museum of New Mexico; Dr. A. J. O. Anderson, in charge of archives at the Museum of New Mexico; Harvey C. Byrd, Grand Secretary of the Grand Lodge of Texas, A. F. and A. M.; General Manuel de J. Solis Andoaga, of the Departamento de Archivo, Secretaria de la Defensa Nacional, Mexico, D. F.; Miss Ruth E. Rambo, assistant librarian at the Museum of New Mexico; Joe B. Lee, librarian, University of Texas; Earleen Holleman, archives assistant, Eugene C. Barker Texas History Center; Mrs. Virginia H. Taylor, now archivist at the Texas State Library; Thomas D. Moorman and Malcolm D. McLean, archives translators at the Eugene C. Barker Texas History Center; Seymour V. Connor, archivist at the Texas State Library; Mrs. Donald Duncan, reference department, the Rosenberg Library; George P. Hammond, director, the Bancroft Library; James W. Arrott, Sapello, New Mexico, who furnished a microfilm copy of the Santa Fé Expedition file at the Texas State Library; William S. Wallace, archivist, New Mexico Highlands University at Las Vegas, who gave permission for use of the Arrott materials; Victor Gondos, Jr., archivist in charge, Old Army Branch, National Archives, Washington, D. C.; R. H. Carruthers, chief of the photographic service at The New York Public Library, who furnished microfilm and photocopies of the *Austin City Gazette;* Mrs. Lilla M. Hawes, director, the Georgia Historical Society; and John Hall Jacobs, librarian of the New Orleans Public

Library. C. Boone McClure, director of the Panhandle-Plains Historical Museum, Canyon, Texas, has been particularly helpful in providing rare illustrative material for the book. This acknowledgment includes also grateful thanks in each and every case.

One other item should be mentioned in connection with the location and gathering of materials. Near the end of this work it was desirable to locate the complete report of Thomas Lubbock, which is only partially quoted by Kendall, and without source or other identification. This report by Lubbock is listed by Raines and by Streeter as appearing in the *Colorado Gazette* for June 4, 1842, a copy of which paper was said to be in the library of the University of Texas, but it could not be located. Months later Fred Folmer, associate librarian, asked Mrs. McLean, who had done some work for Streeter, about the paper. Upon returning to Arkansas, Mrs. McLean examined her notes and located the newspaper (or, rather, one sheet of it) in the Dienst Collection of the library of the University of Texas Archives. Mr. Folmer immediately communicated this welcome information and had the sheet photostated. The one sheet contains all of Lubbock's report, made apparently after he returned to Texas following his escape from Santiago. In such devious ways do historians gather information, and in such delightful ways do some library staff members gladden the hearts of researchers.

Due to the nature of these materials and the fact that a great many of them do not have numbered pages, most of them have been copied by this writer's patient typist, Mrs. Evelyn Girard of Minneapolis, Minn., and these copies have been made into a bound book or "brief" of some one thousand solidly typed pages. Where a reference to the Bancroft Papers sometimes is cumbersome, since the only pagination exists on this writer's microfilm, often a reference is made also to the page of the Brief at which the typed copy appears. Such page references have little value for anybody else—as indeed do page references to the Bancroft Papers—but will enable this writer to locate and identify. Needless to say, where page references useful to other persons are in existence, these have been given preference.

Unpublished Materials

Bancroft Papers. Bancroft Library, Berkeley, Calif. A collection of 150,000 pages of typed transcriptions from Mexican archives, assembled by Herbert E. Bolton.

Bolton Transcriptions. Archives, University of Texas Library, Austin. Selections from the Bancroft Papers, translated by H. Bailey Carroll.

Grand Reference Sheet. Hall of State (Texas Building), Fair Grounds, Dallas, Tex. A list compiled by George W. Grover giving the names of the men in the Sutton-Cooke party and those in the McLeod party.

Grover Materials. Rosenberg Library, Galveston, Tex. One hundred pages of unpublished material.

Lubbock-Tardif List. Archives, Texas State Library, Austin, Tex. A list of Pioneers taken prisoner; dated Aug. 25, 1851.

Payroll List. Archives, Texas State Library, Austin, Tex.; dated 1845 or later.

Reference Sheet. Rosenberg Library, Galveston, Tex. A list compiled by George W. Grover giving the names of the Pioneers who lost their lives on the expedition.

Weakley, Louise. "The Story of Treason in the Republic of Texas." Thesis in the library of Sul Ross State College, Alpine, Tex.

Pamphlets and Government Publications

Bailey, Vernon. *North American Fauna No. 25, Biological Survey of Texas.* Washington, D.C., Government Printing Office, 1905.

Bolton, Herbert E. *Guide to Materials for the History of the*

United States in the Principal Archives of Mexico. Washington, D.C., Carnegie Institution, 1913.

Carter, James D. *Masonry in Texas.* Waco, Grand Lodge of Texas, A.F. and A.M., 1955.

Douglas, Edward M. *Boundaries, Areas, Geographic Centers, and Altitudes of the United States and the Several States.* Washington, D.C., Government Printing Office, 1932. *Geological Survey Bulletin 817.*

Explorations and Surveys for a Railroad Route from the Mississippi River to the Pacific Ocean. Washington, D.C., Government Printing Office, 1854.

Garrison, George P. (ed.). *Diplomatic Correspondence of the Republic of Texas.* 3 vols. Washington, D.C., Government Printing Office, 1908–1911.

Gulick, Charles Adams, and Harriet Smither (eds.). *The Papers of Mirabeau Bonaparte Lamar.* 6 vols. Austin, Texas State Library, 1922–27.

Haggard, J. Villasana. *Handbook for Translators of Spanish Historical Documents.* Austin, University of Texas Archives Collections, 1941.

Hodge, Frederick W. *Handbook of American Indians North of Mexico.* 2 vols. Washington, D.C., Government Printing Office, 1912. *Bulletin 30, Bureau of American Ethnology.*

27 Cong., 2 sess., *House Doc. No. 266.*

Mooney, James. "Calendar History of the Kiowa Indians," *Seventeenth Annual Report of the Bureau of American Ethnology.* 2 vols. Washington, D.C., Government Printing Office, 1898.

Second Report of the United States Board of Geographic Names. Washington, D.C., Government Printing Office, 1901.

27 Cong., 2 sess., *Senate Doc. No. 325.*

Webb, Walter P. (ed.). *The Handbook of Texas.* 2 vols. Austin, The Texas State Historical Association, 1952.

Wislizenus, F. A. *Memoir of a Tour to Northern Mexico.* 30 Cong., 1 sess., *Senate Misc. Doc. No. 26.*

Newspapers

Austin City Gazette, Apr. 28, 1841, and June 23, 1841. (Texas
State Library, Austin.) Also Oct. 30, 1839 to March 2, 1842.
(The New York Public Library.)

Colorado Gazette (Matagorda, Tex.), June 4, 1842. (Dienst
Collection, University of Texas Library.)

Diario del Gobierno, Oct. 16, 1841.

El Siglo XIX, Dec. 14, 1841.

New Orleans *Commercial Bulletin,* Jan. 27, 1842. (Archives
Dept., New Orleans Public Library.)

New Orleans *Picayune,* Aug. 21, 1842.

Niles' National Register (Baltimore), Vols., LXI and LXII
(September, 1841 to August, 1842).

Books

Adams, Ramon. *Western Words.* Norman, University of Oklahoma Press, 1946.

Arnold, Elliott. *The Time of the Gringo.* New York, Alfred A.
Knopf, 1953.

Bancroft, Hubert Howe. *The History of Arizona and New
Mexico.* San Francisco, The History Co., 1889.

———. *History of Mexico.* 6 vols. San Francisco, The History
Co., 1886–88.

———. *History of the North Mexican States and Texas.* 2 vols.
San Francisco, The History Co., 1886–89.

Barca, Calderón de la. *Life in Mexico.* New York, Dutton,
1934.

Bartlett, John Russell. *Dictionary of Americanisms.* Boston,
Little, Brown, 1877.

———. *Personal Narrative of Explorations and Incidents.* 2
vols. New York, D. Appleton, 1854.

Bechdolt, Frederick R. *Tales of the Old-Timers.* New York,
Century Co., 1924.

Bieber, Ralph Paul. *The Papers of James J. Webb, Santa Fé
Merchant, 1844–1861.* 1924.

Billington, Ray Allen. *The Far Western Frontier*. New York, Harper & Brothers, 1956.

Bolton, Herbert E. *Athanase de Mézières and the Louisiana-Texas Frontier, 1768–1780*. 2 vols. Cleveland, Clark, 1914.

Bustamante, Carlos M. *El Gabinete Mexicano*. Vol. II. Mexico, José M. Lara, 1842.

Carroll, H. Bailey. *The Texan Santa Fé Trail*. Canyon, Tex., The Panhandle-Plains Historical Society, 1951.

Castañeda, Carlos E. *The Mexican Side of the Texan Revolution*. Dallas, P. L. Turner Co., 1928.

———. *Our Catholic Heritage in Texas*. 7 vols. Austin, Von Boeckmann-Jones Co., 1936.

Catlin, George. *Letters and Notes on the North-American Indians*. London. 1841.

Chapel, Charles E. *The Gun Collector's Handbook of Values*. New York, Coward McCann, 1947.

Chittenden, Hiram M. *The American Fur Trade of the Far West*. 3 vols. New York, Francis P. Harper, 1902.

Connelley, William E. *Doniphan's Expedition*. Kansas City, Bryant & Douglas, 1907. Volume also includes the Diary of Colonel John T. Hughes.

Copeland, Fayette. *Kendall of the Picayune*. Norman, University of Oklahoma Press, 1943.

Crane, William C. *Life and Select Literary Remains of Sam Houston of Texas*. Philadelphia, J. P. Lippincott, 1884.

Davis, W. W. H. *El Gringo; or, New Mexico and Her People*. New York, Harper & Brothers, 1857.

Day, Donald, and Harry Herbert Ullom (eds.). *The Autobiography of Sam Houston*. Norman, University of Oklahoma Press, 1954.

DeShields, James T. *Border Wars of Texas*. Tioga, Tex., The Herald Co., 1912.

Espinosa, J. Manuel (trans.). *First Expedition of Vargas Into New Mexico, 1692*. Albuquerque, University of New Mexico Press, 1940. Vol. X of *Coronado Quarto Centennial Publications*.

Falconer, Thomas. *Letters and Notes on the Texan Santa Fé Expedition, 1841–1842.* Ed. by F. W. Hodge. New York, Dauber & Pine Bookshops, 1930.

Fergusson, Harvey. *The Conquest of Don Pedro.* New York, Pocket Books, 1955.

Folsom, George F. *Mexico in 1842.* New York, Charles J. Folsom, 1842.

Froebel, Julius. *Seven Years' Travel in Central America.* London, Richard Bentley, 1859.

Gibson, George Rutledge. *Journal of a Soldier Under Kearny and Doniphan, 1846–1847.* Ed. by Ralph P. Bieber. Glendale, Clark, 1935. Vol. III of the Southwest Historical Series.

Grant, U. S. *Personal Memoirs.* Ed. by E. B. Long. New York, World Publishing Co., 1952.

Green, Thomas J. *Journal of the Texian Expedition Against Mier.* New York, Harper & Brothers, 1845.

Gregg, Josiah. *Commerce of the Prairies.* Ed. by Max L. Moorhead. Norman, University of Oklahoma Press, 1954.

———. *Commerce of the Prairies.* Edited by Reuben Gold Thwaites. Cleveland, Clark, 1905. Vols. XIX and XX of Early Western Travels.

Hafen, LeRoy R. (ed.). *Ruxton of the Rockies.* Norman, University of Oklahoma Press, 1950.

Haley, J. Evetts. *Charles Goodnight.* Norman, University of Oklahoma Press, 1949.

Hobbs, James. *Wild Life in the Far West.* Hartford, Wiley, Waterman & Eaton, 1873.

Hollon, W. Eugene, and Ruth Lapham Butler (eds.). *William Bollaert's Texas.* Norman, University of Oklahoma Press, 1956.

Hotten, John C. *The Slang Dictionary, Etymological, Historical, and Anecdotal.* London, Chatto and Windus, 1864.

Hulbert, Archer B. *Forty-Niners; The Chronicle of the California Trail.* Boston, Little, Brown, 1931.

James, Marquis. *The Raven.* Indianapolis, Bobbs-Merrill, 1929.

Johnson, Frank W., and Eugene C. Barker. *History of Texas and Texans.* 5 vols. Chicago and New York, American Historical Society, 1914.

Kane, Joseph N. *Famous First Facts.* New York, H. W. Wilson, 1950.

Keleher, William A. *Turmoil in New Mexico, 1846–1868.* Santa Fe, Rydal Press, 1952.

Kendall, George Wilkins. *Narrative of the Texan Santa Fé Expedition.* 2 vols. New York, Harper & Brothers, 1844.

Kennedy, William. *Texas: The Rise, Progress, and Prospects of the Republic of Texas.* Fort Worth. The Molyneaux Craftsmen, 1925. Reprinted from the second edition, London, 1841.

Lee, Nelson. *Three Years Among the Camanches.* Albany, Baker Taylor, 1859.

LeMar, H. D. *History of the Lamar or LeMar Family in America.* Omaha, 1941.

Magoffin, Susan S. *Down the Santa Fé Trail and Into Mexico.* New Haven, Yale University Press, 1926.

Marcy, Randolph B. *Army Life on the Border.* New York, Harper & Brothers, 1866.

———. *The Prairie Traveler.* New York, Harper & Brothers, 1859.

Margo, Elisabeth. *Taming The Forty-Niner.* New York, Rinehart, 1955.

Marryat, Frederick. *The Travels and Romantic Adventures of Monsieur Violet.* London, Longman, Brown, Green & Longmans, 1843.

Mathews, Mitford M. (ed.). *A Dictionary of Americanisms on Historical Principles.* 2 vols. Chicago, University of Chicago Press, 1951.

Mayer, Brantz. *Mexico As It Was and As It Is.* New York, J. Winchester, 1844.

Mencken, H. L. *The American Language.* New York, Alfred A. Knopf, 1937.

Olmstead, Frederick L. *A Journey Through Texas.* New York, Dix, Edwards, 1857.

Otero, Miguel Antonio. *My Life on the Frontier.* 2 vols. New York, Press of the Pioneers, 1935.

Partridge, Eric. *A Dictionary of Slang and Unconventional English.* New York, Macmillan, 1937.

Pfefferkorn, Ignaz. *Description of the Province of Sonora.* Trans. and annotated by Theodore E. Treutlein, Albuquerque, University of New Mexico Press, 1949. Vol. XII of *Coronado Quarto Centennial Publications.*

Ruxton, George F. *Adventures in Mexico.* London, John Murray, 1847.

Sabin, Edward L. *Kit Carson Days.* New York, Press of the Pioneers, 1935.

Sage, Rufus B. *His Letters and Papers, 1836–1847.* Ed. by LeRoy R. Hafen. 2 vols. Glendale, Clark, 1956. Vols. V and VI, Far West and Rockies.

———. *Rocky Mountain Life.* Boston, Wentworth, 1857.

Schoolcraft, Henry R., *The Indian Tribes of North America.* 6 vols. Philadelphia, Lippincott, Grambo, 1853–1856.

Serven, James E. *Colt Firearms 1836–1954.* Santa Ana, 1954.

Shaw, Reuben C. *Across the Plains in Forty-Nine.* Farmland, Ind., W. C. West, 1896.

Stapp, William P. *The Prisoners of Perote.* Philadelphia, G. B. Zieber, 1845. Facsimile reprint by the Steck Co., Austin, 1935.

Strong, Henry W. *My Frontier Days and Indian Fights On the Plains of Texas.* n. p., n. d.

Thompson, Waddy. *Recollections of Mexico.* New York, Wiley and Putnam, 1846.

Torres, Jacinto G. *Mexico, Memorias Relaciones 1841–1843.* Mexico, 1844.

Twitchell, Ralph E. *The Leading Facts of New Mexican History.* 5 vols. Cedar Rapids, The Torch Press, 1911.

Webb, James Josiah. *Adventures in the Santa Fé Trade, 1844–1847.* Glendale, Clark, 1931. Vol. I in the Southwest Historical Series.

Webb, Walter Prescott. *The Great Plains.* New York, Ginn and Co., 1931.

———. *The Texas Rangers.* Boston, Houghton Mifflin, 1935.

Wharton, Clarence R. *El Presidente; A Sketch of the Life of General Santa Anna.* Austin, Gammel's Book Store, 1926.

Wheat, Carl I. (ed.). *The Letters of Dame Shirley.* San Francisco, The Grabhorn Press, 1933.

Williams, Cleve and Juanita H. *Legends of the Spanish Southwest.* Glendale, Clark, 1938.

Wilson, James G., and Fiske, John (eds.). *Appletons' Cyclopædia of American Biography.* 6 vols. New York, Appleton, 1887–1889.

Winkler, E. W. (ed.). *Manuscripts, Letters and Documents of Early Texians, 1821–1845.* Austin, The Steck Co., 1937.

Wise, Henry A. *Los Gringos.* New York, Baker and Scribner, 1849.

Yoakum, H. *History of Texas.* New York, Redfield, 1855.

Periodicals

Bloom, Lansing. "Texas Aggressions, 1841–1843," *Old Santa Fé,* Vol. II, No. 6 (October, 1914).

Christian, A. K., "Mirabeau Bonaparte Lamar," *The Southwestern Historical Quarterly,* Vol. XXIV, No. 1 (July, 1920).

Grover, George W. "Minutes of Adventure," *Panhandle-Plains Historical Review,* 1936. The complete work is located in the Rosenberg Library, Galveston, Tex.

Hale, Joseph W. "Masonry in the Early Days of Texas," *The Southwestern Historical Quarterly,* Vol. XLIX, No. 3 (January, 1946).

Hobbies, January, 1936; March, 1955.

Illustrated News, 1853.

The Louisiana Historical Quarterly, Vol. XI, No. 2 (April, 1928).

Marshall, Thomas M. "Commercial Aspects of the Texan

Santa Fé Expedition," *The Southwestern Historical Quarterly,* Vol. XX, No. 3 (January, 1917).

New Mexico Historical Review, Vol. XXV, No. 4 (October, 1950).

The Southwestern Historical Quarterly, Vol. IX, No. 3 (January, 1906); Vol. XX, No. 3 (January, 1917); Vol. XXIII, No. 1 (July, 1919); Vol. XXIV, No. 2 (October, 1920); Vol. XXVII, No. 2 (October, 1923); Vol. XXX, No. 1 (July, 1926); Vol. XXXVI, No. 4 (April, 1933); Vol. XLVII, No. 3 (January, 1945).

Texas State Historical Quarterly, Vol. IX, No. 3 (January, 1906).

White, Leslie A. "Punche: Tobacco in New Mexico History," *New Mexico Historical Review,* Vol. XVIII, No. 4 (October, 1943).

Zabel, Charles, and J. L. Beardsley. "Before the Railroad Came," *Outdoor Life,* August, 1933.

INDEX

Acklan: in roster, 202
Acknowledgments: 288–89
Acordada: releases from, 131; Navarro retained in, 132; Navarro in, 141; conditions horrible, 141, 179; near Mexico City, 199; McJunkins sent to, 238; listed, 273
Acquisition of territory by U. S.: 189
Â'dalhabä-k'ia: killed at Camp Resolution, 64n.; listed, 261
Adams, Allensworth: in roster, 202
Adams, Charles W.: escaped north of Paso, 128
Adams, John Quincy: talked against Texas, 164; said the Pioneers had been engaged in a war, 185
Adams, Ramon: *Western Words* cited, 30n.
Adams, Thos. W.: in roster, 202
Advance parties: listed in Appendix H, 281–82
Adventures of Monsieur Violet: mentioned, 220
Ages of Pioneers: *xii*
Ahart, A.: in roster, 202
Ahart, C.: in roster, 202
Akles: in roster, 202
Alameda: McLeod party spent the night at, 278
Alamo: battle at, mentioned, 5
Alcalde: duties of, 78, 78n.
Alexander, J. M.: to be assistant quartermaster, 14; in roster, 202–203
Alexander, Robt. F.: in roster, 203
Algodones: the episodes of the two small rooms, 117–18; McLeod party spent the night at, 278
Alkali water: poisonous, 13

Allande, Pedro María de: governor of New Mexico in 1817, 113n.
Allen, D.: in roster, 203
Allen, David: in Mier action, 187, 203
Allen, H. A.: in roster, 203
Allende: identified, 155n.
Allison: in roster, 203
Allyn, Saml.: in roster, 203
Alsbury, William M.: escaped north of Paso, 128; in Mier action, 187, 203; in roster, 203
Álvarez, Manuel: sent first word of the capture, 183; listed, 261
Amateurs on trip: 15
American stage drivers: gave $500 to $1,000 apiece, 127
Americans (not Pioneers): arrested by Armijo, 73
Amory, Nathaniel: listed, 261
Ampudia, Pedro A.: captured Texans at Mier, 182
Andrade, Juan José de: said their lives were guaranteed, 174; listed, 261
Angosturas: believed seen by Carlos, 49; canyon in New Mexico, 49n.; found by Hunt, 70
Annexation: Texan Congress annexed northern Mexico, 183
Antelope: killed on Llano by Sutton-Cooke, 68
Antipathy: of Mexicans toward *anglos,* 56n.; Arnold suggests reason for, 172; should not have existed, 173
Anton Chico: Van Ness party had dinner there, 74
Apache: *see* Chavis, Antonio

[299]

Apaches, Lipan: complicated existence of republic, 5; guides to be met, 13; failure to meet, 13n.; Apache chief watched them, 121

Archer, B. P.: listed, 261

Archer, Powhatan: in roster, 203

Archuleta, Juan Andrés: demanded surrender of McLeod, 110–11; said their lives were guaranteed, 174; listed, 261

Arista, Mariano: spoke of peaceful nature of expedition, 169; had agents in San Antonio and Austin, 171; believed the expedition commercial, 171; listed, 261

Armijo, Ambrosio: listed, 261–62

Armijo, Manuel: had Americans arrested, 73; propagandized against the Texans, 73; read Kendall's passport, 80; ordered Jesús to bring him their ears, 80; remained safe in San Miguel, 83; fled before Kearny, 83n., 136; ordered prisoners bound in groups, 92; discussed execution of the 90 men, 94; summary of life, 135–36; complained about Conde, 136; court-martialed, 136, 262; died in 1853 near Socorro, 136; avoided the question of Kendall's passport, 143; apparently thought New Mexico would welcome Texans, 168; excited the populace in 1837, 172; an astute propagandist, 172; said their lives were guaranteed, 174; listed, 262–63

Army: traditional methods failed on the plains, 114n.

Arnold, Elliott: speaks of propaganda, 162; suggests reason for antipathy, 172

Arparos: McLeod party spent the night at, 280

Arrangoíz, Francisco de: said Kendall did not have a passport, 144; advises of hostile legislature of Kentucky, 183; listed, 263

Atalantique: listed, 274

Atole: described, 72n.

Attitude of the Mexicans: in New Mexico, 161; expressed by El Siglo XIX, 182

Augusta: public meetings, 183–84

Austin: preparations in, 4; two years old in 1841, 10

Austin City Gazette: call for volunteers, 3; their list is the basis for most figures, 194; list of Jan. 5, 1842, 195, 200, 256, 261; list of June 23, 1841, 196, 199, 255; cited, 10n., 14n., 15n48, 15n49, 23n., 28n., 102n., 148n.

Austin Lodge No. 12, A.F.&A.M.: records burned, 152n.

Austin, Steven F.: outlined Texas' claim, 164

Avant courier: possible author of statement about Kendall, 144n.

Ayers, George: in roster, 204

Baca, Antonio: Burgess party quartered at his ranch, 114; one of his daughters fell in love with one of the prisoners, 116, 263; listed, 263

Bailey, Vernon: North American Fauna No. 25 cited, 33n., 60n.

Bainbridge: listed, 274

Baird, Spruce M.: sent to form the county of Santa Fé, 165

Baker, Alexander: sent ahead to San Miguel, 52; executed at San Miguel, 81–82; in roster, 204

Balle, B. O.: in roster, 204

Bancroft, Hubert Howe: accepted Armijo's version, 161; said no justice to Texas claim, 162; said Armijo was justified in breaking promises, 176; said Thompson said prisoners well enough treated, 176–77; apparently biased, 177n.; considered good historian by Espinosa, 181n.; The History of Arizona and New Mexico cited, 162n., 167n., 176n., 177n17, 177n20

Bancroft Papers: described, 287

Dand: 23n.

Barca, Calderón de la: said conditions were bad, 179

Barchatt, John: in roster, 204

Barker, H.: in roster, 204

Barnard, George: in roster, 204

Barroeta, Francisco: listed, 263

Bartlett, John Russell: Personal Nar-

rative of Explorations and Incidents, 167n.; *Dictionary of Americanisms,* 146

Basman, T. D.: in roster, 204

Bathing: at Ojo Caliente, x; immense natural tub, 35; described by Ruxton, 126n.

Beale, Robt.: on Mier Expedition, 204

Beall, H.: accidentally shot in arm at Camp Resolution, 102; lost Sept. 24, 108; in roster, 204

Beans: black beans of death, xi; drawn at Hacienda Salado, 182

Beardsley, J. L.: "Before the Railroad Came" cited, 55n.

Beardsley, W.: in roster, 204

Bears: men wanted to hunt, 4

Bechdolt, Frederick R.: *Tales of the Old-Timers* cited, 13n., 23n.

Bedbugs: a prison infested with, 130; myriads encountered by Kendall, 232

Bee, Barnard Elliott: listed, 263

Bee Mountain: seen July 10, 32

Beef: 70 head of cattle bought, 10; starting ration 3 pounds a day, 11; Grush sent back for thirty head of oxen, 26; coarser parts thrown away, 27; additional cattle arrived, 29; dried beef thrown away in Cross Timbers, 38, 39; cattle becoming very gaunt, 49; ration reduced to one and one-half pounds per day, 58, 64; weight of animals estimated, 65n., 99n.; seven oxen killed and eaten at Camp Resolution, 99; 19 beef oxen went on the *Jornada* with them, 116; ox killed near Paso, 123; one ox traveled from Austin almost to Paso, 123n.

Beidler, Jonas: in Mier action, 187, 204; in roster, 204

Belgium: had recognized Texas' independence, 175

Bells, N. J.: in roster, 205

Bennet, Valentine: to be quartermaster, 14; in Mier action, 187, 205; in roster, 205

Bernard, J.: in roster, 205

Bestwick, Wm.: in roster, 205

Bickford, P.: court-martialed, 46; in roster, 205–206

Bieber, Ralph P.: *The Papers of James J. Webb* cited, 105n.

Bigby: in roster, 206

Billington, Ray Allen: calls it trading expedition, 175; *The Far Western Frontier* cited, 77n., 175n.

Bissett, Robert P.: in roster, 206

Bissett, William: illness dates list, 200; in roster, 206

Bittler, L.: in roster, 206

Black, John: listed, 263

Blackwell, Chas. M.: in roster, 206

Blake, L. C.: in roster, 206; Mabry was roommate, 236

Blankets: none furnished in San Miguel, 78

Bloom, Lansing: objective in his treatment, 175

Blunt: listed, 263

Boardley, Akles: in roster, 206

Bocanegra, José María de: minister of foreign relations, 130; listed, 263

Bollaert, William: mentions Bonnell report, 286; *William Bollaert's Texas* quoted, 195; cited, 225, 270

Bolton, Herbert E.: transcribed Mexican documents, 199; *Athanase de Mézières and the Louisiana-Texas Frontier 1768–1780* cited, 41n.; *Guide* cited, 152n., 243

Bolton Transcriptions: described, 288; cited, 139n., 157n., 168n24, 168n25, 168n26, 171n.

Bonnell, George W.: in Mier action, 187, 207; in roster, 206–207

Booth, Joshua: in roster, 207

Bosque de los Apaches: McLeod party spent the night at, 278

Bosque River: very difficult crossing, 29

Bowen, Smith: in roster, 207

Bowman, Thos.: in roster, 207

Boxer: listed, 275

Boyd, James: in roster, said not to be a Pioneer, 207

Boyd, M. D.: in roster, 207

Bozeman, Thos.: in roster, 207

Brannard, Jas.: in roster, 207

Brashear, Dr.: died Aug. 17, 58; in roster, 207

Brashear, J. H. L.: in roster, 208

Bratton, Joseph: in roster, 208

Brazos River: reinforcements to join at, 13–14, 14n.; brackish water, 32; plenty of food on, 33; found to be not the Wichita, 56

Bray, John: in Mier action, 187, 208; in roster, 208

Brenham, Richard F.: replaced Burleson, 3; to be commissioner, 14; lost horse to Kiowas, 61; to cross the Llano with Cooke, 66; retaken in San Antonio, 132; in Mier action, 187, 208; in roster, 208

Brenham-Cooke Report: denounced Lewis, 155–56

Brewer, James H.: said he was with Kendall when he got the passport, 143

Brief: described, 289–90

Brignoli, Francisco: deserted with Carlos, 57, 138; in roster, 208

Brinkley, Wm.: in roster, 208

Brock: in roster, 208

Brown, John: in roster, 208

Brown, John H.: in roster, 209

Brown, John M.: in roster, 208–209

Brown, John S.: in roster, 209

Brushy Creek Camp: 10

Bryan, Frank: refers to expedition as "the war of 1841," 175

Bryan, John: in roster, 209

Buchanan, H. R.: in roster, 209

Buchanan, James: referred to by Kinsey, 233–34

Buffalo: men wanted to hunt, 4; first seen on June 22, 25; did not hurt hunters, 26; not used to replace beef, 27; Indians chased cow, 44; Sutton-Cooke men chased buffalo bull on Llano, 68

Buffalo wallows: 106n.

Bullock, J. C.: in roster, 209

Burgess, Charles: dispatched by McLeod, 110; Burgess party came in to San Miguel, 116; (later known as Scott Burgess), in roster, 209

Burgess, C. T.: in roster, 209

Burial: Protestants could not be buried in Mexican cemeteries, 92; Sevey paid $150 to secure, 247; Whitaker confessed to a priest, 254

Burke, James: in Mier action, 187, 209; in roster, 209

Burleson, Edward: announced as commissioner, 3

Burnet, David G.: in charge during Lamar's absence, 9

Burns, Dan: in roster, 209

Bustamante, Anastasio: listed, 263

Bustamante, Carlos M.: said their lives were guaranteed, 174; attacked Kendall, 186; his juvenile writing, 186; see also Gabinete Mexicano

Bustamante, Tomás: acted as intermediary at San Miguel, 79; listed, 263

Butler, Levi: in roster, 209–10

Buzzards: lighted within the lines to get beef, 27, 28

Calaboose: derivation of word, 78n.

Caldwell, Curtis: missing for awhile, 46; in roster, 210

Caldwell, Mathew: battle on the Salado, xi; familiar with conditions, 13; captain, commanded Company D, 15; Company D led march, 22; background, 23n.; tried to get information from Wacos, 47; discovered Brazos River, 56, 138; explored mountains to the north, 58; sent to find Red River, 58; sent to look for Indians Sept. 7, 100; would return to Texas Sept. 20, 101; dispatched to San Miguel, 108; brought into San Miguel, 116; defeated Woll, 182; in Mier action, 187, 211; in roster, 210–11

Calera rancho: McLeod party spent the night at, 280

Campbell, Michael: court-martialed, 29; in roster, 211

Campbell, William: in roster, 211

Camp Bell: 10

Camp Cazneau: 10

Camp Cook: 10

Camp Resolution: massacre at, 63–64; Indians stampeded 83 horses,

98; seven oxen killed and eaten, 99; Glass, Mercer, and a German attacked by Kiowas, 101–102; scurvy seemed imminent, 104; Matías arrived Sept. 17, 104; six wagons and goods burned, 106
Camps: before departure, 10
Canadian River: Sutton-Cooke struck it Sept. 9, 68
Canales, Antonio: fought Davis on the Nueces, 182
Canalizo, Valentín: remitted oath, 187n.; listed, 263
Cannon: brass six-pounder, 15; drawn by mules, 16; got stuck in Cross Timbers, 41; two pieces left San Miguel, 83
Caprock: first seen Aug. 27, 62; Sutton-Cooke ascended, 67; ascended by Caldwell Sept. 7, 100; the only *puerta* for some distance, 106n.; McLeod party ascended Sept. 19, 106; McLeod descended from the Llano Sept. 28, 109
Carazal: McLeod party spent two nights near, 278
Cardmer: in roster, 211
Carlos, Juan: background, 46–47; tried to get information from Wacos, 47; went to Indian village, 48; thought they were above Coffee's Upper Station, 48; thought he recognized the *Angosturas*, 49; criticized for poor guidance, 57; deserted, 57, 138; thought he recognized the Red River, 137; discussion of his actions, 137–40; falsely labeled as a spy, 139; encountered east of San Miguel, 139–40; in roster, 211–12
Carr: in roster, 212
Carrigan: *see* Corrigan
Carrión, Luis: listed, 263
Carroll, H. Bailey: *The Texan Santa Fé Trail* cited, 15n., 106n13, 106n14, 154n.; mentioned, 286
Carter, James D.: *Masonry in Texas* referred to, 202; cited, 210, 254
Casa Colorada: McLeod party spent the night at, 278
Case, Joel T.: in roster, 212

Casey, G. M.: in roster, 212; recognized by García, 259
Castañeda, Carlos E.: *Our Catholic Heritage in Texas* cited, 13n.; *The Mexican Side of the Texas Revolution* cited, 164n.
Catlin, George: *Letters and Notes . . . on the North-American Indians* cited, 48n.
Cavalry: U. S., 11n.; Texas heavy light, 126
Caygües (same as Kiowa): 61n.
Cedar trees: seen for the first time Aug. 12, 54
Celaya: McLeod party spent night at, 280
Cerro Gordo: McLeod party spent the night at, 279
Chalmers, John G.: secretary of the treasury, visited Brushy Camp, 19
Chamberlain, Henry: in roster, 212
Chapel, Charles Edward: *The Gun Collector's Handbook of Values* cited, 63
Chaves, Antonio José: mentioned, 264
Chaves, José: listed, 263
Chaves, Manuel: suggested Texan surrender, 86–87; listed, 263
Chaves, Mariano: listed, 264
Chavis, Antonio: in roster, 212
Cherokees: had been expelled in 1839, 47n.
Chihuahua: area rich in liquid assets, 7; Lewis was not received well, 159; prisoners cruelly whipped, 177; *Salón de los Distinguidos* listed, 273
Chinches: *see* Bedbugs
Chittenden, Hiram M.: *The American Fur Trade of the Far West* cited, 77n., 171n.
Chouteau, Auguste P.: arrested in New Mexico, 113n.
Christian, A. K.: article in *Southwestern Historical Quarterly* cited, 6n., 7n.
Cigarritos: see cigarros
Cigarros: Mexican name for cigarettes, 74n.
Circus: went to Mexico with Connelly, 42n.

Circus proprietor: mentioned, 264

Clark, James W.: in roster, 212

Clark, Richard: talked to Kiowas at Camp Resolution, 103; in roster, 212

Cline, Herr: listed, 264

Coffee, Holland: trading stations, 44; Upper Station, 48n.

Collier, John: in roster, 212–13

Colorado Gazette and Advertiser: cited, 151n., 236

Colorado River: plan to follow, 14

Columbus, Ga., Enquirer: mentioned, 266

Comanche: see Jesús Cuellar and Frank Holmes; escaped, 180

Comanche Peak: actually Bee Mountain, 32

Comancheros: found by Sutton-Cooke party, 72n.

Comanches: complicated existence of republic, 5; controlled the wilderness, 19; captured Thomas Hancock, 223

Companies: had 40 to 50 men each, 15

Company commanders: listed, 14–15

Concert singer: listed, 268

Concha, Fernando de la: advocated Santa Fé trade, 8n.

Conde, García: proclamation of July 28, 1841, 57n.; denied Armijo's charge, 136; listed, 264

Confederacy: Pioneers fought for, xiii

Confiscation: common practice in New Mexico, 112n.

Conn: in roster, 213

Connelley, William E: Doniphan's Expedition cited, 135n.

Connelly, Henry: led the Connelly Expedition, 8, 126n.; Pioneers found his trail, 42; advanced Sutton and Cooke $1,339, 126; listed, 264

Connelly's Expedition: circus proprietor was with, 264

Conquest: actions did not indicate conquest, 52n., 75n., 87n., 151n.; was a military conquest intended? 161ff.; no Texan fired a shot, 161, 172; theory accepted by some historians, 161; Armijo thought New

Mexico would welcome Texans, 168; Lamar's intent, 169ff.; Arista spoke of peaceful purpose of expedition, 169; instructions of the Secretary of State, 169–70; De la Garza said the expedition was commercial, 171; Cortasar said the expedition was commercial, 171; military escorts noted in past, 171n.; Texans did not act like conquerors, 171–72; Lamar possibly mistaken in sending peaceful force, 172

Contraband: to Chihuahua and Santa Fé, 7; trade between Chihuahua and Béxar, 167

Cooke, William G.: call for volunteers, 3; announced as commissioner, 3, 14; instructed to issue call, 10; familiar with conditions, 13; to be over the military, 14; his servant fired on by mistake, 28; had been on Red River, 33; experience in North Texas, 44; lost, 44; knew Carlos, 47; ordered across the Llano, 66; sent four men back to McLeod, 72; held private conversation with Lewis, 88–89; decided not to fight, 90; excoriated Lewis, 91; married Navarro's niece, 142; denounced Lewis, 152–53; not a member of a Texas Blue Lodge, 152n.; in roster, 213

Coolidge, Mr.: Kendall mentioned, 206

Coolidge, T. B.: listed, 264

Coombs, Franklin S.: missing for a while, 46; reported vote on execution, 94n.; to cross the Llano with Cooke, 66; released Jan. 25, 128; statement on treatment, 177; in roster, 213–14; criticised Ellis, 265

Coombs, Leslie: assisted in Texas revolution, 213

Copeland, Fayette: Kendall of the Picayune noted, ix; cited, 210, 240; mentioned, 233

Corrigan, John: in roster, 214

Cortasar, Antonio: said the expedition was commercial, 171; listed, 264

Cortazar, Pedro: listed, 264

Cottonwood bark used for diarrhea: 57n.

"Country unknown from here on": 35

Courts-martial: inquiry over death of Snow, 6; Gates, 27; Glass, 27; Kellett, 27; Campbell, 29; Bickford, 46; Jímerez, 46; Little, 46; Moffitt, 46; Sutton, 51–52; Thompkins, 51; White, 51; ignored by chroniclers, 51n.; McLeod criticised light sentences, 52n.; Moore, 61; Pisarzewski, 61; Watkins, 61; Pisarzewski returned to duty, 97; Willis for selling sword, 97; Willis for stealing meat, 97; Hamrich, 100; Westgate, 100; Houghton requested his own, 109; Salazar, 124, 134–35; Armijo, 136, 262; Navarro tried for treason, 141–42; Andrade was judge, 174

Crane, William C.: *Life and Select Literary Remains of Sam Houston* cited, 138–39

Covington, Hays: in roster, 214

Coyle, Jas. D.: in roster, 214

Cross Timbers: approached July 21, 35; very hard going and dry, 37; John Pope's description, 37n.

Crowder, J. T.: in roster, 214

Cuautitlán: 141, 242

Cuencamé: McLeod party spent the night at, 279

Cuervos, Los: seen, 68–69

Cuesta: Van Ness party surrounded by soldiers, 75

Cuéllar, Jesús: escaped but recaptured, 128; in roster, 214

Cummings, John A.: in Mier action, 187, 214; in roster, 214–15

Cyclopædia of American Biography: cited, 213, 230

Cyprey, Baron Alleye de: listed, 264

Daugherty: in roster, 215

Davidson, Abraham: in roster, 215

Davidson, P.: in roster, 215

Davis, Andrew Jackson: killed, 17; in roster, 215

Davis, James D.: fought Canales on the Nueces, 182

Davis, W. W. H.: says Gregorio Vigil in reduced circumstances, 272; describes propaganda methods, 172; *El Gringo* cited, 113n., 135n., 162n., 172n., 260, 272

Dawson Massacre: xi

Dawson, Nicholas Mosby: men massacred, 182

Day Donald: *The Autobiography of Sam Houston* cited, 8n.

Deaf Smith: Cooke compared to, 213

Debt: public debt in 1841, 6

Declaration of Independence, Texan: drawn up at Washington-on-the-Brazos, 5

Demans: in roster 215

Dennison, James: in roster, 215

Denyer, Samuel I.: in roster, 215

Departure: late in the season, 12; disagreement on date, 17–18; June 10 tentative date, 17n.

DeShields, James T.: summary of the expedition, 186; *Border Wars of Texas* cited, 6n., 21, 21n., 25n., 149n., 186n., 235

Diamond, John: in roster, 215

Diario del Gobierno: cited, 138n.

Diarrhea: specifics for, 57n.

Diggins, Cornelius: in roster, 215

Discipline: fishing and shooting alligators, 24; volunteers broke ranks to shoot buffalo, 26; line of march broken, 35; everyone looking for water in Cross Timbers, 41; nearly all discipline lost, 61, 69; "nearly all discipline lost" at Camp Resolution, 64–65

Distance: St. Louis to Chihuahua, 7; Austin to Chihuahua, 7; thought it was 500 miles to Santa Fé, 14n.; from Austin to Camp Resolution, 101; from San Miguel to Mexico City, 116, 116n.

Division of the command: 65

Dixon: maker of Kendall's rifle, 60n.

Document 266: cited, 175n7, 175n8, 175n9, 177n., 179n.

Document 325: cited, 144n5, 144n6, 144n8, 145n., 178n21, 178n22, 179n., 198, 199, 200, 247, 256; two lists, 195

Dogs: Indian dogs joined them, 45; Indian dogs eaten, 107

Dolores *hacienda:* McLeod party spent the night, 279

Dominican Library at Minneapolis: 131

Donovan, A. A. Stout: missing, 64, 96; in roster, 215

Doran, John: signed a list of prisoners, 200; in roster, 215; list of men, 257

Dorchesey, Burton: in roster, 216

Dorsey: listed, 264

Double compound action: Tweed taught them, 252

Dougherty, B. M.: in roster, 216

Douglas, Edward M.: *Boundaries, Areas, Geographic Centers, and Altitudes of the United States and the Several States* cited, 189n.

Drivers on trip: 15

Dryden, William G.: said Santa Fe would welcome Texans, 168; listed, 264

Dunn, Robert: killed by Kiowas, 63; in roster, 216

Dutch broom girls: 264–65

Dutchman: fired on by mistake, 28; in roster, 216

Dwyer: in roster, 216

Ears: Armijo ordered cut off, 80

Earth: packed by human feet is hard, 78n.

Eberly: in roster, 216

Ebner, Adolphus: in roster, 216

Edgar, James M.: in roster, 216

El Carro: McLeod party spent the night at, 279

Elephant: to see the, *xiii;* "I have seen the elephant" first heard, 36; Kendall's interpretation, 145–47; the true meaning, 146

El Gallo: McLeod party spent the night at, 279

Elías, Col. José María: treated the prisoners kindly in Paso, 124; ordered an investigation of Salazar, 124

El Jaral: McLeod party spent the night at, 280

Elk: said to be in Texas, 33, 33n.

Elliott, Jacob: in roster, 216

Ellis, Powhatan: gave them $1,000

and other money, 127; tried to get them released, 130; said 17 men's names forgotten, 198; criticized by Coombs, 265; listed, 265

Ellison, Theophilus: in roster, 216

El Ojito: McLeod party spent the night at, 279

Emily: the mulatto girl with whom Santa Anna dallied, 270

England: had recognized Texas' independence, 175

Erhart, Antonio: in roster, 216

Erhart, K.: in roster, 216

Ernest, Felix: died during the night, 119; in roster, 216–17

Erwin, Edwin: in roster, 217

Escapes: Van Ness party did not attempt, 77; McLeod party did not attempt near Chihuahua, 124, 180; Alsbury, Hancock, Adams and Sheldon escaped north of Paso but recaptured, 128; Sutton-Cooke party tried to escape south of Chihuahua, 128, 180; "Comanche" escaped but recaptured, 128; McJunkins and a partner escaped but recaptured, 128; Lubbock and Mazur escaped from Santiago, 128; Howard and Hudson escaped from Puebla, 128; Stosoases and Studion escaped from Puebla, 128; Navarro escaped from Vera Cruz, 142; reasons for not trying to escape, 180; either four or six successful, 180

Escarbadas, Las: 107n.

Espinosa, J. Manuel: *First Expedition of Vargas into New Mexico* cited, 181n.; opinions of other writers, 181n.

Espíritu Santo: McLeod party spent the night at, 279

Evans, James M.: in roster, 217

Eve, Joseph: listed, 265

Ewing or Emory: in roster, 217

Executions: Salazar ordered Van Ness party executed, 76; of Baker and Howland, 81–83; Armijo ordered vote on Sutton-Cooke party, 94; 17 men at Hacienda Salado, 182; Howland executed, 227

Expedition: two questions, *viii;* purpose of, 3, 4; reception expected to be good, 4; Lamar broached early, 6; might have saved Texas' finances, 7; amount spent, 9n.; total number of men over three hundred, 11, 23, 23n.; various routes, 13

Explorations and Surveys: cited, 37n.

Failure of expedition: causes summed up by Kendall, 114

Falconer, Thomas: commented on omission of flour, 11; route along the Colorado River, 14; to stay with McLeod, 66; assured McLeod of his support, 102; sent to San Miguel Oct. 7, 114; released Feb. 1, 128; gave wording of the Kendall passport under oath, 144–45; saw pack mules leave Béxar for Río Grande, 167; in roster, 217; writings described, 284; *Letters and Notes on the Texan Santa Fé Expedition* cited, 10n., 12n37, 12n38, 13n., 15n., 27n., 58n., 101n., 102n7, 102n8, 104n., 108n., 112n., 149n., 151n., 158n39, 158n40, 158n42, 158n43, 167n16, 167n19, 175n5, 175n6, 193, 197, 217

Fannin: mentioned, 5

Fardoff: in roster, 218

Farley, Horace H.: in roster, 218

Farmer's Almanack, for the Year of Our Lord 1841: cited, 46n.

Fatigue duty: one company detailed for, 23

Ferguson, James: in roster, 218

Fergusson, Harvey: speaks of the "invasion," 162; *The Conquest of Don Pedro* cited, 162n.

Firearms: Kendall's Dixon was 60-caliber, 60n.; patent 16-shot rifles, 63n.; equipment of Sutton-Cooke party, 67; two Colt pistols in Mexican's waistband, 76; largely muzzleloaders, 90n.; Mexicans were poorly equipped, 156n.

Fitzgerald, Archibald: sent to the Falls of the Brazos to get teams, 27; drove the Jersey wagon in

Cross Timbers, 40; knew Carlos, 47; to cross the Llano with Cooke, 66; sent on to San Miguel, 74; wanted to attack Salazar, 76; tied at the wrists, 79; released Feb. 28, 128; retaken in San Antonio, 132; in Mier action, 187, 218; in roster, 218

Fleming, R. P.: in roster, 219

Flenner, Samuel: killed by Kiowas, 63; in roster, 219

Flint and steel: probably used, 33n.

Flint, Samuel: died of colic, 29; in roster, 219

Flores, Fernando: listed, 258

Flores, Nabor: in roster, 219

Flores, John: in roster, 219

Folsom, Charles J.: *Mexico in 1842* cited, 14n., 47n., 94n., 164n.; list of men, 195; list taken from *Gazette,* 196, 200, 256

Food: one pint of cornmeal a day, x; flour omitted, 11; customary diet on the frontier, 11n.; could have eaten alligators' tails, 24; first buffalo meat eaten, 26; bears and javelinas plentiful on Little River, 28; grapes, plums, honey, duck, elk, deer, bear, wild turkey, buffalo, mustang along the Brazos River, 33; deer, bears, buffalo, and honey found in the Cross Timbers, 37; mesquite beans first used for coffee, 48; pumpkins or watermelons taken from Indian village, 48; fried catfish eaten on the Wichita, 49; sugar and coffee gone, 49; mesquite beans used by Comanches and Mexicans, 51; could not kill enough game on Wichita, 58; prairie dogs eaten, 60; ate broiled antelope, fine mushrooms, and young buffalo, 61; grapes and plums, 61; dried meat found in Kiowa village, 62; hackberries eaten, 63; ate "rough parts" of beef, 65; meat, coffee, sugar and salt gone at Camp Resolution, 64; ate blood, hide and entrails, 65; four days' rations left on Aug. 30, 65; Sutton-Cooke party ate buffalo, horse, grapes, pumpkin, hack-

berries, snakes, terrapins and turkey, 67; plums and grapes found
west of the Llano, 68; turkeys
killed on Llano, 69; Sutton-Cooke
men faced starvation, 69; small
quantity of barley meal for 97
men, 72; Kendall and Fitzgerald
found some wild parsley, 73;
bought twenty sheep on the Gallinas River, 73; bought a sheep on
Sept. 16, 78–79; Falconer got an
armload of biscuits from the Mexicans, 113; very little issued by
Salazar, 117; dry ears of corn were
prized, 117; *see also* Women
Fonley: in roster, 219
Fort Johnson: established by Cooke,
44
Fort Preston: established by Cooke,
44
Foster, Robert: listed, 265
France: had recognized Texas' independence, 175
Francisca: listed, 265
Franco-Texienne Bill: Lamar and
Houston clashed over, 9
Fray Cristóbal: McLeod party spent
the night at, 278
Freeman, Luke: in roster, 219
French widow at Cerro Gordo: listed,
265
French woman at Chihuahua: listed,
265
Fresnillo: McLeod party spent the
night at, 279
Froebel, Julius: said Americans pre-
ferred Texas route, 168; *Seven
Years' Travel in Central America*
cited, 168n.

Gabinete Mexicano: cited, 83n.,
137n., 139n17, 139n18, 174n.,
185n., 186n.; reliability, 181n.
Gadsden purchase: 189
Gallegher-Hoyle *Journal:* cited, 34n.,
112n., 154; mentioned, 227, 231,
239, 256; described, 286
Gallegher, Peter: to stay with
McLeod, 66; sent to San Miguel
Oct. 7, 114; in roster, 219
Galton: in roster, 219

García, Ygnacio: quartered in Casey's
home, 212; listed, 258–59
Garrison, George P.: *Diplomatic
Correspondence of the Republic of
Texas* cited, 18n., 155n., 158n.,
164n., 169n., 170n.
Garza, Antonio de la: said the ex-
pedition was commercial, 171;
listed, 265
Gates: suffered with pneumonia, 118;
died and ears cut off, 123; in
roster, 219
Gates, Thomas: court-martialed, 27;
in roster, 219
Gerlach, Casper: in roster, 220
Gerolte, Federico: listed, 265
Gibson, George N.: in roster, 220
Gibson, George Rutledge: *Journal of
a Soldier Under Kearny and Doni-
phan, 1846–1847* cited, 165n.
Gilliland, Nathan: gave Pioneers
$200, 127
Gilmore, P. W.: in roster, 220
Glass, Thomas: court-martialed, 27;
returned Sept. 2, 97; scalped by
Kiowas, 101–102; in roster, 220
Glenn: in roster, 220
Goldap: in roster, 220
Goliad: massacre at, mentioned, 5;
taken by Mexican detachments,
182
Goliad Massacre: Holliday escaped
from, 225
Gompers: in roster, 220
Gonzales, José María Elías: treated
prisoners kindly, 124; listed, 266
Golpin, Amos A.: unable to ride at
Camp Resolution, 105; ordered
shot by Salazar, 122; in roster, 220
Goodnight, Charles: quoted on to-
bacco, 11n.; quoted on drink for
diarrhea, 57n.; quoted on prickly
pear, 68n.; quoted on starving
men, 99n.
Goods: imported to Chihuahua and
Santa Fé, 7; burned at Camp
Resolution, 105–106; carried by
merchants, 105n.
Gordon, J. L.: in roster, 220–21
Gowan: in roster, 221
Gramont: listed, 266

Grand Lodge of Texas: mentioned, 152n.
Gray, Wm.: in roster, 221
Green, Asa: in roster, 221
Green, Burwell: in roster, 221
Green, Edward: in roster, 221
Green, Thomas: said log chains weighed 20 pounds each, 178; *Mier Expedition* cited, 64n., 201, 273
Gregg, Josiah: went west for his health, *xiii*n.; followed the Arkansas and Canadian rivers, 42n.; said his company had 200 fighting men, 171; *Commerce of the Prairies* cited, 42n., 167n17, 167n18, 171n32, 171n33, 261
Griffith, Edward: attacked by Kiowas at Camp Resolution, 103; brains knocked out, 122–23; in roster, 221
Griswold, S. P.: in roster, 221
Grover, George W.: son lives in Galveston, *xiii*, 187, 222; *Minutes of Adventure* cited, 10n.; to cross the Llano with Cooke, 66; Grand Reference Sheet, 255, 257, cited 15n., 149n., described, 193; Reference Sheet, 193–94, 258; other lists, 195; list of men sailed from Vera Cruz, 200; in roster, 221; materials described, 285–86; handwriting, 286
Grush, H. L.: to be commissary of subsistence, 14; returned for a wagon, 25; in roster, 222
Guadalupe *hacienda*: McLeod party spent the night at, 279
Guajuquilla: McLeod party spent the night at, 279
Guanajuato: money and clothing given the prisoners, 127; 17 left in hospital with smallpox, 128; McLeod party spent night at, 280
Guaymas: supplied goods to Chihuahua, 7; Lewis fled to, 159
Guides: necessary, 13; Howland official guide, 15; lack of, deplored, 19; were available, 102n.; suspected of treachery, 108; did not want to go ahead Sept. 30, 109; Mexicans were excellent, 110n.

Gulick, Charles Adams: *The Papers of Mirabeau Bonaparte Lamar* cited, 9n., 17n., 21n63, 21n64, 102n., 136n9, 136n10, 168n., 203
Gutierres, José Ignacio: listed, 266

Hacienda Salado: 17 men executed, 182
Haddon, G.: in roster, 223
Hafen, Leroy R.: *Ruxton of the Rockies* cited, *xiii*n.; refers to expedition as an attempt to subjugate, 175–76
Haggard, J. Villasana: *Handbook for Translators of Spanish Historical Documents* cited, 179n.
Haines, Ephraim M.: in roster, 223
Haines, John M.: mentioned in court-martial of Hamrich, 100; in roster, 223
Hale, Joseph W.: "Masonry in the Early Days of Texas" cited, 150n.
Haley, J. Evetts: *Charles Goodnight* cited, 11n., 57n., 68n., 99n.
Hall, Edw.: in roster, 223
Hallenbeck, Cleve: *Legends of the Spanish Southwest* cited, 121n.
Hammer, J.: in roster, 223
Hammett, Jacob: in roster, 223
Hamrich, John: court-martialed, 100; in roster, 223
Hancock, Thomas: familiar with conditions, 13; went to Indian village, 47; escaped north of Paso, 128; retaken in San Antonio, 132; attached to Mier prisoners, 187, 224; in roster, 223–24
Handbook of Texas: referred to, 202, 247
Hann, John W.: ordered to find a road Aug. 29, 62–63; returned on Aug. 31, 66; in roster, 224
Harding, T.: in roster, 224
Hargous, L. S.: advanced them $6,253.66, 127; listed, 266
Harris: in roster, 224
Harris, Enoch: in roster, 224
Harrison, Wm. B.: in roster, 224
Hart, Antonio E.: in roster, 224
Hasmann, F.: in roster, 224
Hatch: *see* Hutch
Havana: a wholesale center, 7

Hawaiian Islands: 159n.

Hayes, Henry: in roster, 224–25

Hegewick, Adolph: statement on treatment, 178

Hemridge, J.: in roster, 225

Henry, William Nelson: in roster, 225

Heredia, José C.: gave Pioneers $500 at Durango, 126; said 1,000 men started, 194; listed, 266

Hermann: listed, 275

Hickey, James: in roster, 225

Historians: value varies, 181n.

Hobbies: cited, 42n.

Hobbs, James: Wild Life in the Far West cited, 64n., 135n., 260

Hodge, F. W.: gathered Falconer material, 217; Handbook of American Indians North of Mexico cited, 41n.

Holliday, John J.: died at sea, xii; to be assistant commissary of subsistence, 14; in roster, 225

Holmes, Frank: in roster, 225

Home: in roster, 225

Hoodel, Jacob: in roster, 225

Hoosegow: derivation of word, 78n.

Horace, Bealle: in roster, 225

Horn, Alexander: in roster, 225

Hornsby, C. C.: in roster, 225

Horses: all men mounted, 11; Kendall's evaluation of, 12; first horses stolen by Kiowas Aug. 22, 61; horses and mules missing Aug. 27, 62; shoes were torn off, 68; Howland's horse eaten, 69; had to rest on the Jornada, 122

Hostility: first hint of hostility from Mexicans, 73; see Antipathy

Hotchkiss, Wm.: in roster, 226

Hotten, John Camden: The Slang Dictionary cited, 146

Houghtaling, J. B.: in roster, 226

Houghton, W. D.: captain, commanded Company B, 15; requested his own court-martial, 16, 109; in roster, 226

House: passed bill to authorize expedition, 9; voted to disband army, 9

Houston: preparations in, 4

Houston, Sam: policies in office, 5; opposition to Lamar, 6, 165–67, 267; sitting in the House, 8; opinion of Lamar, 8; clash with Lamar over Franco-Texienne Bill, 9; his supporters opposed the expedition, 20; his policy with Indians, 166; disagreement on his conduct of finances, 166n.; succeeded Lamar, 183; declared naval blockade, 183; invited volunteers from New Orleans, 183; vetoed annexation of northern Mexico, 183

Howard, George Thomas: to New Orleans to buy supplies, 4, 10; familiar with conditions, 13; appointed aide-de-camp, 13, 14; disagreed with McLeod, 13; listed as merchant, 15n.; famous fight with Comanches, 25, 25n.; sent to the Falls of the Brazos for teams, 27; absent when McLeod left, 27; resigned as second in command, 39, 40n.; almost shot Larrabee, 45; to cross the Llano with Cooke, 66; sent on to San Miguel, 74; lame on the road to Santa Fé, 79; escaped from Puebla, 128; on Somervell Expedition, 187, 226; in Civil War, 187; with Kearny, 187; in Mexican War, 187; in roster, 226–27

Howard, John C.: accompanied Burgess, 110; in roster, 227

Howland, Samuel W.: familiar with conditions, 13; to be guide, 14, 15; had not been in the wilderness, 33; advised keeping at a distance from Red River, 41–42; sent ahead to San Miguel, 52; in prison in Santa Fé, 73; execution at San Miguel, 82–83; party escaped but recaptured, 83–84, 83n.; in roster, 227

Hoyle, Stephen, Z.: to stay with McLeod, 66; in roster, 227

Hudson, Joshua: in roster, 227

Hudson, N. G.: in roster, 228

Hudson, Radcliffe: commanded Company C, 15; escaped from Puebla, 128; in roster, 228

Hughes, F.: in roster, 228

Hughes, James H.: in roster, 228

Hulbert, Archer Butler: *Forty-Niners* cited, 146
Hull, G. R.: took astronomical readings, 39; made observations Aug. 25, 61; killed by Kiowas Aug. 30, 63; his horse eaten, 65; in roster, 228
Hunt, George: in roster, 228
Hunt, Thomas W.: assistant guide, 15; had been on Red River, 33; found passage to the mountains, 70; in roster, 229
Hunter, Samuel P.: in roster, 229
Hutch, Joseph T.: in roster, 229

Idger, J. M.: in roster, 229
Illustrated News: cited, 42n.
Imens, José María: in roster, 229
Indas, John T.: in roster, 229
Independence, Mo.: sent goods to Santa Fé and Chihuahua, 7
Independence of Texas: recognized by United States, England, Belgium, and France, 175
Indians: Pioneers expected to meet, 4; Indian fights at time of departure, 28n.; had been on the Brazos in 1840, 33; deserted village found in Cross Timbers, 37; distant fires seen upon the hills, 38; sign on the Wichita River, 42; first seen on July 31, 44; bones of fish, snakes, terrapins, and polecats found in camps, 45; Wacos, well-armed and mounted, 47; Wacos fled at approach of Texans, 48; Wacos' houses looked like beehives, 48; watched them from the distant hills, 49; first hostiles encountered Aug. 22, 61; deserted Kiowa camp found Aug. 28, 62; stampeded 83 horses at Camp Resolution, 98; dangerous after rain, 99n.; used by Archuleta, 113; Houston's policy with, 166
Indignities to prisoners: intensified feelings, 188
Insignia: special emblem for New Mexican soldiers, 188
Invasion: was the expedition an invasion? *see* Conquest

Invitations: issued to men of standing, 14
Irwin, Edward: in roster, 229
Itinerary of prisoners: shown in Appendix G, 275–81
Iturbide: listed, 266

Jackson, Andrew: said expedition was ill-judged, 185
Jackson, J.: in Mier action, 187, 229
Jackson, Wm. H.: in roster, 229
James, Marquis: *The Raven* cited, 6n.
James, Wm.: in roster, 229
Jennison, John: gave Pioneers shoes and cups, 126; possible author of statement about Kendall, 144n.; listed, 266
Jesús, Don: took Van Ness party to San Miguel, 76; Kendall's description of him, 79; listed, 266
Jimerez, Martin José: court-martialed, 46; in roster, 229
Jim the Butcher: description, 12; Kendall fed him bread, 76
Johnson, Chas.: in roster, 229
Johnson, Frank W.: *A History of Texas and Texans* cited, 165n.
Johnson, Thomas: in roster, 229–30
Johnson, Thomas: in roster, 230
Johnson, Wm. J.: in roster, 230
Jones, from Connecticut: listed, 266
Jones: servant, 230
Jones, Calvin: in roster, 230
Jones, C. M.: in roster, 230
Jones, John E.: in Mier action, 187, 230; in roster, 230
Jones, Myers Fisher: in roster, 230
Jones, W. Jefferson: urged Santa Fé trade, 168
Jonesboro, Arkansas: Connelly took party to, 8
Jornada: derivation of name, 121n.; Kendall's description of the march, 122; 40 hours without food or water, 123
Journals: lost, 286
Joya: McLeod party spent the night at, 278
Juan Jérez *hacienda:* McLeod party spent the night at, 279
Justice, Milton M.: in roster, 230–31
Juvero, Julián: listed, 266

Kadogyato: listed, 266

Kane, Joseph Nathan: *Famous First Facts* cited, 146n.

Kangaroo court: convicted man of "simples," x, 228

Kearny: Howard was with, 226

Keenan, Francis: missing Aug. 27, 62; in roster, 231

Keenon, John: in roster, 231

Keleher, William A.: *Turmoil in New Mexico* cited, 267

Kellett, E.: court-martialed, 27; in roster, 231

Kellett, Wm. J.: in roster, 231

Kelly, Wm.: in roster, 231

Kemper, A.: in roster, 231

Kendall, Amos F.: in roster, 231

Kendall, George Wilkins: *Narrative* noted, ixn.; commented on omission of breadstuffs, 11; bought all the bread he could, 11, 75; background and description, 24–25; broke a bone in his right ankle, 24n.; rode in the Jersey wagon, 26; joined spy company Aug. 6, 49; wanted to go on to San Miguel but could not, 52–53; to cross Llano with Cooke, 66; sent on to San Miguel, 74; concealed his valuables, 75; lame on the road to Santa Fé, 79; passport read by Armijo, 80; passport disputed, 80n.; hired seat on a donkey, 81; well impressed by Mexican women's looks, 84; joined main body Oct. 17, 116; feet badly swollen and blistered, 116–17; got out of the two small rooms, 118; tried to crawl into an outdoor oven, 118; bought a pair of shoes at Parrida, 121; broke his water gourd, 121–22; released in April, 131; compares Red and Wichita rivers, 137; describes his meeting with Navarro in the *Acordada*, 141; biography by Copeland, 142; article in the *Louisiana Historical Quarterly*, 142; the question of his passport, 142–45; wording of his passport, 145; interpretation of the phrase, "I have seen the elephant," 145–47; a wagonload of his ma-

terial destroyed, 151n.; a Mason, 153n.; denounced Lewis, 153–55; arrived in New Orleans in May, 186; described priesthood, 186; married a Roman Catholic girl, 186; attacked by Bustamante, 186; statement on treatment, 177–78; was a good friend of Coombs, 214; in roster, 231–33; Olmstead visited in 1856, 232; saved rivet from leg chains, 232; itinerary shown in Appendix G, 275–81; *Narrative* described, 283–84

Kennedy, Robert: in roster, 233

Kennedy, William: *Texas: The Rise, Progress, and Prospects of the Republic of Texas* cited, 5n.

Kennedy, Wm. H.: in roster, 233

Kenneymore, J. C. P.: in roster, 233

Kentucky: legislature hostile to Mexico, 183

Kenyon, John: missing, 64, 96; in roster, 233

Keths, C. R.: in roster, 233

Killett or Kissell (illegible): in roster, 233

Kinsey, Henry M.: in roster, 233–34

Kiowas: complicated existence of republic, 5; controlled the wilderness, 19; massacre, 63; refused to give directions at Camp Resolution, 103; scalped Glass, 220

Klein: missing, 64, 96; in roster, 234

Kordell, B.: in roster, 234

Kuykendall, Henry A.: in Mier action,, 187, 234; in roster, 234

La Caleta: McLeod party spent the night at, 279

La Cruz: McLeod party camped near, 279

Laguna Encinillos: McLeod party camped near, 278

La Luna: quoted by Kendall, 157

Lamar, Mirabeau Bonaparte: call for volunteers, 3; succeeded Houston in 1838, 6; envisioned public improvements, 6; tried to get a loan, 6; advocated expedition in 1839, 6, 7; issued proclamation to Santa Fé in 1840, 7; Houston's opinion of, 8; ineligible to succeed himself, 8n.; clashed with Houston over Franco-Texienne Bill, 9; went to New Orleans for medical treatment, 9; returned by Mar. 8, 1841, 9, 9n.; organized expedition, 9; sent Howard to buy supplies, 10; instructed Cooke to call for volunteers, 10; instructed Shaw to allow bills, 10; appointed McLeod as leader, 10; visited Brushy Camp, 19; made an address, 22; possibly mistaken in sending a peaceful force, 172; his view of Armijo realistic, 172; succeeded by Houston, 183; listed, 266

Lamar, Rebecca: married McLeod, 21n., 239

Lamb, James: in roster, 234

Landers, Wm.: in roster, 234

Landes, David: in roster, 234

Land scrip: *see* Scrip

La Noria: McLeod party spent the night at, 279

La Parada: McLeod party spent the night at, 279

La Puerta: McLeod party spent night at, 280

Lardner, Nicolas: in roster, 234

Larrabee, James B.: almost shot by Howard, 45; worked for Bennet, 45n.; died in a cart at Saucillo, 124; in roster, 234

Las Pilas: McLeod party spent the night at, 280

Laughlin: in roster, 234

Lawrence, Henry E.: listed, 267

Lee, Nelson: *Three Years Among the Comanches* cited, 211, 234; in roster, 234

Legislatures: passed resolutions condemning Mexico, 183

LeMar, H. D.: *History of the Lamar or LeMar Family in America* cited, 21n.

Lemon, John: in roster, 235

Leprosy: Kendall's description, 131

Lewis, John E.: in roster, 235

Lewis, William P.: commanded artillery company, 15; to cross the Llano with Cooke, 66; sent on to San Miguel, 73–74; tied at the wrists, 79; said they were merchants, 80;

went with Armijo as interpreter, 80; persuaded the Texans to surrender, 86–89; his honesty questioned, 87–89; at San Miguel, well dressed, 116; got a share of McLeod's goods, 116; was he a traitor? 148ff.; denounced by Lubbock, 148; a Mason, 150; persuaded Cooke to surrender, 150–52; importance of his Masonic affiliation, 152; denounced by Cooke, 152–53; denounced by Kendall, 153–55; deceived Farley and Houghtaling, 155; denounced by Brenham-Cooke, 155–56; said he was an American merchant, 156; three counts against, 156n.; offered his services to Armijo, 157; his rewards, 157–58; his fate, 158–59; took Farley's watch, 218; in roster, 235

Lewiston, Joseph: in roster, 235

Liceaga, Juan: listed, 267

Liddy, Patrick: in roster, 235

Lie, Luis: listed, 267

Lillie, G.: in roster, 235

Lindley, Jacob: in roster, 235

Line of march: 23

Lists of personnel: total, 33, 196; catalog of (Appendix B), 255ff.

Little, H. P.: court-martialed, 46

Little River: reached on June 24, 26

Little, Robert P.: in roster, 235

Liver ailment: Kendall says Brashear died of, 58n.

Lives guaranteed: 112n24, 112n25, 113n.; discussion, 174; Bancroft said Armijo justified in breaking guarantee, 176

Llano Estacado: no running water in summer, 13; plan to cross, 14; had not been crossed for 200 years, 14n.; dreaded, 19

Lockhart, David: in roster, 235–36

Lockridge, E. B.: shot himself June 25, 28; in roster, 236

Long, F.: in roster, 236

Longcope, Charles L.: in roster, 236

Los Lingos Creek: rendezvous for Indians, 62n.

Los Placeres: McLeod party spent the night at, 278

Louisiana Historical Quarterly: cited, 142, 233
Louisiana Purchase: size, 189
Lovato, Bueno Venturo: listed, 267
Lovey, F.: in roster, 236
Lowter, Ralph: in roster, 236
Lubbock County: named after Thomas S. Lubbock, 151n.
Lubbock-Tardif list: 201, 258
Lubbock, Thomas S.: to cross the Llano with Cooke, 66; spoke of a second traitor, 128; escaped from Santiago, 128; denounced Lewis, 148; original report destroyed, 151n.; statement on treatment, 177; in Mier action, 187, 236; in roster, 236; original printing of his report located, 289
Lumsden, Francis Asbury: said he had seen Kendall's passport, 143; listed, 267
Lyons, Patrick: in Mier action, 187, 236; in roster, 236

Mabee, William: killed by Kiowas, 63; in roster, 236
Mabry, James L.: roommate of L. C. Blake, 206; in roster, 236–37
McAllister, John: shot by Salazar, 120; in roster, 237
McClanahan, John: in roster, 237
McDonald, John: in roster, 237
Macedonian: listed, 275
McElyea: in roster, 238
McGuire, Thomas: in roster, 238
McJunkins, William H.: escaped, 128, 180; in roster, 238
McKaine, Wm.: in roster, 238
McKean: in roster, 238
McKennon: in roster, 238
McLaughlin, John: died Sept. 25, 108; in roster, 239
McLeod, Hugh: appointed leader, 10; set June 5 as starting date, 13; brevet brigadier general, 14; forgave Sutton's men, 17; graduate of West Point, 20; had fought in Texas, 20–21; criticized as commander, 20–21; a brother-in-law of Lamar, 21n63; dissatisfaction over, 21n64; first failure with discipline, 24; returned to settlements

June 25, 27–28; returned to expedition July 12, 33; asked to resign, 39; retained command, 39; not supported by journalists, 39; resigned a commission in United States Army, 39n.; issued orders to speed up the march, 40; certified that Howard had resigned, 40n.; warned Moffit leniency would not be repeated, 46; ordered Pioneers not to molest Indian village, 48; ordered men to drill at Camp Resolution, 97; read funeral service for Sturgess, 101; reached the Arroyo Tucumcari Oct. 3, 110; surrendered to Archuleta, 112; McLeod and officers sent to San Miguel Oct. 7, 114; left San Miguel on Oct. 16, 116; said at San Miguel he had a complete list, 197; in roster, 239
McLeod party: about 180 men, *xii*
McMillen: in roster, 239
McNabb: in roster, 239
Macon (Ga.) *Telegraph:* did not want Texas in the Union, 184
McWilliam: in roster, 239
Magoffin, James Wiley: with Connelly in 1839, 42; wagon train passed the Pioneers, 120; listed, 267
Magoffin, Mrs. James Wiley: fed the Pioneers well in Chihuahua, 126
Manuel: sent on to San Miguel, 74; shot by drummer, 74n.; disappeared from the *Narrative,* 77n.; in roster, 237
Marcy, Randolph B.: *The Prairie Traveler* cited, 12n.; *Army Life on the Border* cited, 114n.
Mardille: in roster, 237
Margo, Elisabeth: *Taming the Forty-Niner* cited, 146
Marguerat, L. F.: in roster, 237
Marryat, Capt. Frank: accused of plagiarism, 220
Marshall, Thomas Maitland: article in *Southwestern Historical Quarterly* cited, 6n.
Martin, Juan Antonio: listed, 267
Maryatte, Charles: in roster, 237

Masonic test of Lewis's honesty: 88–89

Masonry: importance in early Texas, 150; article in the *Southwestern Historical Quarterly*, 150n.

Massacre: at Camp Resolution, 63–64; massacre of Hull's party, 63

Matches: friction matches made in 1833, 33n.

Mathews, Mitford M.: *A Dictionary of Americanisms* cited, 145–46

Matías: sent back to McLeod, 72; arrived at Camp Resolution Sept. 17, 104; accompanied Burgess, 110; in roster, 237

Mayer, Brantz: statement on treatment, 178; listed, 267–68; *Mexico As It Was and As It Is* cited, 268; listed, 273

Mazur, Louis: escaped from Santiago,, 128; in roster, 237

Meade, D. and R.: listed, 268

Mealy, C.: in roster, 239

Meetings, public: held all over U.S., 183–84

Mencken, H. L.: *The American Language* cited, 78n.

Mercer: joined the expedition, 29; wounded by Kiowas, 101–102; in roster, 239–40

Merchants: hoped to make profit in Santa Fé, *xiii*; number on trip, 15

Meriweather, David: mentioned, 112n.

Met, J. C.: in roster, 240

Mexicans: complicated existence of republic, 5

Mexican commanders en route: Appendix C, 258ff.

Mexican War: Pioneers in, *xii*; broke out within four years, 188; Howard was in, 226

Mexico: war with, *xi*, 188

Mexico, Memorias Relaciones 1841–1843: cited, 143n., 144n.

Mexico in 1842: list of men, 200; 306 men enlisted, 258

Miel: identified, 74n.

Mier actions: *xi*; 20 Pioneers in, *xii*; Texans captured Mier, 182; surrender to Ampudia, 182; Wm. A. Wallace was in, 187, 253; Beidler in, 187, 204; David Allen in, 187, 203; Alsbury imprisoned in, 187, 203; Bennet in, 187, 205; Bonnell killed in, 187, 207; Burke was in, 187, 209; Caldwell was in, 187, 211; Robt. Beale in, 204; Bray in, 187, 208; Brenham killed in, 187, 208; John Cummings killed at Salado, 187, 215; Fitzgerald killed, 187, 218; Hancock imprisoned, 187, 218; Van Ness attached to, 218; G. T. Howard in, 187, 226; J. Jackson killed at Mier, 187, 229; John E. Jones killed, 187, 230; Kuykendall was in, 187, 234; Lubbock was in Mier fighting, 187, 236; Patrick Lyons was killed at Salado, 187, 236; John Morgan was captured, 187, 241; John S. Sutton was in, 187, 250; Jas. N. Torrey was executed at Salado, 251; Van Ness attached as a prisoner, 187, 252

Miggins, C. D.: in roster, 240

Military escort: customary, 170–71

Military nature: not known to rank and file, *ix*

Millard, Henry: listed, 268

Miller, A.: in roster, 240

Miller, George D.: in roster, 240

Miller, John M.: in roster, 240

Miller, Washington D.: said times were auspicious, 184–85

Mims, Dignid: in roster, 240

Miranda, Guadalupe: listed, 218

Mission of San Diego de Alcalá: 57

Mississippi: wanted Texas in Union, 184

Mitchell, A. S.: in roster, 240

Mitchell, Wm.: in roster, 241

Mobile: public meetings, 183

Modos, M.: in roster, 241

Moffitt, Spencer: court-martialed, 46; in roster, 241

Money: Texas money devaluated, 6

Moon: eclipse on Aug. 2, 46

Mooney, James: "Calendar History of the Kiowa Indians" cited, 64n.

Moore, Edwin Ward: listed, 268

Moore, J. W.: court-martialed, 61; in roster, 241

Morales: listed, 268

Morale: as Pioneers bad, as prisoners excellent, x; feeling between McLeod and officers, 38–39; argument about having gone through Cross Timbers, 44; McLeod criticized court for leniency, 52; discord between McLeod and Caldwell, 52; men cried "Beef, beef! No drill!" 97; McLeod demanded the court-martial inflict the proper penalties, 101; muttering Sept. 12, 101; growing signs of unrest at Camp Resolution, 102; extreme depression struck McLeod party Sept. 25, 108

More, Kennedy: in roster, 241

Morgan, John D.: in Mier action, 187, 241; in roster, 241

Morlet, Mariano: listed, 268

Morley: in roster, 241

Morris, George W.: saved by Kendall, 240; in roster, 241

Morris, Isaac: in roster, 241

Morton, Js. W.: in roster, 241

Mules: drew cannon, 16

Muñoz: took the Durango dragoons to San Miguel, 122; listed, 268

Munson, Ira: in roster, 241

Murphy, Danl.: in roster, 241

Muster roll: taken, 193; one found on Brazos, 197

Names: Brenham, Cooke, and Coombs wrote names on wall at Cerro Gordo, 208; Hudson carved name in a cathedral in Mexico City, 228

Narrative of the Texan Santa Fé Expedition: ixn.

Narrows: see Angosturas

Naughton, J. W.: in roster, 242

Navarro, Ángela: married Cooke, 213

Navarro, José Antonio: to be commissioner, 3, 14; rode in the Jersey wagon, 26; reason for his lame leg, 26n.; could not ride in the Jersey wagon, 40; pointed out they had no friendly Indians, 102; sent to San Miguel Oct. 7, 114; was not released but escaped in 1845, 132; his sister rejected Santa Anna, 136; separated from the McLeod party and sent to the Acordada, 141; description by Kendall in April, 1842, 141; his background and family, 141–42; summary of his treatment, 141–42; tried for treason by Santa Anna, 141–42; sentenced to death but sentence commuted, 142; escaped, 142; returned to San Antonio, 142; in roster, 242

Navy: Texas lacked, 5

Neighbors, Robert S.: sent to hold elections, 165

Neil, A.: left ill at Paso, 124; in roster, 243

Neldes, S. G.: in roster, 243

Newman, P.: in roster, 243

New Mexico Historical Review: cited, 74n., 135n.

New Orleans: mass meetings in, xi, 183

New Orleans Bee: mentioned, 217

New Orleans Commercial Advertiser: cited, 256

New Orleans Commercial Bulletin: list of Jan. 27, 1842, 196, 200, 256

New Orleans Picayune: cited, 210; established by Kendall and Lumsden, 231

Newspapers: urged Lamar to open trade, 8

Newspapermen: went on trip, xiii

New York: public meetings, 183–84

New York Herald: mentioned, 272

Niles' Register: cited, 94n., 158n., 176n., 183n., 184n5, 184n7, 184n9, 185n., 188n., 256, 257, 275; printed J. Q. Adams' speeches, 185n.

Norris, J.: in roster, 243

Norton, Jas. W.: in roster, 243

Nueces: Canales fought Davis on, 182

Number of men on expedition: 197

Oath: taken not to bear arms, 132, 186–87; apparently remitted, 187n.

Occupations: of Pioneers, 4n.

O'Connor, John: in roster, 243

Ochoa: was kind, xi; listed, 259

Ojo Caliente: where the Mexican girls went in to bathe with them, *x*, 124–25; McLeod party spent the night at, 279

Ojo del Lucero: McLeod party spent the night at, 278

Ojo de San Malayuque: McLeod party spent the night at, 278

Old Santa Fé: cited, 175n.

Olivér, Pedro Pascuela: listed, 268

Olmstead, Frederick Law: went west for his health, *xiii*n.; visited Kendall in 1856, 232–33; *A Journey Through Texas* cited, 233

One-Minute Spring: 58

Opossum Creek: second night's camp, 25

Order Book of Pioneers: 287

Ortega, Blas: listed, 268

Ortis, Felipe: recommended by Armijo, 172n.

Ortiz, Father Ramón: treated the prisoners kindly in Paso, 124; listed, 268

Ortiz, Francisco: listed, 259

Ortiz, Francisco Baca: listed, 268

Ortiz, Juan Felipe: a confidante of Armijo, 136

Ortiz, Juan Raphael: listed, 268

Ortiz, Pedro: listed, 259

Ostrander, Volney: said conditions at Puebla were bad, 178; in roster, 243

Otero, Antonio: *My Life on the Frontier* cited, 262

Outdoor Life: cited, 55n.

Owens, B. W.: in roster, 244

Oxen: not enough draft oxen furnished, 16; many had never been yoked, 24

Pabo P'a: Kiowa name for river at Camp Resolution, 64n.

Pakenham, Richard: listed, 269

Palmer, D. D.: in roster, 244

Palmer, Wm.: in roster, 244

Palo Chino: McLeod party spent the night at, 279

Panhandle-Plains Historical Review: mentioned, 227, 286

Panic of 1837: 5

Pani Piqué: name for Wichitas, 41n.

Parker, Milton: in roster, 244

Parker, Quanah: paraphrased, 202

Parrida: McLeod party spent the night at, 278

Partridge, Eric: *A Dictionary of Slang and Unconventional English* cited, 146

Paso del Norte: not on the left bank, 124n.

Pavón, Francisco G.: listed, 269

Pawnee: *see* Pani Piqué

Payne, Levi: in roster, 244

Pay: of mounted gunmen, 3; needed by many volunteers, 4n.

Payroll list: 200–201, 258

Pecos: McLeod party spent the night at, 278

Perkins, F. R.: in roster, 244

Perote: McLeod party sent to, 128; releases from, 132; no complaint on treatment, 179; Fitzgerald sent to, 218; listed, 273

Perrin, F.: listed, 269

Personnel: total number of men, 11; discussion of total number, 193–202; roster, 193ff.; 19 men unaccounted for between Paso and San Cristóbal, 195; total number lost indefinite, 195

Personnel lists: total 33, 196

Pfefferkorn, Ignaz: *Description of Sonora* cited, 74n.

Philadelphia: public meeting, 183–84

Phillips, Robert D.: in roster, 244

Philpot, J.: in roster, 244

Piedra, José de la: listed, 269

Pient: in roster, 244

Pinder, Daniel: in roster, 244

Pino, Juan Estev012n: listed, 269

Pino, Juan Esteván: listed, 269

Pino, Manuel: listed, 269

Pino, brother of Manuel: listed, 269

Pino, Miguel E.: listed, 269

Pino, Nicolas: listed, 269

Pino *rancho:* McLeod party spent the night at, 278

Pioneers: many returned to fight again, *x*; split into two parties, *xi*; ages and marital status, *xii*; surrendered without firing a shot, *xii*; many died of smallpox or yellow fever, *xii*; denied Christian burial, *xii*; bodies thrown to wolves, *xii*;

some elected to stay in Mexico, *xii;* some fought in Mexican war, *xii;* some fought in Mier Expedition, *xii;* motivations for going to Santa Fé, *xiii;* one has a son living in Galveston, *xiii;* some fought for the Confederacy, *xiii;* call for volunteers, 3; occupations, 4n.; looked like Indians, 45

Pisarzewski, Alphonse: courtmartialed, 61; acquitted, 97; in roster, 244

Pitching: the Texas word for bucking, 30n.

Pitts, J. G.: in roster, 245

Plasmann, Frederick: in roster, 245

Pobrecitos: word noted by Kendall, 77

Polecat: not the same as skunk, 69n.

Politics: taken seriously, 5

Pope, John: description of Cross Timbers, 37n.

Prairie dogs: immense town entered Aug. 20, 60; thought to duck bullets, 60n9; of the squirrel family, 60n10

Prairie fire: on the Brazos, 33–34; second fire on Aug. 13, 54–56

Prats, Salvador: said Kendall never got a passport, 145; listed, 269

Preparations for expedition: 15–16

Prickly pear: specific for diarrhea and dysentery, 57n.; not found on Llano, 68n.

Priests: joined in the propagandizing, 172; described by Kendall, 186

Prisons: listed in Appendix E, 273–74; *see* names of individual prisons

Prisoners: prisoner-of-war status conceded by Mexicans, 113n.; gave up clothing and blankets for rides, 123; discussion of status, 174ff.; status recognized by Armijo, 175; status recognized by Santa Anna, 175; Webster pointed out rights of prisoners of war, 175; began to arrive in New Orleans and Galveston in May, 185–86; required not to take up arms, 186–87; 20 involved in subsequent actions, 187; men from Mier Expedition

mixed with, 199; *see also* Treatment.

Proclamation: issued to Santa Fé in 1840, 7–8

Propaganda: Armijo did a good job, 155n., 161; Elliott Arnold speaks of, 162; Davis describes, 172; described by Armijo, 172n.

Puebla: McLeod men sent to, 128; Stosoases and Studion escaped from, 128; Howard and Hudson escaped from, 128; releases from, 132; treatment of prisoners very bad, 178–79; treatment complained of by Alexander, 203; listed, 273

Puerta: the only one near Camp Resolution, 106n.

Puertecito: home town of Salazar and Jesús, 76

Punche: black tobacco, 74n.

Puros: Mexican name for cigars, 74n.

Quaife, Milo Milton: *Across the Plains in Forty-Nine* cited, 145n.

Querétero: prisoners stoned, 126; McLeod party spent the night at, 280

Quijano, Blasco: listed, 269

Quinlan, John: in roster, 245

Quintana, Teodoro: conducted McLeod to Paso, 116; listed, 259

Quintufue River: reached Aug. 28, 62

Raezer, Westlus: in roster, 245

Rahm, John: in roster, 245

Rain: slept through soaking rain, 46; soaked them through, 50; torrents on Aug. 21, 60; thunderstorms near San Miguel, 81

Ralph, Samuel: in roster, 245

Ramón: scalped at Camp Resolution, 98; in roster, 245

Ramón: a guard who tortured Gates, 269

Rancho Grande: McLeod party spent the night at, 279

Rations: *see* Food

Rats, Jacob: in roster, 245

Rattlesnakes: mentioned, 4; Kendall's first acquaintance with, 32

Reach, T.: in roster, 245
Rebels: discussion of prisoners' status: 174ff.
Reception: expected to be good, 4
Red River: supposedly seen the first time, 41
Red Rivers in the Southwest: 49n.
Re-election of president: unconstitutional, 5
Refugio: McLeod party spent the night at, 279
Reilly, James: listed, 269
Reinforcements: did not arrive, 248
Releases: 26 men released in April, 131; from various prisons, 131–32; general release on June 13, 131–32; oath taken not to bear arms again, 132; Waddy Thompson's description, 133; oath apparently remitted, 187n.
Repercussions: throughout U. S., xi; legislatures passed resolutions, 183; public meetings held in U. S., 183–84
Republic: existence complicated, 5; Texas had been republic for five years, 5; broke in 1841, 6
Results of expedition: summarized by DeShields, 186
Reveille: Kendall tired of, 25
Reyes, Jose J.: listed, 269
Rial: value, 179n.
Rifles: Colt's repeating rifle used, 60; Kendall's Dixon, 60; Colt rifle held by Mabee, 63
Río Flórido: McLeod party spent the night at, 279
Río Grande: land to the river claimed by Texas, 162–65; Texas had asserted her claim, 164; Kearny, recognized the boundary, 165
Rivet: saved from leg chains by Kendall, 232
Roberts, Samuel A.: gave instructions to the commissioners, 169; listed, 269
Robertson, Thompson: in roster, 245
Roblado: listed, 259
Rocha, Gerbacio: listed, 259
Roche: see Reach
Rodger, Wesley: in roster, 245–46

Rodney: in roster, 245
Rogers, Joseph H.: to be wagonmaster, 14; in roster, 246
Romero, Manuel: listed, 259
Rosa Alvina: McLeod was on, 21n.; sailed Aug. 12, 132; 185 men prepared to embark but were quarantined, 132; 139 men left Vera Cruz, 258; listed, 275; 185 embarked July 27, 280; 139 men sailed Aug. 12, 280
Rosenberry, Wm.: sent ahead to San Miguel, 52; in roster, 246
Roster: 193–255
Rousette, Adolf: in roster, 246
Route: north and west, ix; discussion of, 4; to go up the San Saba River, 13; along the Colorado river, 14
Rowland, John T.: listed, 269
Rowland, John T.: listed, 269
Rudge, Fred: in roster, 246
Ruxton, George Frederick: went west for his health, xiiin.; met Armijo with goods, 136, 262; Adventures in Mexico cited, 57n., 126n., 136n.

Sabin, Edward L.: Kit Carson Days cited, 60n.
Sacstee, Geo.: in roster, 246
Saenea: McLeod party spent the night at, 279
Sage, Rufus B.: says the Snively expedition was to bring peace, 176; His Letters and Papers cited, 176n12; Rocky Mountain Life cited, 176n13
Salado: battle on the, xi; Caldwell defeated Woll on, 182
Salamanca: McLeod party spent night at, 280
Salazar, Dámaso: ordered court-martialed, xi; took arms of Van Ness party, 75; ordered Van Ness party executed, 76; requested Cooke and Brenham to parley, 85; surrounded the Sutton-Cooke party, 85–86; took the main body to Paso, 116; treatment of the prisoners, 117; threatened to execute them all on the Jornada, 117; cut off ears, 119; shot McAllister,

120; ordered Golpin shot, 122; slept in one of the wagons, 123; showed Elías the five pairs of ears, 124; investigation at Paso, 134; ordered sentenced 134; summary, 134–35; did not flee from Kearny, 135; asked damages for his son, 135; executed in 1865, 135; severely beat prisoners with sword, 177–78; criticized by *El Siglo XIX*, 182; cruelties inflamed the U. S., 188; listed, 259–60

Salazar, Francisco Antonio: listed, 269

Salazar, José: listed, 269

Salina: McLeod party spent the night at, 279

Salon de los Distinguidos: listed, 273

Salt: meaning when spoken of in connection with water, 64n.

Salton: *see* Galton, 219

San Antonio: invaded by Woll, 182; invaded by Rafael Vasquez, 182

San Antonio: listed, 275

San Bernard: listed, 275

San Cristobal de Ecatepec: most of the McLeod men at San Cristóbal, 128; center of distribution for McLeod and men, 128; treatment of Prisoners, 178; near Mexico City, 199; listed, 273

Sandoval, Antonio: listed, 269–70

Sandoval, Juan: listed, 269–70

Sandwich Islands: Lewis fled to, 159

San Felipe: McLeod party spent the night at, 280

San Gabriel River: first night's camp, 24

San Jacinto: Santa Anna defeated at, 5

San Juan de los Llanos: McLeod party spent the night at, 280

San Juan del Río: McLeod party spent night at, 280

San Lázaro: many gifts brought to the prisoners, 127; used for sick prisoners, 128; a leper's prison, 130; food satisfactory, treatment all right, 178; near Mexico City, 199; listed, 274

San Luis Potosí: purse made up for prisoners, 126–27; smallpox broke out at, 127; McLeod party spent the night at, 280

San Miguel: point at which the Santa Fé caravans turned west, 76n.; Van Ness party in prison, 78; Van Ness party imprisoned, Sept. 17, 81

San Pablo: McLeod party spent the night at, 279

San Saba River: first route projected, 13

San Sebastian: McLeod party spent the night at, 279

Santa Anna, Antonio López de: defeated and captured, 5; provisional president of Mexico, 130; courted Navarro's sister, 136; signed a secret treaty, 136; summary, 136–37; rebuked commutation of Navarro's sentence, 137, 142; signed secret agreement, 163; said his agreement lost its validity, 164, 176; tried Navarro for high treason, 242; listed, 270

Santa Fé: reception at discussed, 4; accent used in, 6n.; got goods from Independence, 7; area rich in liquid assets, 7

Santa Fé Trail: turned west at San Miguel, 76n.

Santa Rosalia: McLeod party spent the night at, 279

Santiago: most of the Sutton-Cooke men were at Santiago, 128; Lubbock and Mazur escaped from, 128; conditions in, 131; releases from, 132; treatment of prisoners, 178; near Mexico City, 199; listed, 274

Sash-Ce-Zinda: listed, 270

Saucillo: McLeod party spent the night at, Larrabee died, 279

Savannah: public meetings, 183

Scarborough, Paul D.: in roster, 246

Schoolcraft, Henry R.: *The Indian Tribes of North America* cited, 33n.

Scott, Robert: accompanied Burgess, 110; in roster, 246

Scrip, land: had little value, 6

Scurvy: imminent at Camp Resolution, 104; broke out at Laguna Colorada, 111

Second Report of the United States Board on Geographic Names: cited, 6n.

Senate: passed bill to open route, 9

Sentinels: McLeod said must be answered, 16

Servants on trip: 15

Serven, James E.: *Colt Firearms 1836–1954* cited, 63n.

Sevey, Theodore: to be adjutant, 14; in roster, 246–47

Shaw, J. B.: refused to allow bills, 9

Shaw, J. D.: in roster, 247

Shaw, J. G. F.: in roster, 247

Sheldon, S. B.: escaped north of Paso, 128; in roster, 247

Ships: listed in Appendix F, 274–75

Short, Ward: in roster, 247

Showdown in the Cross Timbers: 38–40

Sign: meaning of, 42n.

Silao: two men left with smallpox, 128; McLeod party spent the night at, 280

Simon Pure: pen name of George Grover, 221

"Simples": man convicted of, x

Sinvergüenzas: 126n.

Skull of a white woman: found July 18, 35

Skunk: not the same as polecat, 69n.

Small, Matt: listed, 271

Smallpox: broke out on the trail, xii; broke out at San Luis Potosí, 127; three men left at Tula, 128; two men left at Silao, 128; 17 left in hospital at Guanajuata, 128; first sign at La Caleta, 279

Smith, Daniel B.: in roster, 247

Smith, J.: in roster, 247

Smith, Risden: in roster, 247

Smither, Harriet: *see* Gulick, Charles Adams

Snakeroot used as specific for diarrhea, 57n.

Snively, David H.: in roster, 247

Snively, Jacob: in roster, 247

Snow: awoke with three inches of snow on their blankets, 121

Snow, John C.: killed on June 3, 16; McLeod spoke well of him, 16;

had fought in Texas revolution, 16n.; in roster, 247

Socorro: McLeod party spent the night at, 278

Sodomy: Navarro feared, 242

Solway: listed, 275

Somervell Expedition: xi; organized, 182

Southwestern Historical Quarterly: cited, 6n., 7n., 8n., 9n17, 9n19, 14n., 45n., 139n., 143n., 150n., 168n., 184n.; referred to, 202, 208, 214, 234; *Cumulative Index* cited, 247, 273

Sowter, Ralph: in roster, 247–48

Spanish language: the *lingua franca* of the Southwest, 47n.

Speyer, Adolph: Armijo traveled with, 136

Spooner, Thomas H.: joined the expedition, 29; said reinforcements did not appear, 197; in roster, 248

Spotted Pony: listed, 271

Spybuck: listed, 271

Spy company: formed about June 29, 28; law provided three companies of spies, 29n.; not operating efficiently, 38; Kendall joined Aug. 6, 49; broken up, 52; believed it had located Red River, 60

Staff officers listed, 14

Stampede: 30, 32; Indians caused second stampede, 50–51; 83 horses at Camp Resolution, 98

Stapp, William Preston: *Prisoners of Perote* cited, 273, 274

Stegee, Wm.: in roster, 248

Stevenson, Mrs.: treated Pioneers well in Paso, 126; listed, 271

Stickney, Christian R.: in roster, 248

Stokes, Frederic: in roster, 248

Storm: on June 22, 25

Story, Alonzo: in roster, 248

Stosoases, Thomas: escaped from Puebla, 128; in roster, 248

Strain, J. H.: commanded Company E, 15; ordered to contact Indians, 62; returned to the Quintufue, 64; in roster, 248

Street, Charles: in roster, 248

Strong, Henry W.: *My Frontier*

Days and Indian Fights on the Plains of Texas cited, 62n.

Stroud, Charles: in roster, 249

Strouther, James: in roster, 249

Studion, Radulfo: escaped from Puebla, 128; in roster, 249

Stump, John S.: in roster, 249

Sturgess, Benjamin B.: to be paymaster, 14; died of consumption, 101; in roster, 249

Suares, D. W.: in roster, 249

Sully, Theodorick A.: in roster, 249

Supplies: partial listing, 15; furnished by the Republic, 15

Surrender: Van Ness party, 75; Sutton-Cooke, 86–92; McLeod's surrender written out, 112n26; lives guaranteed, 112n24, 112n25, 113n.; did they surrender at discretion? 174; news arrived in January, 183

Sutherland, J.: in roster, 249

Sutton, H. B.: in roster, 249–50

Sutton, John S.: commanded Company A, 14–15; company took up the march, 17; company demanded right to elect own officers, 17; in command until Howard's return, 27; seniority as captain, 27n.; to cross the Llano with Cooke, 66; on Mier Expedition, 187, 250; in roster, 250

Sutton-Cooke party: originally almost 100 men, xii

Swearing: noted by Kendall, 29; by the ox-drivers, 35

Sweed, Jas.: in roster, 250

Sweezy, John: in roster, 250

Tacubaya: near Mexico City, 199; listed, 274

Talbot, Mr.: gave them eight doubloons, 127

Talk, John: assisted Grover on *The True Blue*, 221; in roster, 250

Tanler, D. J.: in roster, 250

Tanler, Jas.: in roster, 250

Tardif, John: in roster, 250

Tarodi, Antonio: listed, 271

Tarrant, Edward H.: found a muster roll, 197

Teamsters: listed by name by Grover, 15n.

Tent: blown away in storm, 25

Territory: acquired by United States bigger than Louisiana Purchase, ix, 189

Teulon, G. K.: editor of the *Austin City Gazette*, 196, 197

Texas: *see* Republic

Texas Military Road: partly laid out by Cooke, 44

Texas State Historical Quarterly: cited, 213

Thickstone, Louis: in roster, 250–51

Thomas, Daniel: in roster, 251

Thomas, John: in roster, 251

Thompkins, John: in roster, 251

Thompson, Waddy: advanced the prisoners $5,000, 127; tried to get them released, 130; misquoted on treatment by Bancroft and Twitchell, 176–77; his true statement on treatment of prisoners, 177; had visited at M. D. Boyd's home, 207; said his appointment gave prestige, 265; listed, 271; *Recollections of Mexico* cited, 57n.; quoted, 131n.; cited, 133n., 247, 254, 270

Tirrell, Charley: listed, 271

Title to land, revolutionary title held superior, 164n.

Tobacco: provided at start, 11; Mexican terms for, 74, 74n.; burned at Camp Resolution, 105

Todd, Robert C.: lost Sept. 24, 108; in roster, 251

Toenails: came off from frostbite, 117

Tompkins, T.: court-martialed, 51; in roster, 251

Tonkawa spies: with Burleson, 102n.

Tóñ-zó' gódal P'a: Kiowa name for river at Camp Resolution, 64n.

Tornel, José María de: minister of war, 130; listed, 271

Torres, Jacinto G.: *see Mexico, Memorias Relaciones 1841–1843*

Torrey, Thos. J.: in roster, 251

Torrey's Trading Houses: George Barnard with, 204; Thos. J. helped establish, 251

Tortillas: described, 74n.

Towler: in roster, 251

Trade: goods listed, 105n.; to Chihuahua in 1846, 167; to New Mexico in 1855, 167; in New Mexico and Chihuahua, 167–68; to Chihuahua in 1852, 168; estimated at $30,000,000 a year, 168; Froebel said Americans preferred Texas route, 168

Traitor: was Lewis a traitor? 148ff.

Trasker, Geo. L.: 251

Treason: Navarro tried for treason to Mexico, 141–42; discussion of Lewis's, 148–60; Louise Weakley's thesis cited, 159n.

Treat, James: listed, 271

Treatment: from San Miguel to Mexico, x; cruel, xi; Mexican civilians kind, xi; protest in Mexican press, xi; prisoners allowed liberty on parole, xi; treated kindly in Paso, 124; stoned at Querétero, 126; Heredia gave them $500 at Durango, 126; Jennison gave them shoes and cups, 126; fed well by Mrs. Magoffin in Chihuahua, 126; treated well by Mrs. Stevenson in Paso, 126; treated kindly by the populace, 126; purse made up in San Luis Potosí, 126–27; miscellaneous gifts, 127; money and clothing given in Guanajuato, 127; $1,000 given in Zacatecas, 127; many gifts brought to San Lázaro, 127; Ellis gave them $1,000 and other money, 127; beggars gave them clothes on their release, 127; Hargous advanced them $6,253.66, 127; Waddy Thompson advanced them $5,000, 127; Nathan Gilliland gave them $200, 127; American stage drivers gave $500 to $1,000 apiece, 127; conditions at Santiago, 131; conditions at the Acordada, 141, 179; Bancroft said Thompson said prisoners well enough treated, 176–77; Thompson's true statement, 177; Twitchell said Thompson said prisoners well enough treated, 177; Lubbock described, 177; Coombs described, 177; cruelly whipped at Chihua-

hua, 177; Salazar severely beat prisoners with sword, 177–78; Kendall described, 177–78; Hegewick described, 178; Ostrander described, 178; conditions at San Cristóbal, 178; conditions at San Lázaro, 178; conditions at Santiago, 178; conditions at Puebla, 178; conditions at Perote, 179; Alexander complained of Puebla, 203

Trenco, Fernando: listed, 271

Trinity River: camped on, 37

Triqueros: listed, 272

Troop: word not used by United States Cavalry, 11n.

Troutz, C.: in roster, 251–52

True Blue, The: published by George Grover, 221; mentioned, 229; Mabry helped Grover edit, 236; subjects for Rogers' lectures, 246; John Talk helped Grover edit, 250; mentions Francisca, 265; mentions Spotted Pony, 271; appearance of 285–86

Tuberculosis: some hoped to cure on trip, xiii; Grover said Brashear died of, 58n.; Sturgess died of, 101

Tucker, Thos. E.: in roster, 252

Tula: three men left with smallpox, 128; listed, 274; McLeod party spent night at, 280

Tweed, James: in roster, 252

Twitchell, Ralph E.: accepted Armijo's version, 161; said Armijo was justified in breaking promises, 176; said Thompson said prisoners well enough treated, 177; Leading Facts of New Mexican History cited, 113n., 176n., 177n.; relies on Davis, 181n.

Ulibarri, Antonio José: listed, 272

Ulibarri, Santiago: listed, 272

Ullom, Harry Herbert: see Day, Donald

Ulúa, San Juan de: Navarro imprisoned at, 242

United States: had recognized Texas' independence, 175; many different opinions in, 184

Valdez, María Gertrudes: married to Magoffin, 267
Valencia: Ernest died and McAllister shot near, 278
Valuables: hid money and watches in cakes, x
Van Buren, Martin: intervened for Houghtaling, 226
Van Ness, George F. X.: to be secretary of commissioners, 3, 14; went to Indian village, 48; to cross the Llano with Cooke, 66; sent on to San Miguel, 73–74; tied at the wrists; 79; pleaded for shelter at Algodones, 117–18; released Feb. 1, 128; gave the wording of the passport under oath, 144–45; attached to Mier prisoners, 187, 252; visited Navarro at Ulúa, 242; in roster, 252; party saved by Vigil, 272
Van Zandt, Isaac: listed, 272
Vasado, Jas.: in roster, 252
Vastida, Miguel la: listed, 260
Vasques, Ciriaco: listed, 272
Vásquez, Rafael: invaded San Antonio, 182
Vega, J. Ignacio: listed, 272
Velasco: listed, 260
Vera Cruz: prisoners sailed from, 131, 132, 200, 202
Vidaurri, Santiago: opinion of Texans, 57n.; listed, 272
Vigil, Francisco: listed, 272
Vigil, Gregorio: objected to execution of Van Ness party, 76; identified, 76n.; Caldwell's party quartered at his ranch, 114; listed, 272
Volunteers: call for, 3; were expected to come from the east, 14n.; very young, 19; 70 left Mobile, 184; 300 left New Orleans, 184
Vrille: listed, 272

Wacos: refused to give directions on the Wichita, 47; first Indians met by the Pioneers, 47n.
Wagons: ten wagons proposed for merchants, 3; 14 merchants' wagons left Brushy Creek, 15; total, 16, 23; not enough fur-
nished, 16; one baggage wagon for each company, 16; two for staff and guests, 16; Jersey carry-all, 16; each drawn by six yoke of oxen, 16; turned over, 24; too heavily loaded, 25; several broken up in Cross Timbers, 40–41; one wagon burned Aug. 13, 55; carried great loads, 55n.; six wagons burned at Camp Resolution, 106; wagon irons found, 106n.; McLeod wagons lined up on the plaza, 116; two of their own wagons went on the *Jornada* with them, 116
Walding, Elisha: in roster, 252
Wallace, Wm.: in roster, 253
Walnut Creek Camp: 10
Walker, John: in roster, 252
Walker, J. L.: in roster, 252
War: between Mexico and U. S., xi
Ward: in roster, 253
Ward, D. S.: in roster, 253
Ward, Jas. E.: in roster, 253
Ware, Ben: in roster, 253
Waring, Thomas: in roster, 253
Water: Brazos River was brackish, 32; dry camp July 14, 34–35; nearly all streams dry in Cross Timbers, 37; dry camp in Cross Timbers July 28, 41; Wichita River was brackish, 48; drinkable water scarce Aug. 12, 54; dry camps Aug. 12 and 13, 54; lack caused suffering Aug. 14, 56–57; gypsum water, Aug. 14, 57; dry camp on Aug. 15, 57; impregnated with gypsum, 57; One-Minute Spring, 58; purgative effect caused sickness, 60; bad for four days, 60; camped at salt springs, Aug. 25, 61; water scarce west of Llano, 68; near the Caprock not as nauseous as the gypsum waters of North Texas, 97; dry camp Sept. 27, 109; traveled without water Sept. 28, 109
Water Witch: listed, 275
Watkins, J. D.: court-martialed, 61; in roster, 253
Weakley, Louise: thesis on treason cited, 159n.

Weather: around Houston, 12n.
Webb, James: quoted, 166n.
Webb, James Josiah: confused over identity of Lewis, 159n.; *Adventures in the Santa Fé Trade* cited, 105n., 159n., 262
Webb, Walter Prescott: *The Great Plains* cited, 114n.; *The Texas Rangers* cited, 29n.
Webster, Daniel: tried to get prisoners released, 130; pointed out Mexico's implicit acceptance of Texas, 175; pointed out rights of prisoners of war, 175; said the facts constituted an outrage, 179; listed, 272
Webster, J.: in roster, 253
Weed, W. A.: listed, 272
Weeder, Johnson: in roster, 253
Westgate, E. C.: court-martialed, 100; in roster, 253-54
Wharton, Clarence R.: *El Presidente* cited, 273
Wheat, Carl I.: *The Shirley Letters* cited, 146
Whisky: given them by a woman at San Miguel, 79
Whitaker, Francis Q.: professed Catholic faith, *xii;* to be surgeon, 14; lost or missing, 42; did not appear, 44; rejoined the expedition Aug. 5, 49; went with the first McLeod party, 118; examined Larrabee's body, 124, 234; in roster, 254
White, Charles: court-martialed, 51; in roster, 254
White, Daniel: in roster, 254
White, Leslie A.: "Punche: Tobacco in New Mexico History" cited, 74n.
Whooping cough: thirty Mexicans had it in the same room, 74
Wichita River: thought to be the Red, 42
Wilkins, W.: lost Sept. 24, 108; in roster, 254
Willett: listed, 272
Williams, Juanita: *see* Hallenbeck, Cleve
Willis: court-martialed, 97;
Willis, C. C.: court-martialed for selling a sword, 97; in roster, 254

Winchell, James H.: in roster, 254
Winkler, E. W.: *Manuscripts, Letters and Documents of Early Texians* quoted, 166n.; cited, 125n.
Winkler, Wm.: in roster, 254-55
Winnebagoes: captured Thomas Hancock, 223
Wise, Henry A.: *Los Gringos* cited, 266
Wiseman, Patrick: listed, 272
Wislizenus, F. A.: *Memoir of a Tour to Northern Mexico* cited, 164n., 170n.
Wm. Bryan: listed, 275
Wolf, C.: in roster, 255
Woll, Adrian W.: attacked San Antonio, xi; invaded San Antonio, 182; defeated by Caldwell, 182; captured Fitzgerald, 218
Women, Mexican: saved prisoners from starvation, *x;* gave tobacco to members of Van Ness party, 74; gave food to the prisoners, 77; one gave them whisky at San Miguel, 79; brought them all the food they could eat, 84; gave them food along the way, 117; Kendall saw a perfect specimen of female loveliness, 118; bathing in canal of Querétaro, 126n.; constantly brought them food, tobacco, and clothing, 127; one helped Grover to get to Vera Cruz, 222
Woodbury: 14 men sailed from Vera Cruz in May, 131, 280; "the rest" sailed Sept. 13, 132, 280; listed, 275
Woods, Samuel: in roster, 255
Woodson, Francis B.: killed by Kiowas, 63; in roster, 255
Woodward, John: in roster, 255
Wright, A. S.: listed, 272
Wright, Jacob: in roster, 255
Wrinkley: in roster, 255

Yarner; pronunciation of Llano, 72n.
Yellow fever: many died of, *xii;* many became ill with, 131; men died in Vera Cruz, 195; *Rosa Alvina* quarantined because of, 132; broke out on board *Rosa Alvina,* 275

Yoakum, H.: *History of Texas* cited, 5n., 6n., 9n., 10n., 163n4, 163n5, 164n., 183n., 185n.

Young, Wm.: in roster, 255

Zabel, Charles: *see* Beardsley, J. L.

Zacatecas: $1,000 given to the prisoners, 127; McLeod party spent the night at, 279

Zavala, Manuel: listed, 273

THE AMERICAN EXPLORATION
AND TRAVEL SERIES

of which *The Texan–Santa Fé Pioneers* is Number 25, was started in 1939 by the University of Oklahoma Press. It follows rather logically the Press's program of regional exploration. Behind the story of the gradual and inevitable recession of the American frontier lie the accounts of explorers, traders, and travelers. which individually and in the aggregate present one of the most romantic and fascinating chapters in the development of the American domain. The following list is complete as of the date of publication of this volume.

1. Captain Randolph B. Marcy and Captain George B. McClellan. *Adventure on Red River:* Report on the Exploration of the Headwaters of the Red River. Edited by Grant Foreman.
2. Grant Foreman. *Marcy and the Gold Seekers:* The Journal of Captain R. B. Marcy, with an account of the Gold Rush over the Southern Route.
3. Pierre-Antoine Tabeau. *Tabeau's Narrative of Loisel's Expedition to the Upper Missouri.* Edited by Annie Heloise Abel. Translated from the French by Rose Abel Wright.
4. Victor Tixier. *Tixier's Travels on the Osage Prairies.* Edited by John Francis McDermott. Translated from the French by Albert J. Salvan.
5. Teodoro de Croix. *Teodoro de Croix and the Northern Frontier of New Spain, 1776–1783.* Translated from the Spanish and edited by Alfred Barnaby Thomas.
6. A. W. Whipple. *A Pathfinder in the Southwest:* The Itinerary of Lieutenant A. W. Whipple During His Ex-

[327]

plorations for a Railway Route from Fort Smith to Los Angeles in the Years 1853 & 1854. Edited and annotated by Grant Foreman.

7. Josiah Gregg. *Diary & Letters.* Two volumes. Edited by Maurice Garland Fulton. Introductions by Paul Horgan. Out of print.

8. Washington Irving. *The Western Journals of Washington Irving.* Edited and annotated by John Francis McDermott. Out of print.

9. Edward Dumbauld. *Thomas Jefferson, American Tourist:* Being an Account of His Journeys in the United States of America, England, France, Italy, the Low Countries, and Germany.

10. Victor Wolfgang von Hagen. *Maya Explorer:* John Lloyd Stephens and the Lost Cities of Central America and Yucatán.

11. E. Merton Coulter. *Travels in the Confederate States:* A Bibliography.

12. W. Eugene Hollon. *The Lost Pathfinder:* Zebulon Montgomery Pike.

13. George Frederick Ruxton. *Ruxton of the Rockies.* Collected by Clyde and Mae Reed Porter. Edited by LeRoy R. Hafen.

14. George Frederick Ruxton. *Life in the Far West.* Edited by LeRoy R. Hafen. Foreword by Mae Reed Porter.

15. Edward Harris. *Up the Missouri with Audubon:* The Journal of Edward Harris. Edited by John Francis McDermott.

16. Robert Stuart. *On the Oregon Trail:* Robert Stuart's Journey of Discovery (1812–1831). Edited by Kenneth A. Spaulding.

17. Josiah Gregg. *Commerce of the Prairies.* Edited by Max L. Moorhead.

18. John Treat Irving, Jr. *Indian Sketches,* Taken During an Expedition to the Pawnee Tribes (1833). Edited and annotated by John Francis McDermott.

19. Thomas D. Clark (ed.). *Travels in the Old South, 1527–1825:* A Bibliography. Two volumes.
20. Alexander Ross. *The Fur Hunters of the Far West.* Edited by Kenneth A. Spaulding.
21. William Bollaert. *William Bollaert's Texas.* Edited by W. Eugene Hollon.
22. Daniel Ellis Conner. *Joseph Reddeford Walker and the Arizona Adventure.* Edited by Donald J. Berthrong and Odessa Davenport.
23. Matthew C. Field. *Prairie and Mountain Sketches.* Collected by Clyde and Mae Reed Porter. Edited by Kate L. Gregg and John Francis McDermott.
24. Ross Cox. *The Columbia River:* Scenes and Adventures During A Residence of Six Years on the Western Side of the Rocky Mountains Among Various Tribes of Indians Hitherto Unknown, Together with a Journey Across the American Continent. Edited by Edgar I. and Jane R. Stewart.
25. Noel M. Loomis. *The Texan–Santa Fé Pioneers.*

THE TEXAN–SANTA FÉ PIONEERS

was designed to convey, in a restrained manner, the typographic treatment of books of the latter part of the nineteenth century. On the title page, set by hand, appear Bulmer Italic, Fry's Ornamented and Alternate Gothic, combined with ornamental borders, which are also used for the chapter titles. The text was set on the Linotype machine in 11 point Caledonia, with 2 points of space between lines for greater legibility.